Inbox - Outlook Data File - Outlook
Microsoft Outlook 2016

File   Home   Send / Receive   Folder   View   Tell me what you want to do...

1 Managing Email Messages with Outlook

Objectives

You will have mastered the material in this module when you can:

- Add a Microsoft account to Outlook
- Set language preferences and sensitivity levels
- Apply a theme
- Compose, address, and send an email message
- Open, read, print, and close an email message
- Preview and save a file attachment
- Display the People Pane
- Reply to an email message

- Check spelling as you type an email message
- Attach a file to an outgoing email message
- Forward an email message
- Copy another person when sending an email message
- Create and move messages into a folder
- Delete an email message
- View the mailbox size

This introductory module covers features and functions common to managing email messages in Outlook 2016.

Roadmap

In this module, you will learn how to perform basic email messaging tasks. The following roadmap identifies general activities you will perform as you progress through this module:

1. CONFIGURE the ACCOUNT OPTIONS
2. COMPOSE AND SEND an email message
3. VIEW AND PRINT an email message
4. REPLY to an email message
5. ATTACH a FILE to an email message
6. ORGANIZE email MESSAGES in folders

At the beginning of the step instructions throughout each module, you will see an abbreviated form of this roadmap. The abbreviated roadmap uses colors to indicate module progress: gray means the module is beyond that activity, blue means the task being shown is covered in that activity, and black means that activity is yet to be covered. For example, the following abbreviated roadmap indicates the module would be showing a task in the View and Print activity.

1 CONFIGURE ACCOUNT OPTIONS | 2 COMPOSE & SEND | 3 VIEW & PRINT | 4 REPLY

5 ATTACH FILE | 6 ORGANIZE MESSAGES

Use the abbreviated roadmap as a progress guide while you read or step through the instructions in this module.

Introduction to Outlook

Outlook 2016 helps you organize and manage your communications, contacts, schedules, and tasks. **Email** (short for **electronic mail**) is the transmission of messages and files between computers or smart devices over a network. An **email client**, such as Microsoft Outlook 2016, is an app that allows you to compose, send, receive, store, and delete email messages. Outlook can access mail servers in a local network, such as your school's network, or on a remote network, such as the Internet. Finally, you can use Outlook to streamline your messages so that you easily can find and respond to them later.

To use Outlook, you must have an email account. An **email account** is an electronic mailbox you receive from an **email service provider**, which is an organization that provides servers for routing and storing email messages. Your employer or school could set up an email account for you, or you can do so yourself through your Internet service provider (ISP) or using a web application such as a Microsoft account, Google Gmail, Yahoo! Mail, or iCloud Mail. Outlook does not create or issue email accounts; it merely provides you with access to them. When you have an email account, you also have an **email address**, which identifies your email account on a network so you can send and receive email messages.

Project — Composing and Sending Email Messages

The project in this module follows the general guidelines for using Outlook to compose, open, and reply to email messages, as shown in Figure 1–1. To communicate with individuals and groups, you typically send or receive some kind of message. Phone calls, letters, texting, and email are examples of ways to communicate a message. Email is a convenient way to send information to multiple people at once.

A work study student in the Pathways Internship Office at Langford College, Sophia Garza, uses Outlook to communicate with faculty and fellow students. This module uses Microsoft Outlook 2016 to compose, send, read, reply to, and forward email messages regarding an upcoming Internship Fair. Sophia has been asked by Ms. Ella Pauley, the director of the internship program, to coordinate the marketing of the Pathways Internship Fair this October. Using Outlook, Sophia reads email messages from her director and students regarding internship opportunities. She replies to email messages and includes a document containing a flyer about the Internship Fair. To organize messages, she also creates folders and then stores the messages in the folders.

BTW

The Outlook Window
The modules in this book begin with the Outlook window appearing as it did at the initial installation of the software. Your Outlook window may look different depending on your screen resolution and other Outlook settings.

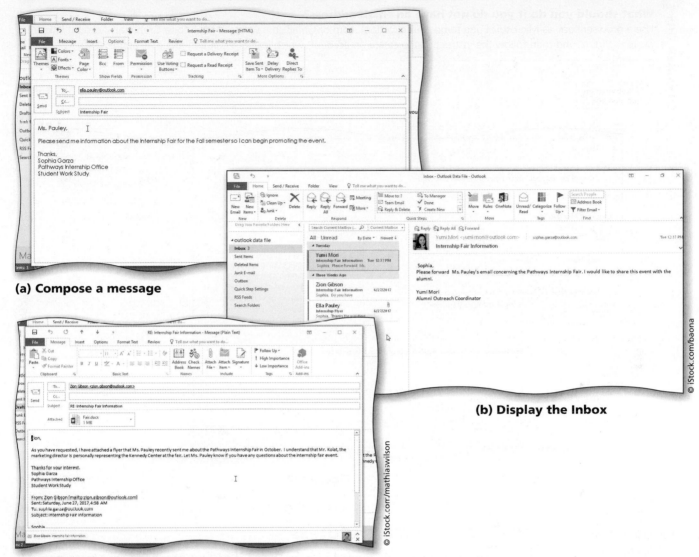

(a) Compose a message

(b) Display the Inbox

(c) Reply and attach a file to a message

© iStock.com/baona

© iStock.com/mathiaswilson

Figure 1–1

Setting Up Outlook

Many computer users have an email account from an online email service provider such as Outlook.com or Gmail.com and another email account at work or school. Instead of using a web app for your online email account and another app for your school account, you can use Outlook 2016 to access all of your email messages in a single location. When you access your email in Outlook 2016, you can take advantage of a full set of features that include social networking, translation services, and file management. You can read your downloaded messages offline and set options to organize your messages in a way that is logical and convenient for you.

The first time you start Outlook on a personal computer, the Auto Account Setup feature guides you to provide information that Outlook needs to send and receive email messages (Figure 1–2). First, the setup feature prompts you to provide your name, which will appear in email messages that you send to other people. Next, the setup feature requests your email address and a password.

What should you do if you do not have an email address?
Use a browser such as Microsoft Edge to go to the Outlook.com or Gmail.com website. Look for a Create an Account link or button, click it, and then follow the instructions to create an account, which includes creating an email address.

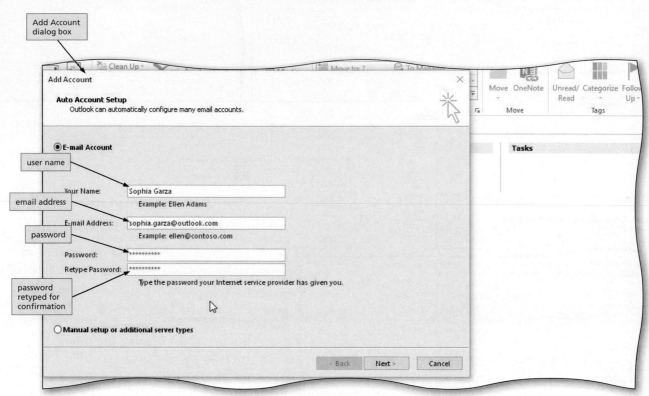

Figure 1–2

For an introduction to Windows and instructions about how to perform basic Windows tasks, read the Office and Windows module at the beginning of this book, where you can learn how to resize windows, change screen resolution, create folders, move and rename files, use Windows Help, and much more.

Parts of an Email Address

An email address is divided into two parts. The first part contains a **user name**, which is a combination of characters, such as letters of the alphabet and numbers, that identifies a specific user. The last part is a **domain name**, which is the name associated with a specific Internet address and is assigned by your email service provider. A user name must be different from other user names in the same domain. For example, the outlook.com domain can have only one user named Sophia.Garza. An email address contains an @ (pronounced *at*) symbol to separate the user name from the domain name. Figure 1–3 shows an email address for Sophia Garza, which would be read as sophia dot garza at outlook dot com.

Figure 1–3

To Run Outlook

If you are using a computer or mobile device to step through the project in this module and you want your screens to match the figures in this book, you should change your screen's resolution to 1366 × 768. For information about how to change a computer's resolution, refer to the Office and Windows module at the beginning of this book.

The following steps, which assume Windows 10 is running, use the Start menu to run Outlook based on a typical installation. You may need to ask your instructor how to run Outlook on your computer. For a detailed example of the procedure summarized below, refer to the Office and Windows module.

1 Click the Start button on the Windows 10 taskbar to display the Start menu.

2 Click All apps at the bottom of the left pane of the Start menu to display a list of apps installed on the computer or mobile device.

3 Scroll to and then click Outlook 2016 in the All apps list to run Outlook.

4 If the Outlook window is not maximized, click the Maximize button on its title bar to maximize the window.

One of the few differences between Windows 8 and Windows 10 occur in the steps to run Outlook. If you are using Windows 8, scroll the Start screen and then click the Outlook 2016 tile.

To Add an Email Account

You can add one or more of your personal email accounts to Outlook. For most accounts, Outlook automatically detects and configures the account after you type your name, email address, and password. Add an email account to Outlook when you are working on your personal or home computer only. You do not want your personal information or email messages on a public computer. Although most people add an email account the first time Outlook runs, you can add email accounts at any time. This module assumes you already set up an email account in Outlook. If you choose to add an email account to Outlook, you would use the following steps.

1. If you started Outlook for the first time, click the Next button to set up an email account. Otherwise, click the File tab, and then click Add Account.

2. If necessary, click the Yes button to add an email account, and then click the Next button to display the Add Account window.

3. Click the Your Name text box, and then type your first and last name to associate your name with the account.

4. Click the E-mail Address text box, and then type your full email address to associate your email address with the account.

5. Click the Password text box, and then type your password to verify the password to your email account.

6. Click the Retype Password text box, and then type your password again to confirm your password.

7. Click the Next button to configure your account settings and sign in to your mail server.

8. Click the Finish button to add your email account.

BTW
The Ribbon and Screen Resolution
Outlook may change how the groups and buttons within the groups appear on the ribbon, depending on the computer or mobile device's screen resolution. Thus, your ribbon may look different from the ones in this book if you are using a screen resolution other than 1366 × 768.

CONSIDER THIS

Will your screen look different if you are using a touch screen?
The Office and Windows interfaces may vary if you are using a touch screen. For this reason, you might notice that the function or appearance of your touch screen differs slightly from this module's presentation.

CONSIDER THIS

How do you remove an email account?
- To remove an email account in Outlook, click the File tab on the ribbon.
- If necessary, click the Info tab in the Backstage view.
- Click the Account Settings button, and then click Account Settings to display the Account Settings dialog box.
- Click the account you want to remove, and then click Remove.
- In the Account Settings dialog box, click the Yes button.

To Change the Navigation Bar Options

1 CONFIGURE ACCOUNT OPTIONS | 2 COMPOSE & SEND | 3 VIEW & PRINT
4 REPLY | 5 ATTACH FILE | 6 ORGANIZE MESSAGES

The first time you start Outlook, the lower-left corner of the screen provides compact navigation by default. To change the Navigation bar from displaying small icons representing Mail, Calendar, Contacts, and Task to a text view, you can disable the compact navigation setting on the Navigation bar. The following steps change the Navigation bar options. **Why?** *Instead of small icons, you can display the Mail, Calendar, Contacts, and Task text labels.*

1

- Click the Navigation Options button (three dots) on the Navigation bar to display a list of Navigation bar options (Figure 1–4).

Q&A

The left pane in my Outlook window is not expanded as it is in Figure 1–4. What should I do?
Click the Expand the Folder Pane button, which is a small arrow button to the left of today's date in the Outlook window.

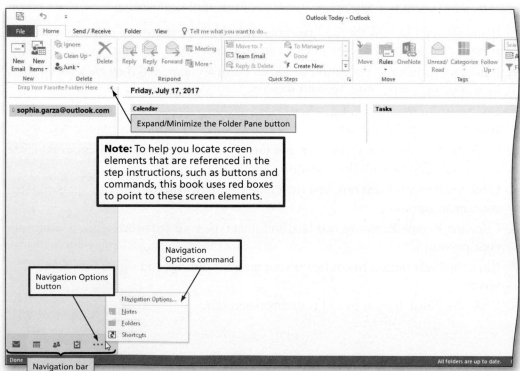

Figure 1–4

- Click Navigations Options to display the Navigation Options dialog box.

- If necessary, click the Compact Navigation check box (Navigation Options dialog box) to remove the check mark and disable the compact navigation setting on the Navigation bar (Figure 1–5).

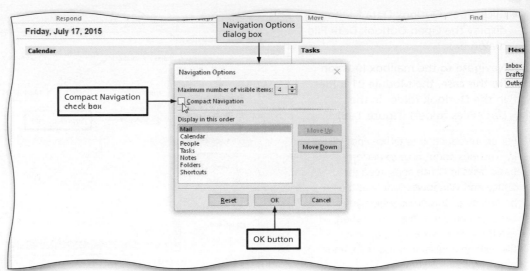

Figure 1–5

- Click the OK button to change the Navigation bar so it displays text labels instead of icons (Figure 1–6).

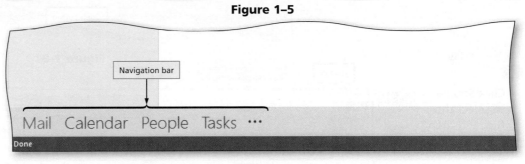

Figure 1–6

To Open an Outlook Data File

Microsoft Outlook uses a special file format called a **personal storage table (.pst file)** to save your email files, calendar entries, and contacts. The email messages with which you work in this module are stored in a personal storage table file named Sophia.pst, which is an Outlook mailbox located with the Data Files. To complete this assignment, you will be required to use the Data Files. Please contact your instructor for information about accessing the Data Files. In this example, the Sophia mailbox is located in the Module 01 folder in the Outlook folder in the Data Files folder. The following steps open the Sophia.pst file in Outlook, display the Inbox for the Sophia file, and then make your Sophia mailbox match the figures in this module. *Why? Opening or importing a .pst file allows you to move your email and other Outlook information to another computer.*

- Click File on the ribbon to open the Backstage view.

- Click the Open & Export tab in the Backstage view to display the Open gallery (Figure 1–7).

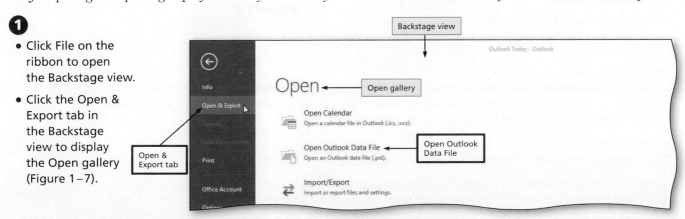

Figure 1–7

- Click Open Outlook Data File to display the Open Outlook Data File dialog box.

- Navigate to the mailbox location (in this case, the Module 01 folder in the Outlook folder in the Data Files folder) (Figure 1–8).

For an introduction to Office and instructions about how to perform basic tasks in Office apps, read the Office and Windows module at the beginning of this book, where you can learn how to run an application, use the ribbon, save a file, open a file, exit an application, use Help, and much more.

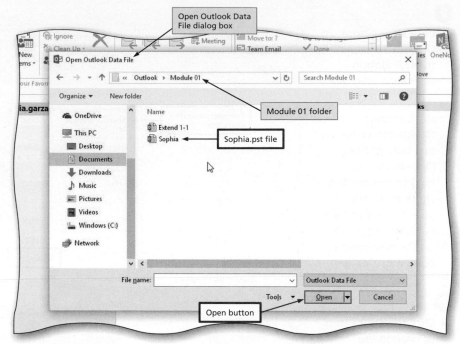

Figure 1–8

- Click Sophia to select the file, and then click the OK button (Open Outlook Data File dialog box) to open the Sophia mailbox in your Outlook window.

- If necessary, click the white triangle next to the outlook data file mailbox in the Navigation Pane to expand the folders.

- Click the Inbox folder below the outlook data file heading in the Navigation Pane to view Sophia's Inbox (Figure 1–9).

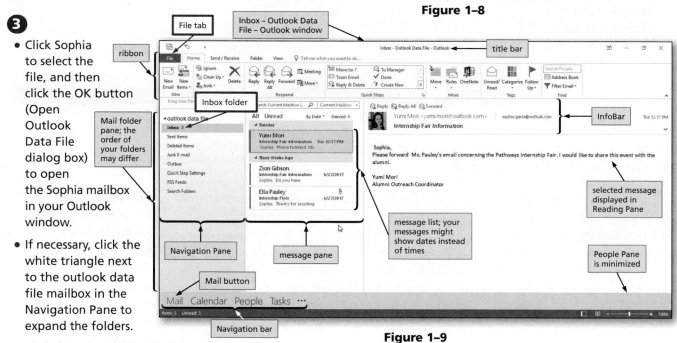

Figure 1–9

Q&A What is the Navigation Pane?

The **Navigation Pane** is a pane along the left side of the Outlook window that contains shortcuts to your Outlook folders and gives you quick access to them. You use the Navigation Pane to browse all your Outlook folders using one of its views: Mail, Calendar, People, or Tasks.

What is the Inbox?

The **Inbox** is the Outlook folder that contains incoming email messages.

The contact photo shown in Figure 1–9 does not appear in my Outlook window. What should I do?

Outlook needs to synchronize the contact photos with the email addresses in the Sophia data file. Click the Close button to close Outlook, restart it, and then expand the outlook data file in the Navigation Pane to have the photos appear. You also might need to import the data file rather than opening it. In Step 2 on this page, click Import/Export instead of Open Outlook Data File.

Outlook Module 1

To Set Language Preferences

You can use the Outlook Options dialog box to set the Office Language Preferences. *Why? You can specify the editing and display languages, such as the languages used in the dictionaries, grammar checking, and sorting.* Usually, Outlook configures the language settings to match your operating system; however, if you want to change those settings, you can adjust the Language preferences. The following steps set the Language preferences.

❶

• Click File on the ribbon to open the Backstage view (Figure 1–10).

Q&A Why does my account information appear in the Backstage view?
If you have already set up an email account in Outlook, it appears on the Info tab in the Backstage view. Other options, such as Rules and Alerts, might also appear.

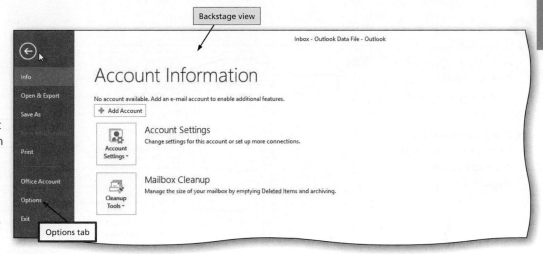

Figure 1–10

❷

• Click the Options tab in the Backstage view to display the Outlook Options dialog box.

• In the left pane, click Language (Outlook Options dialog box) to display the Language options.

• Click the '[Add additional editing languages]' arrow to display a list of editing languages that can be added to Outlook (Figure 1–11).

Q&A How do I set a default language?
After selecting an editing language that you want to use, click the name of the language and then click the 'Set as Default' button.

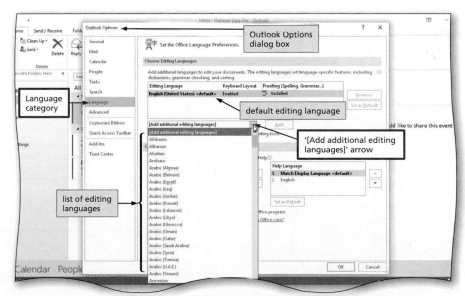

Figure 1–11

❸

• If necessary, scroll the list and then click English (United States) to set the default editing language. Otherwise, click the '[Add additional editing languages]' arrow again to close the list.

To Set the Sensitivity Level for All New Messages

The **Sensitivity level** of a message advises the recipient on how to treat the contents of the message. Sensitivity levels are Normal, Personal, Private, and Confidential. Changing the Sensitivity setting in the Outlook Options dialog box changes the default Sensitivity level of all messages created afterward. ***Why?*** *For example, if you set the Sensitivity level of a message to Confidential, the information should not be disclosed to anyone except the recipient.* The following steps set the default Sensitivity level.

1

- In the left pane, click Mail (Outlook Options dialog box) to display the Mail options.

- Drag the scroll bar to display the Send messages area (Figure 1–12).

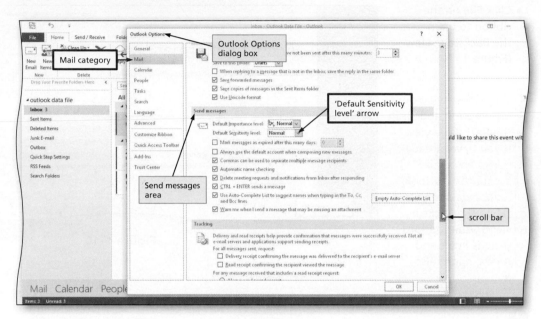

Figure 1–12

2

- Click the 'Default Sensitivity level' arrow to display a list of Sensitivity levels (Figure 1–13).

Q&A Can I set one message to an individual Sensitivity level such as private?
Yes, you can set the Sensitivity level for a single message using the More Options Dialog Box Launcher (Options tab | More Options group) to open the Properties dialog box. Click the Sensitivity button and then click Private to change the sensitivity of a single message to private.

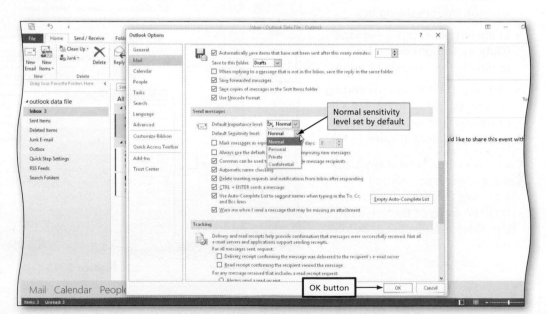

Figure 1–13

- If necessary, click Normal to set the default Sensitivity level of all new messages.
- Click the OK button to close the Outlook Options dialog box.

Q&A
What should I do if the ribbon does not stay open?
Click any tab on the ribbon, and then click the 'Pin the ribbon' button (thumbtack icon) in the lower-right corner of the ribbon to keep the ribbon open.

Composing and Sending Email messages

Composing an email message is the most frequent personal and business task you perform in Microsoft Outlook. Composing an email message consists of four basic steps: open a new message window, enter message header information, enter the message text, and add a signature. When composing an email message, it is best to keep your message text concise and to the point. If you must write a longer, detailed message, break up your message into bullet points or into separate emails each with a clear summary of action.

An email message is organized into two areas: the message header and the message area. The information in the **message header** routes the message to its recipients and identifies the subject of the message. The message header identifies the primary recipient(s) in the To box. If you have multiple recipients in the To box, you can separate each email address with a semicolon. Recipients in the Cc (courtesy copy or carbon copy) and Bcc (blind courtesy copy) boxes, if displayed, also receive the message; however, the names of the recipients in the Bcc box are not visible to other recipients. The **subject line** states the purpose of the message.

The **message area**, where you type an email message, consists of a greeting line or salutation, the message text, an optional closing, and one or more signature lines as shown in Table 1–1.

BTW
Inserting Hyperlinks
To insert a web address in an email message, click where you want to insert the hyperlink, and then click the Hyperlink button (Insert tab | Links group) to display the Insert Hyperlink dialog box. In the Address text box, type the web address you want to insert as a hyperlink, and then click the OK button to insert the hyperlink into the message body.

Table 1–1 Message Area Parts

Part	Description
Greeting line or salutation	Sets the tone of the message and can be formal or informal, depending on the nature of the message. You can use a colon (:) or comma (,) at the end of the greeting line.
Message text	Informs the recipient or requests information.
Closing	Informs the recipient or requests information. A closing signals an end to the message using courtesy words such as *Thank you* or *Regards*. Because the closing is most appropriate for formal email messages, it is optional.
Signature line(s)	Identifies the sender and may contain additional information, such as a job title, business name, and phone number(s). In a signature, the name usually is provided on one line followed by other information listed on separate lines.

To Compose an Email Message

1 CONFIGURE ACCOUNT OPTIONS | 2 COMPOSE & SEND | 3 VIEW & PRINT
4 REPLY | 5 ATTACH FILE | 6 ORGANIZE MESSAGES

An email message from Sophia Garza, the work study student in the Pathways Internship Office, requests information about the Internship Fair from the director named Ella Pauley. The following steps compose a new email message. **Why?** *Composing email messages is a direct and efficient method to connect with personal and professional contacts.*

- Click the New Email button (Home tab | New group) to open the Untitled – Message (HTML) window (Figure 1–14).

What does HTML mean in the title bar?

HTML is the format for the new email message. Outlook messages can use two other formats: Rich Text Format (RTF) and Plain Text. All of these formats are discussed later in this module.

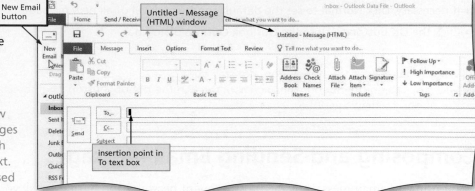

Figure 1–14

- Type `ella.pauley@ outlook.com` (with no spaces) in the To text box to enter the email address of the recipient.

- Click the Subject text box, and then type `Internship Fair` to enter the subject line.

- Press the TAB key to move the insertion point into the message area (Figure 1–15).

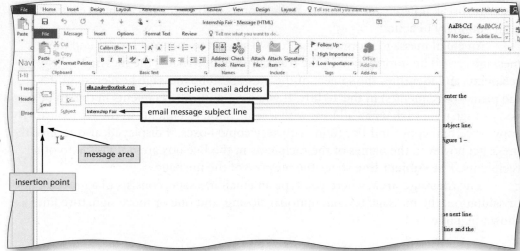

Figure 1–15

3

- Type `Ms. Pauley,` as the greeting line.

- Press the ENTER key to move the insertion point to the beginning of the next line.

- Press the ENTER key again to insert a blank line between the greeting line and the message text (Figure 1–16).

What does it mean if I use all capital letters in my email message?

Writing in all capital letters is considered the same as shouting. Use proper capitalization as you compose your email.

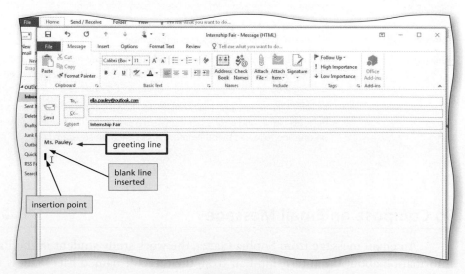

Figure 1–16

4

- Type `Please send me information about the Internship Fair for the Fall semester so I can begin promoting the event.` to enter the message text.

- Press the ENTER key two times to insert a blank line below the message text (Figure 1–17).

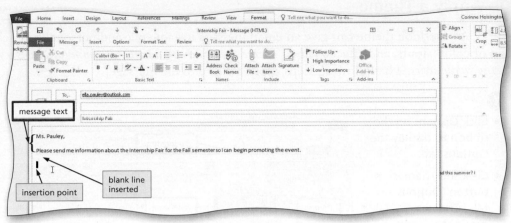

Figure 1–17

5

- Type `Thanks,` to enter the closing for the message.

- Press the ENTER key to move the insertion point to the next line.

- Type `Sophia Garza` as the first line of the signature.

- Press the ENTER key to move the insertion point to the next line.

- Type `Pathways Internship Office` as the second line of the signature.

- Press the ENTER key to move the insertion point to the next line.

- Type `Student Work Study` as the third line of the signature (Figure 1–18).

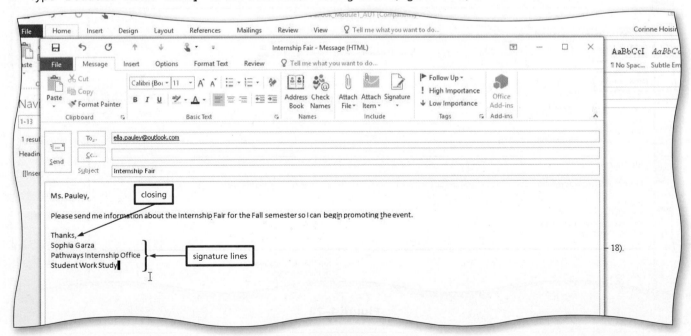

Figure 1–18

Q&A

What if I make an error while typing an email message?

Press the BACKSPACE key until you have deleted the error and then retype the text correctly. You also can click the Undo button on the Quick Access Toolbar to undo your most recent action.

Do I always need to type my last name in the signature of an email message?

No. If you and your recipient know each other, you can type only your first name as the signature.

Other Ways

1. Click Inbox folder, press CTRL+N

To Apply a Theme

An Outlook theme can give an email message instant style and personality. Each theme provides a unique set of colors, fonts, and effects. *Why? Themes give your organization's communications a modern, professional look using subtle styles.* The following steps apply a theme to the message.

- Click Options on the ribbon to display the Options tab.
- Click the Themes button (Options tab | Themes group) to display the Themes gallery (Figure 1–19).

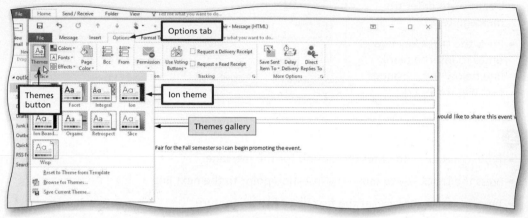

Figure 1–19

2

- Click Ion in the Themes gallery to change the theme of the message (Figure 1–20).

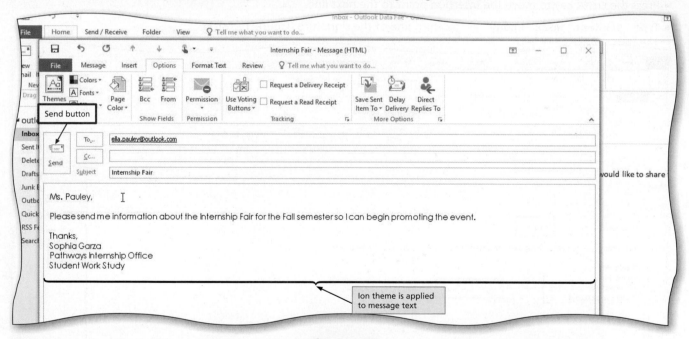

Figure 1–20

CONSIDER THIS

How can you create your own theme for your messages to strengthen your company's brand?

- Format a message with a customized font, colors, and background.
- Click the Themes button (Options tab | Themes group) to display the Themes gallery.
- Click Save Current Theme to display the Save Current Theme dialog box.
- Type a name in the File name text box to name your new theme.
- Click the Save button to save your new theme.

To Send an Email Message

1 CONFIGURE ACCOUNT OPTIONS | 2 COMPOSE & SEND | 3 VIEW & PRINT
4 REPLY | 5 ATTACH FILE | 6 ORGANIZE MESSAGES

Why? After you complete a message, send it to the recipient, who typically receives the message in seconds. The following step sends the completed email message to the recipient.

- Click the Send button in the message header to send the email message and close the message window.

Q&A What happened to the email message?
Outlook automatically sends email messages to their recipient(s) when you click Send in a new message window if you have your own email account set up.

Why did I get an error message that stated that 'No valid email accounts are configured. Add an account to send email'?
If you do not have an email account set up in Outlook, you cannot connect to the Internet to send the email. Click Cancel to close the error message.

Other Ways

1. Press ALT+S

How Email Messages Travel from Sender to Receiver

When you send someone an email message, it travels across the Internet to the computer at your email service provider that handles outgoing email messages. This computer, called the **outgoing email server**, examines the email address on your message, selects the best route for sending the message across the Internet, and then sends the email message. Many outgoing email servers use **SMTP (Simple Mail Transfer Protocol)**, which is a communications protocol, or set of rules for communicating with other computers. An email program such as Outlook contacts the outgoing email server and then transfers the email message(s) in its Outbox to that server. If the email program cannot contact the outgoing email server, the email message(s) remains in the Outbox until the program can connect to the server.

As an email message travels across the Internet, routers direct the email message to a computer at your recipient's email service provider that handles incoming email messages. A **router** is a device that forwards data on a network. The computer handling incoming email messages, called the incoming email server, stores the email message(s) until your recipient uses an email program such as Outlook to retrieve the email message(s). Some email servers use **POP3**, the latest version of **Post Office Protocol (POP)**, a communications protocol for incoming email. Figure 1–21 shows how an email message may travel from a sender to a receiver.

In most cases, the Auto Account Setup feature does not require you to enter the name of your POP or SMTP server, but many businesses require that you manually enter these server settings. You can verify these Internet email settings in the Change Account dialog box, which is displayed by tapping or clicking the File tab on the ribbon to open the Backstage view, tapping or clicking the Account Settings button in the Backstage view, tapping or clicking Account Settings to display the Account Settings dialog box, selecting your email address, and then tapping or clicking the Change button. Figure 1–22 shows the Change Account dialog box for Sophia Garza. Notice that this account uses a mail server named m.hotmail.com.

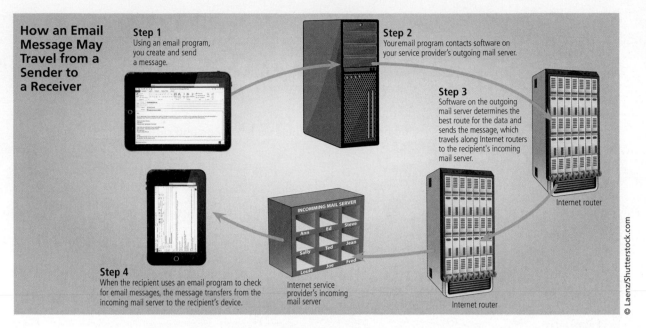

Figure 1–21

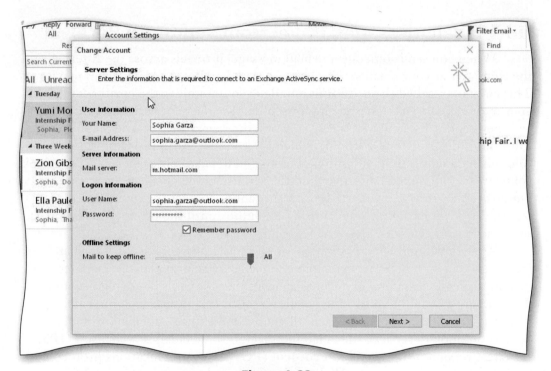

Figure 1–22

Working with Incoming Messages

When you receive email messages, Outlook directs them to your Inbox and displays them in the **message pane**, which lists the contents of the selected folder (Figure 1–23). The list of messages displayed in the message pane is called the **message list**. An unread (unopened) email message in the message list includes a blue vertical bar in front of the message and displays the subject text and time of arrival in a blue bold font. An open envelope icon indicates a previously read (opened) message.

The blue number next to the Inbox folder shows how many unread messages are stored in the Inbox. The email messages on your computer may be different.

You can read incoming messages in three ways: in an open window, in the Reading Pane, or as a hard copy. A **hard copy (printout)** is information presented on a physical medium such as paper.

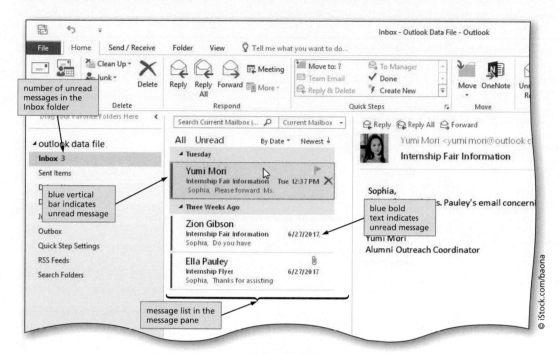

Figure 1–23

BTW

Know the Sender

If you receive an email message from someone you do not know, you should not open it because it might trigger a virus. Unsolicited email messages, known as **spam** or **junk email**, are email messages sent from an unknown sender to many email accounts, usually advertising a product or service such as low-cost medication, low-interest loans, or free credit reports. Do not click a hyperlink in an email message from an unknown sender. A **hyperlink** is a word, phrase, symbol, or picture in an email message or on a webpage that, when tapped or clicked, directs you to another document or website.

To View an Email Message in the Reading Pane

1 CONFIGURE ACCOUNT OPTIONS | 2 COMPOSE & SEND | 3 VIEW & PRINT

4 REPLY | 5 ATTACH FILE | 6 ORGANIZE MESSAGES

Why? *You can preview messages in your Inbox without opening them by using the Reading Pane.* The **Reading Pane** appears on the right side of the Outlook window by default and displays the contents of a message without requiring you to open the message. An advantage of viewing messages in the Reading Pane is that if a message includes content that could be harmful to your computer, such as a malicious script or an attachment containing a virus, the Reading Pane does not activate the harmful content. An **attachment** is a file such as a document or picture you send along with an email message. The attached document can be a file saved to your local computer or from OneDrive, as long as you have Microsoft's cloud service account connected. The instructor Ella Pauley has sent a response to Sophia concerning the Internship Fair. The following step displays an email message from a sender.

1

- Click the message header from Ella Pauley in the Inbox message list to select the email message and display its contents in the Reading Pane (Figure 1–24).

Q&A What happens to the message header when I select another message?
Outlook automatically marks messages as read after you preview the message in the Reading Pane and select another message to view. A read message is displayed in the message list without a vertical blue line or bold text.

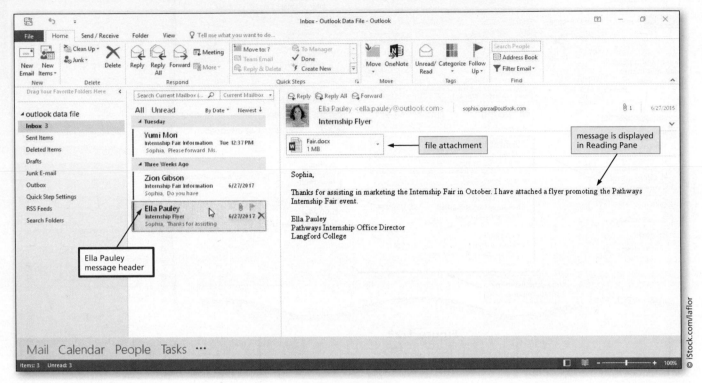

Figure 1–24

To Open an Email Message in a Window

1 CONFIGURE ACCOUNT OPTIONS | 2 COMPOSE & SEND | 3 VIEW & PRINT
4 REPLY | 5 ATTACH FILE | 6 ORGANIZE MESSAGES

Why? To fully evaluate an email message and use additional Outlook tools for working with messages, you display the email message in a window. The following step displays an email message from a sender in a window.

1

- Double-click the Ella Pauley message in the message list to display the selected email message in its own window (Figure 1–25).

Q&A Can I change the status of a message from unread to read without opening the message or displaying its contents in the Reading Pane?
Yes. Right-click the message you want to change, and then click Mark as Read on the shortcut menu.

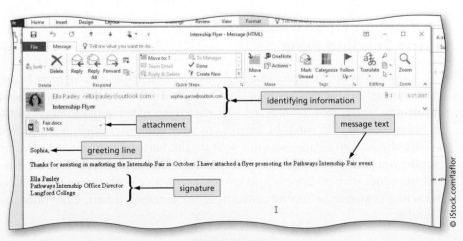

Figure 1–25

Other Ways

1. Click message header, press CTRL+O

Opening Attachments

Email messages that include attachments are identified by a paper clip icon in the message list. Users typically attach a file to an email message to provide additional information to the recipient. An attachment in a message can appear in a line below the subject line or in the message body. To help protect your computer, Outlook does not allow you to receive files as attachments if they are a certain file type, such as .exe (executable) or .js (JavaScript), because of their potential for introducing a virus into your computer. When Outlook blocks a suspicious attachment in a message, the blocked file appears in the InfoBar at the top of your message. An **InfoBar** is a banner displayed at the top of an email message that indicates whether an email message has been replied to or forwarded.

The **Attachment Preview** feature in Outlook allows you to preview an attachment you receive in an email message from either the Reading Pane in an unopened message or the message area of an opened message. Outlook has built-in previewers for several file types, such as other Office programs, pictures, text, and webpages. Outlook includes attachment previewers that work with other Microsoft Office programs so that users can preview an attachment without opening it. These attachment previewers are turned on by default. To preview an attached file created in an Office application, you must have Office installed on your computer. For example, to preview an Excel attachment in Outlook, you must have Excel installed. If an attachment cannot be previewed, you can double-click the attachment to open the file.

BTW
Organizing Files and Folders
You should organize and store files in folders so that you easily can find the files later. For example, if you are taking an introductory technology class called CIS 101, a good practice would be to save all Outlook files in an Outlook folder in a CIS 101 folder. For a discussion of folders and detailed examples of creating folders, refer to the Office and Windows module at the beginning of this book.

To Preview and Save an Attachment

1 CONFIGURE ACCOUNT OPTIONS | 2 COMPOSE & SEND | 3 VIEW & PRINT
4 REPLY | 5 ATTACH FILE | 6 ORGANIZE MESSAGES

Why? *When you receive a message with an attachment, you can preview the attached file without opening it if you are not sure of the contents.* A common transmission method of viruses is by email attachments, so be sure that you trust the sender before opening an attached file. The following steps preview and save an attachment without opening the file. You should save the attachment on your hard disk, OneDrive, or a location that is most appropriate to your situation. These steps assume you already have created folders for storing your files, for example, a CIS 101 folder (for your class) that contains an Outlook folder with a Module 01 folder (for your assignments). Thus, these steps save the attachment in the Module 01 folder in your desired save location. For a detailed example of the procedure for saving a file in a folder or saving a file on OneDrive, refer to the Office and Windows module at the beginning of this book.

1

- Click the Fair.docx file attachment in the message header of the opened email from Ella Pauley to preview the attachment within Outlook (Figure 1–26).

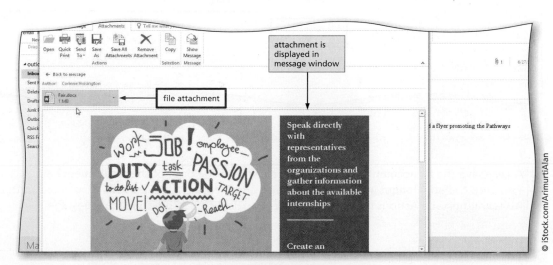

Figure 1–26

© iStock.com/ArimurtiAlan

- Click the Save As button (Attachment Tools Attachments tab | Actions group) to display the Save Attachment dialog box.

- Navigate to the desired save location (in this case, the Module 01 folder in your Outlook folder or your class folder on your computer or OneDrive).

- If requested by your instructor, add your last name to the end of the file name (Figure 1–27).

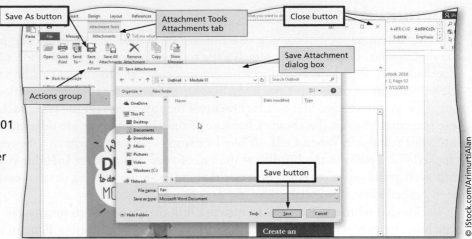

Figure 1–27

- Click the Save button (Save Attachment dialog box) to save the document in the selected folder in the selected location with the entered file name.

- Click the Close button to close the attachment preview window and email message (Figure 1–28).

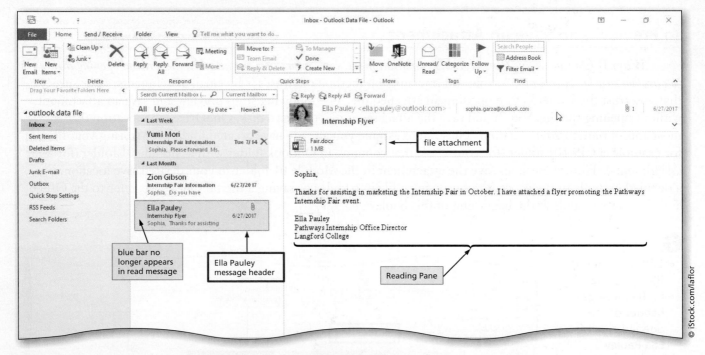

Figure 1–28

Q&A After I save the attachment, can I keep the email message but not the attachment?

Yes. Click the attachment in the Reading Pane, and then click the Remove Attachment button (Attachment Tools Attachments tab | Actions group) to remove the attachment from the email message.

Other Ways

1. Right-click attachment, click Save As

© iStock.com/ArimurtiAlan

© iStock.com/laflor

To Open an Attachment

1 CONFIGURE ACCOUNT OPTIONS | 2 COMPOSE & SEND | 3 VIEW & PRINT | 4 REPLY
5 ATTACH FILE | 6 ORGANIZE MESSAGES

If you know the sender and you know the attachment is safe, you can open the attached file. The following steps open an attachment. *Why? By opening a Word attachment in Microsoft Word, you can edit the document with the full features of Word.*

1

- If necessary, click the message header from Ella Pauley in the Inbox message list to select the email message and display its contents in the Reading Pane.

- Double-click the attachment in the Reading Pane to open the file attachment in Microsoft Word in Protected View (Figure 1–29).

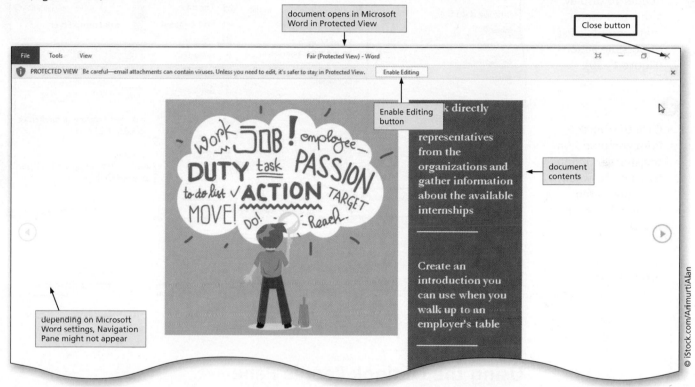

Figure 1–29

 Q&A Why does the attachment open in Protected View in Microsoft Word?
File attachments can contain viruses, worms, or other kinds of malware, which can harm your computer. To help protect your computer, Microsoft Office apps open files from these potentially unsafe locations in Protected View. Click the Enable Editing button if you trust the sender to edit the document.

2

- Click the Close button to close the Word file.

To Print an Email Message

1 CONFIGURE ACCOUNT OPTIONS | 2 COMPOSE & SEND | 3 VIEW & PRINT | 4 REPLY
5 ATTACH FILE | 6 ORGANIZE MESSAGES

Occasionally, you may want to print the contents of an email message. *Why? A hard copy of an email message can serve as reference material if your storage medium becomes corrupted and you need to view the message when your computer is not readily available.* A printed copy of an email message also serves as a **backup**, which is an additional copy of a file or message that you store for safekeeping. You can print the contents of an email message from an open message window or directly from the Inbox window.

You would like to have a hard copy of Ella Pauley's email message for reference about the upcoming internship fair. The following steps print an email message.

- If necessary, click Home on the ribbon to display the Home tab.
- In the message list, right-click the Ella Pauley message header to display a shortcut menu that presents a list of possible actions (Figure 1–30).

- Click the Quick Print command on the shortcut menu to send the email message to the currently selected printer.

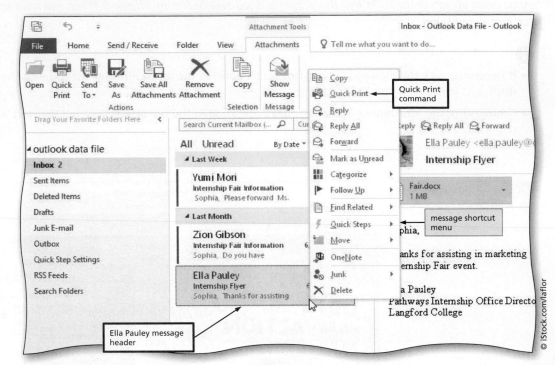

Figure 1–30

Other Ways

1. Press CTRL+P, click Print button

2. Click File tab, click Print tab (Backstage view), click Print button

Using the Outlook People Pane

Outlook provides a means of viewing email history, attachments, and meetings associated with each sender in the Reading pane. The **People Pane** accesses information about each of your contacts. The People Pane can display the photos and contact information of the email sender and recipient at the bottom of the Reading Pane in one location.

To Change the View of the People Pane

1 CONFIGURE ACCOUNT OPTIONS | 2 COMPOSE & SEND | **3 VIEW & PRINT** | **4 REPLY**
5 ATTACH FILE | **6 ORGANIZE MESSAGES**

By default, the People Pane is not displayed in the Reading Pane. By changing the People Pane to the Minimized setting, the contact information is displayed as a one-line bar below an open email message and does not take up a lot of room in the Reading Pane or open message window. To view more details, you can change the People Pane view to Normal. *Why? When you are reading a message in Outlook, you can use the People Pane to view more information about the contacts associated with the message, such as the senders and receivers of the message.* The following steps change the view of the People Pane.

1

- Click View on the ribbon to display the View tab.
- Click the People Pane button (View tab | People Pane group) to display the People Pane gallery (Figure 1–31).

Figure 1–31

2

- Click Normal in the People Pane gallery to display the People Pane in Normal view below the email message in the Reading Pane (Figure 1–32).

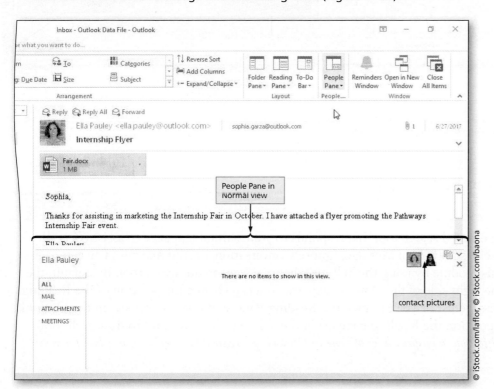

Figure 1–32

If you are using your finger on a touch screen and are having difficulty completing the steps in this module, consider using a stylus. Many people find it easier to be precise with a stylus than with a finger. In addition, with a stylus you see the pointer. If you still are having trouble completing the steps with a stylus, try using a mouse.

 Experiment

- Double-click the first contact picture in the People Pane. A contact card opens that displays the contact information. When you are finished, click the Close button to close the contact card.

 When the People Pane expands to Normal view, should messages from this sender be listed below the sender's name?

Yes. Email messages appear in the People Pane if you have previously corresponded with the sender.

A yellow message appears below Ella Pauley's name in the People Pane. How should I respond to the message?

Close the message by clicking its Close button.

- Click the People Pane button (View tab | People Pane group) to display the People Pane gallery.

- Click Minimized on the People Pane gallery to collapse the People Pane into a single line below the Reading Pane (Figure 1–33).

Q&A Does the People Pane update contact information automatically?
The People Pane automatically updates information about your professional and social network contacts while Outlook is running.

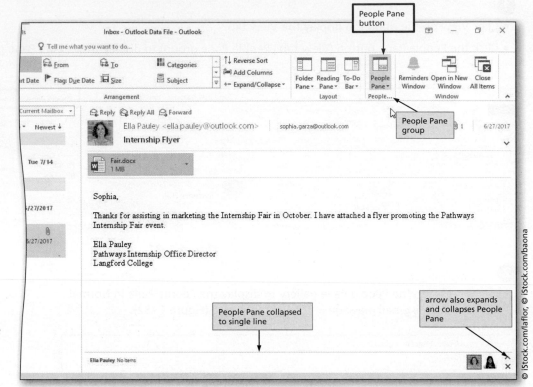

Figure 1–33

Other Ways

1. Click arrow to the right of the People Pane to expand or collapse pane

To Reposition the Reading Pane Using the Tell Me Search Tool

1 CONFIGURE ACCOUNT OPTIONS | 2 COMPOSE & SEND | 3 VIEW & PRINT | 4 REPLY
5 ATTACH FILE | 6 ORGANIZE MESSAGES

Outlook 2016 includes a powerful search tool that responds to your natural language to assist you with most tasks. By typing phrases such as New Mail Message, Ignore Conversation, or Add Account, you can perform the previous tasks in this module by using the Tell me what you want to do search tool. By default, the Reading Pane is displayed on the right side of the Outlook window. You can change the position of the Reading Pane so it appears below the message list or you can hide the Reading Pane so it does not appear in the Outlook window. The following steps reposition the Reading Pane using the Tell me what you want to do search tool. **Why?** *In your work and personal life, you may spend a lot of time in Outlook, so create a layout that works best for your own needs.*

- Click the 'Tell me what you want to do' text box, and then type `Reading Pane` (Figure 1–34).

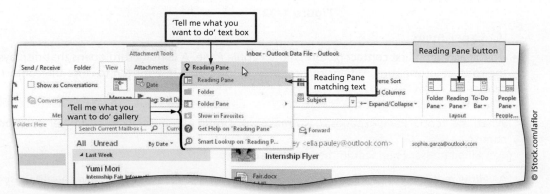

Figure 1–34

2

- Click the Reading Pane matching text option to display the Reading Pane options (Figure 1–35).

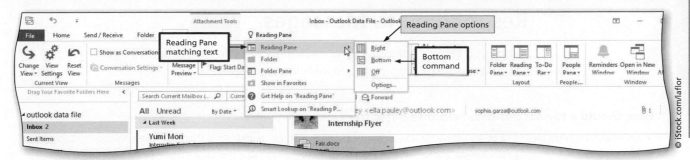

Figure 1–35

3

- Click Bottom in the Reading Pane options to place the Reading Pane for all mail folders at the bottom of the window (Figure 1–36).

message list appears at top of window

Reading Pane appears at bottom of window

Figure 1–36

4

- Using the ribbon, click the Reading Pane button (View tab | Layout group) to display the Reading Pane gallery.

- Click Right on the Reading Pane gallery to return the Reading Pane to the right side of the Outlook window for all mail folders (Figure 1–37).

Q&A Can you hide the Reading Pane completely?
Yes. Click the Reading Pane button and then click Off.

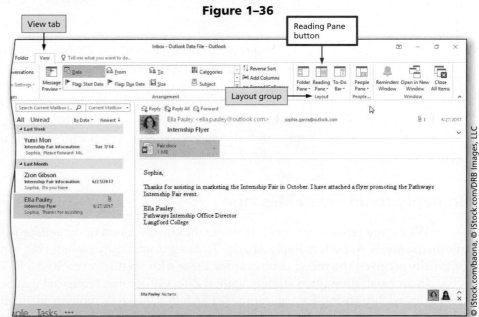

Figure 1–37

Break Point: If you wish to take a break, this is a good place to do so. To resume at a later time, continue to follow the steps from this location forward.

Responding to Messages

When you receive a message, you can send a reply to the sender. You also have the option to forward the message to additional people.

CONSIDER THIS

How should a formal business response differ from a close friend's response?

- An email response you send to an instructor, coworker, or client should be more formal than the one you send to a close friend placing your best foot forward. For example, conversational language to a friend, such as "Can't wait to go out!" is not appropriate in professional email messages.

- A formal email message should be business-like and get to the point quickly. An informal email is more conversational and friendly.

- Most professionals are required to sign a contract with their employer that states that the company has the right to have access to anything on your work computer so do not send personal emails from company email.

- All standard grammar rules apply, such as punctuation, capitalization, and spelling, no matter the audience.

When responding to email messages, you have three options in Outlook: Reply, Reply All, or Forward. Table 1–2 lists the response options and their actions.

Table 1–2 Outlook Response Options	
RESPONSE OPTION	**ACTION**
Reply	Opens the RE: reply window and sends a reply to the person who sent the message.
Reply All	Opens the RE: reply window and sends a reply to everyone listed in the message header.
Forward	Opens the FW: message window and sends a copy of the selected message to additional people, if you want to share information with others. The original message text is included in the message window.

© 2015 Cengage Learning

You reply to messages you already have received. You can forward an email message to additional recipients to share information with others. Based on the situation, you should request permission from the sender before forwarding a message, in case the sender intended the original message to remain private. When forwarding, you send the message to someone other than the original sender of the message. A reply sends the message to the person who sent the message.

To Reply to an Email Message

1 CONFIGURE ACCOUNT OPTIONS | 2 COMPOSE & SEND | 3 VIEW & PRINT | **4 REPLY**
5 ATTACH FILE | **6 ORGANIZE MESSAGES**

When you reply to an email message, the email address of the sender is inserted in the To box automatically. If you select Reply All, the To box automatically includes the sender and the other people who originally received the message (except for those who originally received a BCC message).

In an email message, a student named Zion Gibson has requested that Sophia send him information about the Pathways Internship Fair on campus. The following steps reply to an email message. *Why? When replying to a colleague, responding in a professional manner in an email message indicates how serious you are about your role and enhances your reputation within the organization.*

1

- Click Home on the ribbon to display the Home tab.
- Click the Zion Gibson message header in the message list to select it and display its contents in the Reading Pane (Figure 1–38).

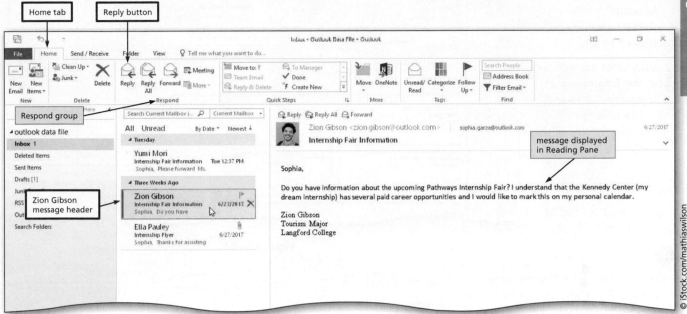

Figure 1–38

2

- Click the Reply button (Home tab | Respond group) to reply to the message in the Reading Pane (Figure 1–39).

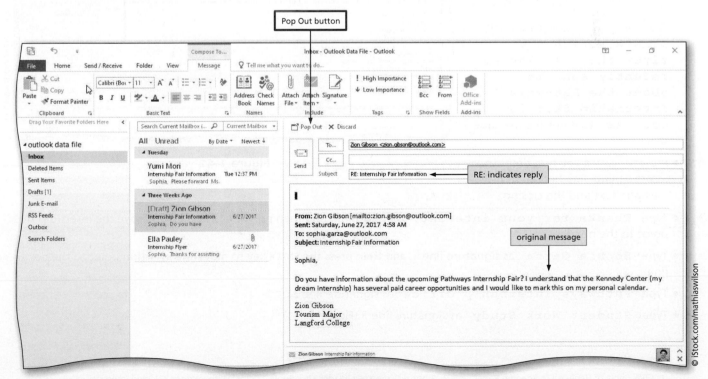

Figure 1–39

- Click the Pop Out button to display the RE: Internship Fair Information – Message (HTML) window (Figure 1–40).

Q&A Why does RE: appear at the beginning of the subject line and in the title bar?
The RE: indicates this message is a reply to another message. The subject of the original message appears after the RE:.

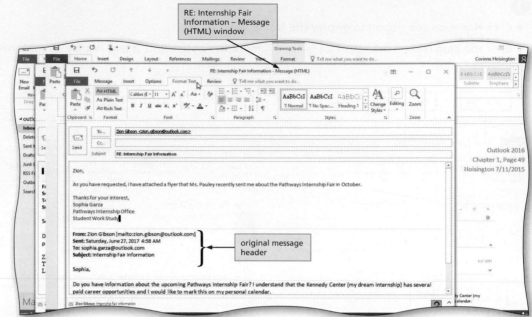

Figure 1–40

- If necessary, click the message area below the message header to position the insertion point at the top of the message area.

- Type **Zion,** as the greeting line.

- Press the ENTER key two times to insert a blank line between the greeting line and the message text.

- Type **As you requested, I have attached a flyer that Ms. Pauley recently sent me about the Pathways Internship Fair in October.** to enter the message text.

- Press the ENTER key two times to insert a blank line between the message text and the closing.

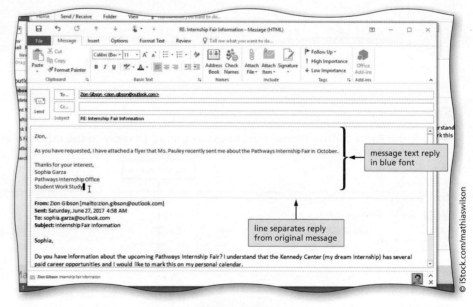

Figure 1–41

- Type **Thanks for your interest,** as the closing, and then press the ENTER key to move the insertion point to the next line.

- Type **Sophia Garza** as signature line 1, and then press the ENTER key to move the insertion point to the next line.

- Type **Pathways Internship Office** as signature line 2.

- Type **Student Work Study** as signature line 3 (Figure 1–41).

Other Ways

1. Click Reply or Reply All in Reading Pane
2. Right-click message header, click Reply
3. With message selected, press CTRL+R

Message Formats

As shown in Figure 1–42, Outlook's default (preset) message format is **HTML (Hypertext Markup Language)**, which is a format that allows you to view pictures and text formatted with color and various fonts and font sizes. **Formatting** refers to changing the appearance of text in a document such as the font (typeface), font size, color, and alignment of the text in a document.

Before you send an email message, reply to an email message, or forward an email message, consider which message format you want to use. A **message format** determines whether an email message can include pictures or formatted text, such as bold, italic, and colored fonts. Select a message format that is appropriate for your message and your recipient. Outlook offers three message formats: HTML, Plain Text, and Rich Text, as summarized in Table 1–3. If you select the HTML format, for example, the email program your recipient uses must be able to display formatted messages or pictures. If your recipient does not have high speed connectivity, a Plain Text format is displayed quickly, especially on a device such as a smartphone. Reading email in plain text offers important security benefits, reducing the possibility of a virus within the email.

Table 1–3 Message Formats	
MESSAGE FORMAT	**DESCRIPTION**
HTML	HTML is the default format for new messages in Outlook. HTML lets you include pictures and basic formatting, such as text formatting, numbering, bullets, and alignment. HTML is the recommended format for Internet mail because the more popular email programs use it.
Plain Text	Plain Text format is recognized by all email programs and is the most likely format to be allowed through a company's virus-filtering program. Plain Text does not support basic formatting, such as bold, italic, colored fonts, or other text formatting. It also does not support pictures displayed directly in the message.
Rich Text	Rich Text Format (RTF) is a Microsoft format that only the latest versions of **Microsoft Exchange** (a Microsoft message system that includes an email program and a mail server) and Outlook recognize. RTF supports more formats than HTML or Plain Text; it also supports hyperlinks. A hyperlink can be text, a picture, or other object that is displayed in an email message.

Can I use plain text formatting to guard against email viruses?
HTML-formatted messages can contain viruses. To minimize the risk of receiving a virus infected email message, change the format of messages you read. You can configure Outlook to format all opened messages in Plain Text. Click File on the ribbon to open the Backstage view. Click the Options tab. Click the Trust Center option in the Outlook Options dialog box, and then click the Trust Center Settings button to display the Trust Center dialog box. Click Email Security (Trust Center dialog box), and in the Read as Plain Text section, click the 'Read all standard mail in plain text' check box.

CONSIDER THIS

1 CONFIGURE ACCOUNT OPTIONS | 2 COMPOSE & SEND | 3 VIEW & PRINT | 4 REPLY
5 ATTACH FILE | 6 ORGANIZE MESSAGES

To Change the Message Format

Why? *You want to make sure that your reply message is not blocked by an antivirus program, so you will change the message format to Plain Text.* The following steps change the message format to Plain Text.

• Click Format Text on the ribbon in the message window to display the Format Text tab (Figure 1–42).

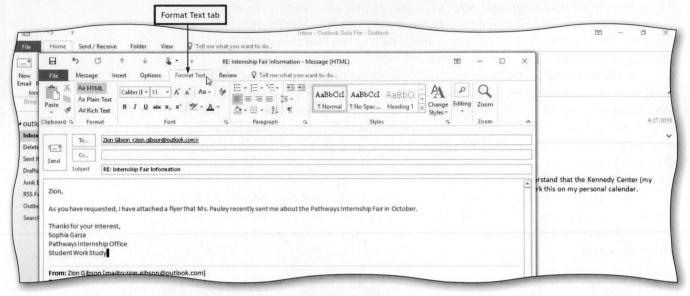

Figure 1–42

• Click the Plain Text button (Format Text tab | Format group) to select the Plain Text message format, which removes all formatting in the message.

• When the Microsoft Outlook Compatibility Checker dialog box is displayed, click the Continue button to change the formatted text to plain text (Figure 1–43).

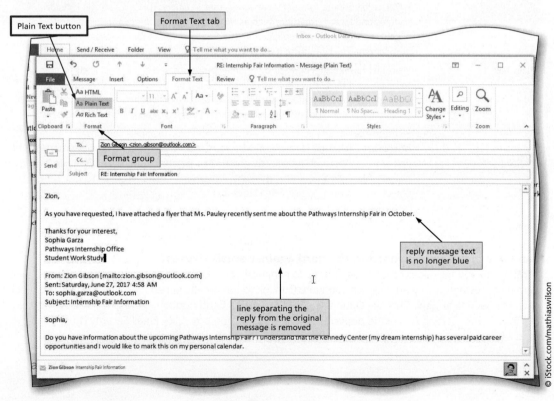

© iStock.com/mathiaswilson

Figure 1–43

Q&A

What happened to the line separating the existing message and the new message?

When Plain Text is selected as the message format, all formatting such as text color, font type, lines, themes, and size is removed.

Checking Spelling and Grammar

Outlook checks your message for possible spelling and grammar errors as you type and flags any potential errors in the message text with a red, green, or blue wavy underline. A red wavy underline means the flagged text is not in Outlook's main dictionary because it is a proper name or misspelled. A green wavy underline indicates the text may be incorrect grammatically. A blue wavy underline indicates the text may contain a contextual spelling error such as the misuse of homophones (words that are pronounced the same but have different spellings or meanings, such as one and won). Although you can check the entire message for spelling and grammar errors at once, you also can check these flagged errors as they appear on the screen.

A flagged word is not necessarily misspelled. For example, many names, abbreviations, and specialized terms are not in Outlook's main dictionary. In these cases, you instruct Outlook to ignore the flagged word. As you type, Outlook also detects duplicate words while checking for spelling errors. For example, if your email message contains the phrase *to the the store*, Outlook places a red wavy underline below the second occurrence of the word, *the*.

BTW

Misspelled Words in an Email Message
When you misspell words in a professional email message, your clients may think you are just sending a quick message and not giving the email your full attention when responding.

Should I remove the original message when replying?

Many email users prefer to reply to a message without including the original email message along with their response. To remove the original message from all email replies, click File to open the Backstage view, and then click the Options tab. Click Mail to display the Mail options. In the Replies and forwards section, click the 'When replying to a message box' arrow, select the 'Do not include original message' option, and then click OK.

CONSIDER THIS

---

1 CONFIGURE ACCOUNT OPTIONS | 2 COMPOSE & SEND | 3 VIEW & PRINT | **4 REPLY**
5 ATTACH FILE | 6 ORGANIZE MESSAGES

To Check the Spelling of a Correctly Typed Word

Sophia adds one more sentence to her email message, recalling that Zion is interested in an internship at the Kennedy Center. In the message, the Kennedy Center employer with the last name of Kolat has a red wavy line below it even though it is spelled correctly, indicating the word is not in Outlook's main dictionary. The following steps ignore the error and remove the red wavy line. *Why? The main dictionary contains most common words, but does not include most proper names, technical terms, or acronyms.*

1

- Click after the first sentence in the email message to Zion to place the insertion point, and then press the SPACEBAR to insert a space.

- Type I understand that Mr. Kolat, the marketing

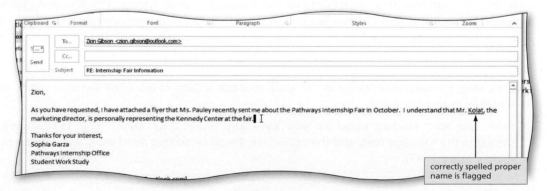

Figure 1–44

director, is personally representing the Kennedy Center at the fair. to enter a second sentence in the message text, and then click a blank spot in the window to have Outlook mark a spelling error (Figure 1–44).

 Why does a red wavy line appear below Kolat even though the last name is spelled correctly?
Outlook places a red wavy line below any word that is not in its main dictionary.

- Right-click the red wavy line below the proper name to display a shortcut menu that presents a list of suggested spelling corrections for the flagged word (in this case, the last name) (Figure 1–45).

Q&A What if Outlook does not flag my spelling and grammar errors with wavy underlines?

To verify that the check spelling and grammar as you type features are enabled, click the File tab on the ribbon to open the Backstage view and then click Options to display the Outlook Options dialog box. Click Mail (Outlook Options dialog box) and click the Editor Options button to display the Editor Options dialog box. In the 'When correcting spelling in Outlook' section, ensure the 'Check spelling as you type' check box contains a check mark. Click the OK button two times to close each open dialog box.

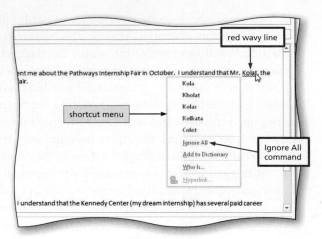

Figure 1–45

- Click Ignore All on the shortcut menu to ignore this flagged error, close the shortcut menu, and remove the red wavy line beneath the proper name (Figure 1–46).

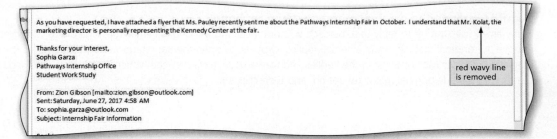

Figure 1–46

To Check the Spelling of Misspelled Text

1 CONFIGURE ACCOUNT OPTIONS | 2 COMPOSE & SEND | 3 VIEW & PRINT | 4 REPLY
5 ATTACH FILE | 6 ORGANIZE MESSAGES

In the following steps, the word *event* is misspelled intentionally as *evnt* to illustrate Outlook's check spelling as you type feature. If you are performing the steps in this project, your email message may contain different misspelled words, depending on the accuracy of your typing. The following steps check the spelling of a misspelled word. *Why? The way you present yourself in email messages contributes to the way you are perceived, so you should be sure to proofread and check the spelling of all communications.*

1

- Click after the second sentence in the email message to Zion to place the insertion point, and then press the SPACEBAR to insert a space.

- Type `Let Ms. Pauley know if you have any questions about the internship fair evnt.` to complete the message text, and then press the SPACEBAR so that a red wavy line appears below the misspelled word (Figure 1–47).

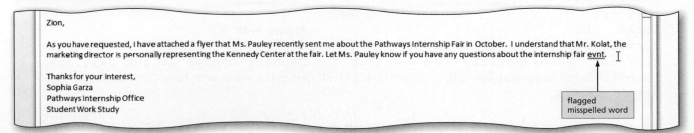

Figure 1–47

- Right-click the flagged word (evnt, in this case) to display a shortcut menu that presents a list of suggested spelling corrections for the flagged word (Figure 1–48).

Q&A What should I do if the correction I want to use is not listed on the shortcut menu? You can click outside the shortcut menu to close it and then retype the correct word.

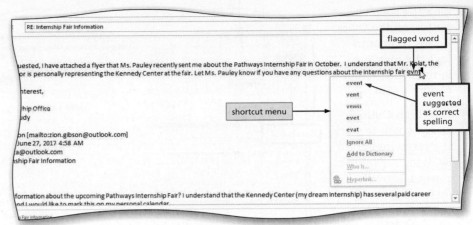

Figure 1–48

- Click the correct spelling on the shortcut menu (in this case, event) to replace the misspelled word in the email message with the correctly spelled word (Figure 1–49).

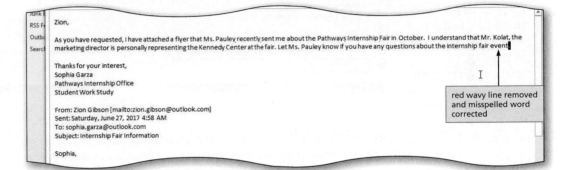

Figure 1–49

Other Ways

1. Click Review tab (message window), click Spelling & Grammar button (Review tab | Proofing group)
2. Press F7

Saving and Closing an Email Message

Occasionally, you begin composing a message but cannot complete it. You may be waiting for information from someone else to include in the message, or you might prefer to rewrite the message later after you have time to evaluate its content. One option is to save the message, which stores the message in the Drafts folder for your email account until you are ready to send it. The Drafts folder is the default location for all saved messages. Later, you can reopen the message, finish writing it, and then send it.

To Save and Close an Email Message without Sending It

1 CONFIGURE ACCOUNT OPTIONS | 2 COMPOSE & SEND | 3 VIEW & PRINT | 4 REPLY
5 ATTACH FILE | 6 ORGANIZE MESSAGES

The Internship Fair information that Zion Gibson requested has been drafted, but Sophia is not ready to send it yet. The following steps save a message in the Drafts folder for completion at a later time. *Why? If you are in the middle of composing a lengthy or important email and get called away, you can save your work so you can resume it later.*

1

- Click the Save button on the Quick Access Toolbar to save the message in the Drafts folder (Figure 1–50).

Q&A How does Outlook know where to store the saved message?
By default, Outlook stores saved messages in the Drafts folder for your email account.

Can I save the message to a location other than the Drafts folder?
To save the message to the Outlook student folder, click the File tab on the ribbon to open the Backstage view, and then click Save As in the Backstage view to display the Save As dialog box. Navigate to the Outlook student folder. In the File name text box, type the name of the message file and then click the Save button. The message is saved with the extension .msg, which represents an Outlook message.

What should I do if Outlook did not save the message in the Drafts folder?
Click the Home tab, click the Move button, click Other Folder, select the Drafts folder for Sophia Garza's Outlook Data File, and then click the OK button.

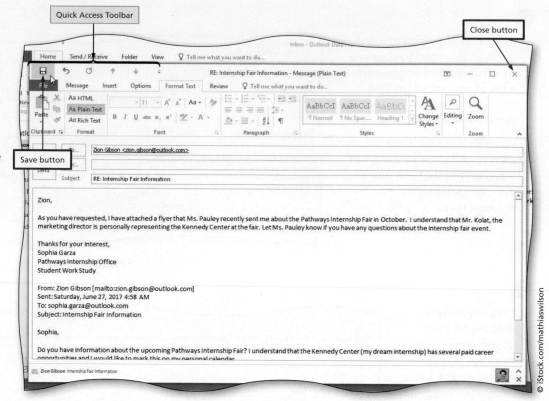

Figure 1–50

© iStock.com/mathiaswilson

2

- Click the Close button on the title bar to close the RE: Internship Fair Information – Message (HTML) window (Figure 1–51).

Q&A How do I know when a message is a draft rather than an incoming message?
The message appears in the message list with [Draft] displayed in red.

What happens if I click the Close button without saving the message?
If you create a message and then click the Close button, Outlook displays a dialog box asking if you want to save the changes. If you click Yes, Outlook saves the file to the Drafts folder and closes the message window. If you click No, Outlook discards the email message and closes the message window.

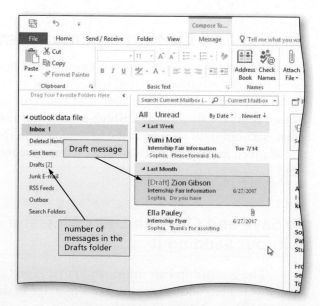

Figure 1–51

Other Ways

1. Click Close button and click Yes to keep saved draft of message   2. Press F12

To Open a Saved Email Message

The following steps open the message saved in the Drafts folder. *Why? By default, Outlook saves any email message in the Drafts folder every three minutes.* You can also save a message and reopen it later.

1

- Click the Drafts folder in the Navigation Pane to display the message header for the Zion Gibson email message in the message list (Figure 1–52).

Q&A

What should I do if the message does not appear in my Drafts folder?

If the message does not appear in the Drafts folder, return to the Inbox, and then click the message header in the message pane.

Figure 1–52

2

- Double-click the Zion Gibson message header in the Drafts folder to open the email message (Figure 1–53).

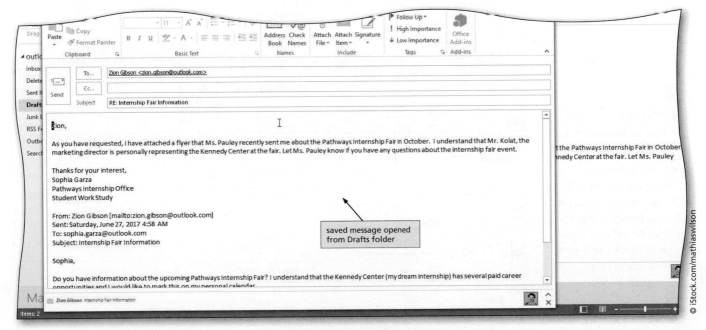

Figure 1–53

Other Ways

1. Right-click message, and click Open
2. With message selected, press CTRL+O

To Attach a File to an Email Message

To share a file such as a photo, flyer, or business document through email, you attach the file to an email message. Outlook does not have a predefined file size limit for attachments, but an email service provider may restrict the size of incoming attachments or the size of the email mailbox. Very large email attachments may be rejected by the recipient's email service provider and returned to the sender as undeliverable. Consider storing large files in OneDrive and sharing a link to the file within an email.

Before you send the email message to Zion, you need to attach a file of a flyer describing the informational meeting about the Internship Fair. The file may be listed on a Recent Items listing when the Attach File button is clicked or you can browse web locations or the local PC for the file attachment(s). The following steps attach a file to an email message. **Why?** *Attaching a file to an email message provides additional information to a recipient.*

1

- Click the Attach File button (Message tab | Include group) to display a listing of Recent Items.

- Click Browse This PC and navigate to the folder containing the data files for this module (in this case, the Module 01 folder in the Outlook folder in the Data Files folder) (Figure 1–54).

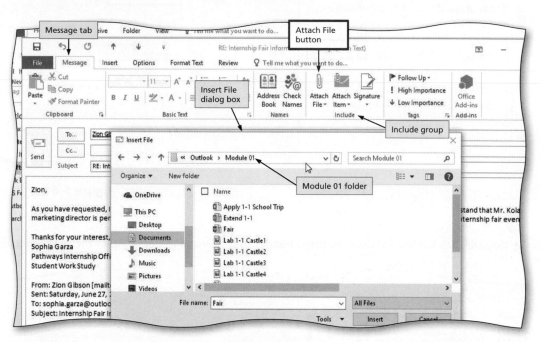

Figure 1–54

2

- Click the document Fair to select the file to attach.

- Click the Insert button (Insert File dialog box) to attach the selected file to the email message and close the Insert File dialog box (Figure 1–55).

Q&A
What should I do if I saved the Fair document to include my last name in the filename?
Select that document and then click the Insert button.

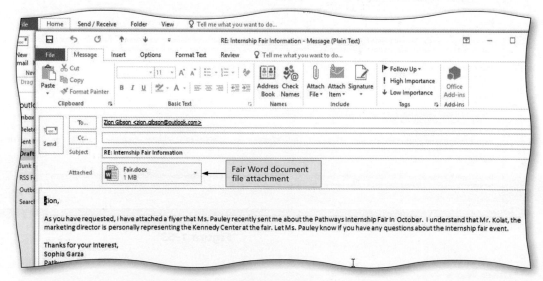

Figure 1–55

Other Ways

1. Click Insert tab, click Attach File button (Insert tab | Include group)
2. Drag file to message area
3. Right-click file attachment, click Copy, right-click message area, click Paste

To Set Message Importance and
Send the Message

1 CONFIGURE ACCOUNT OPTIONS | 2 COMPOSE & SEND | 3 VIEW & PRINT | 4 REPLY
5 ATTACH FILE | 6 ORGANIZE MESSAGES

Why? When you have a message that requires urgent attention, you can send the message with a high importance level. Outlook provides the option to assign an **importance level** to a message, which indicates to the recipient the priority level of an email message. The default importance level for all new messages is normal importance, but you can change the importance level to high or low, depending on the priority level of the email message. A message sent with **high importance** displays a red exclamation point in the message header and indicates to the recipient that the message requires a higher priority than other messages he or she might have received. The **low importance** option displays a blue arrow and indicates to the recipient a low priority for the message. The following steps set the high importance option for a single email message and to send the message.

1

- Click the High Importance button (Message tab | Tags group) to add a high importance level (a red exclamation point) to the email message (Figure 1–56).

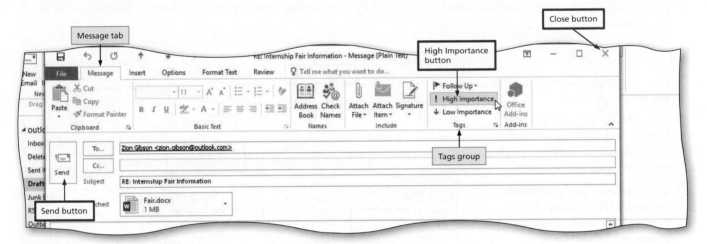

Figure 1–56

Q&A When does a red exclamation point appear in a message with high importance?
The red exclamation point appears in the message header when the message is received.

How would I set a low importance to an email message?
Click the Low Importance button (Message tab | Tags group).

2

- Click the Send button in the message header to send the email message.
- If necessary, click the Cancel button to close the Microsoft Outlook dialog box and then click the Close button to close the message window.

Q&A A message appeared that states 'No valid email accounts are configured. Add an account to send email'. What does this mean?
The Sophia.pst data file is an Outlook Data File, which cannot send an email message. If you are using the Sophia.pst data file, the sent message remains in the Drafts folder unless you configure an email account. You can set up and configure your own email address in Outlook to send an email message.

What happens to the actual email message after I send it?
After Outlook closes the message window, it stores the email message reply in the Outbox folder while it sends the message to the recipient. You might not see the message in the Outbox because Outlook usually stores it there only briefly. Next, Outlook moves the message to the Sent Items folder. The original message in the message list now shows an envelope icon with a purple arrow to indicate a reply was sent.

CONSIDER THIS

Can you place a tag in an email message that requests the recipient to respond within a certain time period?

- If you are sending an email message that requires a timely response, you can click the Follow Up button (Message tab | Tags group) to insert a flag icon indicating that the recipient should respond within a specified period of time.

- Based on your expected response time, you can select the Follow Up flag for Today, Tomorrow, This Week, Next Week, No Date, or Custom.

To Forward an Email Message

1 CONFIGURE ACCOUNT OPTIONS | 2 COMPOSE & SEND | 3 VIEW & PRINT | 4 REPLY
5 ATTACH FILE | 6 ORGANIZE MESSAGES

When you forward an email message, you resend a received or sent email message to another recipient. Yumi Mori, the Alumni Outreach coordinator, sent Sophia an email message requesting that she forward Ms. Pauley's email message about the Internship Fair to advertise on their website. Sophia adds Ms. Pauley as a courtesy copy (cc) recipient to make her aware that Yumi is receiving a copy of her email message. The following steps forward a previously received email message. *Why? Forwarding sends an email to someone who was not on the original recipient list.*

1

- Click the Inbox folder to display the Inbox messages.

- Click the Yumi Mori message header and read her message requesting information about the Pathways Internship Fair.

- Click the Ella Pauley message header in the message list to select the email message (Figure 1–57).

 Why do my message headers show times instead of dates?
Outlook shows today's messages with times in the headers and messages prior to today with dates in the headers.

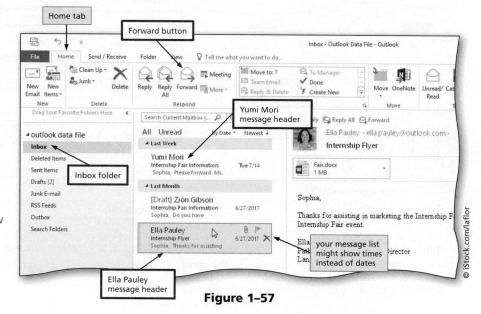

Figure 1–57

2

- Click the Forward button (Home tab | Respond group) to display the message in the Reading Pane (Figure 1–58).

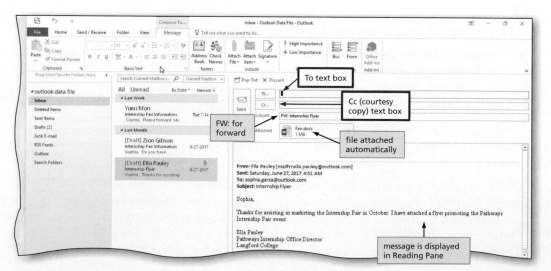

Figure 1–58

- Click the To text box, and then type `yumi.mori@outlook.com` (with no spaces) as the recipient's email address.

- Click the Cc text box, and then type `ella.pauley@outlook.com` (with no spaces) to send a courtesy copy to inform the original sender that you are forwarding her email message (Figure 1–59).

Experiment

- Click the Bcc button (Message tab | Show Fields group) to display the Bcc (blind carbon copy) text box. When you are finished, click the Bcc button (Message tab | Show Fields group) again to hide the Bcc text box.

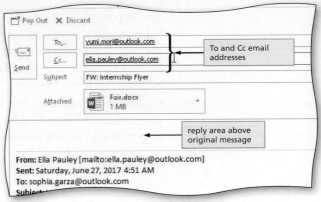

Figure 1–59

Q&A | Why does the original message appear in the message area of the window?
By default, Outlook displays the original message below the new message area for all message replies and forwards.

4

- Click the message area above the original message text, type `Yumi,` as the greeting line and then press the SPACEBAR.

- Right-click Yumi and then click Ignore All to remove the red wavy line.

- Press the ENTER key two times to enter a blank line before the message text.

- Type `Per your request, I am forwarding the email and internship fair flyer from Ms. Pauley about the Pathways Internship event.` to enter the message text.

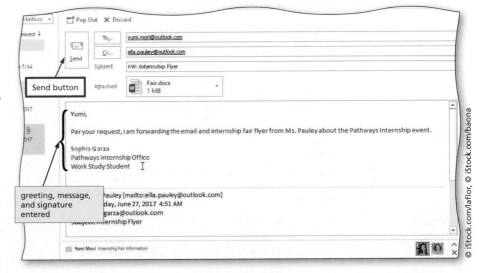

Figure 1–60

- Press the ENTER key two times to place a blank line between the message text and the signature lines.

- Type `Sophia Garza`   as signature line 1, and then press the ENTER key to move the insertion point to the next line.

- Type `Pathways Internship Office,` and then press the ENTER key.

- Type `Work Study Student` as the third line of the signature to represent her title (Figure 1–60).

Q&A | Does Outlook automatically forward the attachment to the recipient?
Yes. Outlook automatically adds the attachment to the forwarded message unless you choose to remove it.

5

- Click the Send button in the message header to forward the message.

- If necessary, click the Cancel button to close the Microsoft Outlook dialog box.

Other Ways
1. Right-click message header, click Forward   2. Click message header, press CTRL+F

Organizing Messages with Outlook Folders

To keep track of your email messages effectively, Outlook provides a basic set of **folders**, which are containers for storing Outlook items of a specific type, such as messages, appointments, or contacts. Email is supposed to help you be more efficient and save time, but if you do not manage it effectively, you can quickly become overloaded with messages. The Inbox is an email folder that stores your incoming email messages. Instead of leaving all of your incoming messages in the Inbox, you can create additional folders and then move messages to these new folders so you can organize and locate your messages easily.

To Create a New Folder in the Inbox Folder

1 CONFIGURE ACCOUNT OPTIONS | 2 COMPOSE & SEND | 3 VIEW & PRINT | 4 REPLY
5 ATTACH FILE | 6 ORGANIZE MESSAGES

By creating multiple folders within the Inbox folder, and then organizing messages in the new folders, you can find a specific email message easily. The following steps create a folder within the Inbox folder. *Why? Folders provide an efficient method for managing your email.*

- If necessary, click the Inbox folder to select it.
- Click Folder on the ribbon to display the Folder tab.
- Click the New Folder button (Folder tab | New group) to display the Create New Folder dialog box (Figure 1–61).

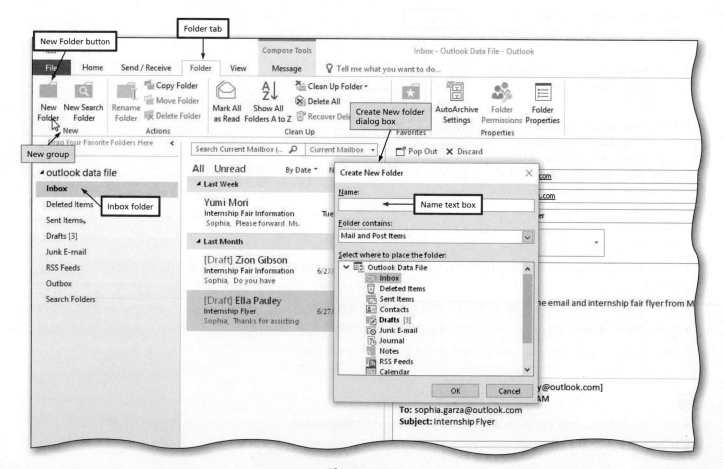

Figure 1–61

2

- Click the Name text box, and then type **Internship Fair** to name the folder within the Inbox folder.

- If necessary, click the Folder contains arrow, and then click 'Mail and Post Items' in the list to place only email messages in the new folder.

- If necessary, click Inbox in the 'Select where to place the folder' list to place the new folder within the Inbox folder (Figure 1–62).

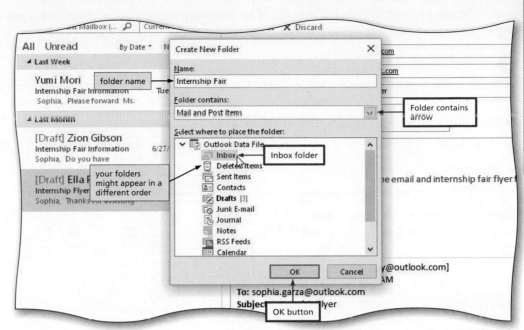

Figure 1–62

3

- Click the OK button to create the Internship Fair folder within the Inbox and close the Create New Folder dialog box (Figure 1–63).

Q&A | Why is the Internship Fair folder indented below the Inbox folder? The Internship Fair folder is stored within the Inbox folder. Outlook indents the folder in the list to indicate that it is within the main folder.

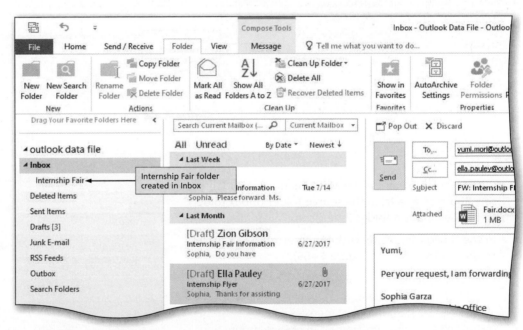

Figure 1–63

Other Ways

1. Right-click folder in Folder pane, click New Folder

To Move an Email Message to a Folder

1 CONFIGURE ACCOUNT OPTIONS | 2 COMPOSE & SEND | 3 VIEW & PRINT | 4 REPLY
5 ATTACH FILE | 6 ORGANIZE MESSAGES

Organizing important email messages about the Internship Fair event into the Internship Fair folder saves time when you search through hundreds or thousands of email messages later. Specifically, you will move the message from Ella Pauley from the Inbox folder to the Internship Fair folder. In this case, the Inbox folder is called the source folder, and the Internship Fair folder is called the destination folder. A **source folder** is the location of the document or message to be moved or copied. A **destination folder** is the location where you want to move or copy the file or message. The following steps move an email message into a folder. *Why? By organizing your emails into topical folders, you can access your messages easily.*

- In the Inbox folder (source folder), click the Ella Pauley message header in the Inbox message list to select the email message.
- Click Home on the ribbon to display the Home tab.
- Click the Move button (Home tab | Move group) to display the Move menu (Figure 1–64).

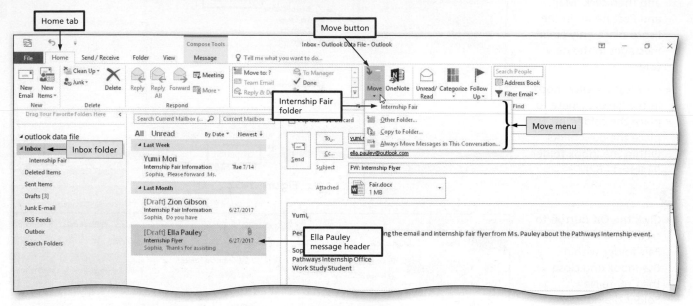

Figure 1–64

2

- Click Internship Fair on the Move menu to move the selected message from the source folder (Inbox folder) to the destination folder (Internship Fair folder).

- In the Navigation Pane, click the Internship Fair folder to display its contents (Figure 1–65).

Q&A Can I move more than one message at a time?
Yes. Click the first message to select it. While holding the CTRL key, click additional messages to select them. Click the Move button (Home tab | Move group) and then click the destination folder to select it.

Can I copy the email messages instead of moving them?
Yes. Select the message(s) to copy, and then click the Move button (Home tab | Move group). Click Copy to Folder on the menu to display the Copy Items dialog box. Select the destination folder, and then click the OK button to copy the selected message to the destination folder.

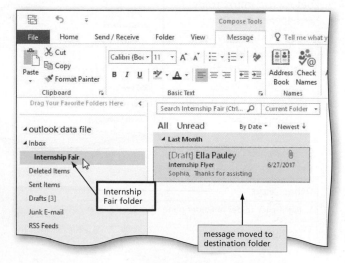

Figure 1–65

Other Ways

1. Right-click selected message, point to Move, click folder
2. Click selected message, drag message into destination folder

Outlook Quick Steps

An Outlook feature called **Quick Steps** provides shortcuts to perform redundant tasks with a single keystroke. For example, you can move an email message to a folder using a one-click Quick Step. You can use the built-in Quick Steps to move a file to a folder, send email to your entire team, or reply and then delete an email message.

1 CONFIGURE ACCOUNT OPTIONS | 2 COMPOSE & SEND | 3 VIEW & PRINT | 4 REPLY
5 ATTACH FILE | 6 ORGANIZE MESSAGES

To Move an Email Message Using Quick Steps

If you frequently move messages to a specific folder, you can use a Quick Step to move a message in one click. The following steps create a Quick Step to move an email message into a specific folder. *Why? Quick Steps allow you to customize email actions that you use most often.*

1

- Click the Inbox folder in the Navigation Pane to select the Inbox folder.
- If necessary, click Home to display the Home tab.
- Click Move to: ? in the Quick Steps gallery (Home tab | Quick Steps group) to display the First Time Setup dialog box (Figure 1–66).

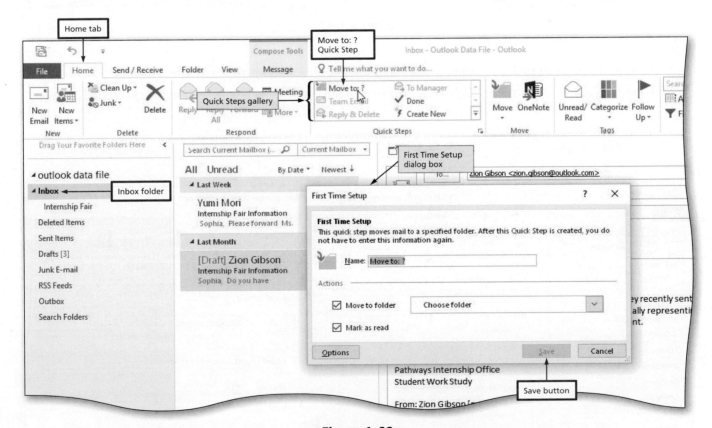

Figure 1–66

Q&A What should I do if Move to: ? does not appear on the Home tab?
Click the More button (Home tab | Quick Steps group), point to New Quick Step, and then click Move to Folder.

- Click the Move to folder arrow (First Time Setup dialog box) to display the list of available folders (Figure 1–67).

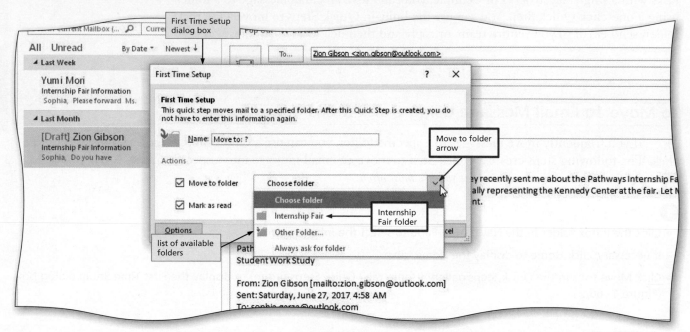

Figure 1–67

- Click the Internship Fair folder to create a Quick Step that moves a message to the specified folder.
- Click the Save button (First Time Setup dialog box) to save the Quick Step and display it in the Quick Steps gallery (Figure 1–68).

Q&A A Save button does not appear in my dialog box. What should I do?
Click the Finish button instead.

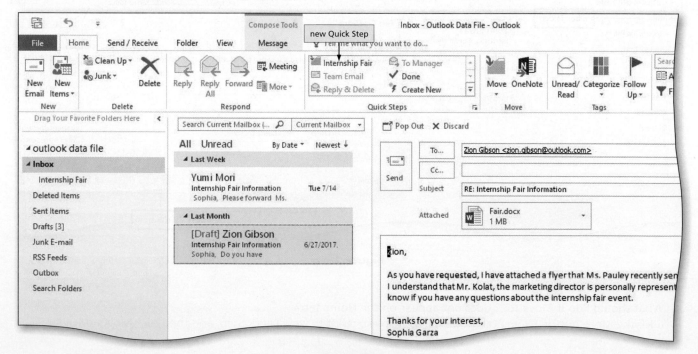

Figure 1–68

4

- In the Inbox folder, click the Yumi Mori message header in the Inbox message list to select the email message.

- Click Internship Fair in the Quick Steps gallery (Home tab | Quick Steps group) to move the message to the Internship Fair folder.

- In the Navigation Pane, click the Internship Fair folder to display its contents (Figure 1–69).

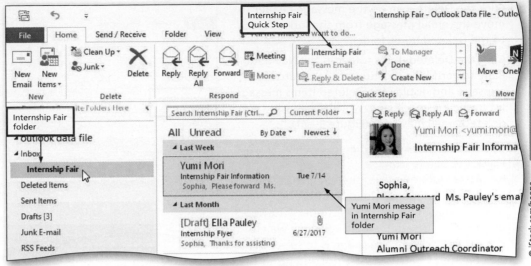

Figure 1–69

To Delete an Email Message

1 CONFIGURE ACCOUNT OPTIONS | 2 COMPOSE & SEND | 3 VIEW & PRINT | 4 REPLY
5 ATTACH FILE | 6 ORGANIZE MESSAGES

When you delete a message from a folder, Outlook moves the message from the folder to the Deleted Items folder. For example, Sophia no longer needs to keep the email message from Zion Gibson in the Inbox and has decided to delete it. The following steps delete an email message. *Why? Delete messages you no longer need so you do not exceed the limits of your mailbox.*

1

- Click the Inbox folder in the Navigation Pane to select the Inbox folder.

- Point to the Zion Gibson message header in the message list to display the Delete icon (Figure 1–70).

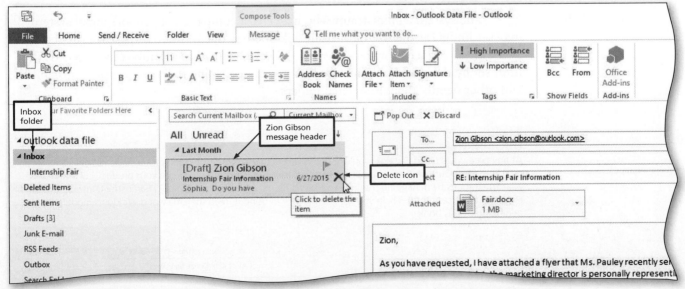

Figure 1–70

2

- Click the Delete icon on the message header to move the email message from the Inbox folder to the Deleted Items folder.

- Click the Deleted Items folder in the Navigation Pane to verify the location of the deleted message and display the Deleted Items message list in the message pane, which shows all deleted email messages (Figure 1–71).

Q&A

Is the email message permanently deleted when I click the Delete icon?

No. After Outlook moves the email message to the Deleted Items folder, it stores the deleted email message in that folder until you permanently delete the message. One way to permanently delete a message is to select the Deleted Items folder to view its contents in the message pane and then select the item to be deleted. Click the Delete icon on the message header and then click the Yes button in the Microsoft Outlook dialog box to permanently delete the selected item from Outlook.

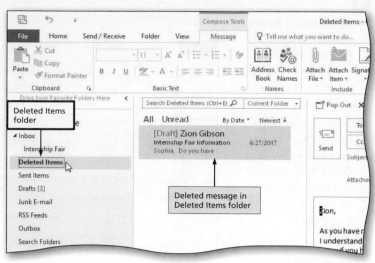

Figure 1–71

Other Ways

1. Drag email message to Deleted Items folder
2. Click email message, press DELETE
3. Click email message, press CTRL+D

How can you ignore future messages in an email thread?

- You can ignore future messages in an email thread through the Ignore Conversation feature. An **email thread** is a message that includes a running list of all the follow-up replies starting with the original email.

- Select an email message header that you no longer wish to view future messages and click the Ignore Conversation button (Home tab | Delete group) to delete this message as well as future messages within the email thread.

Working with the Mailbox

The system administrator who manages a company's or school's email system may set limits for the size of the Outlook mailbox due to limited space on the server. Some email service providers may not deliver new mail to a mailbox that exceeds the limit set by the system administrator. You can determine the total size of your mailbox and other details about individual folders.

BTW

Outlook Help

At any time while using Outlook, you can find answers to questions and display information about various topics through Outlook Help. Used properly, this form of assistance can increase your productivity and reduce your frustrations by minimizing the time you spend learning how to use Outlook. For instructions about Outlook Help and exercises that will help you gain confidence in using it, read the Office and Windows module at the beginning of this book.

To View Mailbox Size

1 CONFIGURE ACCOUNT OPTIONS | 2 COMPOSE & SEND | 3 VIEW & PRINT | 4 REPLY
5 ATTACH FILE | 6 ORGANIZE MESSAGES

The following steps view the amount of space available in the mailbox. *Why? You can determine if you are close to your mailbox size limit.*

1

- Click outlook data file in the Navigation Pane to select the mailbox.
- Click Folder on the ribbon to display the Folder tab (Figure 1–72).

Q&A | What is the outlook data file in the Navigation Pane?
In this case, the outlook data file is the mailbox of Sophia Garza.

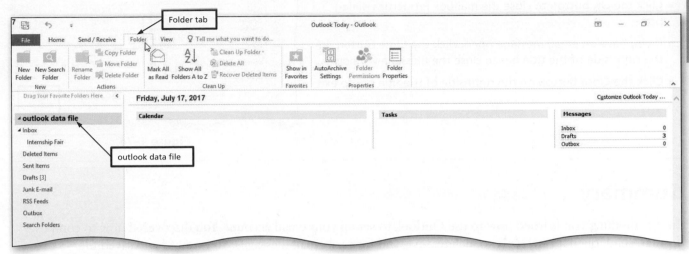

Figure 1–72

2

- Click the Folder Properties button (Folder tab | Properties group) to display the Properties dialog box for the mailbox (Figure 1–73).

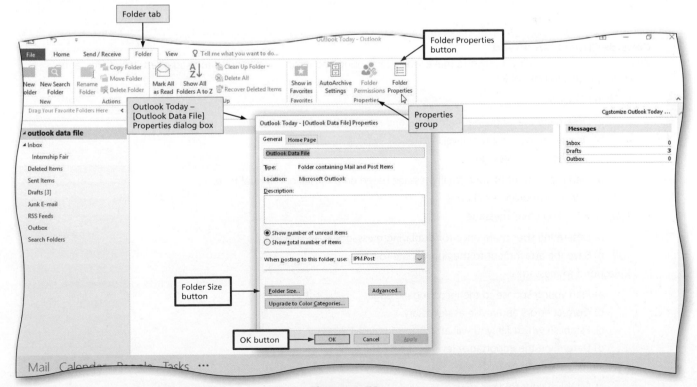

Figure 1–73

- Click the Folder Size button (mailbox Properties dialog box) to display the Folder Size dialog box (Figure 1–74).

4️⃣

- After viewing the folder sizes, click the Close button to close the Folder Size dialog box.

- Click the OK button to close the mailbox Properties dialog box.

- If you have an email message open, click the Close button on the right side of the title bar to close the message window.

- Click the Close button on the right side of the title bar to exit Outlook.

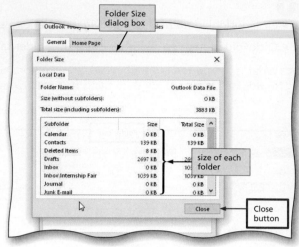

Figure 1–74

Summary

In this module, you learned how to use Outlook to set up your email account. You discovered how to compose, format, send, open, print, reply to, delete, save, and forward email messages. You viewed and saved file attachments and attached a file to an email message. You learned how to add a courtesy copy to an email message and set the sensitivity and importance of email messages. Finally, you created a folder in the Inbox and moved an email message to the new folder.

CONSIDER THIS

Consider This: Plan Ahead

What future decisions will you need to make when composing and responding to email messages, attaching files, and organizing your Outlook folders?

1. Set up Outlook.

   a) Determine the language preferences and sensitivity level.

   b) Decide on the sensitivity level.

2. Compose the email message.

   a) Plan the content of your email message based on a formal or informal tone.

   b) Select an appropriate theme.

3. Open incoming email messages.

   a) Determine your preference for displaying messages.

   b) Save the attachment to the appropriate folder.

4. Respond to messages.

   a) Plan your response to the incoming message.

   b) Correct errors and revise as necessary.

   c) Establish which file you will attach to your email message.

   d) Determine the importance level of the message.

5. Organize your Outlook folders.

   a) Establish your folder names.

   b) Plan where each email message should be stored.

How should you submit solutions to questions in the assignments identified with a symbol?

Every assignment in this book contains one or more questions with a symbol. These questions require you to think beyond the assigned file. Present your solutions to the question in the format required by your instructor. Possible formats may include one or more of these options: write the answer; create a document that contains the answer; present your answer to the class; discuss your answer in a group; record the answer as audio or video using a webcam, smartphone, or portable media player; or post answers on a blog, wiki, or website.

Apply Your Knowledge

Reinforce the skills and apply the concepts you learned in this module.

Note: To complete this assignment, you will be required to use the Data Files. Please contact your instructor for information about accessing the Data Files.

Creating an Email with an Attachment

Instructions: Run Outlook. You are to send an email message addressed to your instructor with information about the French Club's Spring Break trip to Saint Martin. You also attach an Excel workbook called Apply 1-1 School Trip, which is located in the Data Files.

Perform the following tasks:

1. Compose a new email message addressed to your instructor and add your own email address as a courtesy copy address.

2. Type **French Club Spring Break** as the subject of the email message.

3. Type **Greetings,** as the greeting line. Check spelling as you type.

4. Enter the text shown in Figure 1–75 for the message text.

5. Type **Thanks,** as the closing line.

6. Enter your name as the first signature line.

7. Type **French Club Publicity Manager** as the second signature line.

8. If requested by your instructor, type your personal cell phone number as the third signature line.

9. Attach the Excel workbook called Apply 1-1 School Trip, which is located in the Data Files, to the email message.

10. Click the File tab, and then click Save As. Save the message on your hard drive, OneDrive, or a location that is most appropriate to your situation using the file name Apply 1-1 French Club Trip.

11. Submit the email message in the format specified by your instructor.

12. Exit Outlook.

13. The attachment in the email message contained an Excel workbook. What file types are typically not allowed as a file attachment? Name at least two file types and explain why they are not allowed.

Continued >

STUDENT ASSIGNMENTS

Apply Your Knowledge *continued*

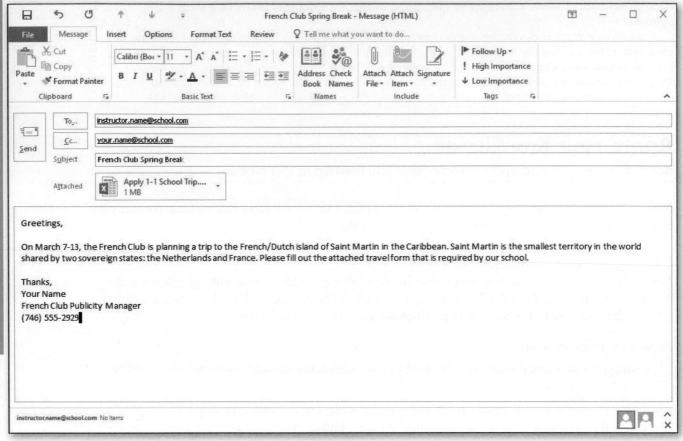

Figure 1–75

Extend Your Knowledge

Extend the skills you learned in this module and experiment with new skills. You may need to use Help to complete the assignment.

Organizing Email Messages

Note: To complete this assignment, you will be required to use the Data Files. Please contact your instructor for information about accessing the Data Files.

Instructions: Run Outlook. You are organizing a trip to Boston for you and your friends where you will participate as a group in an Escape Room activity and stay at a hostel. In the Extend 1-1.pst mailbox file, you will create two folders, add a folder in the Favorites section, and then move messages into the appropriate folders. You also will apply a follow-up flag for the messages in one of the folders. Use Outlook Help to learn how to duplicate a folder in the Favorites section, how to add a flag to a message for follow-up, and how to create an Outlook Data File (.pst file).

Perform the following tasks:

1. Open the Outlook mailbox file called Extend 1-1.pst, which is located in the Data Files.

2. Create two new folders within the Inbox folder. Name the first folder Escape Room and the second folder Hostels. Move the messages into the appropriate folders. Make sure that only mail items are contained in the new folders.

3. The Favorites section is at the top of the Folder Pane on the left. Display a duplicate of the Escape Room folder in the Favorites section.

4. Reply to the Boston Bay Hostel message indicating that you would like to book the hostel for the night of May 11. Sign your name to the email message. Assign high importance to the message.

5. Based on the message headers and content of the email messages in the Extend 1-1 mailbox, move each message to the appropriate folders you created. Figure 1–76 shows the mailbox with the messages moved to the new folders.

6. Export the Inbox mailbox to an Outlook Data File (.pst) on your hard drive, OneDrive, or a location that is most appropriate to your situation using the file name Extend 1-1 Boston.pst, and then submit it in the format specified by your instructor.

7. Exit Outlook.

8. ✸ Saving your mailbox as a .pst file provides a backup copy of your email messages to submit to your instructor. What are other reasons for saving your mailbox as a .pst file?

Figure 1–76

Expand Your World: Cloud and Web Technologies

Opening an Outlook.com Web-Based Email Message in the Outlook Client

Create a solution that uses cloud or web technologies by learning and investigating on your own from general guidance.

Note: To complete this assignment, you will be required to use the Data Files. Please contact your instructor for information about accessing the Data Files.

Instructions: In your Health class, you are presenting the topic, *Using a Health App to Track Your Workout*. Using Outlook, you compose an email message shown in Figure 1–77 and include a PowerPoint file attachment. Save the attachment from your outlook.com account to your OneDrive and edit the PowerPoint slides as a web app. Share the PowerPoint slides by providing a link to your OneDrive. Sharing files in the cloud as links can eliminate large attachments and saves email storage space.

Continued >

Expand Your World *continued*

Perform the following tasks:

1. If necessary, create a Microsoft account at outlook.com.

2. Compose a new email message from the client program, Outlook (not outlook.com). Address the email message to your Microsoft account with the message text shown in Figure 1–77. Select a theme of your choice. Replace the signature with your name and school name.

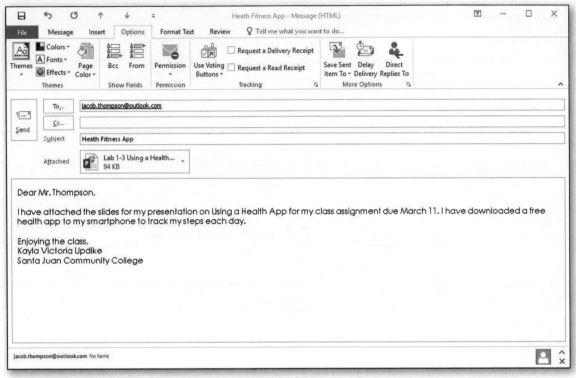

Figure 1–77

3. Attach the PowerPoint presentation called Lab 1-3 Using a Health App, which is located in the Data Files, to the email message.

4. Send the email message with high importance.

5. Open your Microsoft account at outlook.com. Open the email message that you sent from Outlook, click the attachment, and then click View online to view the PowerPoint file attachment.

6. Click Edit and Reply to edit the PowerPoint presentation in Microsoft PowerPoint Online.

7. If requested by your instructor, change the name on the first slide to your name on the first line and the name of your hometown on the second line.

8. Add a fourth slide to the PowerPoint presentation showing how far you have to walk to burn the calories in a typical slice of pizza. (*Hint:* Research this statistic on the web.)

9. Click the Insert tab, and then add a clip art image about walking to the fourth slide.

10. Click the File tab, and then click Share to share the PowerPoint file.

11. Click 'Share with people', and then type your instructor's email address and a short message describing how sharing a file by sending a link to your OneDrive can be easier than sending an attachment. Include your name at the end of the message.

12. Click the Share button to send the shared link of the completed PowerPoint file to your instructor.

13. Exit PowerPoint Online, and then exit Outlook.

14. ✴ In this exercise, you sent an email message from the Outlook client to your web-based email service provider at outlook.com. What are the advantages of using a Microsoft account with Outlook on your personal computer and checking the same email address at outlook.com when you are on a public computer?

In the Labs

Design, create, modify, and/or use files following the guidelines, concepts, and skills presented in this module. Labs 1 and 2, which increase in difficulty, require you to create solutions based on what you learned in the module; Lab 3 requires you to apply your creative thinking and problem-solving skills to design and implement a solution.

Lab 1: **Composing an Email Message with Attachments**

Note: To complete this assignment, you will be required to use the Data Files. Please contact your instructor for information about accessing the Data Files.

Problem: On a recent trip to Europe, your aunt took photos of castles using a digital camera. Because your aunt is new to technology, she asks you to extract the castle photos (provided in the Data Files) from her camera's memory card. She would like you to send them to her using email, because she is not on Facebook. Compose an email message to your aunt as shown in Figure 1–78 with the four picture attachments of castles.

Perform the following tasks:

1. Compose a new email message. Address the message to yourself with a courtesy copy to your instructor.

2. Enter the subject, message text, and signature shown in Figure 1–78. Insert blank lines where they are shown in the figure. If Outlook flags any misspelled words as you type, check their spelling and correct them.

3. Change the theme of the email message to the Integral theme.

4. If requested by your instructor, change the city and state from Zagreb, MN, to the city and state of your birth. Also change the signature to your name.

5. Attach the four image files called Lab 1-1 Castle1, Lab 1-1 Castle2, Lab 1-1 Castle3, and Lab 1-1 Castle4, which are located in the Data Files, to the email message.

6. Send the email message.

7. When you receive the message, open it, and then save the message on your hard drive, OneDrive, or a location that is most appropriate to your situation using the file name Lab 1-1 Castles. Submit the file in the format specified by your instructor.

8. ✴ Using one of your own email service providers, determine the maximum allowed mailbox size. Report the name of your email service provider, the maximum size, and whether you feel that is enough storage space.

Continued >

In the Labs *continued*

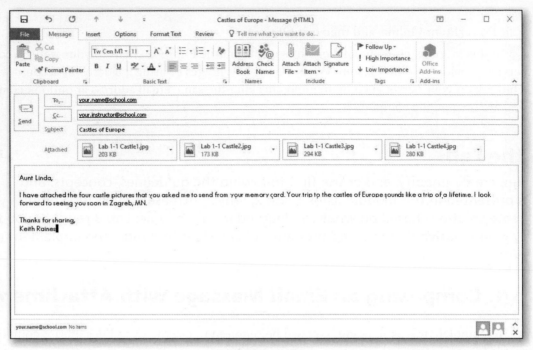

Figure 1–78

Lab 2: **Composing and Replying to an Email Message**

Problem: You recently moved into a new apartment. To turn on the electricity in your new apartment and place the bill in your name, you must fill out the request for electricity form. You need to send your completed form to the Compton Electric Company. First, you compose the email message shown in Figure 1–79a, and then you attach a file. Compton Electric Company responds to your email as shown in Figure 1–79b.

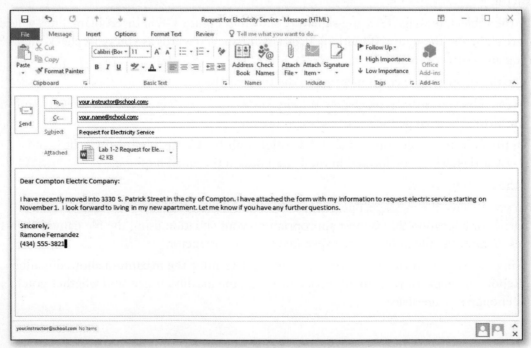

(a) Composed Email Message

Figure 1–79 (Continues)

(b) Response to Email Message
Figure 1–79

Perform the following tasks:

1. Create a new email message. Address the message to your instructor with a courtesy copy to yourself.

2. Enter the subject, message text, and signature shown in Figure 1–79a. Check spelling and grammar.

3. If requested by your instructor, change the address in the email message to your own address.

4. Change the theme of the email message to the Slice theme.

5. Change the importance of this email to high importance because you would like to move in immediately.

6. Attach the document called Lab 1-2 Request for Electricity, which is located in the Data Files, to the email message. You do not need to fill out this form.

7. Send the email message and use the HTML format for the message.

8. When you receive the email message, move it to a new folder in your Inbox named Apartment.

9. Open the message in the Apartment folder, and then compose the reply. Figure 1–79b shows the reply from Compton Electric Company. Reply using the text in the email message shown in Figure 1–79b. If Outlook flags any misspelled words as you type, check their spelling and correct them.

10. If necessary, change the format of the email message to Plain Text, and then send the message to yourself.

11. When you receive the RE: Request for Electric Service message, move it to the Apartment folder in your Inbox folder.

12. Select the original Request for Electricity message in the Sent Items folder. Save the message on your hard drive, OneDrive, or a location that is most appropriate to your situation using the file name Lab 1-2 Electric. Submit the file in the format specified by your instructor.

13. ⬢ Some company and utility websites do not include a phone number or a physical address. Why do you think that these business and utility sites only include an email address for correspondence?

Continued >

In the Labs *continued*

Lab 3: Consider This: Your Turn
Composing an Introductory Email Message to an Online Class Instructor and Attaching a File

Problem: For an online class, your instructor requests that you send an email message to introduce yourself. You decide to compose a new message and attach a file containing your favorite song.

Part 1: The email message you write should be addressed to yourself and your instructor. Insert an appropriate subject line based on the content of your message. Write a paragraph of at least 50 words telling the instructor about yourself (age, career interest, hobbies, and so forth). Next, attach one of your favorite songs to share your personality. In a second paragraph in the email message, explain why the attached song is your favorite. Apply a theme other than the Office theme. You can use your own digital music file as an attachment. Use the concepts and techniques presented in this module to create this email message. Be sure to check spelling and grammar before you send the message. Submit your assignment in the format specified by your instructor.

Part 2: ☀ You made several decisions while creating the email message in this assignment. When you decide on the subject of an email message, what considerations should you make? Why is it important that the email subject be eye-catching and informative? Why should you not use the following subject lines: FYI, Hey You, or Open This?

Inbox - Outlook Data File - Outlook
Microsoft Outlook 2016

File   Home   Send / Receive   Folder   View   Tell me what you want to do.

2 Managing Calendars with Outlook

Objectives

You will have mastered the material in this module when you can:

- Describe the components of the Outlook Calendar
- Add a personal calendar to Outlook
- Add a city to the calendar Weather Bar list
- Navigate the calendar using the Date Navigator
- Display the calendar in various views
- Add national holidays to the default calendar
- Enter, save, move, edit, and delete appointments and events
- Organize your calendar with color categories

- Set the status of and a reminder for an appointment
- Import an iCalendar and view it in overlay mode
- Schedule and modify events
- Schedule meetings
- Respond to meeting requests
- Peek at a calendar
- Print a calendar
- Save and share a calendar

Managing Calendars with Outlook

This introductory module covers features and functions common to managing calendars in Outlook 2016.

Roadmap

In this module, you will learn how to perform basic calendar tasks. The following roadmap identifies general activities you will perform as you progress through this module:

1. CONFIGURE the CALENDAR OPTIONS
2. CREATE AND MANIPULATE APPOINTMENTS
3. SCHEDULE EVENTS
4. SCHEDULE MEETINGS
5. PRINT a CALENDAR
6. SAVE AND SHARE a CALENDAR

Microsoft Outlook 2016

File   Home   Send / Receive   Folder   View   ♀ Tell me what you want to do...

Inbox - Outlook Data File - Outlook

At the beginning of step instructions throughout the module, you will see an abbreviated form of this roadmap. The abbreviated roadmap uses colors to indicate module progress: gray means the module is beyond that activity, blue means the task being shown is covered in that activity, and black means that activity is yet to be covered. For example, the following abbreviated roadmap indicates the module would be showing a task in the Schedule Events activity.

1 CONFIGURE CALENDAR OPTIONS | 2 CREATE & MANIPULATE APPOINTMENTS | 3 SCHEDULE EVENTS

4 SCHEDULE MEETINGS | 5 PRINT CALENDAR | 6 SAVE & SHARE CALENDAR

Use the abbreviated roadmap as a progress guide while you read or step through the instructions in this module.

Introduction to the Outlook Calendar

Plan your day, keep track of your deadlines, and increase your daily productivity. Whether you are a student, club organizer, or business professional, you can take advantage of the Outlook Calendar to schedule and manage appointments, events, and meetings. In particular, you can use Calendar to keep track of your class schedule and appointments and to schedule meetings. If you are traveling and do not have electronic access to your calendar, you can print a copy to keep with you. You can use Outlook to view a daily, weekly, or monthly calendar.

In addition to using Calendar in your academic or professional life, you will find it helpful for scheduling personal time. Most people have multiple appointments to keep each day, week, or month. Calendar can organize activity-related information in a structured, readable manner. You can create a calendar folder for a specific project and share it with your friends and professional colleagues.

Project — Appointments, Events, and Meetings in Calendar

By creating a daily time management schedule, you can stay organized and reduce your stress level. Managing your schedule using a calendar can increase productivity while maximizing free time. Outlook is the perfect tool to maintain both a professional and a personal schedule. The **Calendar** is the Outlook folder that contains your personal schedule of appointments, events, and meetings. In this project, Sophia Garza, the student work study employee for the Pathways Internship Office, sets up the basic features of Calendar to create her calendar for her appointments, classes, work schedules, and meetings (Figure 2 – 1).

People use a calendar to keep track of their schedules and to organize and manage their time. For students, a class list with room numbers and class times would be a good start toward managing their school schedule. For business professionals, the calendar is a dynamic tool that requires frequent updating to keep track of appointments and meetings. You also may want to keep track of personal items, such as doctor appointments, birthdays, and family gatherings.

BTW
Using Calendars
You can share your calendar with others online using OneDrive to make appointments, check free times, schedule meetings, and refer to contact information. This is especially useful when you are arranging and syncing events that depend on other people's schedules.

BTW
Deleting Items Permanently
Items you delete, including events and email messages, are stored in the Deleted Items folder in Mail view until you empty the folder by right-clicking the Deleted Items folder and then clicking Empty Folder on the shortcut menu.

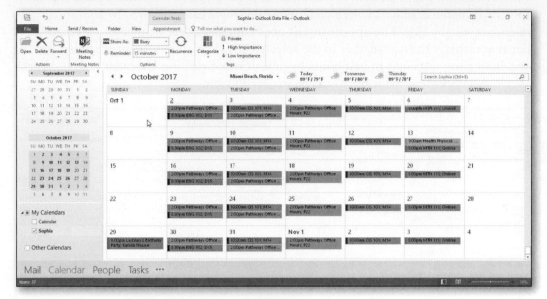

Figure 2–1

Configuring the Outlook Calendar

When you start Outlook, the Mail view appears. The Navigation bar displays four views — Mail, Calendar, People, and Tasks. You changed the Navigation bar icons to text in Module 1. By selecting Calendar, you can create a customized calendar to assist in scheduling your day, week, and month. Before scheduling your first calendar appointment, you can add a personal calendar and customize your settings to fit the way you work. Each day as you check your calendar for the day's events, the Weather Bar displays your local weather so you can plan whether you need an umbrella or take other weather precautions. By adding national holidays to your Outlook calendar, you can make sure these dates are prominent in your calendar.

BTW
The Ribbon and Screen Resolution
Outlook may change how the groups and buttons within the groups appear on the ribbon, depending on the computer's screen resolution. Thus, your ribbon may look different from the ones in this book if you are using a screen resolution other than 1366 × 768.

What advantages does a digital calendar like Outlook provide compared to a paper planner or wall calendar?

A digital calendar provides access from any location by synching your computer or smartphone with the cloud to view your appointments and meetings. You can view your schedule within an email meeting invitation. You can view more than one calendar at a time, share others' calendars, and overlay calendars to plan a meeting date with colleagues.

CONSIDER THIS

Calendar Window

The Calendar - Outlook Data File - Microsoft Outlook window shown in Figure 2–2 includes a variety of features to help you work efficiently. It contains many elements similar to the windows in other Office programs, as well as some that are unique to Outlook. The main elements of the Calendar window are the Navigation Pane and the appointment area.

The Navigation Pane includes two panes: the Date Navigator and the My Calendars pane. The **Date Navigator** includes the present month's calendar and the future month's calendar in Figure 2–2. The calendar displays the current month with a blue box around the current date, scroll arrows to advance from one month to another, and any date on which an item is scheduled in bold. The **My Calendars pane** includes a list of available calendars where you can view a single calendar or view additional calendars side by side. The **appointment area** contains a date banner and a Weather Bar that displays today's weather in the selected city. The appointment area displays one-hour time slots split in half hours by default when viewing Calendar in Day, Work Week, or Week view and is not available in Month view.

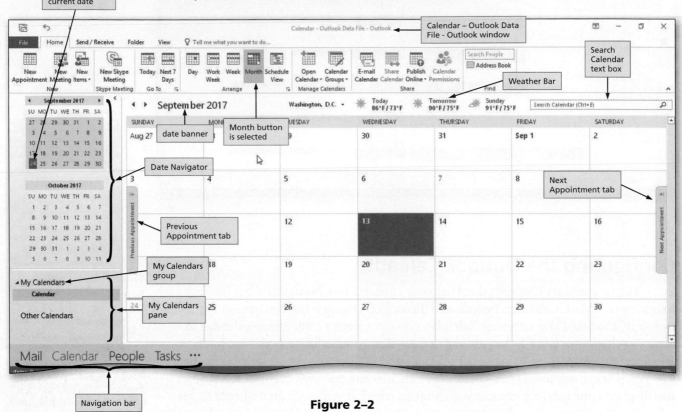

Figure 2–2

Calendar Items

BTW

Searching for Calendar Items
To find a calendar item, click the Search *Calendar Name* text box, and then type a word or phrase in the calendar item you are seeking. Items that contain the text you typed are listed with the search text highlighted. When you are finished, click the Close Search button (Search Tools Search tab | Close group).

An **item** is any element in Outlook that contains information. Examples of calendar items include appointments, events, and meetings. All calendar items start as an appointment. Outlook defines an **appointment**, such as a doctor's appointment, as an activity that does not involve other people or resources, such as conference rooms. Outlook defines an **event**, such as a seminar or vacation, as an activity that occurs at least once and lasts 24 hours or longer. An appointment becomes an event when you schedule it for the entire day. An annual event, such as a birthday, anniversary, or holiday, occurs yearly on a specific date. Events do not occupy time slots in the appointment area and, instead, are displayed in a banner below the day heading when viewing the calendar in Day, Work Week, or Week view. An appointment becomes a **meeting** when people and other resources, such as meeting rooms, are invited.

When you create items on your calendar, it is helpful to show your time using the appointment status information. You set the appointment status for a calendar item using the Show As button, which provides four options for showing your time on the calendar: Free, Tentative, Busy, and Out of Office. For example, if you are studying or working on a project, you might show your time as busy because you are unable to perform other tasks at the same time. On the other hand, a dental appointment or a class would show your time as Out of Office because you need to leave your home or office to attend. Table 2–1 describes the items you can schedule on your calendar and the appointment status option associated with each item. Each calendar item also can be one-time or recurring.

Table 2–1 Calendar Items

Calendar Item	Description	Show as Default
One-time appointment	Default calendar item, involves only your schedule and does not invite other attendees or require resources such as a conference room	Busy
Recurring appointment	Occurs at regular intervals, such as weekly, biweekly, monthly, or bimonthly	Busy
One-time event	Occurs at least once and lasts 24 hours or longer, such as a vacation or conference	Free
Recurring event	Occurs at regular intervals, such as weekly, biweekly, monthly, or bimonthly, such as holidays	Free
One-time meeting	Includes people and other resources, such as meeting rooms	Busy
Recurring meeting	Occurs at regular intervals, such as weekly, biweekly, monthly, or bimonthly, such as staff meetings or department meetings	Busy

To Create a Calendar Folder

1 CONFIGURE CALENDAR OPTIONS | 2 CREATE & MANIPULATE APPOINTMENTS | 3 SCHEDULE EVENTS
4 SCHEDULE MEETINGS | 5 PRINT CALENDAR | 6 SAVE & SHARE CALENDAR

When you schedule an appointment, Outlook adds the appointment to the Calendar folder by default. Sophia Garza plans to keep track of her work study business tasks at the job at the Pathways Internship Office as well as her personal and academic items instead of creating separate calendars for every aspect of her life. Users often create multiple calendars to keep personal items separate from academic or business items. As in other Outlook folders, such as the Inbox, you can create multiple folders within the Calendar folder that each contains one or more calendars. The following steps create a calendar to store your personal and school-related information separate from your default Calendar within the same calendar group. *Why? In certain situations, you may need to keep more than one calendar, such as one for business items and another for personal items.*

- Run Outlook 2016.

- Click Calendar on the Navigation bar to display the Outlook Calendar.

- Click Folder on the ribbon to display the Folder tab (Figure 2–3).

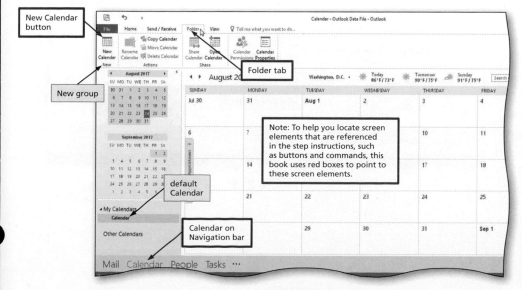

Figure 2–3

For an introduction to Office and instructions about how to perform basic tasks in Office apps, read the Office and Windows module at the beginning of this book, where you can learn how to run an app, use the ribbon, save a file, open a file, exit an app, use Help, and much more.

One of the few differences between Windows 8 and Windows 10 occur in the steps to run Outlook. If you are using Windows 8, scroll the Start screen and then click the Outlook 2016 tile.

BTW

Outlook and Screen Resolution
If you are using a computer or mobile device to step through the project in this module and you want your screens to match the figures in this book, you should change your screen's resolution to 1366 x 768. For information about how to change a computer's resolution, refer to the Office and Windows module at the beginning of this book.

2

- Click the New Calendar button (Folder tab | New group) to display the Create New Folder dialog box.

- Type **Sophia** in the Name text box (Create New Folder dialog box) to enter a name for the new folder.

- Click the Folder contains arrow button to display a list of items the folder will contain.

- If necessary, click Calendar Items to specify what the folder will contain.

- If necessary, click Calendar in the 'Select where to place the folder' list to specify where the folder will be stored (Figure 2–4).

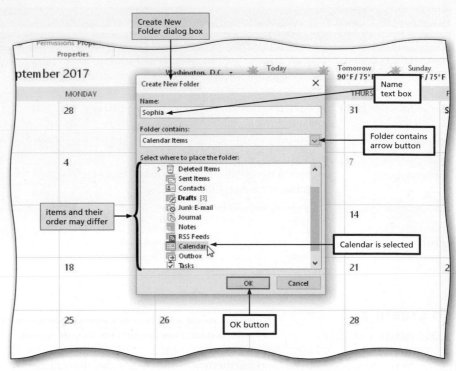

Figure 2–4

3

- Click the OK button to close the Create New Folder dialog box and add the new folder to the My Calendars group (Figure 2–5).

Q&A

Why is the named Sophia calendar not displayed in the Outlook window?
Outlook does not automatically display the newly created calendar until you select it.

I received an error message indicating that calendars cannot be created in Exchange ActiveSync accounts. What should I do?
Use a browser to sign into your email account at outlook.com. Use the Calendar feature at outlook.com to create a calendar. Restart Outlook 2016. After syncing, the new calendar should appear in Outlook 2016.

Figure 2–5

- In the My Calendars pane, click Sophia to insert a check mark in the check box, so that both the default Calendar and the Sophia calendars are selected and displayed in the appointment area of the Outlook window (Figure 2–6).

Q&A Why is the default calendar displayed in a different color from Sophia's calendar?

Outlook automatically assigns a different color to each new calendar you create to make it easier to distinguish one calendar from the other. Your calendar colors might be different from those shown in Figure 2–6.

Can I select a color for the calendar?

Yes. Click the View tab, click the Color button (View tab | Color group), and then select a color from the Color gallery.

Figure 2–6

- Click Calendar in the My Calendars pane to remove the check mark from the Calendar check box so that the default calendar no longer is displayed in the appointment area (Figure 2–7).

Q&A Why does my view look different from what is shown?

Figure 2–7 shows Month view, which is the default view for Calendar. If this is not the current view, click the Month button (Home tab | Arrange group).

What is the purpose of the colored tabs on each side of the appointment area?

The tabs are for navigating to the previous and next appointments.

Figure 2–7

Other Ways

1. Press CTRL+SHIFT+E

To Add a City to the Calendar Weather Bar

Outlook provides a Weather Bar so you can view the current three-day weather forecast when you open the calendar. By default, Washington, D.C. is displayed. You can customize the Weather Bar to display weather symbols such as cloud or snow symbols and today's high and low temperatures for your local weather conditions. When you click the forecast, further details appear such as the wind condition, humidity level, precipitation, and a link to a detailed weather forecast online. *Why?* *Each morning as you view your schedule, the Weather Bar informs you about the day's weather so you can plan your day accordingly.* The following steps add a city to the calendar Weather Bar to display the current forecast.

- Click the arrow button to the right of the current city in the Weather Bar to display the Add Location command (Figure 2–8).

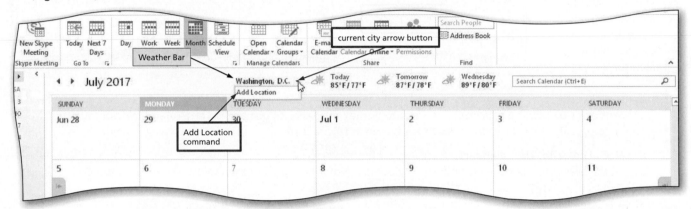

Figure 2–8

My Weather Bar does not appear in the calendar. What should I do?

Click the File tab to display Backstage View, click Options, and then click the Calendar category. Scroll down to the Weather section, and then click the Show weather on the calendar check box to insert a check mark.

❷

- Click Add Location to display a search text box.
- Type **Miami Beach** and then press the ENTER key to search for the city location (Figure 2–9).

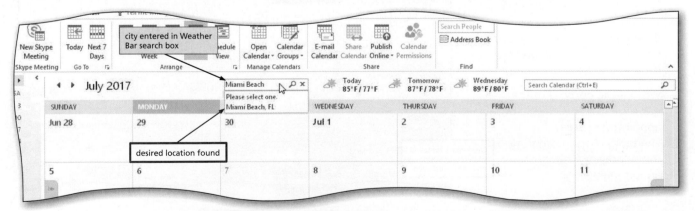

Figure 2–9

Can I search for a city using a postal code?

Yes. Type the postal code to search for the location in the Weather Bar search text box.

- Click Miami Beach, FL to select the location and display its three-day forecast in the Weather Bar.
- If requested by your instructor, replace Miami Beach, FL with your hometown in the Weather Bar (Figure 2–10).

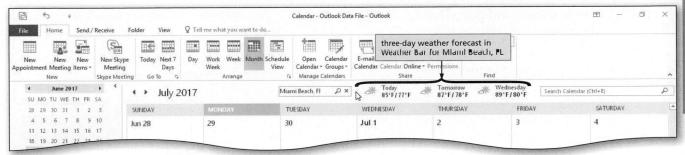

Figure 2–10

Q&A | Why does my Weather Bar display the message 'Weather service is not available'?
Most likely, you are not connected to the Internet. You must have Internet connectivity to display the weather forecast.

For an introduction to Windows and instructions about how to perform basic Windows tasks, read the Office and Windows module at the beginning of this book, where you can learn how to resize windows, change screen resolution, create folders, move and rename files, use Windows Help, and much more.

Navigating the Calendar

Each Microsoft Outlook folder displays the items it contains in a layout called a view. The **calendar view** is the arrangement and format of the folder contents by day, work week, week, month, or schedule, which is a horizontal layout. Recall that the default view of the Calendar folder is Month view. Some people prefer a different view of their calendar, such as weekly or daily. For instance, you might want to view all the items for a day at one time, in which case Day view would work best. Although the Outlook window looks different in each view, you can accomplish the same tasks in each view: you can add, edit, or delete appointments, events, and meetings.

To Go to a Specific Date

1 CONFIGURE CALENDAR OPTIONS | 2 CREATE & MANIPULATE APPOINTMENTS | 3 SCHEDULE EVENTS

4 SCHEDULE MEETINGS | 5 PRINT CALENDAR | 6 SAVE & SHARE CALENDAR

To display a date that is not visible in the current view so that you can view that date in the appointment area, one option is to use the Go to Date Dialog Box Launcher. The following steps display a specific date in the appointment area in a calendar. *Why? Rather than scrolling through your calendars in Outlook to find a specific date, you can quickly find a date in Outlook by using the Go To Date dialog box.*

- Click Home on the ribbon to display the Home tab.
- Click the Go to Date Dialog Box Launcher (Home tab | Go To group) to display the Go To Date dialog box (Figure 2–11).

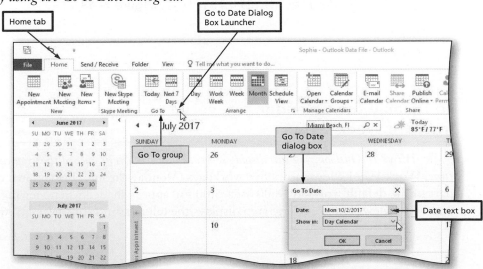

Figure 2–11

- Type 10/2/2017 in the Date text box to enter the date you want to display in the current calendar.

- Click the Show in button, and then select Day Calendar to show the calendar in Day view (Figure 2–12).

Q&A

Why did 'Mon' appear next to the date in the Date box?

Outlook automatically includes the day of the week (Monday, in this case) when you enter a date in the Date box.

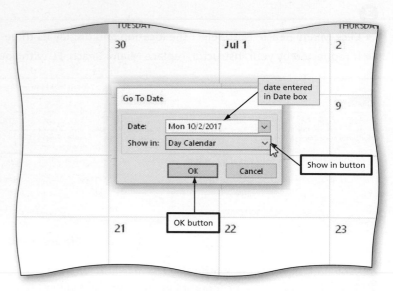

Figure 2–12

❸

- Click the OK button to close the Go To Date dialog box and display the selected date in Day view (Figure 2–13).

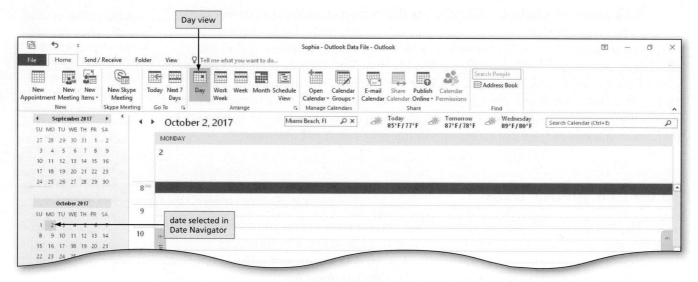

Figure 2–13

Other Ways

1. Press CTRL+G

To Display the Calendar in Work Week View

1 CONFIGURE CALENDAR OPTIONS | 2 CREATE & MANIPULATE APPOINTMENTS | 3 SCHEDULE EVENTS
4 SCHEDULE MEETINGS | 5 PRINT CALENDAR | 6 SAVE & SHARE CALENDAR

Why? In Outlook, you can display several calendar days at once so that you can see multiple appointments at the same time. **Work Week view** shows five workdays (Monday through Friday) in a columnar style. Hours that are not part of the default workday (8:00 AM – 5:00 PM) appear shaded when viewing the calendar in Day, Work Week, and Week view. The following step displays the calendar in Work Week view.

1

- Click the Work Week button (Home tab | Arrange group) to display the work week in the appointment area for the selected date (Figure 2–14).

**Experiment**

- Scroll up and down in Work Week view to see how the color changes to reflect hours outside the default workday.

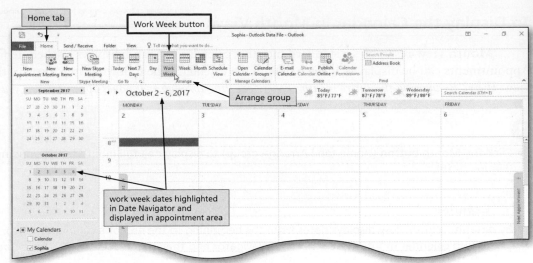

Figure 2–14

Q&A Why is Monday through Friday highlighted on the Date Navigator?

The calendar days displayed in the appointment area are highlighted on the Date Navigator.

Other Ways

1. Press CTRL+ALT+2

To Display the Calendar in Week View

1 CONFIGURE CALENDAR OPTIONS | 2 CREATE & MANIPULATE APPOINTMENTS | 3 SCHEDULE EVENTS
4 SCHEDULE MEETINGS | 5 PRINT CALENDAR | 6 SAVE & SHARE CALENDAR

Why? *The advantage of displaying a calendar in Week view is to see how many appointments are scheduled for any given week, including weekends.* In **Week view**, the seven days of the selected week appear in the appointment area. The following step displays the calendar in Week view.

1

- Click the Week button (Home tab | Arrange group) to display the full week, including weekends, in the appointment area (Figure 2–15).

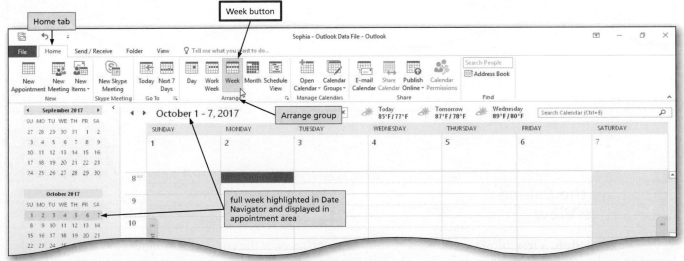

Figure 2–15

Other Ways

1. Press CTRL+ALT+3

To Display the Calendar in Month View

Month view resembles a standard monthly calendar page and displays a schedule for an entire month. Appointments can be displayed in each date in the calendar. The following step displays the calendar in Month view. *Why? By viewing the entire month without scrolling through individual appointments, you can see when you have an open day.*

- Click the Month button (Home tab | Arrange group) to display one full month in the appointment area (Figure 2–16).

🔎 Experiment

- By default, Month view displays dates from the beginning to the end of a calendar month. To select several weeks across two calendar months, click the Date Navigator and then drag to select the weeks you want to view.

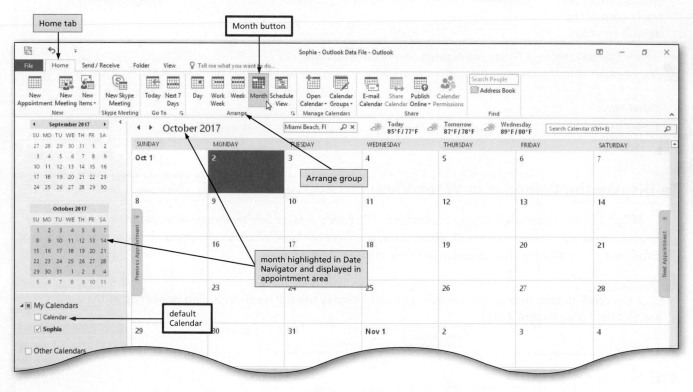

Figure 2–16

Other Ways

1. Press CTRL+ALT+4

To Display the Calendar in Schedule View

The **Schedule View** allows you to view multiple calendars over the course of a single day in a horizontal layout to make scheduling meetings easier. The following steps display the default Calendar and the Sophia calendar in Schedule View. *Why? Schedule View is useful when trying to see multiple calendars so that you can check for overlapping items.*

①

- Click Calendar (default Calendar) in the My Calendars pane to insert a check mark in the check box and to display both the default Calendar and Sophia's calendar in the appointment area (Figure 2–17).

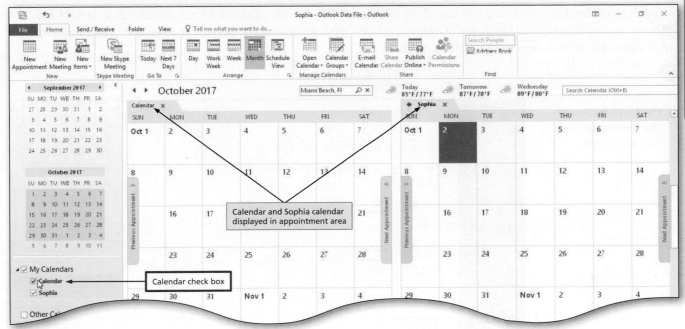

Figure 2–17

Q&A | Why are both calendars displayed in Month view?
Outlook uses the view of the existing calendar for a newly displayed calendar. In this case, Sophia's calendar was displayed in Month view, so the default Calendar also is displayed in Month view.

②

- Click the Schedule View button (Home tab | Arrange group) to display both calendars in Schedule View (Figure 2–18).

Q&A | Why does Schedule View show a single day instead of multiple days?
Schedule View displays one day at a time.

What does the dark blue shaded area in the calendar represent?
The dark blue shaded area represents the time slot selected in Day view.

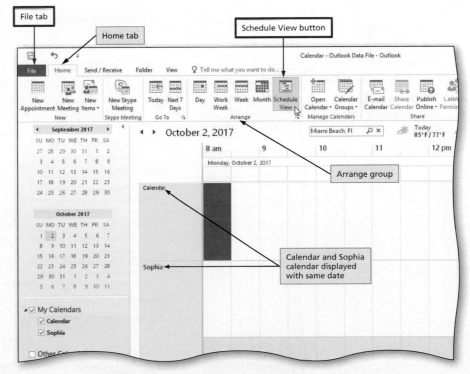

Figure 2–18

Other Ways

1. Press CTRL+ALT+5

To Add Holidays to the Default Calendar

Before you add appointments to a calendar, you can mark the standard holidays for one or more countries. You can add holidays to your default calendar folder only, not to a public folder or nondefault calendar such as Sophia's calendar. However, you can drag holidays from your default calendar to nondefault calendars. *Why? International businesses should be aware of national holidays within each country where they do business.* The following steps add national holidays to the default calendar.

• Click the File tab on the ribbon to open the Backstage view (Figure 2–19).

Figure 2–19

• Click Options to display the Outlook Options dialog box.

• Click Calendar in the left pane to display the options in the Calendar category (Figure 2–20).

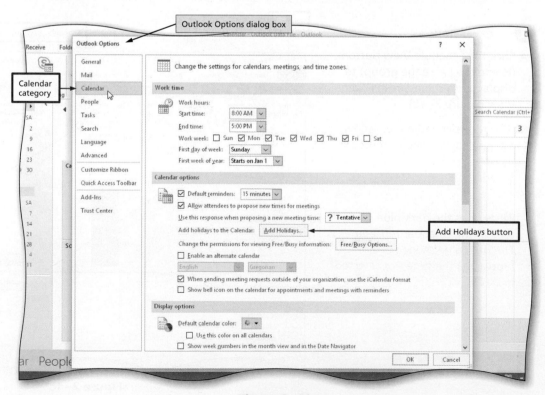

Figure 2–20

3

- Click the Add Holidays button to display the Add Holidays to Calendar dialog box (Figure 2–21).

Can I select multiple countries to display more than one set of national holidays? Yes. You can select the holidays of multiple countries to display in the default calendar.

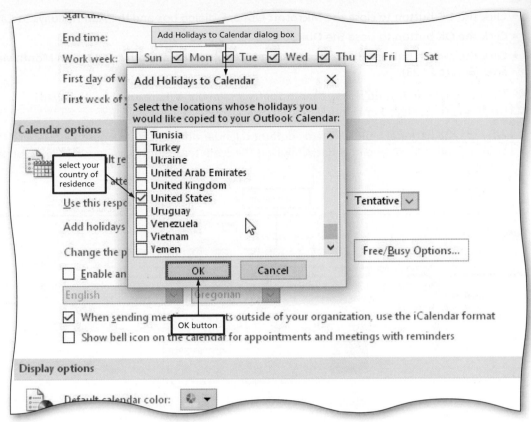

Figure 2–21

4

- If necessary, click the check box for your country of residence to add that country's national holidays to the default calendar.

- Click the OK button to close the dialog box, import the holidays, and display the confirmation message that the holidays were added to your calendar (Figure 2–22).

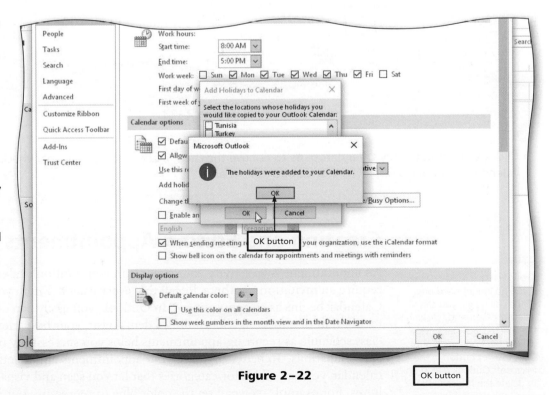

Figure 2–22

- Click the OK button to close the Microsoft Outlook dialog box and the Add Holidays to Calendar dialog box.
- Click the OK button to close the Outlook Options dialog box.
- Click the Month button (Home tab | Arrange group) to display both calendars in Month view in the appointment area (Figure 2–23).

Q&A

The national holidays do not appear in Sophia's calendar. Where are they displayed?
Holidays are displayed only in the default calendar.

Why are the national holidays on my default calendar different from Figure 2–23?
Your default calendar holiday dates might differ from those shown in Figure 2–23 if you selected a different country.

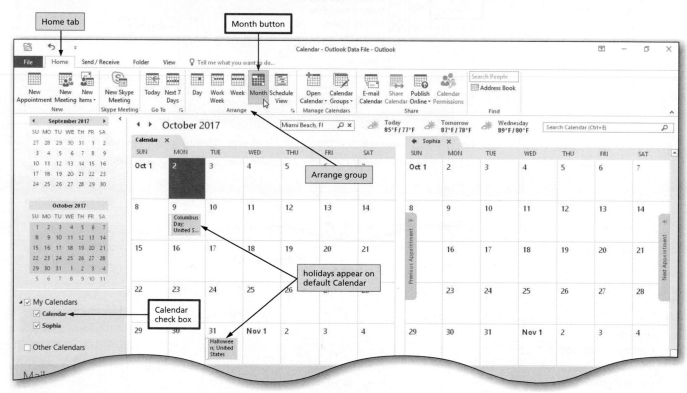

Figure 2–23

- Click Calendar in the My Calendars pane to remove the check mark from the Calendar check box so that the default calendar no longer is displayed in the appointment area.

Creating and Editing Appointments

BTW

Deleting a Calendar
If you no longer need one of the calendars, you can delete a calendar by clicking the Delete Calendar button (Folder tab | Actions group). Click the Yes button in the Microsoft Outlook dialog box to delete the folder. Outlook sends the deleted folder to the Deleted Items folder.

An appointment is an activity you schedule in your Outlook calendar that does not require an invitation to others. Recall that every calendar item you schedule in Outlook Calendar begins as an appointment. In Outlook, you easily can change an appointment to an event or a meeting. Scheduling a dental visit, your best friend's birthday, or a class schedule as recurring appointments helps you successfully manage your activities and obligations. To better organize your appointments and meetings in your Outlook calendar, you can add color categories that let you scan and visually associate similar items. For example, you can set the color blue to represent your academic classes and the color green for doctor's appointments.

Creating Appointments in the Appointment Area

A **one-time appointment**, such as a concert event, conference call, or course exam date, is an appointment that occurs only once on a calendar. A **recurring appointment**, such as a class throughout an academic course, repeats on the calendar at regular intervals. Appointments can be created in two ways: using the appointment area, where you enter the appointment directly in the appropriate time slot, or using the Untitled – Appointment window, where you can enter more specific details about the appointment such as the location or address of the activity.

BTWs
Touch Screen Differences
The Office and Windows interfaces may vary if you are using a touch screen. For this reason, you might notice that the function or appearance of your touch screen differs slightly from this module's presentation.

To Create a One-Time Appointment Using the Appointment Area

1 CONFIGURE CALENDAR OPTIONS | 2 CREATE & MANIPULATE APPOINTMENTS | 3 SCHEDULE EVENTS
4 SCHEDULE MEETINGS | 5 PRINT CALENDAR | 6 SAVE & SHARE CALENDAR

When you click a day on the calendar in the Navigation Pane, Outlook displays the calendar for the date selected in Day view in the appointment area. Day view shows a daily view of a specific date in half-hour increments. The following steps use the appointment area to create a one-time appointment for Sophia's yearly health physical. *Why? If you are scheduling a one-time activity such as a doctor's appointment, you can type directly in the appointment area because you do not need a detailed description.*

1

- Click the month name October on the Date Navigator to display a list of months with the associated year (Figure 2–24).

 Experiment

- View several dates that are not consecutive by clicking a date in the Date Navigator, holding down the CTRL key, and then clicking additional days.

Figure 2–24

2

- If necessary, click October 2017 on the Date Navigator to display the selected month in the appointment area.

- Click 13 in the October 2017 calendar on the Date Navigator to display the selected date in the appointment area in Day view (Figure 2–25).

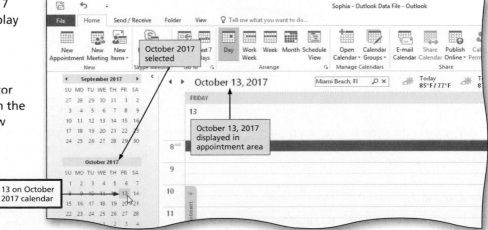

Figure 2–25

• Drag to select two half-hour increments from the 9:00 AM to the 10:00 AM time slot in the appointment area (Figure 2–26).

Q&A What if I select more or less than two half-hour increments?
If you incorrectly select the appointment time, repeat this step to try again.

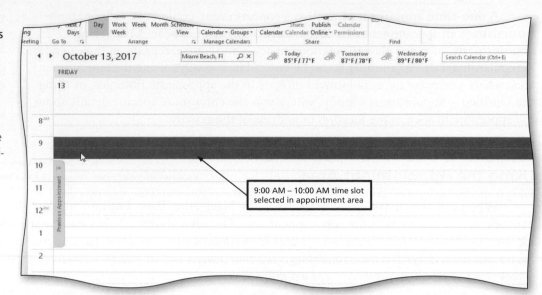

Figure 2–26

• Type Health Physical: Dr. Bolton as the appointment subject and then press the ENTER key to enter the appointment in the appointment area (Figure 2–27).

Q&A Do I have to perform another step to save the appointment entry?
No, the appointment entry is saved automatically when you press the ENTER key.

Why is Busy displayed in the Show As box (Calendar Tools Appointment tab | Options group)?
When you create an appointment, Outlook assigns your time as busy by default.

Why does the date of the health physical appointment appear in bold on the Date Navigator?
Outlook displays in bold any date with a time allocated on your calendar as busy to indicate that you have something scheduled on that day.

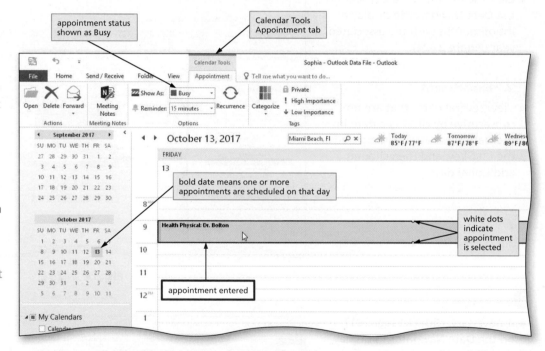

Figure 2–27

Other Ways

1. Select beginning time slot, hold down SHIFT, click ending time slot, type appointment name, press ENTER

Organize the Calendar with Color Categories

As you add appointments to the Outlook Calendar, you can use categories to color-code the appointments by type. Adding color categories allows you to quickly scan and visually group similar items such as classes or work-related appointments. For example, Sophia can assign her work tasks to a blue category, doctor's appointments to green, classes to orange, and all friends- and family-related activities to purple. After you associate each category with a color, she can categorize each appointment. The associated color is used as the item's background color on the calendar in the appointment area.

BTW

Adding a Calendar Group
To organize multiple calendars, you can create calendar groups. Click the Calendar Groups button (Home tab | Manage Calendars group) and then click Create New Calendar Group. Type a name for the new calendar group, and then click the OK button.

To Add Color Categories

1 CONFIGURE CALENDAR OPTIONS | 2 CREATE & MANIPULATE APPOINTMENTS | 3 SCHEDULE EVENTS
4 SCHEDULE MEETINGS | 5 PRINT CALENDAR | 6 SAVE & SHARE CALENDAR

Why? *Color categories enable you to easily identify and group associated items in the Outlook Calendar.* The following steps add color categories in the calendar.

- Click the Categorize button (Calendar Tools Appointment tab | Tags group) to display the Categorize list of color categories (Figure 2–28).

Q&A
Can you use color categories for any type of email account?
You should use a Microsoft account as your Outlook email account to take advantage of categories and other special features.

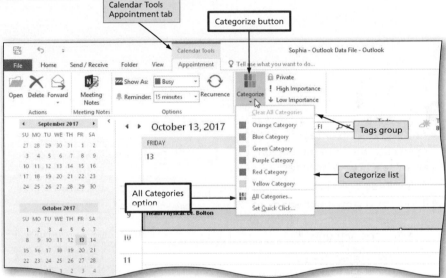

Figure 2–28

- Click All Categories to display the Color Categories dialog box (Figure 2–29).

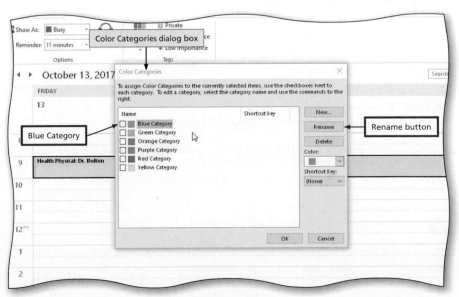

Figure 2–29

- Click the Blue Category to select the category.
- Click the Rename button to select the category for renaming.
- Type `Work` and then press the ENTER key to rename the category (Figure 2–30).

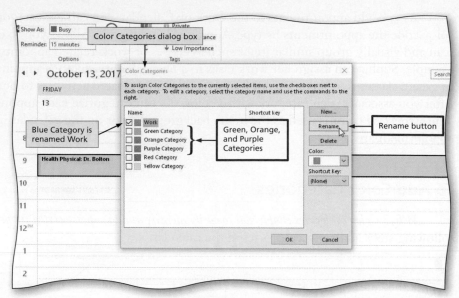

Figure 2–30

- Click the Green Category, and then click the Rename button to select the category for renaming.
- Type `Dr. Appointments` and then press the ENTER key to rename the category.
- Click the Orange Category, and then click the Rename button to select the category for renaming.
- Type `Friends & Family` and then press the ENTER key to rename the category.
- Click the Purple Category, and then click the Rename button to select the category for renaming.
- Type `Classes` and then press the ENTER key to rename the category (Figure 2–31).

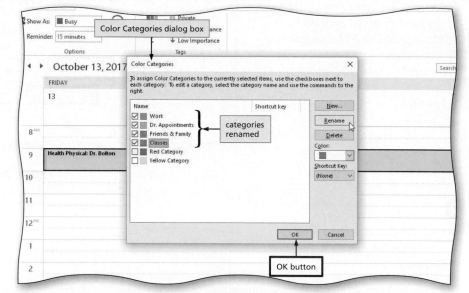

Figure 2–31

 How many color categories can I set?

You can assign fifteen color categories in Outlook Calendar. Click the New button in the Color Categories dialog box to select colors not shown in the dialog box by default.

5

- Click the OK button to close the Color Categories dialog box.

To Assign a Color Category to an Appointment

The following steps assign a color category to a calendar appointment. *Why? By color coding your Outlook calendar appointments, you can quickly distinguish among your assigned categories such as class, work, or birthdays.*

1

- If necessary, click the Health Physical appointment at 9:00 AM to select the appointment.
- Click the Categorize button (Calendar Tools Appointment tab | Tags group) to display the Categorize list of color categories (Figure 2–32).

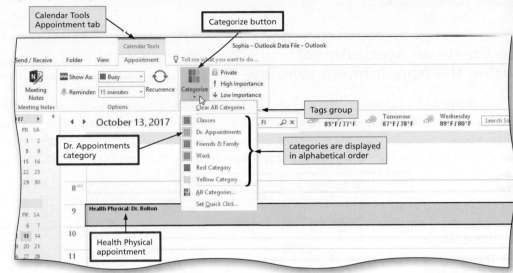

Figure 2–32

2

- Click the green Dr. Appointments category to display the selected appointment with a medium-green background (Figure 2–33).

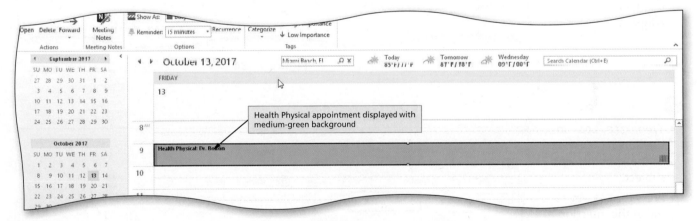

Figure 2–33

Creating Appointments Using the Appointment Window

Another way to create an appointment is by using the Appointment window, which provides additional options for entering an appointment, such as the location of the appointment and a recurrence pattern. When you set a **recurrence pattern**, Outlook schedules the appointment on the calendar at regular intervals for a designated period of time, such as a class that Sophia takes for an entire semester on Tuesdays and Thursdays.

Outlook also allows you to configure a **reminder**, similar to an alarm clock reminder, which is an alert window that briefly appears on your screen to remind you of an upcoming appointment. You also can set a chime or other sound to play as part of the reminder.

BTW
Entering Locations
As you enter calendar items, you can include location information by clicking the Location box arrow and selecting a location on the list.

Another option when creating an appointment is to set the **appointment status**, which is how the time for a calendar item is marked on your calendar. The default appointment status setting is Busy, as indicated in the previous steps, but you can change the status to reflect your availability as appropriate.

To Create an Appointment Using the Appointment Window

1 CONFIGURE CALENDAR OPTIONS | 2 CREATE & MANIPULATE APPOINTMENTS | 3 SCHEDULE EVENTS
4 SCHEDULE MEETINGS | 5 PRINT CALENDAR | 6 SAVE & SHARE CALENDAR

Why? *Instead of directly entering an appointment in the appointment area, you can specify various details such as the location by using the Appointment window.* To schedule an appointment such as Sophia's CIS 101 computer class that meets repeatedly over the semester in a particular room on campus, you decide to use the Appointment window. The following steps create an appointment using the Appointment window.

1

• Click Home on the ribbon to display the Home tab.

• Click the New Appointment button (Home tab | New group) to open the Untitled – Appointment window (Figure 2–34).

Figure 2–34

2

• Type CIS 101 in the Subject text box as the appointment subject.

• Press the TAB key to move the insertion point to the Location box.

• Type M14 as the room number of the class (Figure 2–35).

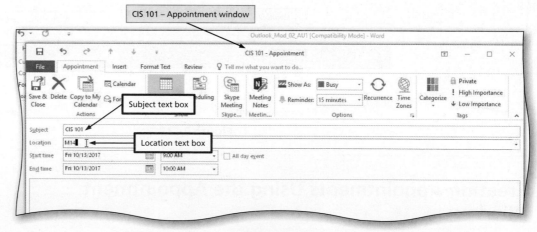

Figure 2–35

Q&A

Why did the title of the window change from Untitled – Appointment to CIS 101 – Appointment?
The title bar displays the name of the appointment. Because the name of the appointment has changed, the name on the title bar also changes.

Why are the date and time already specified?
When you start to create a new appointment, Outlook sets the start and end times using the time selected in the appointment area.

- Click the Start
  time calendar
  button to display
  a calendar for the
  current month
  (Figure 2–36).

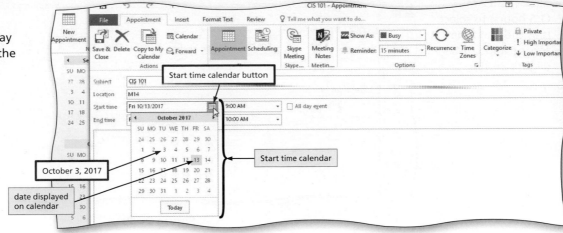

Figure 2–36

4

- Click 3 on the
  calendar to select
  the next CIS 101
  class as October 3,
  2017.
- Click the Start
  time box arrow
  to display a list
  of time slots
  (Figure 2–37).

Figure 2–37

5

- Click 10:00 AM
  to select it as the
  Start time for the
  appointment.
- Click the End time
  box arrow to display
  a list of time slots
  (Figure 2–38).

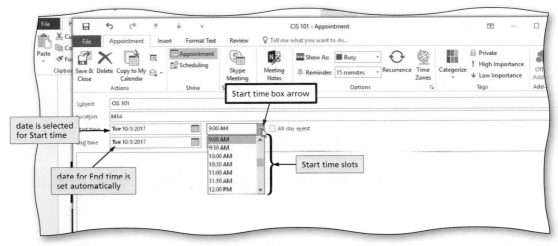

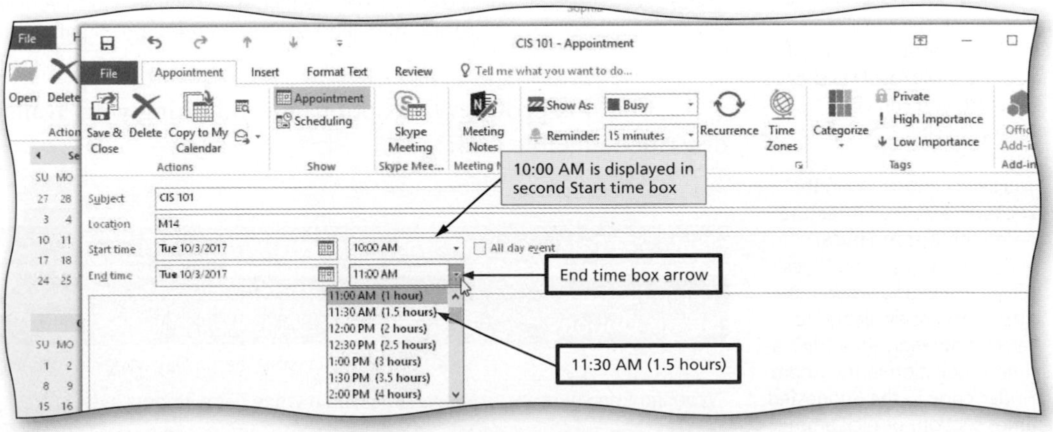

Q&A
Why did the End
time change to the
same date as the
Start time?
Outlook
automatically sets
appointments to occur during a single day.

Why does the second end time list have a duration for each time?
Outlook automatically displays the duration next to the end time to help you set the length of the appointment.

Figure 2–38

- Click 11:30 AM (1.5 hours) to select it as the End time for the appointment (Figure 2–39).

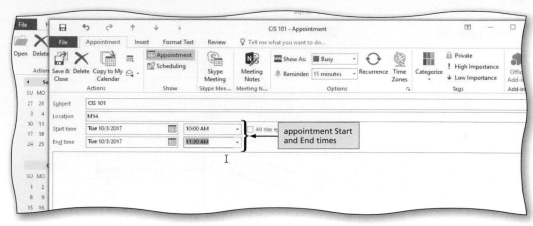

Figure 2–39

Other Ways

1. Press CTRL+SHIFT+A

BTW
Time Zones
Use the Time Zones button (Appointment tab | Options group) to specify a time zone for the start and end times of an appointment.

BTW
Room Finder
Some features in Outlook 2016 require a Microsoft Exchange Server account. **Exchange** is a collaborative communications server that many organizations use. Microsoft Office 365 includes Exchange Online, and some Internet hosting providers offer Exchange accounts. If you use a Microsoft Exchange account, you can click Rooms to check availability and reserve rooms when you select a location in the Location text box. A feature called the **Room Finder** assists you in locating times for your meeting when most attendees are available. To select a meeting time, click a time suggestion in the Room Finder pane in the Suggested times section, or pick a time on the free/busy calendar.

Setting Appointment Options

When creating appointments on the Outlook calendar, you can set a number of options that determine how the appointment is handled. Table 2–2 lists the options available when creating an item on your calendar.

Table 2–2 Calendar Window Options	
Option	**Description**
Show As	Indicates your availability on a specific date and time; if you want to show others your availability when they schedule a meeting with you during a specific time, this must be set accurately
Reminder	Alerts you at a specific time prior to the item's occurrence
Recurrence	If an item on your calendar repeats at regularly scheduled intervals, sets the recurring options so that you only have to enter the item once on your calendar
Time Zone	Shows or hides the time zone controls, which you can use to specify the time zones for the start and end times of the appointment

Outlook provides five options for indicating your availability on the Calendar, as described in Table 2–3.

Table 2–3 Calendar Item Status Options	
Calendar Item Status Options	**Description**
Free	Shows time with a white bar in Day, Week, Work Week, or Month view
Working Elsewhere	Shows time with a white bar with dots in Day, Week, Work Week, or Month view
Tentative	Shows time with a slashed bar in Day, Week, Work Week, or Month view
Busy	Shows time with a solid bar in Day, Week, Work Week, or Month view
Out of Office	Shows time with a purple bar in Day, Week, Work Week, or Month view

To Change the Status of an Appointment

To make sure your time is displayed accurately on the calendar, you can change the appointment status from the default of Busy to Out of Office, meaning Sophia is not in the internship office during class time while attending CIS 101. The following steps change the status of an appointment. *Why? You can display time indicators such as Busy or Out of Office to show calendar entries that reflect your availability. If you share your calendar, others can see at a glance if you are available.*

- Click the Show As box arrow (Appointment tab | Options group) in the CIS 101 appointment to display the Show As list of appointment status options (Figure 2–40).

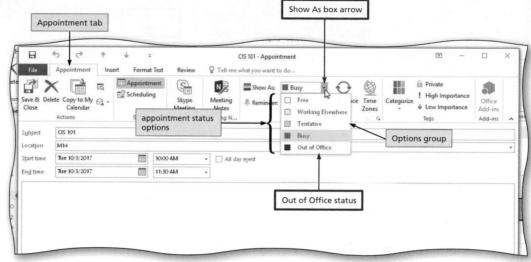

Figure 2–40

- Click Out of Office to change the appointment status (Figure 2–41).

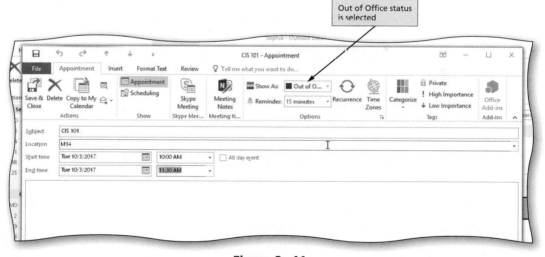

Figure 2–41

To Set a Reminder for an Appointment

With the start and end dates and times for the class set and the appointment status selected, Sophia wants to schedule a reminder so that she does not forget class. *Why? Your Outlook Calendar can be your personal alarm clock by displaying reminders of your appointments with options such as snooze and dismiss.* When the reminder is displayed, you can open the appointment for further review. The following steps set a 30-minute reminder for an appointment.

- Click the Reminder box arrow (Appointment tab | Options group) to display the Reminder list of available reminder intervals (Figure 2–42).

What does the Sound option in the Reminder list do?
In addition to a visual reminder, Outlook allows you to set an auditory alarm, much like an alarm clock.

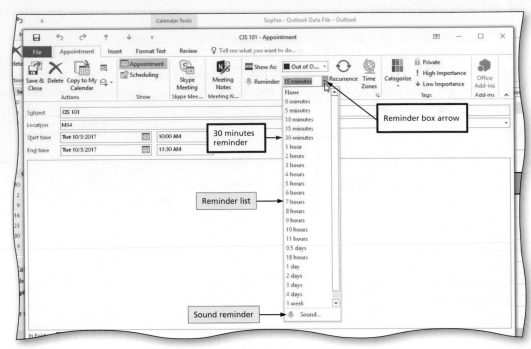

Figure 2–42

- Click 30 minutes to set a reminder for 30 minutes prior to the start time of the appointment (Figure 2–43).

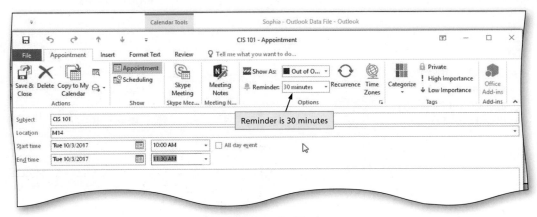

Figure 2–43

Why was the reminder time originally scheduled for 15 minutes?
By default, a Reminder is set to occur 15 minutes before the start of an appointment. However, you can increase or decrease the default reminder time.

Can you customize the sound that is played when a reminder is displayed?

- When you click the Reminder box arrow (Calendar Tools Appointment tab | Options group), click Sound to open the Reminder Sound dialog box.
- Click the Browse button, and then select the sound .wav file that you want played.
- Click the Open button. Click the OK button to select the custom reminder sound.
- A reminder time must be selected before the Sound command appears.

Creating Recurring Appointments

Many appointments are recurring appointments, meaning they happen at regular intervals for a designated period of time. The recurring appointment is configured with a recurrence pattern designating the rate of recurrence, for example, weekly, and on what day(s) of the week the appointment occurs.

To Set Recurrence Options for an Appointment

1 CONFIGURE CALENDAR OPTIONS | 2 CREATE & MANIPULATE APPOINTMENTS | 3 SCHEDULE EVENTS
4 SCHEDULE MEETINGS | 5 PRINT CALENDAR | 6 SAVE & SHARE CALENDAR

The next CIS 101 class is on October 3 and is held every Tuesday and Thursday from 10:00 AM to 11:30 AM at regular intervals for the rest of the semester, making it a recurring appointment. The following steps configure a recurrence pattern for an appointment. *Why? By establishing a recurrence pattern, you do not have to enter each class into the schedule for the entire semester.*

• Click the Recurrence button (Appointment tab | Options group) to display the Appointment Recurrence dialog box (Figure 2–44).

Q&A Why are the start and end times and the duration already set in the Appointment time area of the Appointment Recurrence dialog box?
Outlook uses the settings you already selected for the appointment.

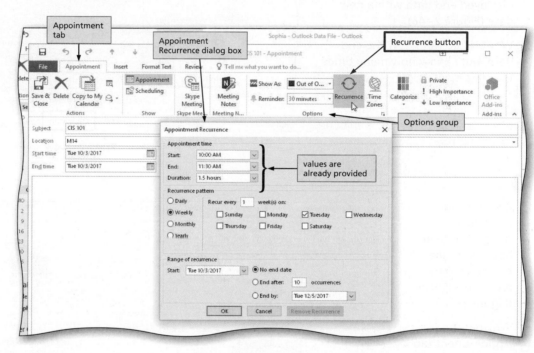

Figure 2–44

• If necessary, in the Recurrence pattern area, click the Weekly option button (Appointment Recurrence dialog box) to set the recurrence pattern.

• If necessary, in the Recur every text box (Appointment Recurrence dialog box), type 1 to schedule the frequency of the recurrence pattern.

• Click Thursday to insert a check mark in the check box and to schedule the class two times per week (in this case, Tuesday and Thursday) (Figure 2–45).

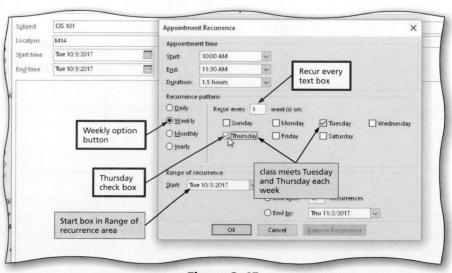

Figure 2–45

Q&A

Why is the Tuesday check box already selected in the Recurrence pattern area?
Tuesday is already selected because the class starts on that day of the week.

Why does the Start box in the 'Range of recurrence' area contain a date?
When you display the Appointment Recurrence dialog box, Outlook automatically sets the range of recurrence with the date the appointment starts.

3

- In the Range of recurrence area, click the End by option button (Appointment Recurrence dialog box), and then press the TAB key two times to select the End by box.

- Type 12/14/2017 as the day the class ends to replace the displayed end date with a new date (Figure 2–46).

What if I do not know the end date, but I know how many times the class meets?
You can click the End after option button and then type the number of times the class meets in the End after text box.

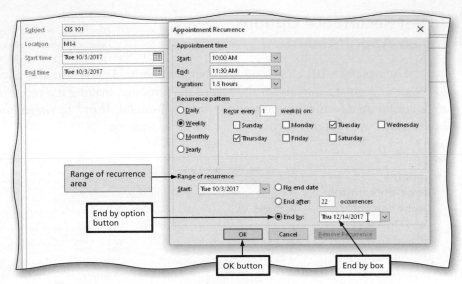

Figure 2–46

4

- Click the OK button to close the Appointment Recurrence dialog box and set the recurrence pattern (Figure 2–47).

Why did the Appointment tab change to the Appointment Series tab?
When you set a recurrence pattern, the tab name changes to reflect that you are working with a series.

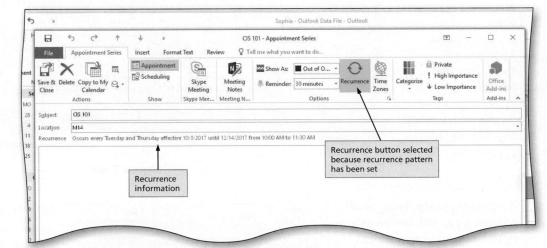

Figure 2–47

To Save an Appointment

1 CONFIGURE CALENDAR OPTIONS | 2 CREATE & MANIPULATE APPOINTMENTS | 3 SCHEDULE EVENTS
4 SCHEDULE MEETINGS | 5 PRINT CALENDAR | 6 SAVE & SHARE CALENDAR

With the details entered for the CIS 101 class, you can assign the appointment to a color category and then save the appointment. The following steps categorize the appointment, save the appointment series, and close the window. **Why?** *By changing the color-coded category and saving the appointment, your recurring appointment is scheduled.*

1

- Click the Categorize button (Appointment Series tab | Tags group) to display a list of color-coded categories (Figure 2–48).

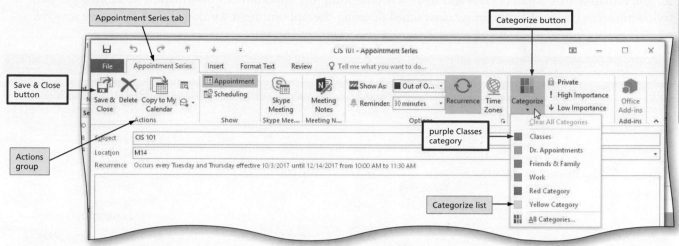

Figure 2–48

BTW

Organizing Files and Folders

You should organize and store files in folders so that you easily can find the files later. For example, if Sophia is taking an introductory computer class called CIS 101, a good practice would be to save all Outlook files in an Outlook folder in a CIS 101 folder. For a discussion of folders and detailed examples of creating folders, refer to the Office and Windows module at the beginning of this book.

2

- Click the purple Classes category to assign this appointment to a category.
- Click the Save & Close button (Appointment Series tab | Actions group) to save the recurring appointment on the calendar and close the window.
- Click Home on the ribbon to display the Home tab.
- Click the Month button (Home tab | Arrange group) to display the calendar in Month view (Figure 2–49).

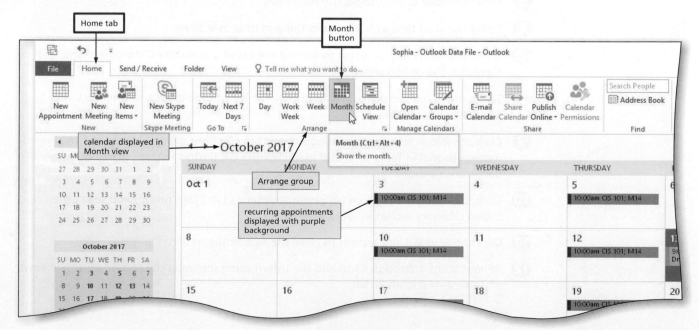

Figure 2–49

To Add More Recurring Appointments

With the CIS 101 class appointment series created, the next step is to create recurring appointments for the remainder of Sophia's class and work schedule using the appointment information in Table 2–4. The following steps create the remaining class schedule using the Appointment window. *Why? By adding your full schedule to the Outlook calendar, you will not miss any important appointments.*

Table 2–4 Recurring Appointments

Appointment	Location	Start Date	End Date	Start Time	End Time	Show As	Reminder	Recurrence	Category
ENG 102	D15	10/02/2017	Set in Recurrence	5:30 PM	8:30 PM	Out of Office	30 minutes	Weekly, every Monday; end by Monday, 12/11/2017	Classes
MTH 111	Online	10/06/2017	Set in Recurrence	5:00 PM	5:00 PM	Busy	1 hour	Weekly, every Friday; end by Friday, 12/08/2017	Classes
Pathways Office Hours	P22	10/02/2017	Set in Recurrence	2:00 PM	5:00 PM	Busy	15 minutes	Weekly, every Monday, Tuesday, & Wednesday; end by Wednesday 12/13/2017	Work

1 If necessary, click Home to display the Home tab.

2 Click the New Appointment button (Home tab | New group) to open the Appointment window.

3 Type ENG 102 as the appointment subject.

4 Type D15 as the location.

5 Select October 2, 2017 to set the start date.

6 Select the start time as 5:30 PM and the end time as 8:30 PM.

7 Select the Show As box arrow to display the list of appointment status options, and then click the option shown in Table 2–4.

8 Select the Reminder box arrow to display the list of time slots, and then click the option shown in Table 2–4.

9 Click the Recurrence button (Appointment tab | Options group) and set the recurrence pattern shown in Table 2–4, and then click the OK button to close the Appointment Recurrence window.

10 Click the Categorize button (Appointment Series tab | Tags group) and select the color-coded category shown in Table 2–4.

11 Click the Save & Close button to close the Appointment Series window.

12 Repeat Steps 1 through 11 to add the information shown in the second and third rows of Table 2–4 (Figure 2–50).

Q&A Why is the Calendar Tools Appointment Series tab displayed instead of the Calendar Tools Appointment tab?

The Calendar Tools Appointment Series tab is displayed when you select an appointment that is part of a series. This tab provides tools for working with recurring appointments.

What if I have appointments that recur other than weekly?

You can set daily, weekly, monthly, or yearly recurrence patterns in the Appointment Recurrence dialog box. A recurring appointment can be set to have no end date, to end after a certain number of occurrences, or to end by a certain date.

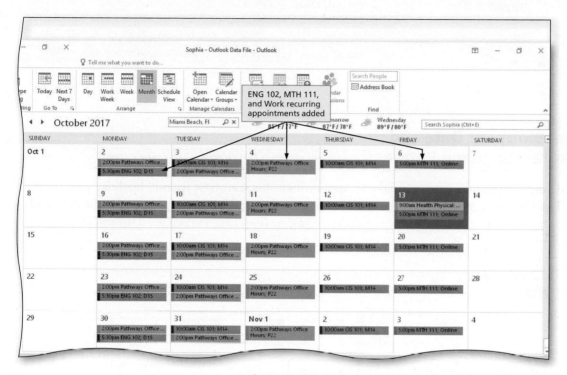

Figure 2–50

Using Natural Language Phrasing

In the previous steps, you entered dates and times in the Appointment window using standard numeric entries, such as 10/08/2017. You also can specify appointment dates and times using natural language. A **natural language phrase** is a phrase closely resembling how people speak during normal conversation. For example, you can type a phrase, such as "next Thursday" or "two weeks from yesterday," or you can type a single word, such as "midnight," and Outlook will calculate the correct date and time relative to the current date and time on the computer's system clock.

Outlook also can convert abbreviations and ordinal numbers into complete words and dates. For example, you can type "Feb" instead of "February" or "the first of May" instead of "5/1." Outlook's Calendar also can convert words such as "yesterday" and "tomorrow" and the names of holidays that occur on the same date each year, such as Valentine's Day. Table 2–5 lists various natural language options.

BTW

Outlook Help

At any time while using Outlook, you can find answers to questions and display information about various topics through Outlook Help. Used properly, this form of assistance can increase your productivity and reduce your frustrations by minimizing the time you spend learning how to use Outlook. For instructions about Outlook Help and exercises that will help you gain confidence in using it, read the Office and Windows module at the beginning of this book.

Table 2–5 Natural Language Options	
Category	**Examples**
Dates Spelled Out	July twenty-third, March 17th, first of May This Fri, next Sat, two days from now
Times Spelled Out	Noon, midnight Nine o'clock AM, five-twenty
Descriptions of Times and Dates	Now Yesterday, today, tomorrow
Holidays	Cinco de Mayo Christmas Day, Christmas Eve
Formulas for dates and times	10/15/2017 + 12d converts the date to 10/27/2017; use *d* for day, *m* for month, or *y* for year and add that amount of time to any date

To Create an Appointment Date and Time Using Natural Language Phrases

1 CONFIGURE CALENDAR OPTIONS | 2 CREATE & MANIPULATE APPOINTMENTS | 3 SCHEDULE EVENTS
4 SCHEDULE MEETINGS | 5 PRINT CALENDAR | 6 SAVE & SHARE CALENDAR

Using a natural language phrase, you can make an appointment for your best friend's birthday party next Monday at 8:00 PM. The following steps create an appointment using natural language phrases for the date and time. **Why?** *If you are not sure of the exact date for next Tuesday or 36 days from now, you can use a natural language phrase.*

- Click the New Appointment button (Home tab | New group) to open the Untitled – Appointment window.

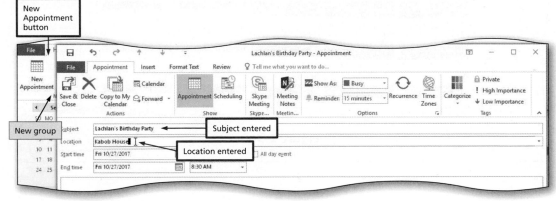

Figure 2–51

- Type **Lachlan's Birthday Party** in the Subject text box, and then press the TAB key to move the insertion point to the Location text box.

- Type **Kabob House** to add the location (Figure 2–51).

- Press the TAB key to select the first Start time text box, and then type **next sunday** to enter the start date.

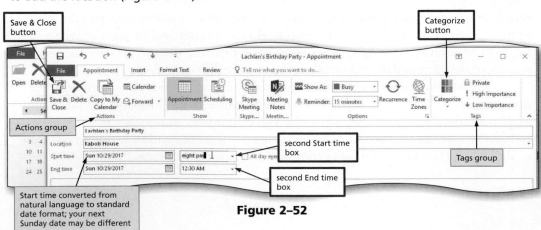

Figure 2–52

- Press the TAB key to convert the phrase to a start date and to select the second Start time text box.
- Type **eight pm** as the time in the second Start time text box to enter the start time (Figure 2–52).

Q&A

Do I need to use proper capitalization when entering natural language phrases?
No. Outlook converts the text to the proper date or time, regardless of the capitalization.

Why did the text change to a numeric date when I pressed the TAB key?
If you enter the date using natural language phrasing, Outlook converts typed text to the correct date format when you click to move the insertion point to a different box.

3

- Press the TAB key two times to convert the Start time entry to 8:00 pm.
- Type **eleven pm** as the time in the second End time box.
- Press the ENTER key to convert the end time text to 11:00 pm.
- Click the Categorize button (Appointment tab | Tags group) to display the Categorize list.
- Click the orange Friends & Family category to assign this appointment to a category.
- Click the Save & Close button (Appointment tab | Actions group) to save the appointment and close the window.
- If necessary, scroll to next Sunday's date (Figure 2–53).

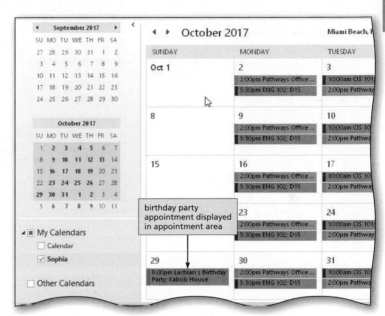

Figure 2–53

Editing Appointments

Schedules often need to be rearranged, so Outlook provides several ways to edit appointments. You can change the subject or location by clicking the appointment and editing the information directly in the appointment area. You can change the subject, location, date, or time by double-clicking the appointment and making corrections using the Appointment window. You can specify whether all occurrences in a series of recurring appointments need to be changed, or only a single occurrence should be altered.

BTW
Emailing Calendar Items
To send a calendar item to someone else, click the item, such as an appointment, and then click the Forward button (Calendar Tools Appointment tab | Actions group). Enter the email address of the recipient and send the message.

To Move an Appointment to a Different Time on the Same Day

1 CONFIGURE CALENDAR OPTIONS | 2 CREATE & MANIPULATE APPOINTMENTS | 3 SCHEDULE EVENTS
4 SCHEDULE MEETINGS | 5 PRINT CALENDAR | 6 SAVE & SHARE CALENDAR

Suppose that you cannot attend the Health Physical appointment at 9:00 AM on October 13, 2017. The appointment needs to be rescheduled to 11:00 AM for the same amount of time. *Why? Instead of deleting and then retyping the appointment, you can drag it to a new time slot.* The following step moves an appointment to a new time slot.

- If necessary, click a scroll arrow on the Calendar in the Navigation Pane until October 2017 is displayed in the calendar on the Date Navigator.

- Click 13 in the October 2017 calendar on the Date Navigator to display the selected date in the appointment area.

- Drag the Health Physical appointment from 9:00 AM to the 11:00 AM time slot on the same day to reschedule the appointment (Figure 2–54).

Figure 2–54

Other Ways

1. Double-click appointment, change time	2. Press CTRL+O, change time

BTW
Moving a Recurring Appointment
If you move a recurring appointment, you move only the selected instance of the appointment. To move all instances of a recurring appointment, open the appointment, click the Recurrence button (Appointment Series tab | Options group), and then change the recurrence pattern.

To Move an Appointment to a Different Date

1 CONFIGURE CALENDAR OPTIONS | 2 CREATE & MANIPULATE APPOINTMENTS | 3 SCHEDULE EVENTS
4 SCHEDULE MEETINGS | 5 PRINT CALENDAR | 6 SAVE & SHARE CALENDAR

Why? If you are moving an appointment to a new date at the same time, you can drag the appointment to the new date on the Date Navigator instead of retyping it. The following step moves an appointment to a new date in the same time slot.

- Drag the Health Physical appointment on October 13, 2017 to October 20, 2017 on the Date Navigator to move the appointment to a new date (Figure 2–55).

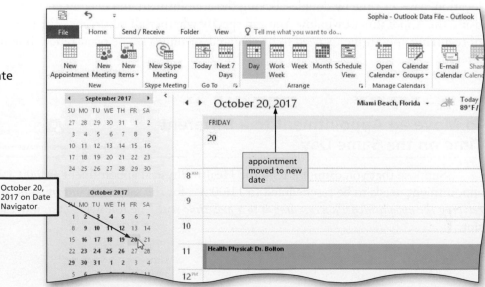

Figure 2–55

To Delete a Single Occurrence of a Recurring Appointment

Because your school is closed for a Fall Break holiday on November 6, 2017, no classes will meet during that day. The following steps delete a single occurrence of a recurring appointment. *Why? Occasionally, appointments are canceled and must be deleted from the schedule.*

1

- Click the forward navigation arrow in the Date Navigator until November 2017 is displayed.

- Click 6 in the November 2017 calendar on the Date Navigator to display the selected date in the appointment area.

- If necessary, scroll down and click the class, ENG 102, scheduled for November 6, 2017, to select the appointment and display the Calendar Tools Appointment Series tab (Figure 2–56).

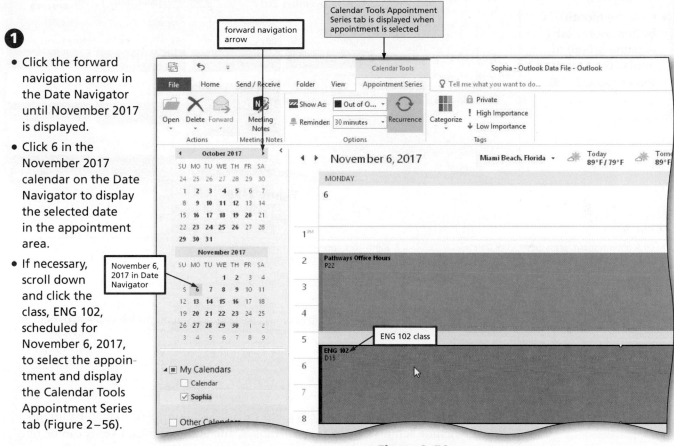

Figure 2–56

2

- Click the Delete button (Calendar Tools Appointment Series tab | Actions group) to display the Delete list (Figure 2–57).

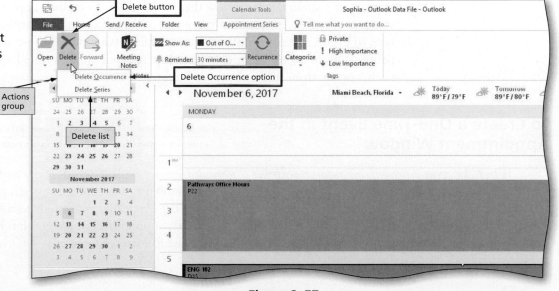

Figure 2–57

- Click Delete Occurrence on the Delete list to delete only the selected occurrence (single appointment) from the calendar.

- Click the Month button (Home tab | Arrange group) to display the Month view (Figure 2–58).

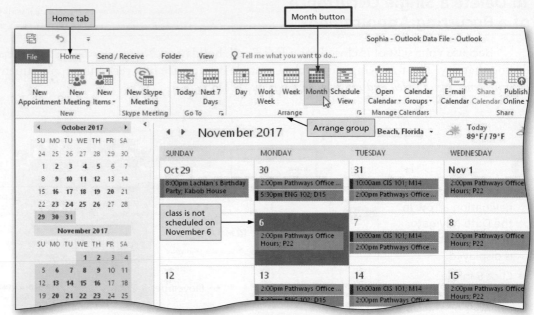

Figure 2–58

Other Ways

1. Click appointment, press DELETE, click Delete this occurrence, click OK

2. Right-click appointment, click Delete on shortcut menu, click Delete Occurrence

Break Point: If you wish to take a break, this is a good place to do so. To resume at a later time, continue to follow the steps from this location forward.

Scheduling Events

Similar to appointments, events are activities that last 24 hours or longer. Examples of events include seminars, vacations, birthdays, and anniversaries. Events can be one-time or recurring and differ from appointments in one primary way — they do not appear in individual time slots in the appointment area. Instead, the event description appears in a small banner below the day heading. As with an appointment, the event status can be free, busy, tentative, or out of the office and categorized according to the type of event. An all-day appointment displays your time as busy when viewed by other people, but an event or annual event displays your time as free. By default, all-day events occur from midnight to midnight.

To Create a One-Time Event in the Appointment Window

1 CONFIGURE CALENDAR OPTIONS | 2 CREATE & MANIPULATE APPOINTMENTS | 3 SCHEDULE EVENTS
4 SCHEDULE MEETINGS | 5 PRINT CALENDAR | 6 SAVE & SHARE CALENDAR

Why? *An event represents an appointment that is scheduled over a period of days such as a conference.* The Pathways Internship Fair is being held at Hamblen Hall on October 6 but Sophia is assisting with the setup starting on October 5, so she wants to block out both days for the event. Because the Internship Fair will last for a couple days, Outlook will schedule the conference as an event. Sophia will be at Hamblen Hall both days, so she decides to show her time for the event as Out of Office. The following steps create an event on the calendar.

1

- Click the New Items button (Home tab | New group) to display the New Items list (Figure 2–59).

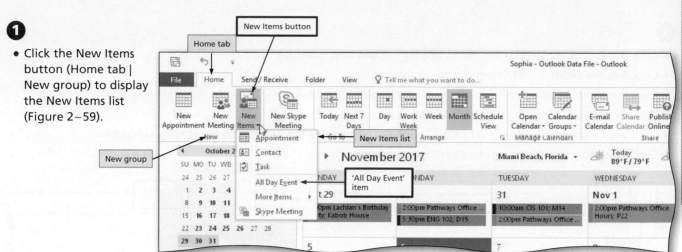

Figure 2–59

2

- Click 'All Day Event' to open the Untitled – Event window.
- Type **Internship Fair** in the Subject text box, and then press the TAB key to move the insertion point to the Location text box.
- Type **Hamblen Hall** as the location of the event.
- Click the Start time calendar button to display the Start time calendar.
- If necessary, display the October 2017 calendar.
- Click 5 in the October 2017 calendar to display Thu 10/5/2017 as the day the Internship Fair setup begins (Figure 2–60).

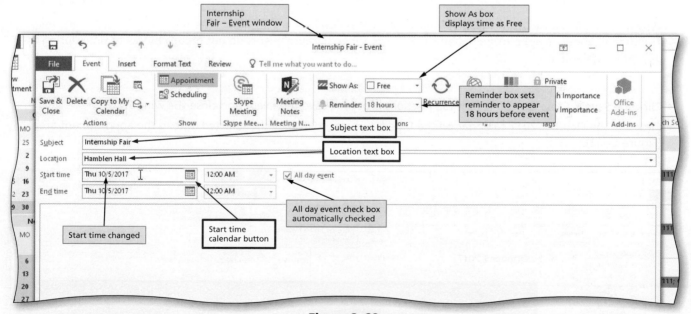

Figure 2–60

Q&A | Can I create an event by checking the 'All day event' check box in an appointment?
| Yes. Click the New Appointment button (Home tab | New group) and then click 'All day event' to create an event.

- Click the End time calendar button to display the End time calendar.
- Click 6 in the October 2017 calendar to set the end date.
- Click the Show As box arrow (Event tab | Options group) to display the Show As list of event status options.
- Click Out of the Office to set the event status.
- Click the Categorize button (Event tab | Tags group) to display the Categorize list of color categories.
- Click Work to assign the event to a category (Figure 2–61).

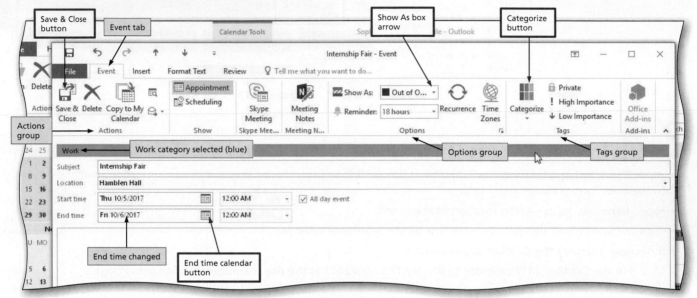

Figure 2–61

Q&A Why does the Show As box originally display the time as Free?

The default Show As appointment status for events is Free because events do not occupy blocks of time during the day on the calendar.

- Click the Save & Close button (Event tab | Actions group) to save the event and close the window.
- Click 5 in the October 2017 calendar on the Date Navigator to display the selected date in the appointment area (Figure 2–62).

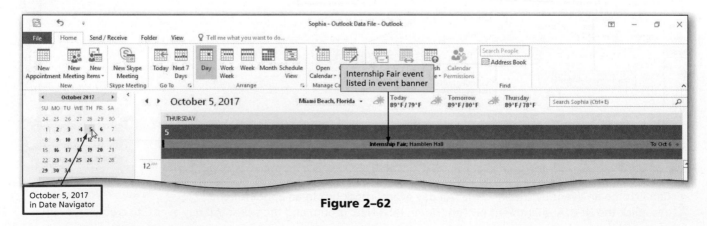

Figure 2–62

Q&A Why is the Internship Fair event displayed at the top of the Day view of the calendar?

Events do not occupy time slots on the Day view of the calendar, so they appear as banners at the top of the calendar on the day they occur.

To Delete a One-Time Event

1 CONFIGURE CALENDAR OPTIONS | 2 CREATE & MANIPULATE APPOINTMENTS | 3 SCHEDULE EVENTS
4 SCHEDULE MEETINGS | 5 PRINT CALENDAR | 6 SAVE & SHARE CALENDAR

Ms. Pauley, the Internship Office director, decides that the Internship Fair must be cancelled due to a conflict with another event in the local area. *Why? Because the schedule has changed, the Internship Fair event is cancelled but will be rescheduled later in the semester.* The following step deletes an event from your calendar.

- Click the Internship Fair event banner in the appointment area of the calendar to select it and to display the Calendar Tools Appointment tab on the ribbon.
- Click the Delete button (Calendar Tools Appointment tab | Actions group) to delete the Internship Fair event from the calendar (Figure 2–63).

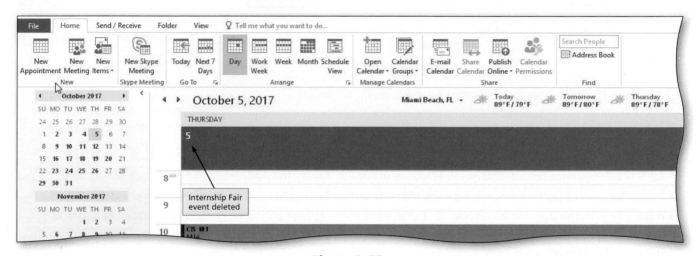

Figure 2–63

Other Ways

1. Select event, press DELETE

To Create a Recurring Event Using the Appointment Window

1 CONFIGURE CALENDAR OPTIONS | 2 CREATE & MANIPULATE APPOINTMENTS | 3 SCHEDULE EVENTS
4 SCHEDULE MEETINGS | 5 PRINT CALENDAR | 6 SAVE & SHARE CALENDAR

A recurring event is similar to a recurring appointment in that it occurs at regular intervals on your calendar. However, editing a recurring event is slightly different from editing one-time events. You can specify whether all occurrences in a series of recurring events need to be changed or if a single occurrence should be altered.

On the first day of each month, the college highlights an internship opportunity that Sophia wants to add to the calendar to keep track of when to prepare the marketing campaign for the internship. The following steps create a recurring event for the internship opportunity. *Why? To keep up with a periodic event such as your monthly or weekly occasion, the recurring event feature gives you a way to remind yourself of important dates.*

- Click the New Items button (Home tab | New group) to display the New Items list.
- Click 'All Day Event' to open the Untitled – Event window.
- In the Subject text box, type `Pathways Internship Ad` as the subject.
- In the first Start time text box, type `10/01/2017` as the date, and then press the ENTER key (Figure 2–64).

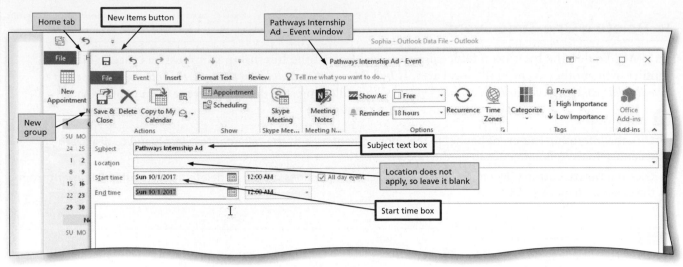

Figure 2–64

Q&A
Do I need to add a location to the Pathways Internship Ad event?
No, an event such as a marketing campaign, payday, birthday, or anniversary does not have a location.

2

- Click the Recurrence button (Event tab | Options group) to display the Appointment Recurrence dialog box.
- In the Recurrence pattern section, click the Monthly option button to set the Recurrence pattern to Monthly.
- If necessary, in the Day text box, type 1 to have the event appear on the calendar at the first of each month.
- If necessary, in the Range of recurrence section, click the 'No end date' option button so that the event remains on the calendar indefinitely (Figure 2–65).

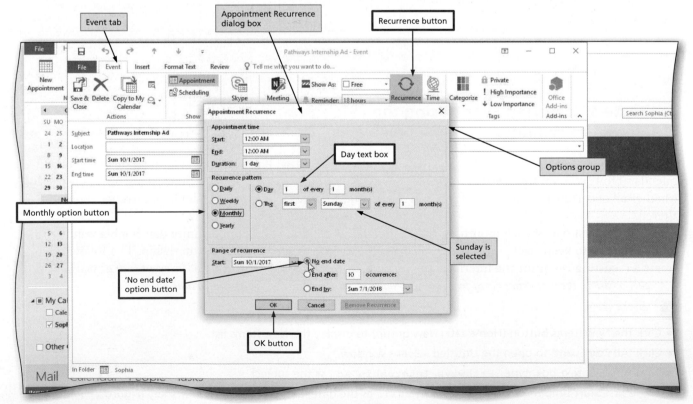

Figure 2–65

❸

- Click the OK button to accept the recurrence settings and close the Appointment Recurrence dialog box.
- Click the Reminder box arrow (Recurring Event tab | Options group) to display the Reminder list of reminder time slots.
- Click None to remove the reminder from the event.
- Click the Categorize button (Recurring Event tab | Tags group) to display the Categorize list of color categories.
- Click the blue Work category to assign the event to a category (Figure 2–66).

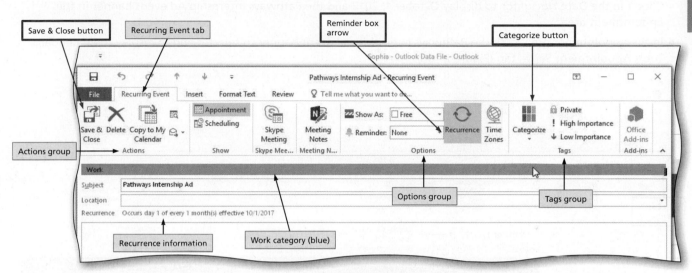

Figure 2–66

❹

- Click the Save & Close button (Recurring Event tab | Actions group) to save the event and close the window.
- Click the Month button (Home tab | Arrange group) to view the Pathways Internship Ad event on the calendar (Figure 2–67).

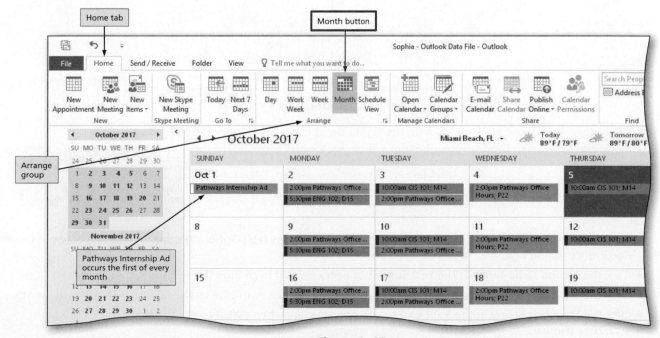

Figure 2–67

To Move a Recurring Event to a Different Day

Why? A recurring date may change to a different day or duration. The Internship Office Sophia works for is changing the internship ad rollout to the first Monday of each month. The recurring Pathways Internship Ad event must be changed for the entire series. The following steps change the date for all occurrences in a series.

- Click the Day button (Home tab | Arrange group) to display the Day view.
- Click 1 in the Date Navigator to display October 1, 2017 and the Pathways Internship Ad event banner in the appointment area.
- In the appointment area, click the Pathways Internship Ad event banner to select it and to display the Calendar Tools Appointment Series tab (Figure 2–68).

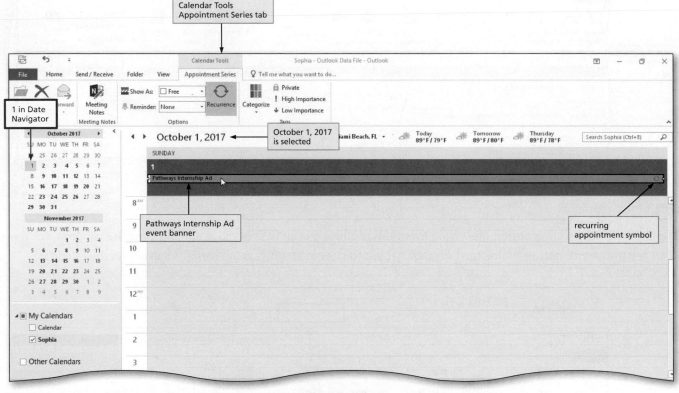

Figure 2–68

Q&A What does the double arrow symbol on the right side of the event banner represent?
The event appears in the Outlook calendar with a double arrow symbol to show that it is a recurring appointment.

- Click the Recurrence button (Calendar Tools Appointment Series tab | Options group) to display the Appointment Recurrence dialog box.
- Click the second radio button 'The first Sunday of every month' to change the recurrence pattern.
- Click the Sunday box arrow and then click to Monday to set the recurrence to the first Monday of each month.
- Click the Start box arrow in the Range of recurrence area, and then click 2 to change the start date to Mon 10/2/2017 (Figure 2–69).

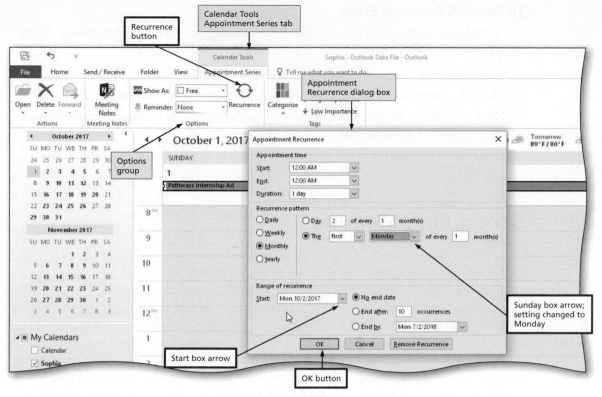

Figure 2–69

❸

- Click the OK button to close the Appointment Recurrence dialog box and change the event day.
- Click the Month button (Home tab | Arrange group) to view the full month calendar (Figure 2–70).

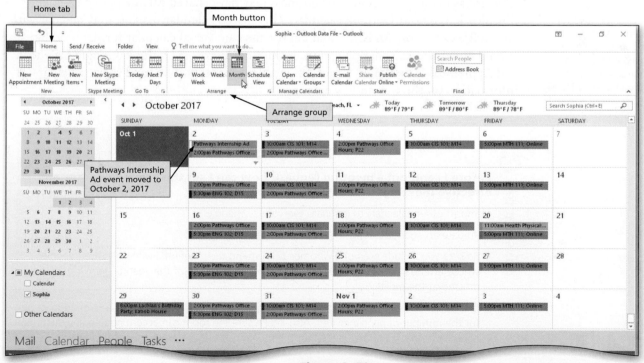

Figure 2–70

Other Ways

1. Double-click event, click entire series option button, click Recurrence button

2. Click event, press CTRL+O, click entire series option button, click Recurrence button

TO DELETE A RECURRING EVENT

Deleting a recurring event is similar to deleting a recurring appointment. If you choose to delete a recurring event, you would use the following steps.

1. Click the scroll arrow on the Date Navigator to display the date of the event.
2. Click the event to display the Calendar Tools Appointment Series tab.
3. Click the Delete button (Calendar Tools Appointment Series tab | Actions group) to display the Delete menu.
4. Click Delete Series on the Delete menu to delete the event from the calendar.

Scheduling Meetings

As defined earlier, a meeting is an appointment that you invite other people to attend. Each person who is invited can accept, accept as tentative, or decline a meeting request. A meeting also can include resources such as conference rooms. The person who creates the meeting and sends the invitations is known as the **meeting organizer**. The meeting organizer schedules a meeting by creating a **meeting request**, which is an email invitation to the meeting and arrives in each attendee's Inbox. Responses to a meeting request arrive in the Inbox of the meeting organizer. To create a meeting request, you use the Untitled – Meeting request window, which is similar to the Untitled – Appointment window with a few exceptions. The meeting request window includes the To text box, where you enter an email address for **attendees**, who are people invited to the meeting, and the Send button, which sends the invitation for the meeting to the attendees. When a meeting request arrives in the attendee's Inbox, it displays an icon different from an email message icon.

Before you invite others to a meeting, confirm that the meeting date and time are available. Your school or business may have shared calendars that can be downloaded to your Outlook calendar. This shared calendar may be an iCalendar with an .ics file extension. An **iCalendar** represents a universal calendar format used by several email and calendar programs, including Microsoft Outlook, Google Calendar, and Apple iCal. The iCalendar format enables users to publish and share calendar information on the web and by email.

If you are using your finger on a touch screen and are having difficulty completing the steps in this module, consider using a stylus. Many people find it easier to be precise with a stylus than with a finger. In addition, with a stylus you see the pointer. If you still are having trouble completing the steps with a stylus, try using a mouse.

BTW
Scheduling Assistant
If you have an Exchange account, you can use the **Scheduling Assistant** to find a meeting time when attendees and resources, such as rooms, are available. When you set up a meeting and are connected to an Exchange server, click the Scheduling button (Meeting tab | Show group) and add attendees to view their schedules.

CONSIDER THIS

Before I send out a meeting request, how can I set the groundwork for an effective meeting?

- Import other calendars to compare everyone's schedule.

- Prepare an agenda stating the purpose of the meeting.

- Be sure you include everyone who needs to attend the meeting. Invite only those people whose attendance is absolutely necessary to ensure that all of the agenda items can be addressed at the meeting.

- Confirm that the location of the meeting is available and that the room is the appropriate size for the number of people invited. Also, make sure the room can accommodate any multimedia equipment that might be needed for the meeting, such as a projector or telephone.

To Import an iCalendar File

Before scheduling a meeting, you can open your school's calendar to view your availability. Your school has a shared calendar in the iCalendar format that contains the school's master schedule. The following steps import an iCalendar file into Outlook. *Why? By importing another calendar, you can compare available dates for a meeting.*

1
- Click the File tab on the ribbon to open the Backstage view.
- Click Open & Export to display the Open gallery (Figure 2–71).

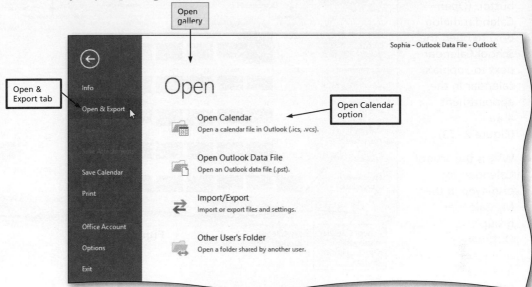

Figure 2–71

2
- Click Open Calendar in the Open gallery to display the Open Calendar dialog box.
- Navigate to the mailbox location (in this case, the Module 02 folder in the Outlook folder) (Figure 2–72).

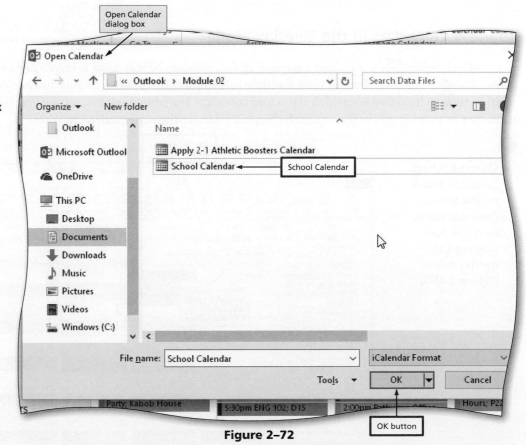

Figure 2–72

3

- Click School Calendar to select the file, and then click the OK button (Open Calendar dialog box) to open the School Calendar next to Sophia's calendar in the appointment area (Figure 2–73).

Q&A
Why is the School Calendar not displayed in the My Calendar group?
Outlook organizes multiple calendars in groups. If you frequently work with a set of calendars, you can view them in groups. When you open an iCalendar, it initially might appear in an Other Calendars group.

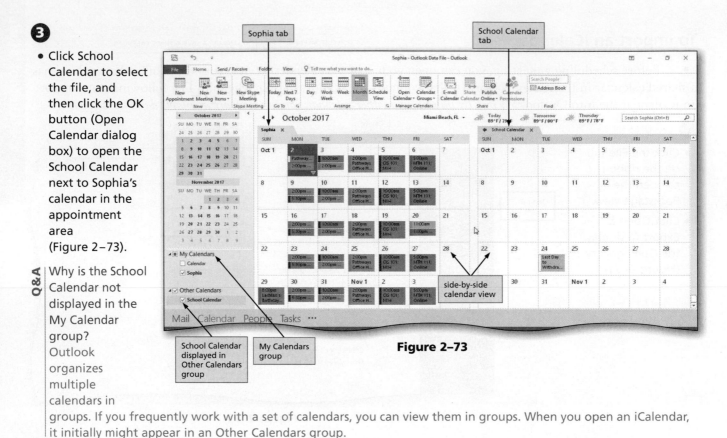

Figure 2–73

___

To View Calendars in the Overlay Mode

1 CONFIGURE CALENDAR OPTIONS | 2 CREATE & MANIPULATE APPOINTMENTS | 3 SCHEDULE EVENTS
4 SCHEDULE MEETINGS | 5 PRINT CALENDAR | 6 SAVE & SHARE CALENDAR

Why? Before Sophia schedules a meeting on her calendar, she may want to review her school's official calendar to avoid scheduling conflicts. You can view multiple calendars at the same time side-by-side or combined into an overlay view to help you see which dates and times are available in all calendars. The following steps display both calendars in overlay mode and make the Sophia calendar the active calendar.

1

- Click the School Calendar arrow on the School Calendar tab to view the two calendars in overlay mode (Figure 2–74).

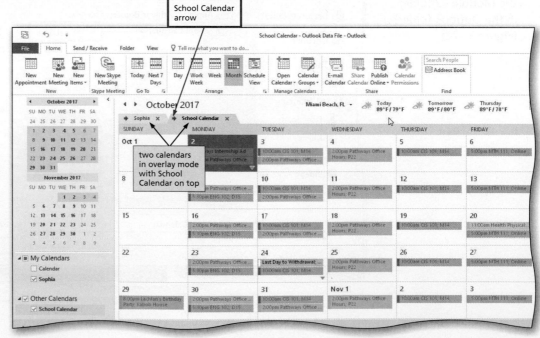

Figure 2–74

2

- Click the Sophia tab to display the Sophia calendar in front of the School Calendar (Figure 2–75).

Q&A What happens if I click the arrow on Sophia's calendar at this point? Outlook again displays the calendars side by side.

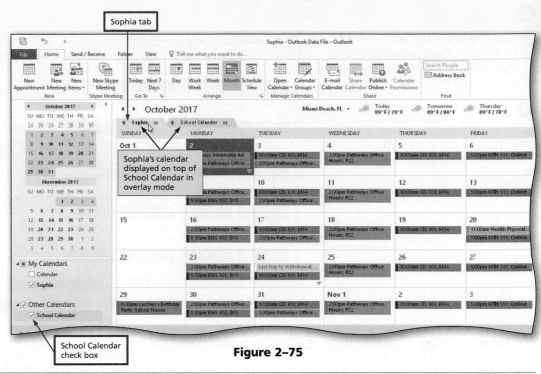

Figure 2–75

To View and Dock the Peek Calendar

1 CONFIGURE CALENDAR OPTIONS | 2 CREATE & MANIPULATE APPOINTMENTS | 3 SCHEDULE EVENTS
4 SCHEDULE MEETINGS | 5 PRINT CALENDAR | 6 SAVE & SHARE CALENDAR

The Outlook Navigation bar provides a **Peek** feature, a pop-up window that provides access to email, calendar, people, and tasks. **Why?** *Using the Peek feature, you can take a quick glance at your schedule without having to rearrange windows or lose your train of thought.* When you hover over Calendar in the Navigation Pane, a Peek calendar of the current month opens and the current date is highlighted with a blue background. The Peek calendar can be docked in the right pane of the calendar. Appointments and meetings scheduled for today appear below the calendar. The following steps view, dock, and remove the Peek calendar.

1

- Click the School Calendar check box in the Navigation Pane to remove the School Calendar from the Outlook window.
- Point to Calendar on the Navigation bar to display the Peek calendar with today's appointments or meetings (Figure 2–76).

Q&A Why do I not see any appointments or meetings in the Peek calendar?
If you do not have any appointments or meetings today in the default Calendar, the Peek calendar does not display any calendar items.

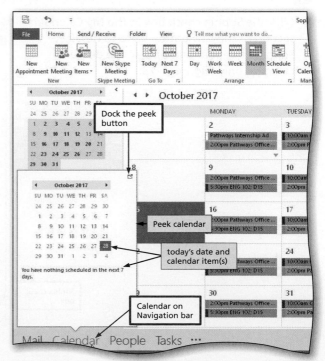

Figure 2–76

- Click the 'Dock the peek' button to dock the Peek calendar in the right pane of the Outlook window (Figure 2–77).

- Click the 'Remove the peek' button on the docked Peek calendar to remove the Peek calendar.

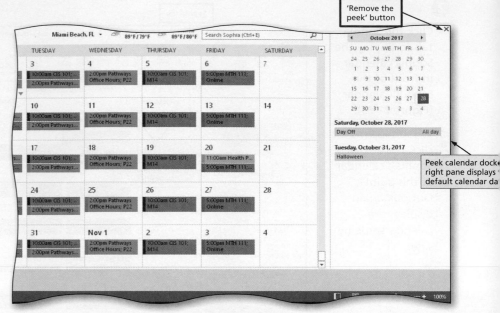

Figure 2–77

To Create and Send a Meeting Request

1 CONFIGURE CALENDAR OPTIONS | 2 CREATE & MANIPULATE APPOINTMENTS | 3 SCHEDULE EVENTS
4 SCHEDULE MEETINGS | 5 PRINT CALENDAR | 6 SAVE & SHARE CALENDAR

Why? *To find the best time to meet with other people, request a meeting, and keep track of the meeting date in your Inbox, you can send a meeting request in Outlook.* Sophia needs to meet with Ms. Pauley to discuss rescheduling the Pathways Internship Fair. Rather than send an email message requesting the meeting, she decides to use Outlook Calendar to create this meeting. Meetings can be scheduled on your default calendar or supplemental calendars. The following steps display the default calendar, create a meeting request, and send an invitation to the financial aid office. If you are completing this project on a personal computer, your email address must be set up in Outlook (see Module 1) so you can send an email meeting invitation. Use the email address of your instructor instead of the Ms. Pauley's email address.

- Click the Sophia check box in the My Calendars section of the Navigation Pane to deselect Sophia's calendar and display the default calendar only (Figure 2–78).

Figure 2–78

2

- Click the New Meeting button (Home tab | New group) to open the Untitled – Meeting window.
- Click the To text box and then type `ella.pauley@outlook.com` (substitute your instructor's email address for the email address) as the invitee to this meeting.
- Press the TAB key to move the insertion point to the Subject text box.
- Type `New Date for Pathways Internship Fair` as the subject of the meeting.
- Press the TAB key to move the insertion point to the Location text box.
- Type `P22` as the location of the meeting (Figure 2–79).

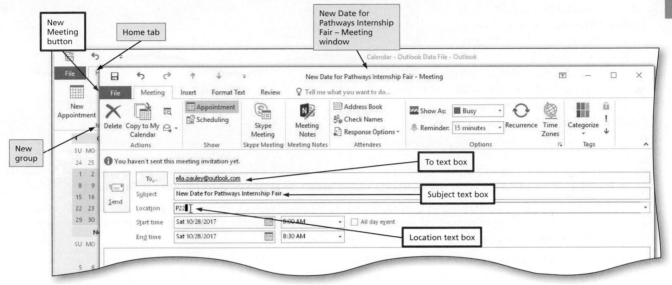

Figure 2–79

Q&A

Why does the message header include the text, "You haven't sent this meeting invitation yet"?

This notice reminds you that you have not yet sent the invitation to the meeting. If you review this invitation after sending it, the notice no longer appears.

3

- Press the TAB key to select the date in the first Start time box.
- Type `10/2/2017` as the start date of the meeting, and then press the TAB key to select the time in the second Start time box.
- Type `1:30 PM` as the start time for the meeting, and then press the TAB key two times to select the time in the second End time box.
- Type `2:30 PM` as the end time for the meeting (Figure 2–80).

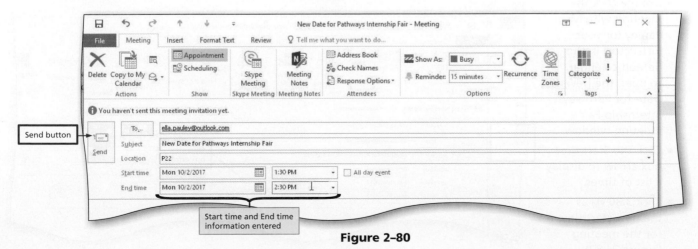

Figure 2–80

4

- Click the Send button to send the invitation and add the meeting to the calendar.

- If necessary, add an email account to Outlook to send the invitation to view the meeting on the calendar (Figure 2–81).

Q&A

When I sent the meeting request, an error message appeared that states "No valid email accounts are configured." Why did I get this error message?

A meeting request sends an email to each of the invitees. You must have an email account set up in Outlook to send the meeting request.

Figure 2–81

CONSIDER THIS

Is it possible to connect with my contacts using video or audio within Microsoft Outlook?

- Skype Meetings are integrated within Outlook by clicking the New Skype Meeting button (Home tab | Skype Meeting group). Using your Outlook contact list, you can call someone on their mobile, landline, or computer using video and audio capabilities. You do not need to be friends within Skype.

- Skype requires credit or subscription to reach landlines.

To Change the Time of a Meeting and Send an Update

1 CONFIGURE CALENDAR OPTIONS | 2 CREATE & MANIPULATE APPOINTMENTS | 3 SCHEDULE EVENTS
4 SCHEDULE MEETINGS | 5 PRINT CALENDAR | 6 SAVE & SHARE CALENDAR

Your schedule has changed, which means you need to change the time of the meeting about the Pathways Internship Fair and send an update about the change. Though the invitee can propose a new time, only the originator can change or delete the meeting. *Why? You can update any meeting request to add or remove attendees or resources, change the meeting to a recurring series, or move the meeting to a different date or time.* The following steps change the time of the meeting and send an update to the attendee. If you are completing this project on a personal computer, your email account must be set up in Outlook (see Module 1) to be able to view the meeting request.

1

- Double-click the meeting with Ms. Pauley (or your instructor) in the default calendar to open the New Date for Pathways Internship Fair – Meeting window.

- Click the Start time box arrow to display a list of times.

- Click 3:30 PM as the new start time for the meeting (Figure 2–82).

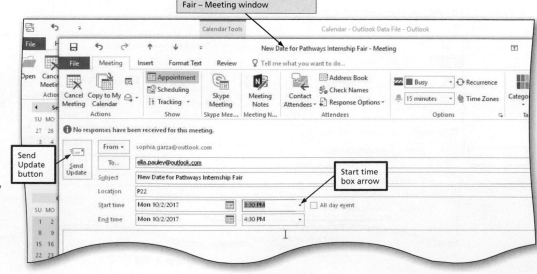

Figure 2–82

2

- Click the Send Update button in the message header to send the new information, close the meeting request, and view the updated meeting in the appointment area (Figure 2–83).

Q&A What if I need to cancel the meeting?
To remove a meeting, click the meeting in the appointment area to display the Calendar Tools Meeting tab, click the Cancel Meeting button (Calendar Tools Meeting tab | Actions group), and then click the Send Cancellation button to send the cancellation notice to the attendee and remove the meeting from the calendar.

Figure 2–83

Other Ways

1. Drag meeting to new time, click 'Save changes and send update', click OK, click Send Update

To Reply to a Meeting Request

1 CONFIGURE CALENDAR OPTIONS | 2 CREATE & MANIPULATE APPOINTMENTS | 3 SCHEDULE EVENTS
4 SCHEDULE MEETINGS | 5 PRINT CALENDAR | 6 SAVE & SHARE CALENDAR

Ms. Pauley has received Sophia's meeting request in an email message and wants to respond. *Why? Outlook allows invitees to choose from four response options: Accept, Tentative, Decline, or Propose New Time.* The following steps accept the meeting request. If you have a meeting request in your personal email that is set up using Outlook, substitute your meeting request in the following steps. If you do not have any meeting requests, read these steps without performing them.

1

- Click Mail on the Navigation bar to display the Inbox folder.
- Double-click the email message header to open the meeting invitation (Figure 2–84).

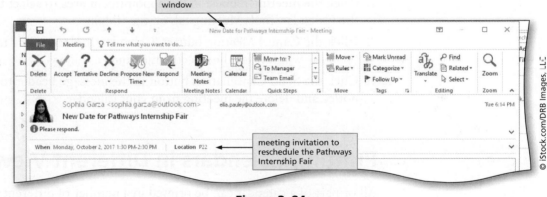

Figure 2–84

2

- Click the Accept button (Meeting tab | Respond group) to display the options for accepting the meeting (Figure 2–85).

3

- Click Send the Response Now to send the accept response and add the meeting to the calendar.

Q&A What happened to the meeting invitation in the Inbox?
When you accept or tentatively accept a meeting request, the invitation is deleted from the Inbox and the meeting is added to your calendar. The meeting response is in the Sent Items folder.

What happens when I decline a meeting request?
When a meeting request is declined, it is removed from your Inbox and the meeting is not added to your calendar. The reply is placed in the Sent Items folder.

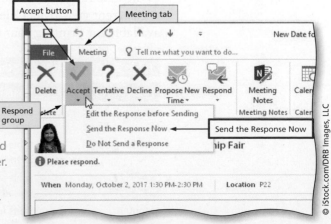

Figure 2–85

TO PROPOSE A NEW MEETING TIME

When you receive a meeting invitation, you can propose a new time if the original time is not available in your calendar. When you propose a new time, a proposal is sent to the meeting originator via email, indicating that you tentatively accept the request, but propose the meeting be held at a different time or on a different date. To propose a new time for a meeting, you would perform the following steps.

1. Click the appropriate meeting request to display the Calendar Tools Meeting Occurrence tab on the ribbon.
2. Click the Propose New Time button (Calendar Tools Meeting Occurrence tab | Respond group) to display the Occurrence menu.
3. Click the Tentative and Propose New Time option to display the Propose New Time dialog box for the selected meeting.
4. Drag through the time slot that you want to propose, or enter the appropriate information in the Meeting start and Meeting end boxes (Propose New Time dialog box).
5. Click the Propose time button to open the New Time Proposed – Meeting Response window.
6. Click the Send button.

TO CANCEL A MEETING

To cancel a meeting, you would perform the following steps.

1. Click the meeting request in the appointment area to select the meeting and display the Calendar Tools Meeting tab on the ribbon.
2. Click the Cancel Meeting button (Calendar Tools Meeting tab | Actions group) to open the window for the selected meeting.
3. Click the Send Cancellation button in the message header to send the cancellation notice and delete the meeting from your calendar.

Printing Calendars in Different Views

All or part of a calendar can be printed in a number of different views, or **print styles**. You can print a monthly, daily, or weekly view of your calendar and select options such as the date range and fonts to use. You also can view your calendar in a list by changing the current view from Calendar view to List view. Table 2–6 lists the print styles available for printing your calendar from Calendar view.

Table 2–6 Print Styles for Calendar View	
Print Style	**Description**
Daily	Prints a daily appointment schedule for a specific date including one day per page, a daily task list, an area for notes, and a two-month calendar
Weekly Agenda	Prints a seven-day weekly calendar with one week per page and a two-month calendar
Weekly Calendar	Prints a seven-day weekly calendar with one week per page and an hourly schedule, similar to the Daily style
Monthly	Prints five weeks per page of a particular month or date range
Tri-fold	Prints a page for each day, including a daily task list and a weekly schedule
Calendar Details	Prints a list of calendar items and supporting details

To Print the Calendar in Weekly Calendar Style

Why? *Printing a calendar enables you to distribute the calendar to others in a form that can be read or viewed, but cannot be edited.* Sophia can print her calendar to create a hard copy of her first week of classes. The following steps print a calendar in a weekly calendar style.

1

- Click Calendar on the Navigation bar to display the Outlook calendar.
- If necessary, click the Sophia check box to display Sophia's calendar.
- If necessary, click the other check boxes to close the other calendars.
- Click the Go to Date Dialog Box Launcher (Home tab | Go To group) to display the Go To Date dialog box.
- Type 10/1/2017 in the Date text box to select that date.
- If necessary, click the Show in button, and then click Month Calendar to show the month view in the appointment area.
- Click the OK button to close the Go To Date dialog box (Figure 2–86).

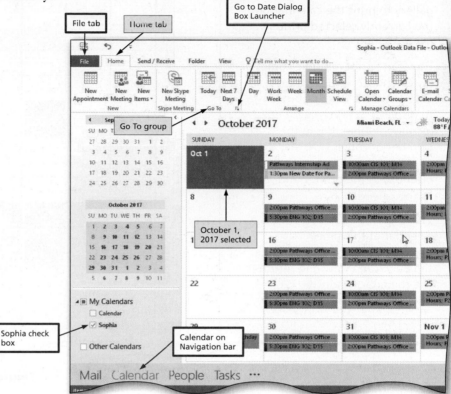

Figure 2–86

2

- Click File on the ribbon to open the Backstage view.
- Click the Print tab in the Backstage view to display the Print gallery.
- Click Weekly Calendar Style in the Settings list to preview how the printed calendar will look in Weekly Calendar Style (Figure 2–87).

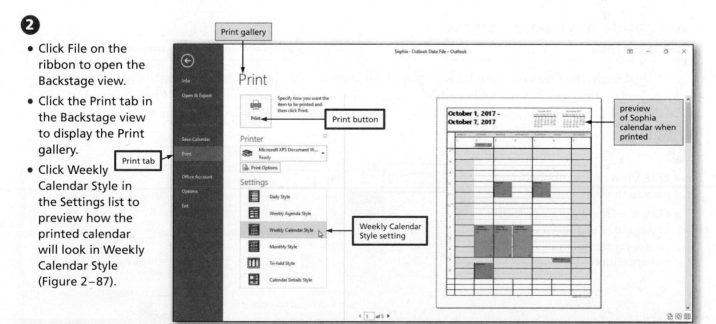

Figure 2–87

Experiment

- Click the other settings to preview the different print styles. When finished, select Weekly Calendar Style.

- If necessary, click the desired printer to change the currently selected printer.
- Click the Print button in the Print gallery to print the calendar on the currently selected printer (Figure 2–88).

Q&A

How can I print multiple copies of my calendar?

Click the Print Options button to display the Print dialog box, increase the number in the Number of copies box, and then click the Print button to send the calendar to the printer and return to the calendar.

What if I decide not to print the calendar at this time?

Click File on the ribbon to close the Backstage view and return to the calendar window.

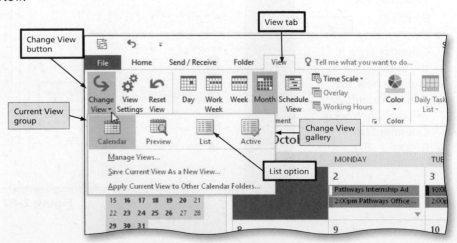

Figure 2–88

Other Ways

1. Press CTRL+P, press ENTER

To Change the Calendar View to List View

1 CONFIGURE CALENDAR OPTIONS | 2 CREATE & MANIPULATE APPOINTMENTS | 3 SCHEDULE EVENTS
4 SCHEDULE MEETINGS | 5 PRINT CALENDAR | 6 SAVE & SHARE CALENDAR

By default, the Outlook calendar is displayed in Calendar view, but other options include a List view, which displays the calendar as a table with each row displaying a unique calendar item. *Why? To display all of your calendar appointments, events, and meetings, change the current Calendar view to List view.* The following steps change the view from Calendar view to List view.

- Click View on the ribbon to display the View tab.
- Click the Change View button (View tab | Current View group) to display the Change View gallery (Figure 2–89).

Figure 2–89

- Click List in the Change View gallery to display a list of calendar items in the appointment area (Figure 2–90).

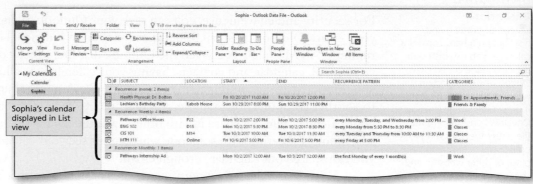

Sophia's calendar displayed in List view

Figure 2–90

To Print the Calendar in List View

To print a list of your calendar items in a table, print the List view display. The following steps print the calendar in Table style.

1. Click File on the ribbon to open the Backstage view.

2. Click the Print tab in the Backstage view to display the Print gallery.

3. Click the Table Style option in the Settings list to preview the calendar in Table Style.

4. If necessary, click the Printer box to display a list of available printer options, and then click the desired printer to change the selected printer.

5. Click the Print button to send the list of appointments to the selected printer (Figure 2–91).

Q&A When I changed the view from List view to Calendar view, why did the Calendar display the current date and not the date I printed?

The calendar always displays the current date when you change from List view to Calendar view.

BTW
Changing Settings before Printing
To change the margins, page orientation, or paper size before printing, click the Print Options button in the Print gallery and then click the Page Setup button to display the Page Setup: Table Style dialog box.

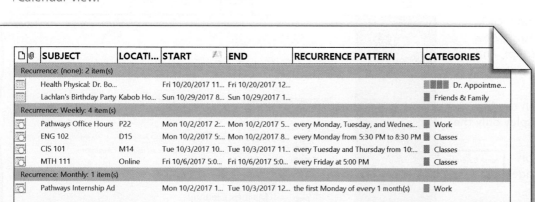

Figure 2–91

Other Ways

1. Press CTRL+P, click Print

BTW
**Distributing a
Calendar**
Instead of printing and
distributing a hard copy of a
calendar, you can distribute
the calendar electronically.
Options include sending the
calendar via email; posting
it on cloud storage (such as
OneDrive) and sharing the
file with others; posting it
on a social networking site,
blog, or other website; and
sharing a link associated with
an online location of the
calendar. You also can create
and share a PDF or XPS image
of the calendar, so that users
can view the file in Acrobat
Reader or XPS Viewer instead
of in Outlook.

Saving and Sharing the Calendar

For security and convenience, you can save your Outlook calendar by backing up your entire Outlook personal folder files (.pst) or an individual calendar (.ics). As a reminder, in Module 1 you saved the Outlook .pst file, which contained a backup of your email, calendar, and contacts. Saving your calendar file allows you to back up your appointments, events, and meetings in a single file. You can then move your calendar to another computer, for example, and continue to schedule items there. Besides saving your calendar, you can share it with others, whether they use Outlook or not. Finally, scheduling a meeting with someone who cannot see your calendar can be difficult, so you can share your calendar through email.

With Outlook, each appointment, task, or contact can be saved as a separate iCalendar file or you can save the whole calendar to your local computer or external storage device. An iCalendar file with the .ics file extension can be imported by other programs such as Google Calendar. Instead of emailing an iCalendar file as an attachment to share your calendar, you can share portions of your entire calendar through a built-in function in Outlook.

To Save a Calendar as an iCalendar File

1 CONFIGURE CALENDAR OPTIONS | 2 CREATE & MANIPULATE APPOINTMENTS | 3 SCHEDULE EVENTS
4 SCHEDULE MEETINGS | 5 PRINT CALENDAR | **6 SAVE & SHARE CALENDAR**

You have performed many tasks while creating this calendar and do not want to risk losing work completed thus far. Accordingly, you should save the calendar on your hard disk, OneDrive, or a location that is most appropriate to your situation.

The following steps assume you already have created folders for storing your files, for example, an Outlook folder (for your class) that contains a Module 02 folder (for your assignments). Thus, these steps save the calendar in the Module 02 folder in the Outlook folder in your desired save location. For a detailed example of the procedure for saving a file in a folder or saving a file on OneDrive, refer to the Office and Windows module at the beginning of this book.

Why? By saving a copy of your calendar to an iCalendar format, you can back up or share your calendar with your business colleagues or friends. The following steps save a calendar. They assume you already have created folders for storing your files, for example, an Outlook folder (for your class) that contains a Module 02 folder (for your assignments).

• Click View on the ribbon, click the Change View button (View tab | Current View group), and then click Calendar to return to Calendar view.

• Use the check boxes in the My Calendars pane to display only the Sophia calendar.

• Click File on the ribbon to display the Backstage view (Figure 2–92).

Figure 2–92

● Click the Save Calendar tab to
display the Save As dialog box.

● Navigate to the desired save
location (in this case, the Module
02 folder in the Outlook folder or
your class folder) (Figure 2–93).

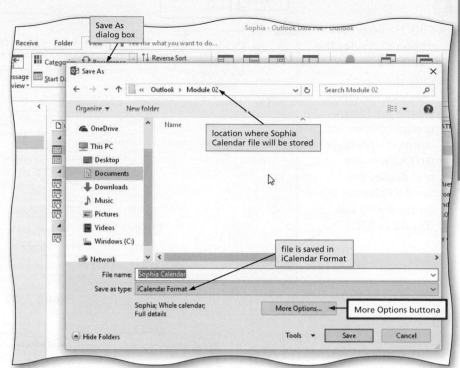

Figure 2–93

● Click the More Options button to display the
Save As dialog box.

● Click the Date Range arrow to display the Date
Range list (Figure 2–94).

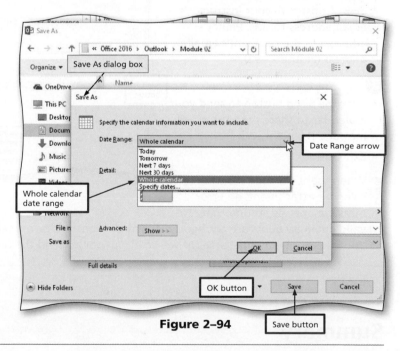

● If necessary, click Whole calendar on the Date
Range list to save the calendar's full details.

● Click the OK button (Save As dialog box) to
specify the whole calendar date range.

● Click the Save button to save the calendar as an
iCalendar file in the selected location.

Figure 2–94

1 CONFIGURE CALENDAR OPTIONS | 2 CREATE & MANIPULATE APPOINTMENTS | 3 SCHEDULE EVENTS
4 SCHEDULE MEETINGS | 5 PRINT CALENDAR | 6 SAVE & SHARE CALENDAR

To Share a Calendar

Ms. Pauley, the director of the Pathways Internship Office, needs to meet with Sophia to reschedule
the fair. She requests a copy of Sophia's calendar. *Why? Sophia can send a copy of her calendar in an email message
directly from Outlook to inform Ms. Pauley when she is available for a meeting.* The following steps share a calendar by
forwarding the selected calendar. These steps assume you have an email account set up in Outlook.

1

- Click Home on the ribbon to display the Home tab.

- Click the E-mail Calendar button (Home tab | Share group) to open the Untitled – Message (HTML) window and display the Send a Calendar via E-mail dialog box (Figure 2–95).

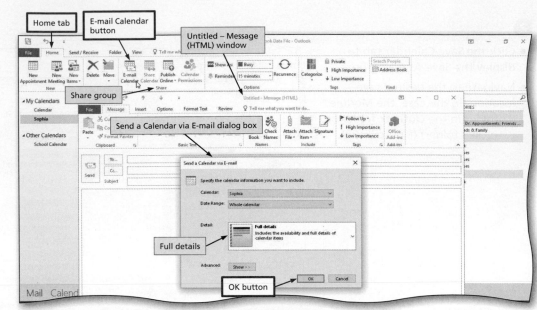

Figure 2–95

2

- Click the OK button to attach the Sophia calendar to the email message.

- Click the To text box, and then type `ella.pauley@outlook.com` (substitute your instructor's email address for Ms. Pauley's address) as the recipient's email address (Figure 2–96).

3

- Click the Send button to send your iCalendar to share with the email message recipient.

- Exit Outlook.

Q&A When I sent the email with the calendar attachment, an error message opened stating that "No valid email accounts are configured." Why did I get this error message?
You must have an email account set up in Outlook to send the calendar.

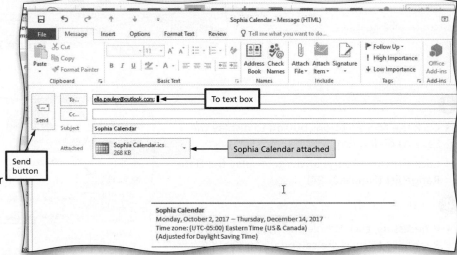

Figure 2–96

Summary

In this module, you have learned how to use Outlook to create a personal schedule by entering appointments, creating recurring appointments, moving appointments to new dates, and scheduling events. You also learned how to invite attendees to a meeting, accept a meeting request, and change the time of a meeting. To review your schedule, you learned to view and print your calendar in different views and print styles. Finally, you learned how to save your calendar and share your schedule with others.

What decisions will you need to make when configuring the Outlook calendar; scheduling appointments, events, and meetings; printing calendars; and saving and sharing your calendar in the future?

CONSIDER THIS

1. Configure the Outlook Calendar:
    a. Determine the purpose of your calendar — personal, professional, or for a group.
    b. Determine the city displayed on the Weather Bar and if you prefer holidays in your default calendar.
2. Schedule appointments, events, and meetings:
    a. Determine if each calendar item is an appointment, event, or a meeting.
    b. Determine which appointments and events are one-time or recurring.
    c. Plan which color-coded categories would best organize your calendar items.
3. Edit appointments, events, and meetings:
    a. Update the details of your calendar items as your schedule changes.
    b. Respond to meeting requests.
4. Print your calendar:
    a. Plan which calendar style would best fit your needs.
5. Save and share your calendar:
    a. Plan where your calendar should be stored.
    b. Determine how you will share your calendar with friends and colleagues.

How should you submit solutions to questions in the assignments identified with a ❄ symbol?

CONSIDER THIS

Every assignment in this book contains one or more questions identified with a ❄ symbol. These questions require you to think beyond the assigned file. Present your solutions to the questions in the format required by your instructor. Possible formats may include one or more of these options: write the answer; create a document that contains the answer; present your answer to the class; discuss your answer in a group; record the answer as audio or video using a webcam, smartphone, or portable media player; or post answers on a blog, wiki, or website.

Apply Your Knowledge

Reinforce the skills and apply the concepts you learned in this module.

Note: To complete this assignment, you will be required to use the Data Files. Please contact your instructor for information about accessing the Data Files.

Updating a Calendar

Instructions: Run Outlook. You are updating the Athletic Boosters iCalendar named Apply 2-1 Athletic Boosters Calendar, which is located in the Data Files, by revising the scheduled activities.

Perform the following tasks:
1. Open the Apply 2-1 Athletic Boosters Calendar.ics file from the Data Files.
2. Display only this iCalendar in the Outlook Calendar window. Use Month view to display the calendar for March 2017.
3. Add a monthly Athletic Boosters Meeting appointment for the first Wednesday of each month starting at 2 PM and lasting for one hour from March through December 2017.
4. Change the color category of the monthly Athletic Boosters Meeting to orange.
5. Change the Senior Night appointment from March 10 to March 17. Move the appointment to one hour later with the same duration.
6. Change the location of the Ladies Basketball Awards appointment on March 18 to Hanel Hall.

Continued >

Apply Your Knowledge *continued*

7. Reschedule the Fundraising Meeting appointment from Thursdays starting on February 23 until April 13 to meet at the same time on Mondays starting on March 6 until April 17.

8. Change the starting and ending time of the Athletic Booster Picnic on May 6 to two hours later.

9. If requested by your instructor, change the location of the picnic from Morristown Park to a park named after your birth city.

10. Save the Calendar as Apply 2-1 Athletic Boosters Updated and submit the iCalendar in the format specified by your instructor.

11. Print the final calendar in Month view, shown in Figure 2–97, and then submit the printout to your instructor.

12. Delete this calendar from Outlook and exit Outlook.

13. ✷ Most calendar programs save files with the .ics format. Why is it convenient that most calendar programs use the same format?

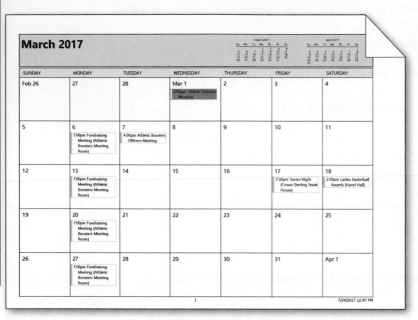

Figure 2–97

Extend Your Knowledge

Extend the skills you learned in this module and experiment with new skills. You may need to use Help to complete the assignment.

Creating and Sharing a Calendar

Instructions: Run Outlook. You are volunteering at a local animal shelter a couple days a week. Create a new calendar to share your availability to help at the shelter. Use Outlook Help to learn how to create a calendar group, change the color of the calendar, and create a private appointment.

Perform the following tasks:

1. Create a new calendar group called Pet Shelter.

2. Create a blank calendar named Volunteers and then move it to the Pet Shelter calendar group.

3. Change the color of the entire calendar to brown.

4. Add a recurring Feed Animals appointment from 5:00 PM to 6:30 PM on Monday and Wednesday beginning on June 5, 2017 and continuing for 20 occurrences at the Laredo Animal Shelter.

5. Create an event named Adoption Week starting on June 26, 2017 at the Laredo Animal Shelter lasting 7 days from this Monday to next Monday.

6. Add a recurring Post Animal of the Week Online as an All Day event starting on June 2 and lasting for 12 months on the first Friday of each month.

7. If requested by your instructor, change the Weather Bar to display weather information for your hometown. The completed calendar is shown in Figure 2–98.

8. Save the Calendar file as Extend Your Knowledge 2-1 Pet Shelter and submit the iCalendar in the format specified by your instructor.

9. Exit Outlook.

10. ✻ Think about the reason you might share your Outlook Calendar. In the case of sharing your schedule and other volunteer's calendars with the animal shelter, why would a digital calendar be more helpful to the director of the shelter instead of a paper schedule?

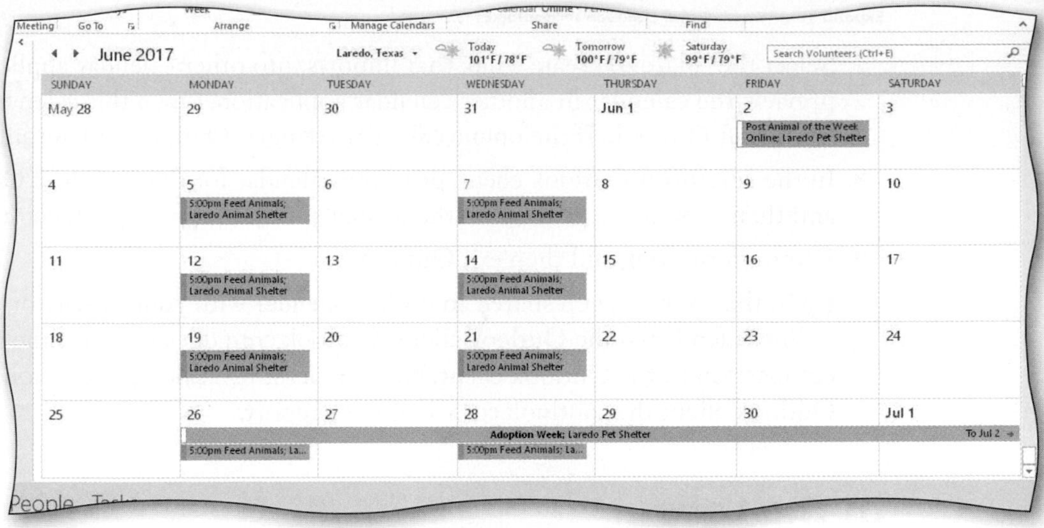

Figure 2–98

Expand Your World: Cloud and Web Technologies

Opening a Web-Based Calendar in the Outlook Client

Instructions: In your role as a barista at a new local coffee shop, you have been asked by the manager to assist with marketing the café on social media by posting to Facebook and Twitter. Use the calendar dates shown in Table 2–7 to create an online calendar at Outlook.com using your Microsoft account. Share the online calendar with your instructor. Using Outlook, open the online calendar and print the calendar in the Outlook client. Sharing your calendar in the cloud as a link allows anyone to see your calendar such as the café's manager, even if they do not have their own calendar established.

Perform the following tasks:

1. If necessary, create a Microsoft account at outlook.com.

2. Open the calendar option at outlook.com and add a calendar named Social Media for Coffee Shop Calendar with the description, **Online Marketing** .

3. Open the Social Media for Coffee Shop Calendar only and add the items shown in Table 2–7 to the online calendar.

4. If requested by your instructor, add a promotional calendar item on your birthday in 2017 titled Barista's Birthday — 1 Free Scone per Coffee Order.

5. Click the Share button to view the sharing options for this calendar. Select the option to send people a view-only link to access this calendar online. Select the ICS option to import into another calendar application to show event details.

6. Submit the outlook.com calendar link to view in a web browser in a format specified by your instructor.

Table 2–7 Social Media for Coffee Shop Calendar Items			
Description	**Recurrence**	**Due Date**	**Availability**
Pumpkin Latte Promotion	None	First Sunday in October 2017 at 5 AM	Free
Join the Jolt Frequent Customer Program	Monthly	First day of each month starting in October 2017 at midnight, never ends	Free
Happy Caffeine Hours	Mondays	Every Monday in October 2017 from 4:00 PM for 2 hours	Busy
Halloween Coffee Roasters 20% Off	None	October 31, 2017 All Day Event	Busy

Continued >

Expand Your World: Cloud and Web Technologies *continued*

7. Select the 'share to create a link that imports into other calendar applications (ICS)' option to preview the calendar in another calendar application. Open this calendar link in the calendar in Microsoft Outlook. If the online calendar changes, Outlook will automatically update.

8. In the Microsoft Outlook client, print the calendar for the month of October in Monthly style, and then submit the printout in the format specified by your instructor.

9. Exit outlook.com, and then exit Outlook.

10. ✳ In this exercise, you shared an online calendar with your instructor and also imported the online calendar to the Outlook client. Outlook.com does not have the full functionality in comparison to the Outlook client. Name at least five calendar functions that are part of the Outlook client that outlook.com does not support.

In the Labs

Design, create, modify, and/or use files following the guidelines, concepts, and skills presented in this module. Labs 1 and 2, which increase in difficulty, require you to create solutions based on what you learned in the module; Lab 3 requires you to apply your creative thinking and problem-solving skills to design and implement a solution.

Lab 1: Creating Recurring Events

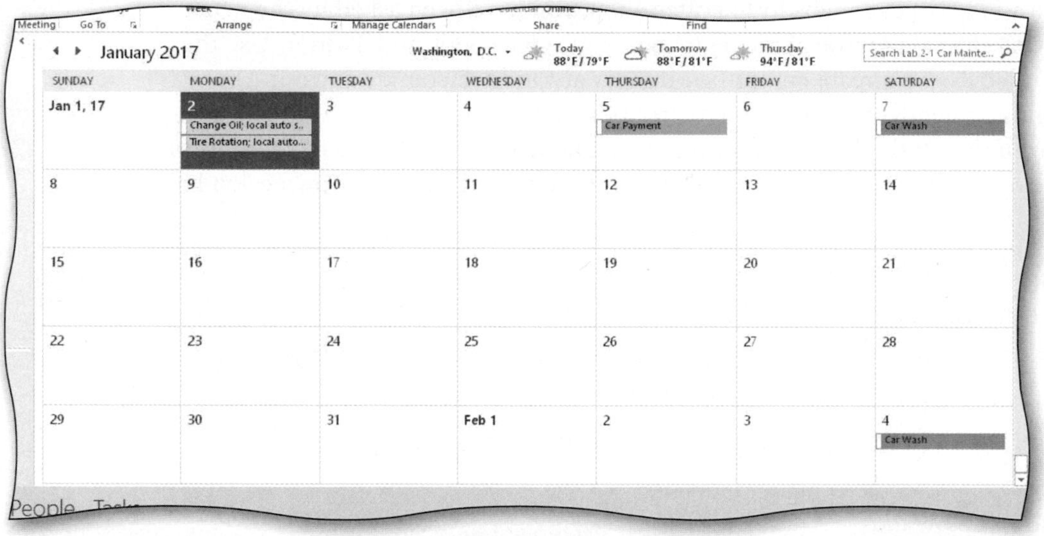

Problem: You would like to set up a calendar to remember to take care of your car scheduled maintenance, loan, cleaning, and, inspection as shown in Figure 2–99.

Figure 2–99

Perform the following tasks:

1. Create a Calendar named Lab 2-1 Car Maintenance Calendar in Outlook.

2. Create the events in the calendar in the year 2017, using the information listed in Table 2–8.

3. For each event, enter the location as local auto shop for the category Schedule Maintenance, otherwise leave the location blank.

4. For each event, show the time as Free.

5. For each event, set the reminder to one day.

6. For each monthly event, set the event to recur every month during 2017.

7. Each event should be an All Day event.

8. If requested by your instructor, add your favorite car model as a car show (for example, Mustang Car Show) on your birthday as an event in your 2017 Calendar.

9. Save the calendar as an .ics file and submit it in a format specified by your instructor.

10. Print the month of May using the Monthly Style and submit it in a format specified by your instructor.

11. ✳ A calendar can keep you organized. In the case of scheduling your car payment, how can a digital calendar assist in increasing your credit score?

Table 2–8 Car Maintenance Schedule			
Calendar Item	**Due Date**	**Category**	**Color Code**
Car Wash	First Saturday of each month	Cleaning	blue
Change Oil	Starting on January 2 and occurring every 120 days	Scheduled Maintenance	yellow
Car payment	5th day of the month	Payment	green
Add Antifreeze	October 15th	Scheduled Maintenance	yellow
Tire Rotation	January 2 and July 2	Scheduled Maintenance	yellow
New Tires	August 1	Scheduled Maintenance	yellow
Car inspection	May 30th	Tax and Scheduled Maintenance	red, yellow

Lab 2: Creating a Calendar

Problem: You were recently hired part-time by your local news station as a restaurant and events reviewer. By taking the time to develop a plan for your restaurant and event visits, as shown in Figure 2–100, you will remember to produce regular reviews for the news station.

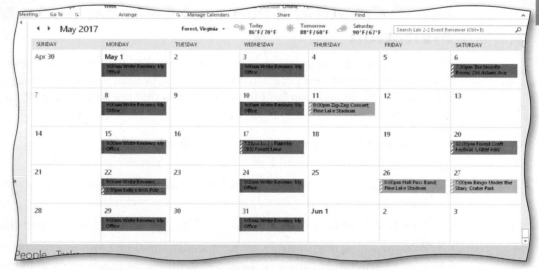

Figure 2–100

Instructions: Open Outlook. Perform the following tasks:

1. Create a calendar named Lab 2-2 Event Reviewer Calendar in Outlook.

2. Create the appointments in the calendar, using the information listed in Table 2–9.

Table 2–9 Local Restaurant and Events Table				
Restaurant or Event	**Location**	**Event Date**	**Category**	**Color Code**
The Noodle Room	256 Adams Ave	May 6, 2017	Restaurant	red
Zig-Zag Concert	Pine Lake Stadium	May 11, 2017	Concert	green
Lori's Pizzeria	7800 Forest Lane	May 17, 2017	Restaurant	red
Forest Craft Festival	Crater Park	May 20, 2017	Festival	purple
Kelly's Irish Pub	129 45th St	May 22, 2017	Restaurant	red
Hall Pass Band	Pine Lake Stadium	May 26, 2017	Concert	green
Bingo Under the Stars	Crater Park	May 27, 2017	Other	yellow

Continued >

3. For each event in the table, set the reminder as 2 hours.

4. For each event, show the time as Tentative.

5. Set each restaurant dinner for 7:30 PM for one hour, concerts at 8 PM for two hours, festivals at noon for two hours, and other events at 7 PM for 2.5 hours.

6. For each Monday and Wednesday throughout the month of May 2017, add a recurring appointment. Enter **Write Reviews** as the subject. For location, enter **My Office**. Show the time as Busy. The appointment should start at 9:00 AM and end two hours later. Add all four color-coded categories and set a 10-minute reminder.

7. Delete the one occurrence of the recurring appointment on May 17.

8. If requested by your instructor, change your Weather Bar to show the weather for your hometown.

9. Save the calendar as an .ics file and submit it in a format specified by your instructor.

10. Print the calendar for the month of May in Monthly style, and then submit the printout in the format specified by your instructor.

11. ✸ What are the advantages of syncing your Outlook Calendar to a mobile phone?

Lab 3: Creating a Personal Calendar and a Meeting Invitation

Problem: You are meeting with your school advisor to plan next year's course schedule. She has requested that you create a personal calendar of the present semester listing your present classes, time, room numbers. In addition, add five other events that are scheduled with work, hobbies, or other activities.

Instructions: Open Outlook. Perform the following tasks:

1. Create a calendar named Lab 2-3 Personal Calendar in Outlook.

2. Create the appointments in the calendar based on your present class schedule with class names, locations, times, and a 10-minute reminder for each class.

3. Create at least four categories for your class types and associate each class type to the category.

4. Add the following meetings to the calendar and then send invitations for upcoming meetings to your instructor, as shown in Table 2–10. All the meetings are held in the Advisor's Office. Send a meeting invitation to yourself.

Table 2–10 Advisor Calendar Meetings				
Description	**Date**	**Time**	**Show As**	**Reminder**
Discuss Career Interest	June 3	1:00 PM – 2:00 PM	Out of Office	30 minutes
Class Schedule Selection	June 8	12:00 PM – 2:00 PM	Tentative	30 minutes

5. If requested by your instructor, add a third meeting titled **Class Performance** on June 2nd at 9:00 AM for one to meet with your instructor; include a one-day reminder and show as working elsewhere.

6. Save your calendar as an iCalendar named Lab 3-3 Personal Calendar. Submit your assignment in the format specified by your instructor.

Part 2: ✸ If you receive a meeting request, you can respond in several ways. What are the four ways to respond to a meeting request? You can add comments with each of these responses. Provide comments to each of the four meeting requests responses explaining why you can or cannot attend the meeting with your advisor.

3 | Managing Contacts and Personal Contact Information with Outlook

Objectives

You will have mastered the material in this module when you can:

- Create a new contact
- Create a contact from an email message
- Modify a contact
- Add a contact photo
- Delete a contact
- Manipulate attachments to contacts
- Display contacts in different views
- Sort a contact list

- Find contacts using complete or partial information
- Find contacts from any Outlook folder
- Create a contact group
- Modify a contact group
- Add and remove names in a contact group
- Preview a contact list
- Print a contact list

Managing Contacts and Personal Contact Information with Outlook

This introductory module covers features and functions common to managing contacts in Outlook 2016.

Roadmap

In this module, you will learn how to perform basic contact management tasks. The following roadmap identifies general activities you will perform as you progress through this module:

1. CREATE a NEW CONTACT
2. MODIFY a CONTACT

Microsoft Outlook 2016

File   Home   Send / Receive   Folder   View   Q Tell me what you want to do...

Inbox - Outlook Data File - Outlook

3. CHANGE the VIEW OF CONTACTS

4. FIND a CONTACT

5. CREATE a CONTACT GROUP

6. PRINT the CONTACT LIST

At the beginning of the step instructions throughout each module, you will see an abbreviated form of this roadmap. The abbreviated roadmap uses colors to indicate module progress: gray means the module is beyond that activity, blue means the task being shown is covered in that activity, and black means that activity is yet to be covered. For example, the following abbreviated roadmap indicates the module would be showing a task in the Change View of Contacts activity.

1 CREATE NEW CONTACT | 2 MODIFY CONTACT | 3 CHANGE VIEW OF CONTACTS

4 FIND CONTACT | 5 CREATE CONTACT GROUP | 6 PRINT CONTACT LIST

Use the abbreviated roadmap as a progress guide while you read or step through the instructions in this module.

Introduction to Outlook Contacts

To keep track of your friends, business partners, family, and others with whom you communicate, you can use Outlook to create contact lists and contact groups. A **contact list** lets you record information about people, such as their email address, phone number, birthday, physical address, and photo. Each person's information is stored in a **contact record** in the contact list. If you have several colleagues at work whom you email frequently, you can add them to a **contact group**. You then can send email messages to all of your colleagues using the contact group rather than having to select each contact individually.

Project — Contact List with Groups

People and businesses create contact lists to keep track of people who are important to them or their business. A contact list may contain groups so that several contacts can be identified with a group name rather than individual contact names. Managing your contacts using a contact list can increase productivity greatly.

The project in this module follows general guidelines and uses Outlook to create the contact list shown in Figure 3–1. This contact list displays individual contacts and contact groups by name. A photograph of each contact helps you associate a face to a name. The contact groups display the name of the group, have a group label, and include a different graphic from the individual contacts.

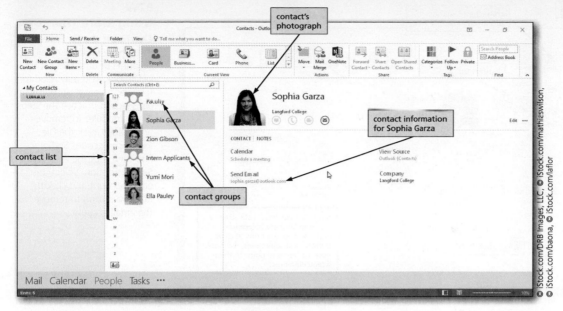

Figure 3–1

Creating a Contact List

The first step in creating a contact list is to enter information such as names, email addresses, and phone numbers for the people you communicate with regularly. After you enter and save contact information, that information is available as you compose email messages. You can type the first few letters of a contact's name into an email message, and Outlook will fill in the rest of the email address for you. If you are working on a mobile device that can make and receive phone calls, you also can use contact information to call someone on your contact list.

What advantages does an Outlook contact list provide for marketing a new business such as a gym?

Creating a contact list of your customer contacts lets you reach more people who can help your business grow by becoming repeat customers and spreading the word about your business. A gym can provide an email sign-up form on its website so that customers can choose to keep up with the latest schedule and deals. For example, a gym might send monthly email messages to advertise specials such as 50 percent off kickboxing classes on a certain date.

CONSIDER THIS

Contacts – Outlook Window

The Contacts – Outlook window shown in Figure 3–2 includes a variety of features to help you work efficiently with a contact list. The Contacts – Outlook window contains many elements similar to the windows in other Office programs, as well as some elements that are unique to Outlook. The main elements of the Contacts window are the My Contacts pane, the contact list, and the People pane.

For an introduction to Windows and instructions about how to perform basic Windows tasks, read the Office and Windows module at the beginning of this book, where you can learn how to resize windows, change screen resolution, create folders, move and rename files, use Windows Help, and much more.

For an introduction to Office and instructions about how to perform basic tasks in Office apps, read the Office and Windows module at the beginning of this book, where you can learn how to run an application, use the ribbon, save a file, open a file, print a file, exit an application, use Help, and much more.

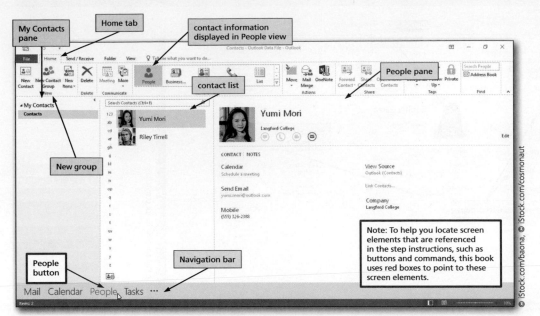

Figure 3–2

BTW

Using More Than One Outlook Data File
If you have multiple email accounts or data files set up in Outlook, you may need to remove the email accounts or data files to practice the steps in this module. To remove an account, click the File tab, click Account Settings, and then click the Account Settings option. Select the email account and click the Remove button to remove the email account.

To Create a New Contact

1 CREATE NEW CONTACT | 2 MODIFY CONTACT | 3 CHANGE VIEW OF CONTACTS
4 FIND CONTACT | 5 CREATE CONTACT GROUP | 6 PRINT CONTACT LIST

    To create the contact list in this module, you start by adding Sophia Garza as the first contact. In Modules 1 and 2, you set up Sophia's email account and calendar in Outlook. When you create or update a contact, you add the contact's name, company name, email address, and other information, such as a Twitter username. The following steps create a new contact in the People view. *Why? To organize the contact information of your friends, clients, and colleagues, you should keep an Outlook contact list to communicate efficiently without having to search for information in multiple locations. Sophia is adding herself to her contact list to organize her contact information in a central place.*

- Run Outlook and open the Sophia Module 3.pst Outlook Data File from the Data Files.

- Click People (shown in Figure 3–2) on the Navigation bar to display the Outlook Contacts.

- Click the New Contact button (Home tab | New group) to display the Untitled – Contact window (Figure 3–3).

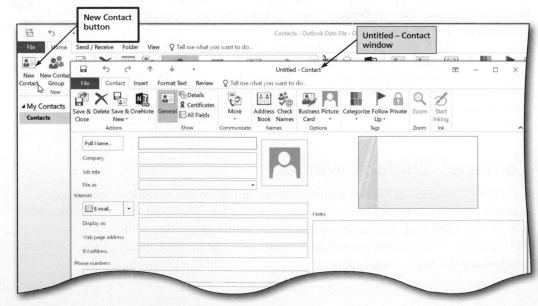

Figure 3–3

Q&A   What should I do if I have more than one Outlook data file open in the Navigation Pane?
Open only the Sophia Module 3.pst Outlook data file, which appears as outlook data file in the Navigation Pane. Close any other Outlook data files open in the Navigation Pane, and then repeat Step 1.

2

- Type `Sophia Garza` in the Full Name text box to enter a name for the contact.
- Type `Langford College` in the Company text box to enter a company (or in this case, a school) for the contact.
- Type `sophia.garza@outlook.com` in the E-mail text box, and then press the TAB key to enter an email address for the contact (Figure 3–4).

Q&A Why did the title of the Contact window change after I entered the name?

As soon as you enter the name, Outlook updates the Contact window title to reflect the information you have entered. Outlook also displays the name in the File as text box. The contact is not saved, however; only the window title and File as text boxes are updated.

Can I add information to other fields for a contact?

Yes. As long as you have the information, you can fill out the fields accordingly. You even can add fields besides those listed by clicking the All Fields button (Contact tab | Show group).

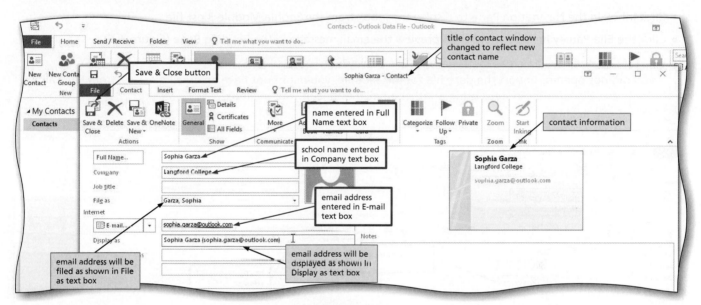

Figure 3–4

3

- Click the Save & Close button (Contact tab | Actions group) (shown in Figure 3–4) to save the contact record and close the Contact window (Figure 3–5).

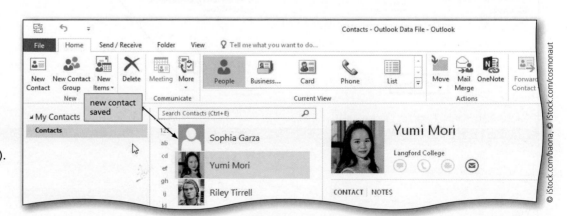

© iStock.com/baona, © iStock.com/cosmonaut

Figure 3–5

Other Ways

1. Right-click contact list, click New Contact

2. Press CTRL+SHIFT+C

To Create Contacts from Email Messages

Sophia frequently emails Ella Pauley, the director of the Pathways Internship Office. In addition, as a student worker in the Internship Office, Sophia contacts another student named Zion Gibson, who is actively applying for an internship. Creating contacts for Ella and Zion will simplify communications for Sophia. Outlook can create a contact based on the information located within email messages. The following steps create contacts from email messages. *Why? You can quickly add a contact from an email message to better keep track of the sender's information. If you type the first few letters of a contact's name into a new email message, Outlook fills in the email address for you.*

- Click the Mail button in the Navigation bar to display your mailbox from the Sophia Module 3.pst file.
- Click Inbox in the Navigation Pane to display the Inbox from the Sophia Module 3.pst file.
- Click the Ella Pauley message header to preview the email message in the Reading Pane (Figure 3–6).

Q&A What if I do not have an email message from Ella Pauley?
If you did not open or import the data file for this module, you might not have an email message from Ella Pauley. In that case, perform these steps using another email message in your mailbox.

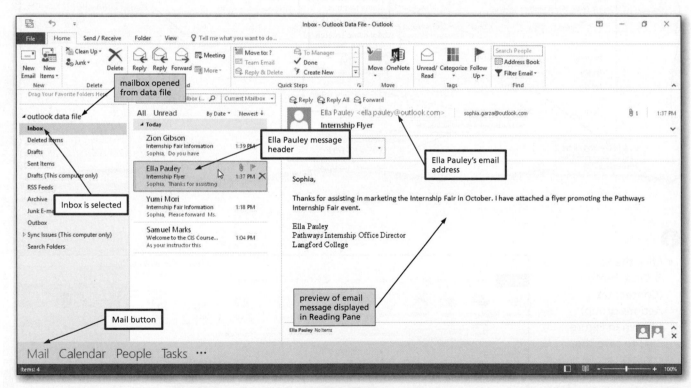

Figure 3–6

BTW

Contacts Window

By default, clicking the People button in the Navigation bar displays the contacts in the Microsoft Outlook window. To display the contacts in a new window, right-click the People button in the Navigation bar, and then click Open in New Window on the shortcut menu.

2

- Right-click Ella Pauley's email address (shown in Figure 3–6) in the message header of the Reading Pane to display a shortcut menu (Figure 3–7).

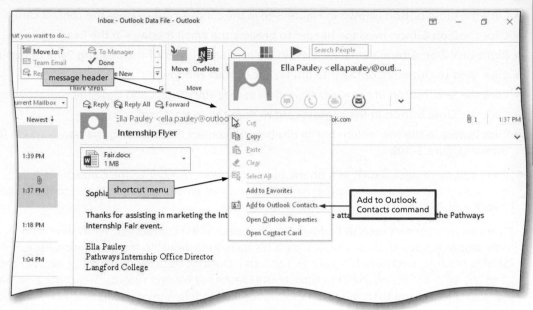

Figure 3–7

3

- Click Add to Outlook Contacts (shown in Figure 3–7) to display the contact window (Figure 3–8).

Q&A Why does the contact window already have Ella's Pauley's name and email address entered into the Name and Email text boxes? Outlook automatically detects the name and the email address for the contact from the existing email message.

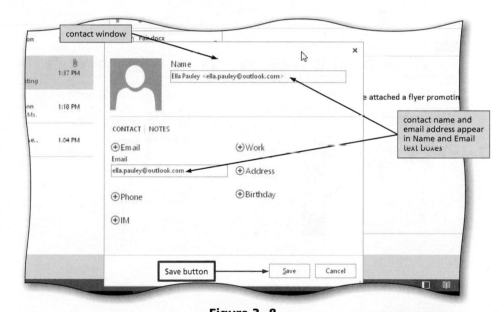

Figure 3–8

4

- Click the Save button (shown in Figure 3–8) in the contact window to save the contact and open the contact card for Ella Pauley (Figure 3–9).

Q&A What can you do with the contact card? The contact card includes shortcuts to tasks typically performed with contacts, such as scheduling a meeting, sending an email message, and editing contact information.

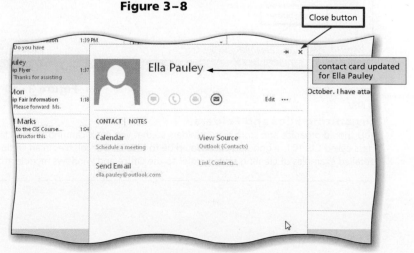

Figure 3–9

- Click the Close button (shown in Figure 3–9) in the contact card to close the contact card.
- Click the Zion Gibson message header to preview the email message in the Reading Pane.
- Right-click Zion Gibson's email address in the message header of the Reading Pane to display a shortcut menu.
- Click 'Add to Outlook Contacts' to display the contact window.
- Click the Save button in the contact window to save the contact and close the contact window.
- Click the Close button in the contact card to close the contact card.
- Click People in the Navigation bar to display your contact list, including the new contacts for Ella Pauley and Zion Gibson (Figure 3–10).

Q&A

Can I add more details such as a phone number or work number to the contact window?
You always can add more information such as another email address or photo to the contact window when you create a contact or later when you have more time.

The two new contact records I added do not appear in the contact list. What should I do?
You probably have another Outlook data file open in Outlook. In the Navigation Pane, note the name of the Sophia Module 3.pst data file, such as Contacts – Outlook Data File. Click other items in the Navigation pane to find the one containing the Zion Gibson and Ella Pauley contact records. Select the Zion Gibson and Ella Pauley contact records, and then drag them to the Sophia Module 3.pst data file, such as the Contacts – Outlook Data File in the Navigation Pane.

Figure 3–10

BTW

Organizing Files and Folders
You should organize and store files in folders so that you easily can find the files later. For example, if you are taking an introductory technology class called CIS 101, a good practice would be to save all Outlook files in an Outlook folder in a CIS 101 folder. For a discussion of folders and detailed examples of creating folders, refer to the Office and Windows module at the beginning of this book.

How can I import contacts from an external source such as an iPhone or Android smartphone?

To create a master list of all your contacts in one location in Outlook, you can import your contacts from your smartphone's address book, Internet-based email addresses such as your Gmail contacts, or from within another program such as an Access database. To import your contacts from an external address book:

1. Click the Address Book button (Home tab | Find group) to open the Address Book: Contacts dialog box.

2. Click the Address Book arrow to view a list of Other Address Books.

3. Click Other Address Books, such as Contacts (Mobile), to display a list of external contacts.

4. Click the first contact, press the SHIFT key, and click the last contact to select the entire list of contacts.

5. Click File to display the File menu. Click Add to Contacts to add the selected contacts to your Outlook contact list.

6. Click the Close button to close the Address Book: Contacts dialog box.

Editing a Contact

After setting up your contact list, you need to keep the information current and add new information, such as a new work phone number, Twitter account username, or picture, to help you interact with your contact. You can attach one or more files to a contact to store documents, tables, pictures, or clip art, for example, along with their contact information. If your colleagues transfer to other companies, remove contact information that you no longer need unless you will continue to interact with them on a regular basis.

BTW
Importing Contacts from External Sources
If you need to copy an existing contact list into Outlook, click the File tab and then click Open & Export. Next, click Import/Export to open the Import and Export Wizard. Based on the type of contact file, select the import file type and follow the steps for the appropriate import type.

When I maximize the Contact window, I noticed a Map It button next to addresses. What is the purpose of the Map It button?

The Map It button opens a Bing map within a browser to show the address listed in the Addresses text box. You could use the map to find directions to the address.

BTW
Touch Screen Differences
The Office and Windows interfaces may vary if you are using a touch screen. For this reason, you might notice that the function or appearance of your touch screen differs slightly from this module's presentation.

To Edit a Contact

1 CREATE NEW CONTACT | 2 MODIFY CONTACT | 3 CHANGE VIEW OF CONTACTS
4 FIND CONTACT | 5 CREATE CONTACT GROUP | 6 PRINT CONTACT LIST

When you created a contact record for Ella Pauley, it did not include her job title, work phone number, or picture. Ms. Pauley has given you the name of her school, proper title, work phone number, and photo, and you want to edit her contact record to include the new information. In addition, you need to include contact pictures for Sophia and Zion. The following steps edit a contact by entering additional information including pictures. To perform the steps, you will be required to use the Data Files. Please contact your instructor for information about accessing the Data Files. *Why? The more information you have about a business contact, the better you can provide personalized service. For example, including a business photo of your contact associates a name with a face. A company logo also could be used instead of a professional photo.*

• Click the Ella Pauley contact to display Ella Pauley's contact information in the People pane (Figure 3–11).

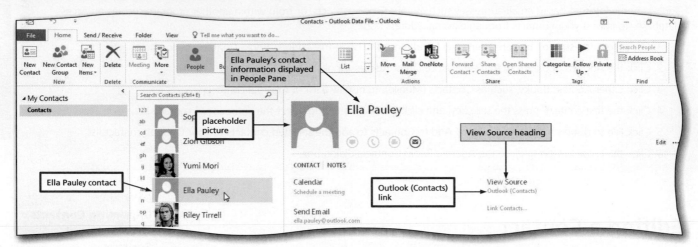

Figure 3–11

• Click Outlook (Contacts) below the View Source heading (shown in Figure 3–11) to display the Ella Pauley – Contact window.

• Type **Langford College** in the Company text box to enter a company or school name for the contact.

• In the Phone numbers section, type **(954) 555-1890** in the Business text box, and then press the ENTER key to enter a business phone number for the contact (Figure 3–12).

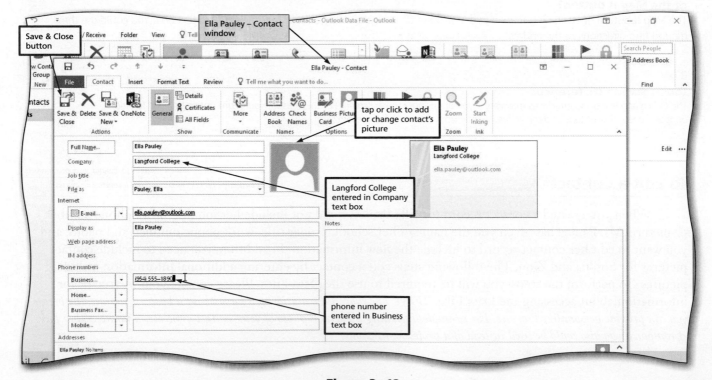

Figure 3–12

3

- Click the placeholder picture to open the Add Contact Picture dialog box.

- Navigate to the file location, in this case, the Module 03 folder in the Outlook folder provided with the Data Files.

- Click Ella to select the photo of Ella (Figure 3–13).

Q&A Why do I only see filenames and not actual pictures of the contacts?
An image is displayed if the Large icons option is set in your Windows settings.

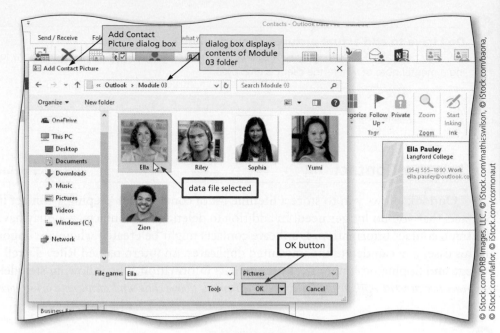

Figure 3–13

4

- Click the OK button (shown in Figure 3–13) to add an image to the contact record.

- Click the Save & Close button (Contact tab | Actions group) to save the contact and close the Contact window (Figure 3–14).

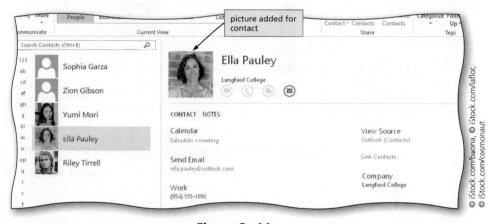

Figure 3–14

5

- Click the Sophia Garza contact to display Sophia Garza in the People pane.

- Click Outlook (Contacts) below the View Source heading to display the Sophia Garza – Contact window.

- Click the placeholder picture to open the Add Contact Picture dialog box.

- Click Sophia to select the photo of Sophia.

- Click the OK button to add an image to the contact record.

Figure 3–15

- Click the Save & Close button (Contact tab | Actions group) to save the contact and close the Contact window.

- Repeat these steps to add the contact photograph named Zion for the Zion Gibson contact (Figure 3–15).

Do I have to add actual pictures of every client?

You may not have access to images of every client, but consider adding at least a company logo, which could assist you in making a mental note of where the client is employed.

To Delete a Contact

1 CREATE NEW CONTACT | 2 MODIFY CONTACT | 3 CHANGE VIEW OF CONTACTS
4 FIND CONTACT | 5 CREATE CONTACT GROUP | 6 PRINT CONTACT LIST

Outlook allows you to store a lifetime list of contacts, but keeping a contact list current involves deleting contacts that you no longer need. In addition to deleting old contacts, you may have duplicate contacts that have the same contact information. Duplicate contacts might be created when you import contacts into Outlook. In this case, you can delete the unwanted duplicates. An intern named Riley Tirrell has transferred to another college and Sophia no longer needs his contact information. The following step deletes a contact. *Why? Keeping a contact list current makes your activities with email, phone calls, and social networks more efficient.*

1

- Click the Riley Tirrell contact (shown in Figure 3–15) to select the contact.

- Press the DELETE key to delete the contact information for Riley Tirrell (Figure 3–16).

Figure 3–16

Other Ways

1. Click contact, click Delete (Home tab | Delete group)

2. Right-click contact, click Delete

To Add an Attachment to a Contact

1 CREATE NEW CONTACT | 2 MODIFY CONTACT | 3 CHANGE VIEW OF CONTACTS
4 FIND CONTACT | 5 CREATE CONTACT GROUP | 6 PRINT CONTACT LIST

Zion Gibson sent you his resume, which he plans to send to apply to a marketing internship position at the Kennedy Center. You want to attach the resume document to his contact record. *Why? Including this document as part of his contact record will help you find the document easily.* Any files you attach to a contact are displayed in the Notes section of the Contact window. You also can insert items such as financial spreadsheets, pictures, and meeting slides to the Notes section. The following steps add an attachment to a contact.

1

- Click the Zion Gibson contact to display Zion Gibson in the People pane.
- Click Outlook (Contacts) below View Source to display the Zion Gibson – Contact window (Figure 3–17).

Figure 3–17

2

- Click Insert on the ribbon to display the Insert tab (Figure 3–18).

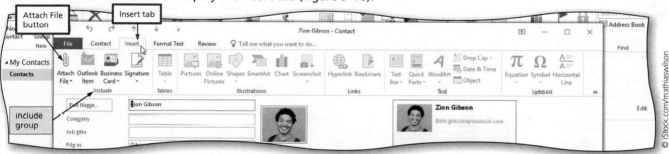

Figure 3–18

3

- Click the Attach File button (Insert tab | Include group) to display a list of Recent Items.

- Click Browse This PC to display the Insert File dialog box.

- If necessary, navigate to the file location, in this case, the Module 03 folder in the Outlook folder provided with the Data Files.

- Click Zion Gibson Resume to select the Word document (Figure 3–19).

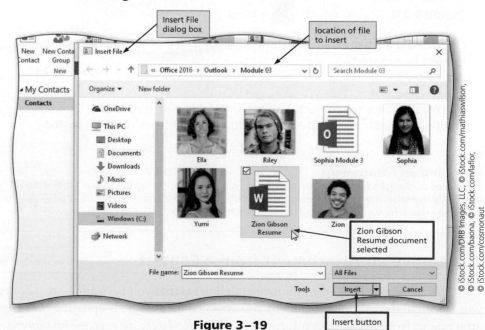

Figure 3–19

4

- Click the Insert button (Insert File dialog box) to attach the document to the contact record in the Notes area (Figure 3–20).

Q&A

Can I add more than one attachment?
Yes; you can add as many attachments as you want.

How do I view an attachment after I have added it?
Open the contact and then double-click the attachment to open it.

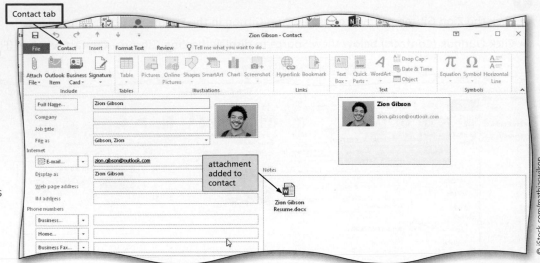

Figure 3–20

5

- Click Contact on the ribbon to display the Contact tab.
- Click the Save & Close button (Contact tab | Actions group) to save the contact record and close the Contact window (Figure 3–21).

Q&A

Can I send a meeting request to a contact?
Yes. To send a meeting request to a contact, click the contact to select it, click Meeting (Home tab | Communicate group), enter the details of the meeting in the Untitled – Meeting window, and then click the Send button.

Figure 3–21

BTW

Changing an Attachment

If you need to change an attachment to another file within a contact, select the original file and then click the Insert tab on the ribbon. Click Attach File and select the new attachment. Because the original file was selected before attaching the new file, the new file replaces the original file. If the original file were not selected, Outlook would add the new file while keeping the original file.

To Remove an Attachment from a Contact

1 CREATE NEW CONTACT | 2 MODIFY CONTACT | **3 CHANGE VIEW OF CONTACTS**
4 FIND CONTACT | 5 CREATE CONTACT GROUP | 6 PRINT CONTACT LIST

Sometimes you need to remove attachments that you have added to a contact. Zion Gibson has asked you to delete the original document you attached because he is updating his resume. You need to remove the attachment from his contact information. *Why? Removing an outdated attachment is important to keep your contact information current.* The following steps remove the attachment from a contact.

1

- If necessary, click the Zion Gibson contact to display Zion Gibson in the People pane.

- Click Outlook (Contacts) below View Source to display the Zion Gibson – Contact window.

- Click the Zion Gibson Resume document to select it (Figure 3–22).

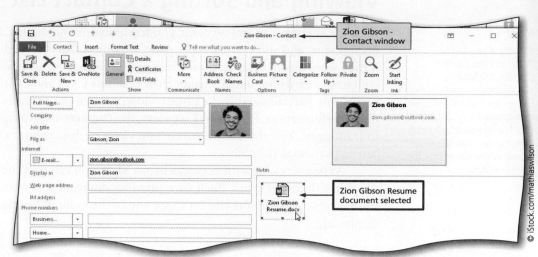

Figure 3–22

2

- Press the DELETE key to remove the attachment (Figure 3–23).

3

- Click the Save & Close button (Contact tab | Actions group) to save the contact and close the Contact window.

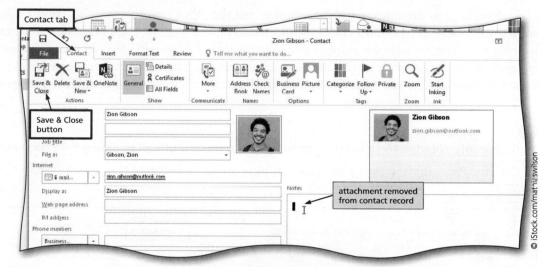

Figure 3–23

Other Ways

1. Click file icon, click Delete (Contact tab | Actions group)

CONSIDER THIS

How can I tag a contact to include a color-coded category or follow-up flag to remind me to follow up with a contact later?

To search through your contacts more efficiently, add color-coded categories such as a green tag to remind you of a new intern in the Pathways Internship program, for example. You may want to tag a contact with a Follow Up Tomorrow flag to remind you to email that person in the next day. To add a tag to a contact:

1. Click a contact to display the contact in the People pane.

2. Click Outlook (Contacts) below View Source to display the Contact window.

3. Click Categorize or Follow Up (Contact tab | Tags group) to display a list of color-coded categories or follow-up flags.

4. Click the color-coded category or follow-up flag that you want to use. You can use multiple tags on each contact if needed.

Viewing and Sorting a Contact List

BTW
Filing Contacts
When creating a new
contact, Outlook
automatically inserts in the
File as box the contact's full
name, usually in Last Name,
First Name format. Outlook
sorts contacts on the value
stored in the File as box for
each contact.

Outlook supports several ways for you to view your contact list. **People view** is the default view and shows the People pane. **Business Card view** displays the contacts as if they were business cards, a well-recognized format in business. **Card view** shows the contacts as cards but much smaller than Business Card view, with most information being only partially visible. In **Phone view**, you see the contacts in a list displaying phone information. Finally, in **List view**, the contacts are arranged in a list according to businesses. You also can create custom views to display your contacts in a way that suits a particular purpose.

When working with contacts in any view, you can sort the contacts to display them in a different order. Each view provides different sort options. For example, in Phone view, you can sort the list using any of the column heading buttons that are displayed.

To Change the Current View

1 CREATE NEW CONTACT | 2 MODIFY CONTACT | 3 CHANGE VIEW OF CONTACTS
4 FIND CONTACT | 5 CREATE CONTACT GROUP | 6 PRINT CONTACT LIST

People view provides useful information, but the other views also can be helpful. Changing the view sometimes can help you find a contact's information more quickly. Use Phone view, for example, when you are looking for a contact's phone number in a long list. *Why? Phone view provides a tabular layout with each contact in one row, and each column containing one contact's information.* The following steps change the current view to Phone view and then to Business card view to display the contact information on digital business cards.

1
- If necessary, click the More button (Home tab | Current View group) to display the Phone button.

- Click the Phone button (Home tab | Current View group) to switch to Phone view (Figure 3–24).

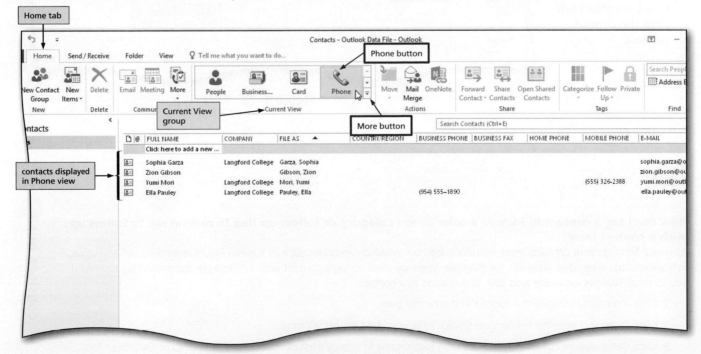

Figure 3–24

2

• If necessary, click the More button (Home tab | Current View group), and then click Business Card to switch to Business Card view (Figure 3–25).

Q&A What if the More button is not displayed in the Current View group?
You likely are using a lower resolution than 1366 × 768, so the ribbon hides additional buttons. Click the Business Card button in the Current View group to switch to Business Card view.

Experiment

• Click the other views in the Current View group to view the contacts in other arrangements. When you are finished, click Business Card to return to Business Card view.

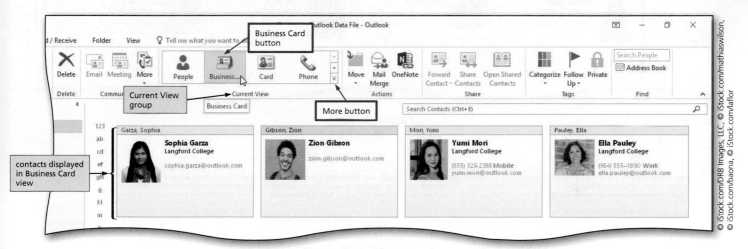

Figure 3–25

To Sort Contacts

1 CREATE NEW CONTACT | 2 MODIFY CONTACT | 3 CHANGE VIEW OF CONTACTS
4 FIND CONTACT | 5 CREATE CONTACT GROUP | 6 PRINT CONTACT LIST

Business Card view lists contacts in alphabetical order by default; however, you can sort the contacts to view them in reverse order. *Why? Reverse order is especially helpful if you want to quickly open a record for a contact at the end of a long contact list.* The following steps sort the contact list in reverse order, and then switch back to alphabetical order.

1

• Click View on the ribbon to display the View tab.

• Click the Reverse Sort button (View tab | Arrangement group) to display the contact list in reverse alphabetical order (Figure 3–26).

Figure 3–26

2

- Click the Reverse Sort button (View tab | Arrangement group) to display the contact list in the original order (Figure 3–27).

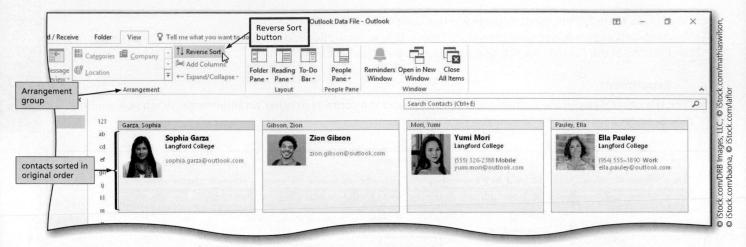

Figure 3–27

Break Point: If you wish to take a break, this is a good place to do so. To resume at a later time, continue to follow the steps from this location forward.

Using Search to Find a Contact

Over time, contact lists can grow quite large, making them difficult to navigate. In addition, you sometimes may not remember details about a contact you want to find. For example, you may remember that someone works for a particular company, but not their name. Alternatively, you may remember a phone number but nothing else. If this happens, you can use the Search People text box to search your contact list.

You also can find contacts using the Search People search box in the Find group on the Home tab. This works no matter which folder you are using (such as Mail, Calendar, People, or Tasks). This means that anytime you need to find your contacts, you can look them up quickly.

You can maximize your search efforts if you create a list of keywords that you can assign to contacts. The more general the keyword, the more results you will find. Using more specific keywords will reduce the number of results.

To Find a Contact by Searching for Text

1 CREATE NEW CONTACT | 2 MODIFY CONTACT | 3 CHANGE VIEW OF CONTACTS
4 FIND CONTACT | 5 CREATE CONTACT GROUP | 6 PRINT CONTACT LIST

If you only know partial information such as the area code in a phone number, the first word in a school name, or the domain name in an email address, you can use it to find matching contacts. Note that you might find many contacts that contain the text for which you are searching. The text you are using as the search term could be part of an email address, a school name, or a Twitter username, for example. Therefore, you may have to examine the results further. The following steps find all contacts that contain the text, langford. *Why? To save time, you can search for text or tags such as the college name Langford to locate the correct contact(s) quickly.*

1

- Click the Search Contacts text box to display the Search Tools Search tab (Figure 3–28).

Q&A Why is the Search Tools Search tab displayed when I click the Search Contacts text box?
The Search Tools Search tab contains buttons and commands that can help you search contacts.

Figure 3–28

2

- Type `langford` in the Search Contacts text box to search for all contacts containing the text, langford (Figure 3–29).

Q&A Can I modify a search further after getting the initial results?
Certainly. You can use the Search Tools Search tab to refine your search by specifying a name or phone number, for example. You also can expand the search to include all of the Outlook folders.

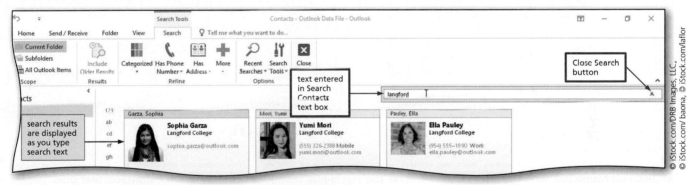

Figure 3–29

3

- Click the Close Search button (shown in Figure 3–29) in the Search Contacts text box to close the search and return to the Contacts – Outlook Data File – Outlook window (Figure 3–30).

Figure 3–30

Other Ways

1. Press CTRL+E

To Refine a Search

If you type a full name or email address in the Search Contacts text box, you will find your contact, but the information need not be only in the E-mail field or the Company field. The results might contain contacts where the name or email address is part of the Notes field, for example. In that case, you can find a contact by searching only a particular field. *Why? The results will contain only contacts with the search term in the specified field. No contacts will appear that contain the search term in a different field.*

You want to update the Zion Gibson contact record by searching only the Full Name field. The following steps search for an exact name in a particular field.

1
- Click the Search Contacts text box to display the Search Tools Search tab.

- Click the More button (Search Tools Search tab | Refine group) to display a list of common properties for refining a search (Figure 3–31).

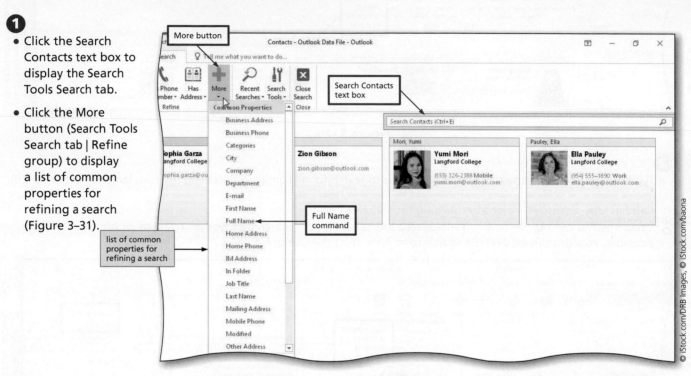

Figure 3–31

2
- Click Full Name (shown in Figure 3–31) to display the Full Name text box below the Search Contacts text box.

- Type `Zion Gibson` in the Full Name text box to search for the Zion Gibson contact (Figure 3–32).

Q&A | Why might Outlook display search results that do not seem to contain the search text?
When you perform a search, Outlook searches all specified fields for a match. However, the matching fields might not be displayed in the list of search results, although the contact record does contain the search text.

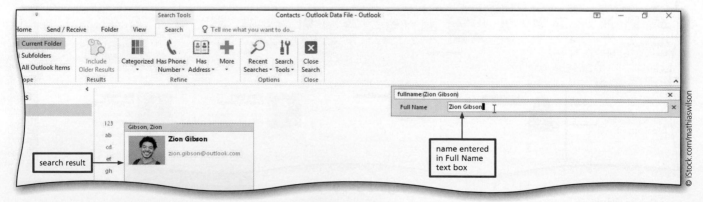

Figure 3–32

3

- Double-click the Zion Gibson contact to open it.
- Type `Interested in the Kennedy Center internship` in the Notes field to update the contact (Figure 3–33).

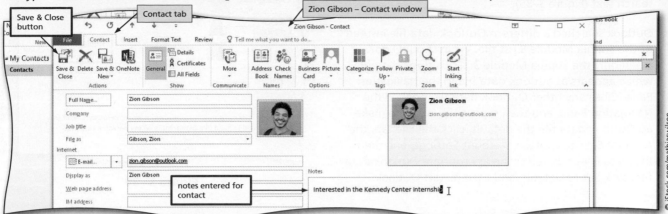

Figure 3–33

4

- Click the Save & Close button (Contact tab | Actions group) (shown in Figure 3–33) to save the contact and close the Contact window.
- Click the Close Search button in the Search Contacts text box to close the search and return to the Contacts – Outlook Data File – Outlook window.

To Find a Contact from Any Outlook Window

1 CREATE NEW CONTACT | 2 MODIFY CONTACT | 3 CHANGE VIEW OF CONTACTS
4 FIND CONTACT | 5 CREATE CONTACT GROUP | 6 PRINT CONTACT LIST

You do not have to be working in the Contacts – Outlook window to search for contacts. You can use the Search People text box in the Find group on the Home tab to search for contacts when you are working with email or performing other Outlook tasks. If what you type in the search box matches a single contact, that entry will be displayed in a contact window. If what you type matches more than one entry, you will be asked to select the contact that you want to view. *Why? For example, if you search for a contact using part of the company name, more than one contact may appear in the search results. You then can select a single contact from the results.*

The following steps search for a contact from the Inbox – Outlook Data File – Outlook window using only part of the company name, college. In this case, you are searching through your college contacts for the information about Yumi Mori.

1

- Click the Mail button on the Navigation bar to display the Sophia Module 3.pst mailbox.
- Click the Inbox folder to display the Inbox from the Sophia Module 3.pst file (Figure 3–34).

Figure 3–34

2

- Type `college` in the Search People text box (Home tab | Find group) to search for contacts containing the search text (Figure 3–35).

Q&A

Outlook searched a different Outlook data file instead of the Sophia Module 3.pst file. What should I do?
Open only the Sophia Module 3.pst Outlook data file, which appears as outlook data file in the Navigation Pane. Close any other Outlook data file open in the Navigation Pane, and then repeat the steps. To make an Outlook data file the default, click the File tab, the Account Settings button, Account Settings, and then the Data Files tab, select the appropriate Outlook data file, click Set as Default, and then restart Outlook.

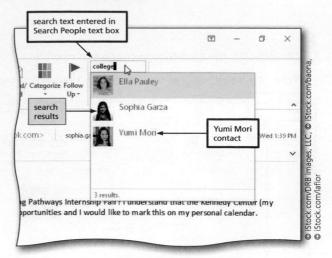

Figure 3–35

3

- Click Yumi Mori to select the contact and display her contact card (Figure 3–36).

Figure 3–36

4

- Click the Close button to close the window.

- Click the People button on the Navigation bar to return to the Contacts – Outlook Data File – Outlook window (Figure 3–37).

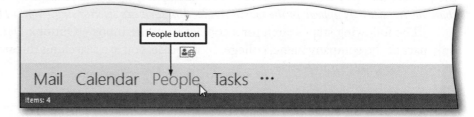

Figure 3–37

Creating and Editing a Contact Group

BTW

Contact Groups
If you receive an email message sent to a contact group, you can add the contact group to Microsoft Outlook. To add the contact group, right-click the name of the contact group in the To or Cc box, and then select Add to Outlook Contacts.

When you have several contacts that you frequently email or work with as a group, you can create a contact group and add contacts to it. A **contact group**, also called a distribution list, provides a single name for you to use when working with two or more contacts. You are not creating subfolders for contacts, but rather another way to reference multiple contacts at one time. For example, you could create a group called Inner Circle and then add all your closest family and friends to the group. Whenever you want to send an email message to your closest family and friends at one time, you could enter the contact group name, Inner Circle, as the recipient of the email message — and every contact in the group would receive the email message.

To Create a Contact Group from Existing Contacts

1 CREATE NEW CONTACT | 2 MODIFY CONTACT | 3 CHANGE VIEW OF CONTACTS
4 FIND CONTACT | 5 CREATE CONTACT GROUP | 6 PRINT CONTACT LIST

Why? *A message sent to a contact group goes to all recipients listed in the group. If your contact list gets too cluttered, you can use a contact group to communicate with friends, family, and coworkers more quickly.* When creating contact groups, you choose the name for your contact group and then add the contacts you want to have in the group. To quickly send an email to all the members of the Student Internship Club, you want to create a group of all the members who are part of your contact list and name the group Intern Applicants. The following steps create a contact group and then add the related contacts to the group.

1

- Click the New Contact Group button (Home tab | New group) to display the Untitled – Contact Group window (Figure 3–38).

Figure 3–38

2

- Type Intern Applicants in the Name text box to enter a name for the group (Figure 3–39).

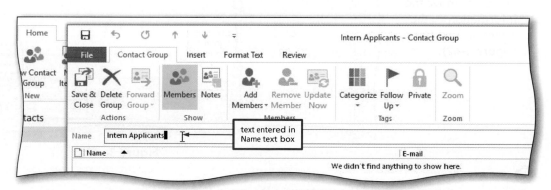

Figure 3–39

3

- Click the Add Members button (Contact Group tab | Members group) to display the Add Members menu (Figure 3–40).

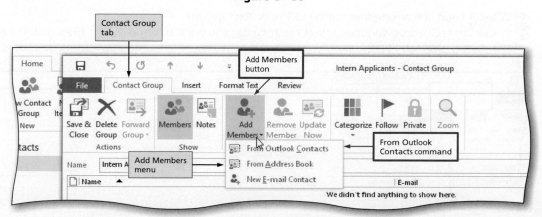

Figure 3–40

- Click From Outlook Contacts to display the Select Members: Contacts dialog box (Figure 3–41).

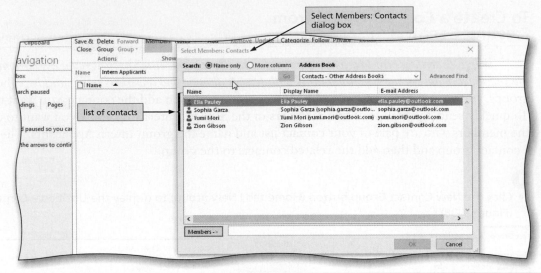

Figure 3–41

- Click the Zion Gibson contact to select it, press and hold the CTRL key, and then click the Yumi Mori contact to select both contacts.

- Click the Members button to move the information to the Members text box (Figure 3–42).

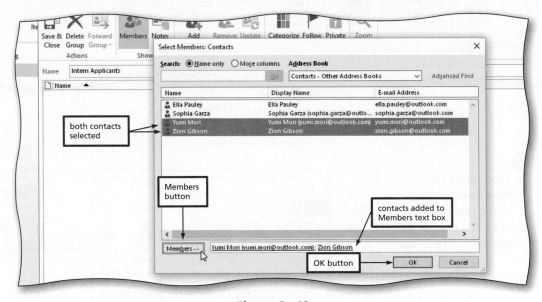

Figure 3–42

6

- Click the OK button to add the contacts to the group (Figure 3–43).

Q&A What if I add the wrong member(s) to the contact group?

In the Contact Group window, select the member you want to remove, and then click the Remove Member button (Contact Group tab | Members group). Next, repeat Steps 3–6 to add any missing members.

Figure 3–43

7
- Click the Save & Close button (Contact Group tab | Actions group) to save the contact group and close the window (Figure 3–44).

Q&A | Why are the contacts and the group displayed in the Contacts window?
You use a contact group to send email messages to a set of contacts using the group name; it does not replace or move the existing contacts.

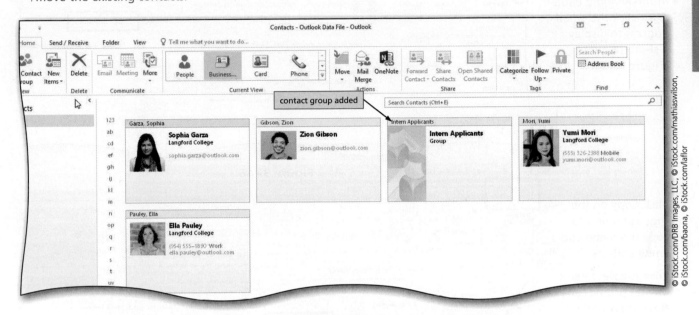

Figure 3–44

To Create a Contact Group from an Existing Email Message

1 CREATE NEW CONTACT | 2 MODIFY CONTACT | 3 CHANGE VIEW OF CONTACTS
4 FIND CONTACT | 5 CREATE CONTACT GROUP | **6 PRINT CONTACT LIST**

Outlook allows you to create a group for individuals who are not in your contact list but have sent you an email message. To do this, you copy a name from an email message and then paste the name in the Select Members dialog box when creating the group. The following steps create a contact group named Faculty and then add a member by using information in an email message from Samuel Marks. ***Why?*** *You can create a group and add a new contact right after reading an email.*

1
- Click the Mail button on the Navigation bar to display your mailbox (Figure 3–45).

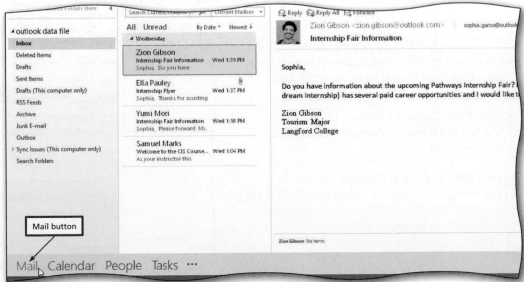

Figure 3–45

2

- Click the Samuel Marks message header to preview the email message in the Reading Pane.

- In the Reading Pane, right-click the email address to display a shortcut menu (Figure 3–46).

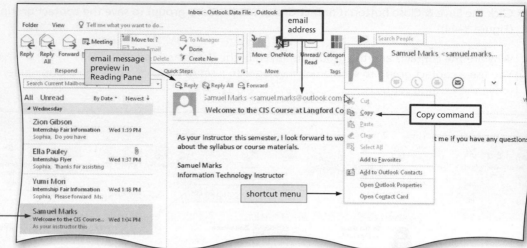

Figure 3–46

3

- Click Copy on the shortcut menu to copy the name and email address.

- Click the New Items button (Home tab | New group) to display the New Items menu.

- Click More Items to display the More Items submenu (Figure 3–47).

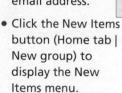

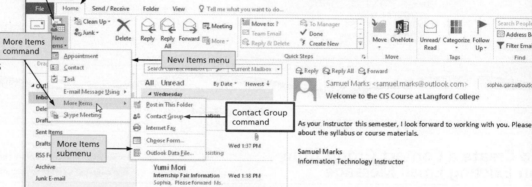

Figure 3–47

4

- Click Contact Group to display the Untitled – Contact Group window.

- Type **Faculty** in the Name text box to enter a name for the group.

- Click the Add Members button (Contact Group tab | Members group) to display the Add Members menu.

- Click From Outlook Contacts to display the Select Members: Contacts dialog box (Figure 3–48).

Q&A Why did I click From Outlook Contacts?
You need to display the Select Members dialog box, and you click the From Outlook Contacts menu option to open it. You also could have clicked From Address Book to display the dialog box.

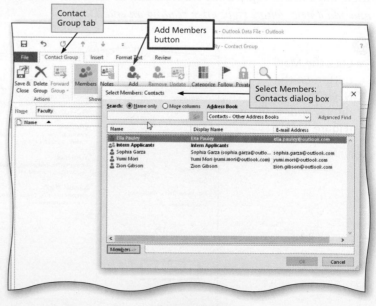

Figure 3–48

5

- Right-click the Members text box to display a shortcut menu.

- Click Paste on the shortcut menu to paste the copied name and email address (Figure 3–49).

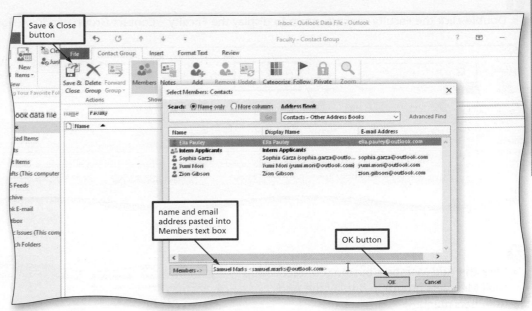

Figure 3–49

6

- Click the OK button to add the contact to the group.

- Click the Save & Close button (Contact Group tab | Actions group) to save the contact and close the window.

- Click the People button on the Navigation bar to display your contacts (Figure 3–50).

Q&A | Can I forward a contact group to someone else?
Yes. You can forward a contact group by selecting the contact group, clicking Forward Contact (Home tab | Share group), and then selecting the option you want to use to forward the contact group.

Figure 3–50

To Add a Name to a Contact Group

1 CREATE NEW CONTACT | 2 MODIFY CONTACT | 3 CHANGE VIEW OF CONTACTS
4 FIND CONTACT | 5 CREATE CONTACT GROUP | 6 PRINT CONTACT LIST

As you meet and work with people, you can add them to one or more contact groups. You have been contacting the instructor Ella Pauley and you want to add her to the Faculty contact group. *Why? By adding people to a group, you can send email messages and meeting invitations to groups of people that you contact frequently without having to enter each individual email address.* The following steps add a new contact to the Faculty contact group.

- Double-click the Faculty contact group to display the Faculty – Contact Group window (Figure 3–51).

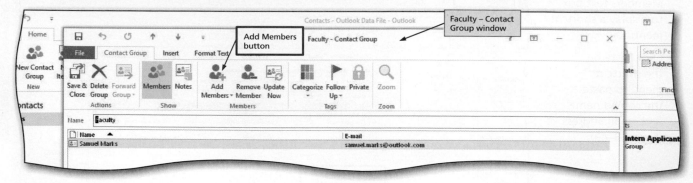

Figure 3–51

2

- Click the Add Members button (Contact Group tab | Members group) to display the Add Members menu.

- Click From Outlook Contacts to display the Select Members: Contacts dialog box.

- If necessary, click Ella Pauley to select her contact record.

- Click the Members button to add Ella Pauley to the Members text box (Figure 3–52).

3

- Click the OK button to add Ella Pauley to the contact group.

- Click the Save & Close button (Contact Group tab | Actions group) to save the contact and close the Faculty – Contact Group window.

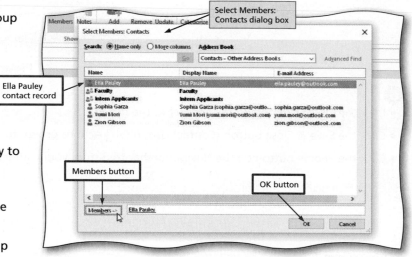

Figure 3–52

To Add Notes to a Contact Group

1 CREATE NEW CONTACT | 2 MODIFY CONTACT | 3 CHANGE VIEW OF CONTACTS
4 FIND CONTACT | 5 CREATE CONTACT GROUP | **6 PRINT CONTACT LIST**

You can add reminder notes to a contact group. *Why? As you create groups, you may have trouble remembering who is part of the group and why.* The contact group notes are only displayed in the Contacts list when Card view is selected. You would like to add a note to the Intern Applicants contact group that their internship placements must be assigned by November 1. The following steps add a note to a contact group and display the note in the Card view.

1

- Double-click the Intern Applicants contact group to display the Intern Applicants – Contact Group window (Figure 3–53).

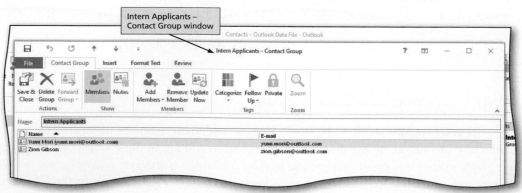

Figure 3–53

2

- Click the Notes button (Contact Group tab | Show group) to display the Notes page.

- Type **The internship placements must be assigned by November 1.** in the Notes page to create a reminder (Figure 3–54).

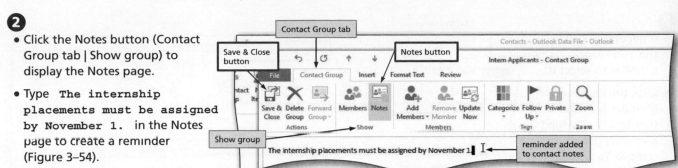

Figure 3–54

3

- Click the Save & Close button on the Notes page to close the Intern Applicants – Contact Group window.

- Click the Card button (Home tab | Current View group) to display the contact list in Card view, which in this case includes the contact group note for the Intern Applicants (Figure 3–55).

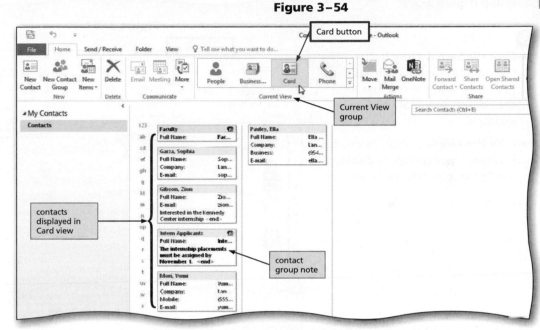

Figure 3–55

To Remove a Name from a Contact Group

1 CREATE NEW CONTACT | 2 MODIFY CONTACT | 3 CHANGE VIEW OF CONTACTS
4 FIND CONTACT | 5 CREATE CONTACT GROUP | **6 PRINT CONTACT LIST**

Why? Periodically, you may need to remove someone from a contact group. For example, contacts may switch jobs or ask to be removed from your list because they no longer are working on or participating in a club or project. Yumi Mori has decided to transfer and will no longer be participating in the Pathways Internship program. You have decided to remove her from the Intern Applicants contact group so that she will not receive email messages sent to the group. The following steps remove a contact from a group.

1

- If necessary, scroll in the Contacts window until the Intern Applicants contact group is visible.

- Double-click the Intern Applicants contact group to display the Intern Applicants – Contact Group window (Figure 3–56).

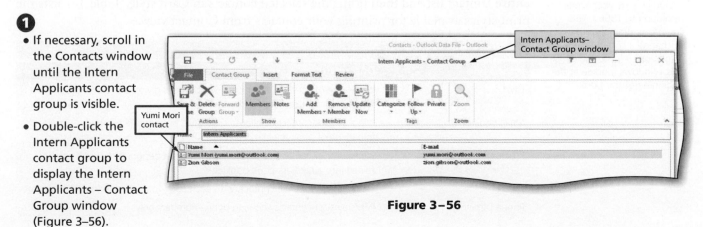

Figure 3–56

2

- If necessary, click the Yumi Mori member to select it.

- Click the Remove Member button (Contact Group tab | Members group) to remove Yumi Mori from the contact group (Figure 3–57).

3

- Click the Save & Close button (Contact Group tab | Actions group) to save the changes to the contact group and close the window.

- Click the People button (Home tab | Current View group) to display the Contact list (Figure 3–58).

Q&A

When you remove a contact from a contact group, does it also remove the contact from Outlook?
No. The contact remains in Outlook, even after removing it from a contact group.

How can I delete a contact group?
To delete a contact group, select the contact group to delete, and then click the Delete button (Home tab | Delete group).

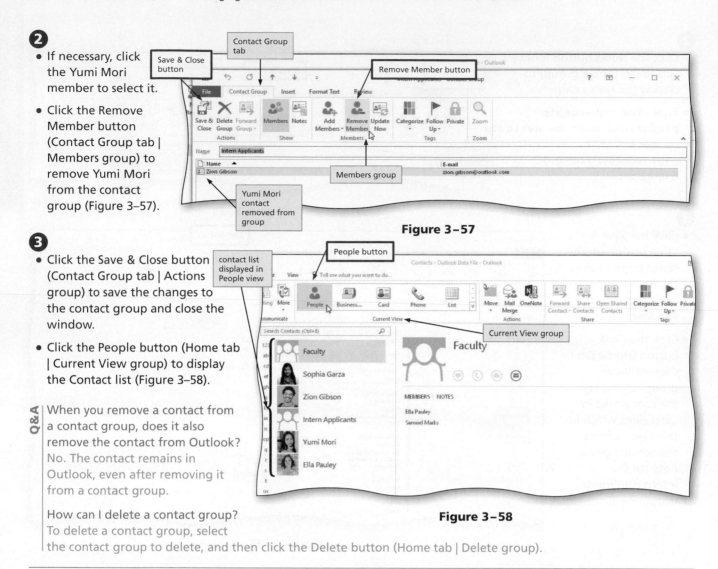

Figure 3–57

Figure 3–58

BTW

Outlook Screen Resolution

If you are using a computer or mobile device to step through the project in this module and you want your screens to match the figures in this book, you should change your screen's resolution to 1366 x 768. For information about how to change a computer's resolution, refer to the Office and Windows module at the beginning of this book.

Printing Your Contacts

All or part of your contacts can be printed in a number of different views, or **print styles**. You can distribute a printed contact or contact list to others in a form that can be read or viewed, but cannot be edited. You can choose to print only one contact or the entire list. To print only part of your contacts, select one or more contacts and then change the print options so that you print your selection. This section previews the entire contact list and then prints the selected contacts in Card style. Table 3–1 lists the print styles available for printing your contacts from Contact view.

Table 3–1 Print Styles for Contact View	
Print Style	**Description**
Card	Prints a list of contacts separated by alphabetic dividers and provides a sheet for adding more contact information
Small Booklet	Prints a list of contacts similar to Card style but designed so that it can be folded into a small booklet
Medium Booklet	Prints a list of contacts similar to Card style but designed so that it can be folded into a medium-sized booklet
Memo	Prints a page for each contact, with each page formatted to look like a memo
Phone Directory	Prints a list of contacts showing phone numbers only

To Preview a Contact List

You can print preview a single contact or multiple pages of contacts displayed as cards or in phone lists. The following steps preview the contact list in various print styles. *Why? Unless you change the print options, you will see all your contacts when you preview the list before printing.*

1

Filo tab • In the Contacts window, select the Zion Gibson and Ella Pauley contacts (Figure 3–59).

two contacts selected

Figure 3–59

2

• Click the File tab on the ribbon (shown in Figure 3–59) to open the Backstage view.

• Click the Print tab in the Backstage view to display the Print gallery.

• Click Small Booklet Style in the Settings area to change the print style (Figure 3–60).

Q&A Why are all the contacts displayed when I selected only two contacts?
By default, the print range is set for all items to display and print. You can change the Print Options to print only the selected items.

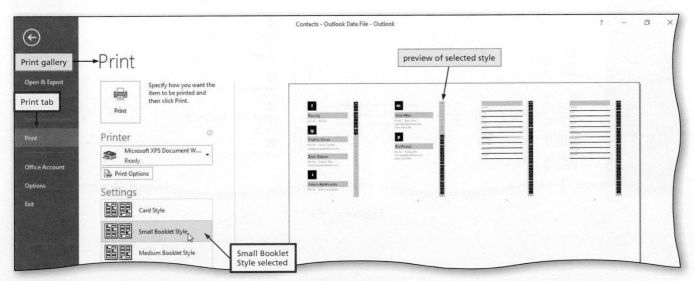

Print gallery

Print tab

preview of selected style

Small Booklet Style selected

Figure 3–60

❸
- Click Phone Directory Style in the Settings area to change to Phone Directory Style (Figure 3–61).

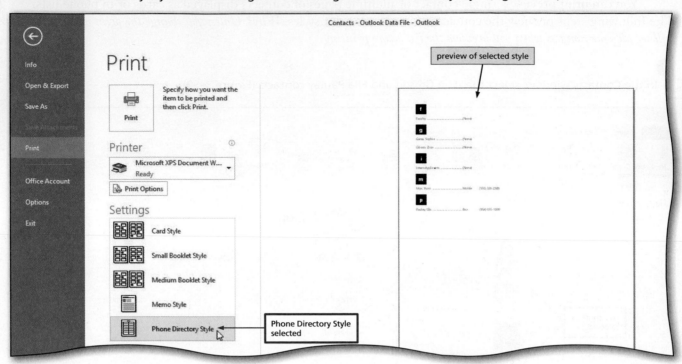

Figure 3–61

❹
- Click Card Style in the Settings area to change to Card Style (Figure 3–62).

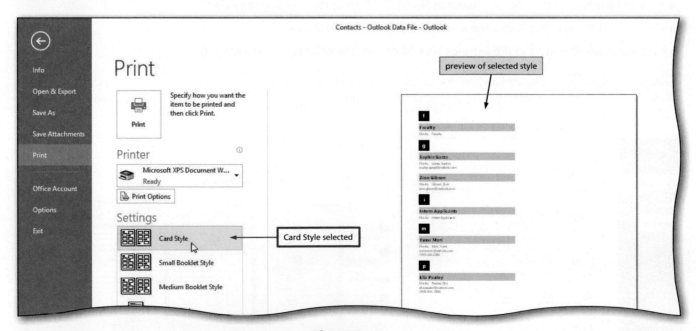

Figure 3–62

5
- Click the Print Options button to display the Print dialog box.

- Click the 'Only selected items' option button (Print dialog box) to preview only the selected contacts (Figure 3–63).

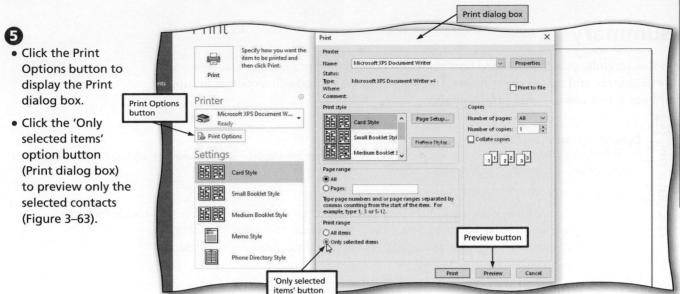

Figure 3–63

6
- Click the Preview button (Print dialog box) to close the dialog box and preview only the selected contacts.

- Click the print preview to zoom in to view the selected contacts (Figure 3–64).

Q&A
If I click the other styles, will they only show selected contacts?
No. If you change the style, the preview returns to showing all contacts. To see the selected contacts in a particular style, you select the style and then change the print options.

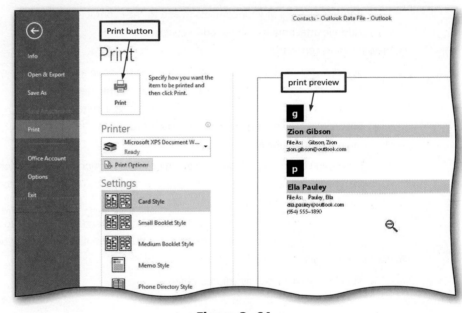

Figure 3–64

BTW
Printing Contacts
Contacts can be printed directly to paper, saved as a PDF file, or sent to OneNote using the Printer button arrow.

To Print a Contact List

1 CREATE NEW CONTACT | 2 MODIFY CONTACT | 3 CHANGE VIEW OF CONTACTS
4 FIND CONTACT | 5 CREATE CONTACT GROUP | 6 PRINT CONTACT LIST

Why? *Before heading to a meeting, you may want a printed list of contacts for reference.* The following steps print the selected contacts in Card style, and then exit Outlook.

1 Click the Print button to print the selected contacts (Figure 3–65).

2 If you have a contact open, click the Close button on the right side of the title bar to close the Contact window.

3 Click the Close button on the right side of the title bar to exit Outlook.

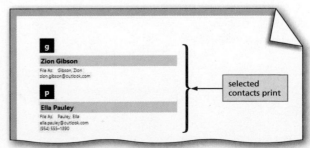

Figure 3–65

Summary

In this module, you have learned how to use Outlook to create a contact list, view and sort contacts, and search for contacts. You learned to create and edit a contact group, add notes to a contact, and print contacts.

CONSIDER THIS

Consider This: Plan Ahead

What decisions will you need to make when creating contacts from friends, family, and coworkers, editing contacts, creating a contact group, and printing contacts in the future?

1. Create contacts.

   a. Determine the people with whom you plan to interact on a regular basis, such as your friends, family, and coworkers. Adding too many contacts can make it difficult to manage your contact list.

   b. Determine the information that would be most helpful about each of your contacts.

2. Edit contacts.

   a. Determine if any additional contact information should be added to a contact.

   b. Determine which contacts should be deleted, such as those with whom you no longer have regular communication.

   c. Request pictures of your contacts to add to their contact information.

   d. Add file attachments as needed to contacts.

3. View and sort contact lists.

   a. Select a view that displays the information you need in a contact list.

   b. Switch views as necessary to have quick access to people's information.

   c. Create a custom view if none of the built-in views is suitable for you.

   d. Sort contacts to display them in a different order.

4. Use Search to find contacts.

   a. Determine the preferred way to view the contacts to find the information you are seeking.

   b. Determine the sort order to use for your contacts, considering what information you are trying to find.

5. Create and edit contact groups.

   a. Plan the relationship of the contacts that are organized under the group name.

   b. Consider a good name for a contact group that will make it easier for you to remember the purpose of the group.

6. Print your contacts.

   a. Plan how best to display your contacts.

CONSIDER THIS

How should you submit solutions to questions in the assignments identified with a ⚙ symbol?

Every assignment in this book contains one or more questions with a ⚙ symbol. These questions require you to think beyond the assigned file. Present your solutions to the question in the format required by your instructor. Possible formats may include one or more of these options: write the answer; create a document that contains the answer; present your answer to the class; discuss your answer in a group; record the answer as audio or video using a webcam, smartphone, or portable media player; or post answers on a blog, wiki, or website.

Apply Your Knowledge

Reinforce the skills and apply the concepts you learned in this module.

Note: To complete this assignment, you will be required to use the Data Files. Please contact your instructor for information about accessing the Data Files.

Updating a Contact List

Instructions: Run Outlook. Edit the contact list provided in the file called Apply Your Knowledge 3-1 Contacts, located on the Data Files for Students. The Apply Your Knowledge 3-1 Contacts file contains five contacts and a contact group. Many of the contacts have changed and some are incomplete. You now need to revise these contacts and print them in Card view (Figure 3–66).

Perform the following tasks:

1. Import the Apply Your Knowledge 3-1 Contacts file into Outlook.

2. Change Kelly Updike's company to **Adventure Tours**. Move Kelly's Business phone number to the Mobile text box. Change her job title to **Sales Manager**. Add an email address of **kelly.updike@ email.com**.

3. Change Hugo Arenas' company to **Whitewater Rafting Tours**. Type **hugo.arenas@email.com** as his new email address, and change his phone number to **555-0610**. Add the following as his webpage address: **http://www.hugorafting.com/whitewater**.

4. Change Chelsea Nash's email address to **cnash@ adventure.com**. Add a Home phone of **555-9965**.

5. Change the job title for Hansen Jacobs to **Tour Guide**.

6. Change the Adventure contact group name to Adventure Tours. Add the Kelly Updike contact to the contact group and remove the Lauren Mariel contact from the contact group.

7. Add a new contact using your name, email address, and photo.

8. Print the final contact list in Card Style, as shown in Figure 3–66, and then submit the printout to your instructor.

9. Export the Apply Your Knowledge 3-1 Contacts file to a USB flash drive, and then delete the file from the hard disk.

10. ✳ Outlook can display your contacts in a variety of views. Which view do you prefer, and why?

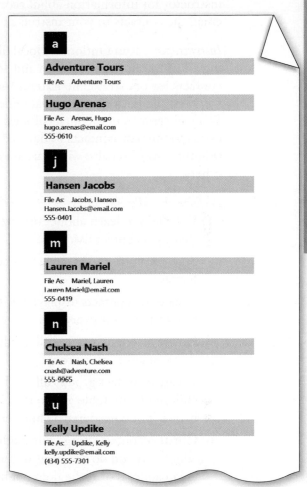

Figure 3–66

Extend Your Knowledge

Extend the skills you learned in this module and experiment with new skills. You may need to use Help to complete the assignment.

Creating a Contact Folder

Note: To complete this assignment, you will be required to use the Data Files. Please contact your instructor for information about accessing the Data Files. An active email account is necessary to email the contacts to your instructor.

Instructions: Run Outlook. A local filmmaker is creating a feature film in your town and needs to create a contacts list of extras. The Extend Your Knowledge 3-1 Contacts file located on the Data Files has no contacts. You will create a new contacts folder, add the names of extras to the new contacts folder, and print the contact list (Figure 3–67). You also will share the contacts folder with others.

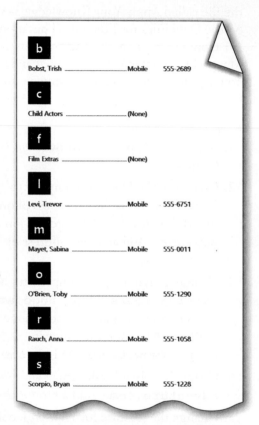

Perform the following tasks:

1. Use Help to learn about creating a contacts folder and sharing a contact list.

2. Start Outlook and create a new contacts folder named Extras.

3. Create the contacts displayed in Table 3–2. Add the job title of Extra for everyone.

4. Create a contact group called Film Extras. Add all of the contacts to this group.

5. Create a contact group called Child Actors. Add the children from Table 3–2 to the Child Actors group. A baby is not considered a child actor.

6. Create a contact using your mother's name and email address. If you do not want to disclose your mother's email address or if she does not have one, replace it with your email address.

Figure 3–67

7. Print the contact list in Phone Directory view, as shown in Figure 3–67, and then submit the printout to your instructor.

Table 3–2 Film Extras Information			
Full Name	**Notes**	**Email Address**	**Mobile Phone**
Bryan Scorpio	College-Aged Male	bryan.scorpio@email.com	555-1228
Toby O'Brien	Middle-Aged Male	mrobrien@world.net	555-1290
Anna Rauch	Girl, Age 10	anna.rauch@earth.com	555-1058
Trevor Levi	Boy, Age 12	tlevi@agent.com	555-6751
Sabina Mayet	Mother with Baby	sabinam@earth.net	555-0011
Trish Bobst	Dog Handler	trish@pupactors.com	555-2689

8. Select all the contacts. Use the Forward Contact button (Home tab | Share group) and click As an Outlook Contact to email the contact list to your instructor.

9. ✸ Why might it be advantageous to create separate folders within your contacts?

Expand Your World: Cloud and Web Technologies

Create a solution that uses cloud or web technologies by learning and investigating on your own from general guidance.

Opening Contacts in Microsoft OneNote 2016

Note: To complete this assignment, you will be required to use the completed Module 3 files from this text.

Instructions: A program named OneNote is part of the Microsoft Office 2016 suite that gathers users' digital notes (handwritten or typed), contacts, drawings, screen clippings, and audio/video commentaries. In this assignment, you will set up a OneNote notebook and copy contacts from Outlook into a OneNote notebook to add contact references that will allow you to take detailed notes about each contact (Figure 3–68).

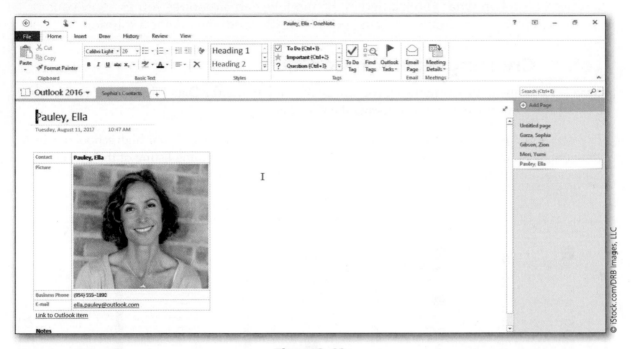

Figure 3–68

Perform the following tasks:

1. Open Outlook with the completed Sophia contacts for Module 3 displayed and then open OneNote.

2. In OneNote, create a notebook named Outlook 2016 and then create a OneNote section named Sophia's Contacts.

3. In Outlook, click People on the Navigation bar to display Sophia's contacts. Select the four individual contacts including Sophia, Zion, Yumi, and Ella.

4. Open Microsoft OneNote if you have never opened the program before to confirm that Microsoft OneNote is set up. Close Microsoft OneNote.

5. Click OneNote (Home tab | Actions group) to open the Select Location in OneNote dialog box.

6. In the Select Location in OneNote dialog box, click the plus sign in front of Outlook 2016 and then click Sophia's Contacts.

7. Click the OK button in the Select Location in OneNote dialog box to copy the contacts into four separate pages in OneNote (Figure 3–68).

Continued >

8. Click the Sophia Garza page in the right pane, press the SHIFT key and click Ella Pauley to select all four contact pages.

9. Click the File tab and click Send. Next, click Send to Word to open Microsoft Word, which displays all four contacts.

10. Submit the Microsoft Word document in the format specified by your instructor.

11. ✸ Why would you copy contacts into OneNote? Write at least three ideas in sentence format.

In the Labs

Design, create, modify, and/or use files following the guidelines, concepts, and skills presented in this module. Labs 1 and 2, which increase in difficulty, require you to create solutions based on what you learned in the module; Lab 3 requires you to apply your creative thinking and problem-solving skills to design and implement a solution.

Lab 1: **Creating Reunion Contacts**

Note: To complete this assignment, you will be required to use the Data Files. Please contact your instructor for information about accessing the Data Files.

Problem: You have agreed to create a contact list of your senior class of your high school in which you graduated for an upcoming reunion. Table 3–3 provides a beginning listing of the classmates' contact information. Enter the contacts into the contacts list. The contact list you create will look like that in Figure 3–69.

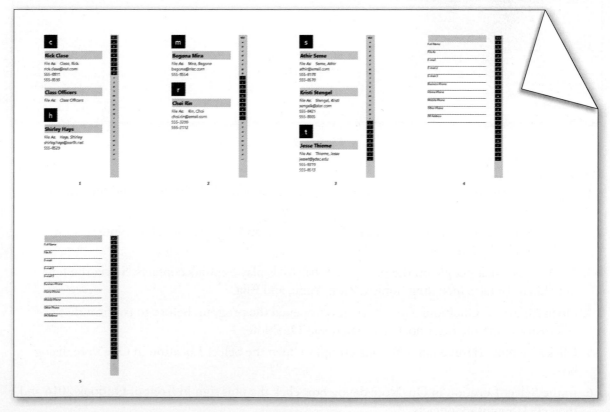

Figure 3–69

Perform the following tasks:

1. Create a new Outlook Data File named Lab 3-1 Reunion Contacts.

2. Create the contacts in the Contacts window, using the information listed in Table 3–3.

Table 3–3 Reunion Contact Information			
Classmate	**Email Address**	**Business**	**Mobile**
Jesse Thieme	jesset@ydac.edu	555-8319	555-0513
Shirley Hays	shirley.hays@earth.net		555-8529
Athir Seme	athir@email.com	555-8178	555-8570
Kristi Stengel	stengelk@star.com	555-8421	555-8005
Begona Mira	begona@nlsc.com		555-8554
Rick Clase	rick.clase@net.com	555-8111	555-8593
Choi Rin	choi.rin@email.com	555-3200	555-2112

3. For each contact, list the webpage address as http://www.classmate.com/rhs.

4. Create a group named Class Officers. Add Athir, Rick, and Choi.

5. Add the following note to Kristi's contact information — **Owns an event coordination company.**

6. Create a contact for yourself with your email address and mobile phone number.

7. Print the contacts list using Small Booklet Style as shown in Figure 3–69, and submit it in a format specified by your instructor.

8. ⚙ What other information might be useful to include in the reunion contact list if you plan to share this with the rest of your classmates at the reunion?

Lab 2: **Creating an Employee Contact List**

Problem: You are the owner of Rock Salt Seafood Supply, a local fresh seafood store. Your store has decided to email reminders to their best customers about weekly specials. You need to create a contacts list and add contact groups so that you send specific information for local restaurant owners and regular customers (Figure 3–70).

Perform the following tasks:

1. Create a new Outlook Data File named Lab 3-2 Rock Salt Contacts.

2. Create two contact groups called Restaurant Owners and Regular Customers.

3. Enter the contacts in the Contacts list, using the information listed in Table 3–4.

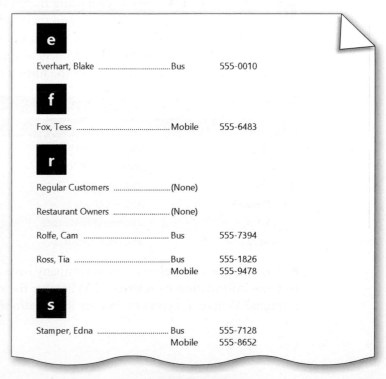

Figure 3–70

Continued >

In the Labs *continued*

4. Add the contacts to the appropriate contact group.

5. Add the following note to Edna's contact information: `Give us a call if Rock Point Oysters available.`

Table 3–4 Rock Salt Seafood Supply Mailing List				
Name/Business Name	**Email Address**	**Business Phone**	**Mobile Phone**	**Customer Type**
Cam Rolfe (Company: Blue Marlin)	bluemarlin@blue.com	555-7394		Restaurant Owner
Tia Ross	tia.ross@email.com	555-1826	555-9478	Regular Customer
Tess Fox	tess09@earth.com		555-6483	Regular Customer
Edna Stamper (Company: Sea Mist)	seamist@email.com	555-7128	555-8652	Restaurant Owner
Blake Everhart (Company: Hard Shell)	hardshell@earth.net	555-0010		Restaurant Owner

6. Add the title of owner to the restaurant owner contacts.

7. Print the contacts list in Phone Directory style as a PDF file and save the Outlook data file as a .pst file. Submit both files in the format specified by your instructor.

8. ✳ What additional information about your customers might be useful to add to your contacts folder?

Lab 3: Scheduling Employees for the Gelato Shop

Professional

Part 1: At the Dolce Gelato Shop, you are in charge of scheduling your team of employees. You need a contact list of all part-time and full-time employees. Using the contacts and techniques presented in this module, create an Outlook Data File named Lab 3-3 Dolce Gelato and add contacts for each member of your team using the information in Table 3–5. The gelato shop is located at 75 Beach Dr., Westlake, FL, 33022 and their website is http://dolcegelatoshop.com. Add three additional contacts using your friends' names and information. Create two contact groups called Part-Time and Full-Time. Add the contacts to appropriate group. Save the contact list and print the contacts in Card style and submit it in the format specified by your instructor.

Table 3–5 Team List Contacts			
Full Name	**Email Address**	**Mobile Phone**	**Part/Full Time**
Titus Angel	titus@dolcegelato.com	555-6667	Part Time
Ben Cohen	ben@dolcegelato.com	555-8221	Full Time
Rob Ruiz	rob@dolcegelato.com	555-9856	Part Time
Nina Inwood	nina@dolcegelato.com	555-3846	Full Time
Stan Silver	stan@dolcegelato.com	555-2877	Full Time
Aiko Kuro	aiko@dolcegelato.com	555-8745	Part Time

Part 2: ✳ Should everyone in the company have access to all contact information, or should access to some information be restricted? What was the rationale behind each of these decisions and suggestions? Where did you obtain your information?

4 | Creating and Managing Tasks with Outlook

Objectives

You will have mastered the material in this module when you can:

- Create a new task
- Create a task with a status
- Create a task with a priority
- Create a task with a reminder
- Create a recurring task
- Categorize a task
- Configure Quick Clicks
- Categorize email messages

- Update a task
- Attach a file to a task
- Assign a task
- Forward a task
- Send a status report
- Print tasks
- Create a note
- Change the view of notes

Creating and Managing Tasks with Outlook

This introductory module covers features and functions common to creating and managing tasks in Outlook 2016.

Roadmap

In this module, you will learn how to create and manage tasks. The following roadmap identifies general activities you will perform as you progress through this module:

1. CREATE a NEW TASK
2. CATEGORIZE a TASK
3. CATEGORIZE an EMAIL MESSAGE
4. ASSIGN a TASK
5. PRINT a TASK
6. CREATE AND USE NOTES

At the beginning of step instructions throughout the module, you will see an abbreviated form of this roadmap. The abbreviated roadmap uses colors to indicate module progress: gray means the module is beyond that activity, blue means the task being shown is covered in that activity, and black means that activity is yet to be covered. For example, the following abbreviated roadmap indicates the section would be about categorizing an email message.

1 CREATE NEW TASK | 2 CATEGORIZE TASK | 3 CATEGORIZE EMAIL MESSAGE
4 ASSIGN TASK | 5 PRINT TASK | 6 CREATE AND USE NOTES

Use the abbreviated roadmap as a progress guide while you read or step through the instructions in this module.

Introduction to Outlook Tasks

Whether you are keeping track of your school assignments that are due next week or the action items that your boss needs completed as soon as possible, you can use Outlook tasks to manage your to-do list by generating a checklist and tracking activities. Instead of keeping a paper list of the things you need to do, you can use Outlook to combine your various tasks into one list that has reminders and tracking. A **task** is an item that you create in Outlook to track until its completion. A **to-do item** is any Outlook item such as a task, an email message, or a contact that has been flagged for follow-up later.

Creating and managing tasks in Outlook allows you to keep track of projects, which might include school assignments, work responsibilities, or personal activities. Using a task, you can record information about a project such as start date, due date, status, priority, and percent complete. Outlook can also remind you about the task so that you do not forget to complete it. If you are managing a project, for example, you can assign tasks to people so that everyone can complete their portion of the project.

Project — Managing Tasks

People and businesses create tasks to keep track of projects that are important to them or their organizations. Tasks can be categorized and monitored to ensure that all projects are completed in a timely fashion. You can track one-time tasks as well as tasks that recur over a period of time. You can also prioritize tasks so that you can decide which ones must be completed first.

The project in this module follows general guidelines and uses Outlook to create the task list shown in Figure 4–1. The task list in the Sophia Module 4 mailbox includes tasks that are organized using class, personal, and project team categories.

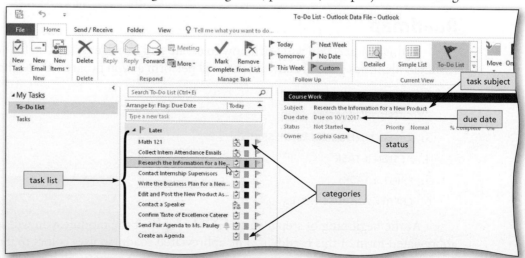

Figure 4–1

Creating a Task

The first step in creating a task for your to-do list is to open the Tasks category in Outlook. After you create a list of tasks, you can sync your tasks across multiple devices such as your smartphone and laptop, staying up to date and improving your productivity.

BTW

The Ribbon and Screen Resolution
Outlook may change how the groups and buttons within the groups appear on the ribbon, depending on the computer or mobile device's screen resolution. Thus, your ribbon may look different from the ones in this book if you are using a screen resolution other than 1366 × 768.

CONSIDER THIS

What advantages does an Outlook task list provide beyond a basic to-do list?
Many business employees use an Outlook task list to detail their hours, business expenses, and mileage. Instead of jotting down how many hours you worked on Tuesday to report later, remembering the tolls paid on a business trip, or how many miles you must list on your expense report, you can store this information in a task. When it is time to turn in your work hours or expense report, you can easily retrieve the details from your task list.

To-Do List Window

The To-Do List - Outlook Data File - Outlook window shown in Figure 4–2 includes features to help you manage your tasks. The main elements of the To-Do List window are the Navigation Pane, the To-Do list pane, and the Preview pane. The My Tasks folder in the Navigation Pane displays the To-Do list link and Tasks folder. Clicking the To-Do list link displays the tasks in the To-Do list view, and clicking Tasks displays the tasks in the task folder in Simple List view.

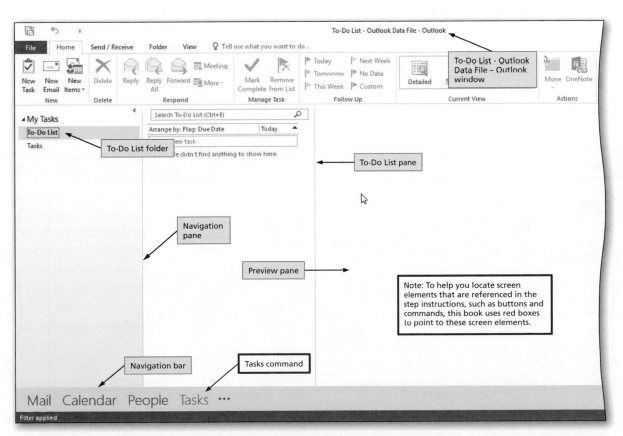

Figure 4–2

Creating a To-Do List

The first step in creating a To-Do list is to select a folder for storing your tasks. By default, Outlook stores tasks in the Tasks folder, but you can also create a personal folder in which to store your tasks, using the technique presented in Module 2. In this module, you will create tasks in the Tasks folder.

To Create a New Task

1 CREATE NEW TASK | 2 CATEGORIZE TASK | 3 CATEGORIZE EMAIL MESSAGE
4 ASSIGN TASK | 5 PRINT TASK | 6 CREATE AND USE NOTES

Sophia Garza, a student work study employee in the Pathways Internship Office, wants to create a task list to keep track of the internships and her own classes. The first task is to invite the internship supervisors to the rescheduled Pathways Internship Fair at least a month before the meeting now scheduled on November 3 so that she does not forget to complete the task. The following steps create a new task. *Why? To stay organized, you should create Outlook tasks to make sure you complete all the items on your to-do list.*

- Run Outlook 2016.
- Open the Sophia Module 4.pst Outlook Data File from the Data Files for Module 4.
- Click Tasks (shown in Figure 4–2) on the Navigation bar to display the Outlook Tasks.
- Click the New Task button (Home tab | New group) to display the Untitled – Task window (Figure 4–3).

Q&A | Why is my screen different? My Untitled – Task window does not have the two buttons named Assign Task and Send Status Report in the Manage Task group as shown in Figure 4–3.
If you do not have an email account connected to Outlook (covered in Module 1), you will not have these two buttons.

The New Task button does not appear on the Home tab. What should I do?
Click the New Items button (Home tab | New group), and then click Task. Now the New Task button should appear on the Home tab.

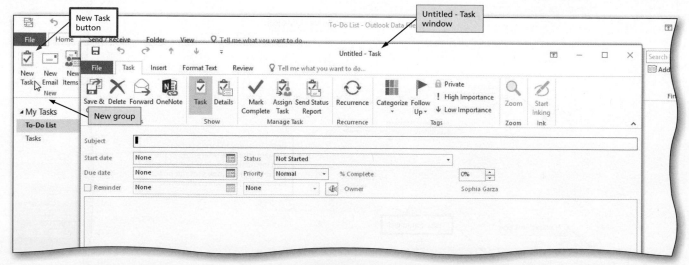

Figure 4–3

2

- Type `Contact Internship Supervisors` in the Subject text box to enter a subject for the task.

- Type `Pathways Internship Fair rescheduled for November 3` in the task body area to enter a description for the task (Figure 4–4).

Q&A Why did the title of the Task window change after I entered the subject?
As soon as you enter the subject, Outlook updates the Task window title to reflect the information you entered. The task is not saved, however; only the window title is updated.

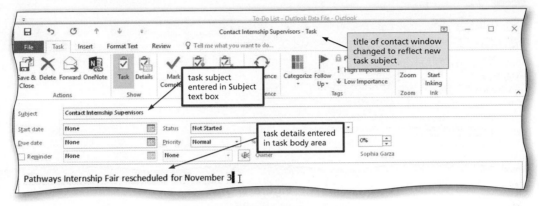

Figure 4–4

3

- Click the Start date Calendar button to display a calendar for the current month (Figure 4–5).

Q&A Why does my calendar display a different month?
Depending on the actual calendar month, your current month may be different.

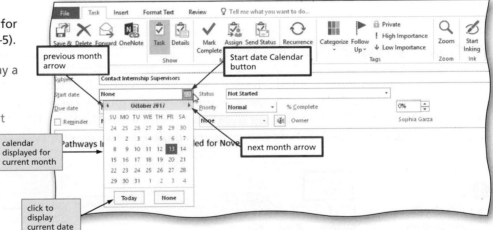

Figure 4–5

4

- If necessary, click the next month arrow or previous month arrow an appropriate number of times to advance to October 2017.

- Click 3 to select Tues 10/3/2017 as the start date (Figure 4–6).

Q&A Why did the due date change?
If you enter a start date, the due date automatically changes to match the start date. You can change the due date if needed.

Can I just type the date?
Yes, you can type the date. Using the calendar allows you to avoid potential errors due to typing mistakes.

What if October 2017 is in the past?
If October 2017 is in the past, click the previous month arrow an appropriate number of times until you reach October 2017.

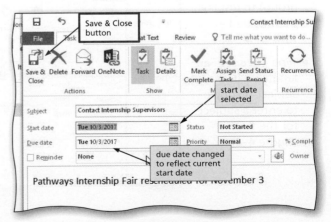

Figure 4–6

- Click the Save & Close button (Task tab | Actions group) (shown in Figure 4–6) to save the task and close the Task window (Figure 4–7).

Q&A My tasks are displayed in an arrangement different from the one in Figure 4–7. What should I do?
Click the Change View button or the More button (Home tab | Current View group), and then click To-Do List.

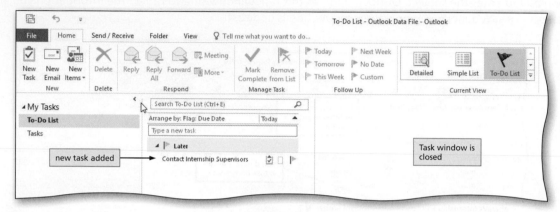

Figure 4–7

Other Ways
1. Press CTRL+N

To Create a Task with a Due Date

1 CREATE NEW TASK | 2 CATEGORIZE TASK | 3 CATEGORIZE EMAIL MESSAGE
4 ASSIGN TASK | 5 PRINT TASK | 6 CREATE AND USE NOTES

When you create the first task, the due date is set automatically after you enter the start date. If you have a specific due date, you can enter it when you create a task. Sophia needs to create a meeting agenda before the meeting on November 3. The following steps create a task with a due date. *Why? You can quickly add a specific due date to set a deadline for a task. You also can sort by the due date, placing the most urgent tasks at the top of your list.*

- Click the New Task button (Home tab | New group) to display the Untitled – Task window.

- Type **Create an Agenda** in the Subject text box to enter a subject for the task (Figure 4–8).

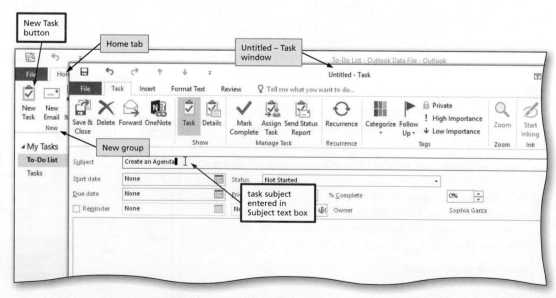

Figure 4–8

2

- Click the Due date Calendar button to display a calendar for the current month.

- Click the next or previous month arrow an appropriate number of times to display November 2017.

- Click 3 to select Fri 11/3/2017 as the due date (Figure 4–9).

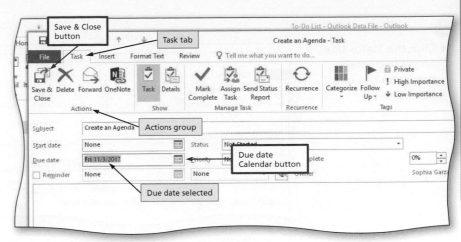

Figure 4–9

3

- Click the Save & Close button (Task tab | Actions group) to save the task and close the Task window (Figure 4–10).

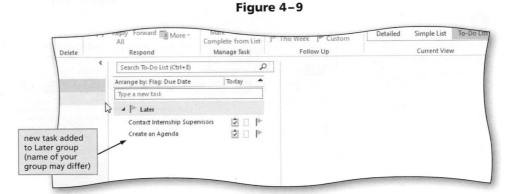

Figure 4–10

To Create a Task with a Status

1 CREATE NEW TASK | 2 CATEGORIZE TASK | 3 CATEGORIZE EMAIL MESSAGE
4 ASSIGN TASK | 5 PRINT TASK | 6 CREATE AND USE NOTES

You can assign a status to a task using any of five status indicators: Not Started, In Progress, Completed, Waiting on someone else, and Deferred. Sophia is planning to provide a speaker for the Land Your Perfect Internship event on 10/27/2017 and wants to create a task to remind herself to contact a speaker. She has already started working on a few speaker ideas, so the task status should be set to In Progress. The following steps create a task with a status. *Why? You can reflect your current progress by changing the status of a task.*

1

- Click the New Task button (Home tab | New group) to display the Untitled – Task window.

- Type `Contact a Speaker` in the Subject text box to enter a subject for the task.

- Type `Speaker needed for the Land Your Perfect Internship event` in the task body area to enter a description for the task.

- Click the Due date Calendar button to display a calendar for the current month.

- Click the appropriate month arrow button to go to October 2017.

- Click 27 to select Fri 10/27/2017 as the due date (Figure 4–11).

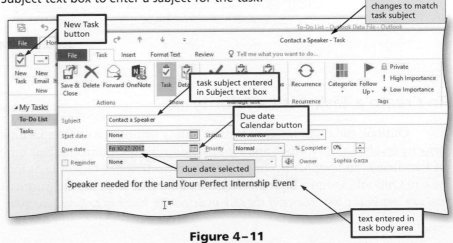

Figure 4–11

2
- Click the Status box arrow to display the status options (Figure 4–12).

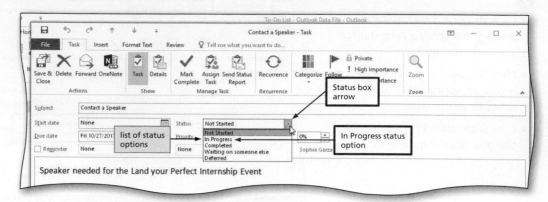

Figure 4–12

3
- Click In Progress to change the status of the task (Figure 4–13).

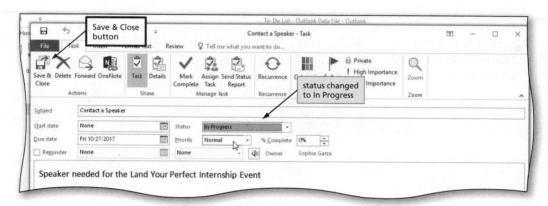

Figure 4–13

4
- Click the Save & Close button (Task tab | Actions group) to save the task and close the Task window (Figure 4–14).

Figure 4–14

To Create a Task with a Priority

1 CREATE NEW TASK | 2 CATEGORIZE TASK | 3 CATEGORIZE EMAIL MESSAGE
4 ASSIGN TASK | 5 PRINT TASK | 6 CREATE AND USE NOTES

Outlook can organize each task by setting priorities to reflect its importance. Outlook allows for three priority levels: Low, Normal, and High. The Pathways Internship Fair on November 3 will be catered by Taste of Excellence, and Sophia needs to confirm the catering details at least four days in advance. As you enter the task in Outlook, assign a high priority. The following steps set the priority of a task. *Why? After setting priorities, you can sort by the importance of the task to determine how best to focus your time.*

1

- Click the New Task button (Home tab | New group) to display the Untitled – Task window.

- Type `Confirm Taste of Excellence Caterer` in the Subject text box to enter a subject for the task.

- Click the Due date Calendar button to display a calendar for the current month.

- Click the next or previous month arrow an appropriate number of times to display October 2017.

- Click 30 to select Mon 10/30/2017 as the due date (Figure 4–15).

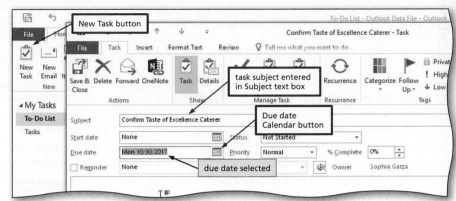

Figure 4–15

2

- Click the Priority box arrow to display the priority options (Figure 4–16).

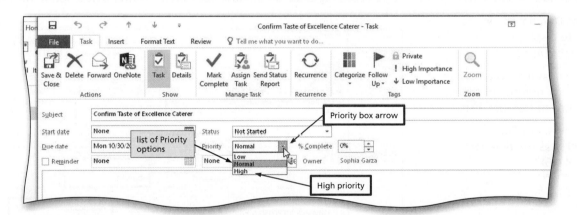

Figure 4–16

3

- Click High to set the priority (Figure 4–17).

4

- Click the Save & Close button (Task tab | Actions group) to save the task and close the Task window.

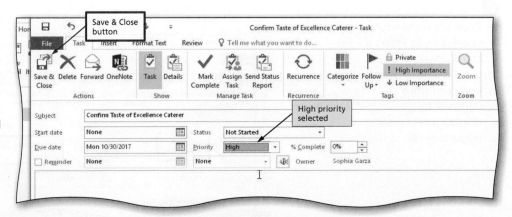

Figure 4–17

Can a project manager in a business team assign tasks in Outlook to keep track of what work the team has completed?

Outlook provides an easy way for project managers to assign tasks. For example, a manager might want to receive status reports and updates on the progress of a task. If the person who is assigned a task rejects it, the manager can reassign the task to someone else and set a high priority for the task.

To Create a Task with a Reminder

1 CREATE NEW TASK | 2 CATEGORIZE TASK | 3 CATEGORIZE EMAIL MESSAGE
4 ASSIGN TASK | 5 PRINT TASK | 6 CREATE AND USE NOTES

To make sure you remember to complete a task, set a reminder before the task is due so you have enough time to complete the task. Ms. Pauley, the faculty advisor, asked Sophia to send her the Pathways Internship Fair agenda by the end of October. Sophia can create a task with a reminder to respond to Ms. Pauley's request. *Why? By adding a reminder to a task, Outlook can remind you about the task automatically.* The following steps add a task and set the reminder option for a week before the task is due.

- Click the New Task button (Home tab | New group) to display the Untitled – Task window.

- Type `Send Fair Agenda to Ms. Pauley` in the Subject text box to enter a subject for the task.

- Type `Pathways Internship Fair detailed agenda` in the task body area to enter a description for the task.

- Click the Due date Calendar button to display a calendar for the current month.

- Click the next month arrow an appropriate number of times to advance to October 2017.

- Click 31 to select Tue 10/31/2017 as the due date (Figure 4–18).

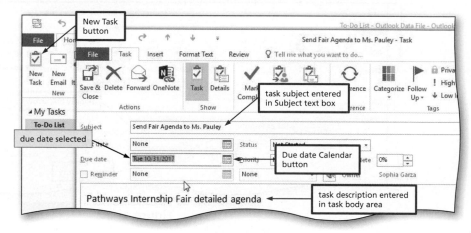

Figure 4–18

- Click the Reminder check box to insert a check mark, enable the Reminder boxes, and configure Outlook to display a reminder (Figure 4–19).

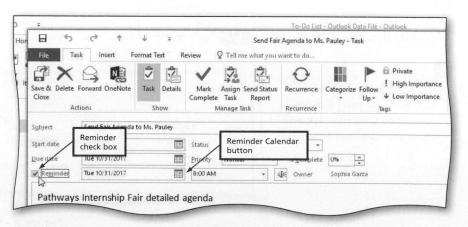

Figure 4–19

❸

- Click the Reminder Calendar button to display a calendar for October.

- Click 24 to select Tue 10/24/2017 as the Reminder date (Figure 4–20).

Q&A Can I change the time that Outlook displays the reminder?

Yes. When you set a reminder, Outlook automatically sets the time for the reminder to 8:00 AM. You can change the time by clicking the Reminder box arrow and then selecting a time. You can also use the Outlook Options dialog box to change the default time.

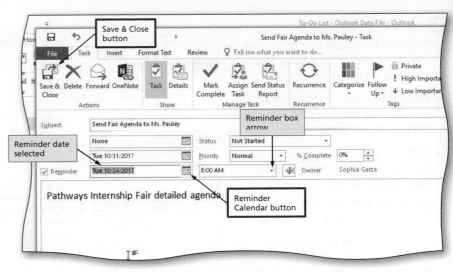

Figure 4–20

❹

- Click the Save & Close button (Task tab | Actions group) to save the task and close the Task window (Figure 4–21).

Q&A How does Outlook remind me of a task?

Outlook displays the Task window for the task at the specified time. If you used the Sound icon to set an alarm for the reminder, Outlook also plays the sound when it displays the Task window.

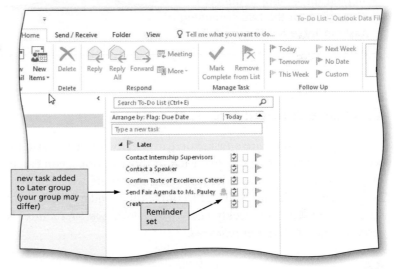

Figure 4–21

To Create More Tasks

1 CREATE NEW TASK | 2 CATEGORIZE TASK | 3 CATEGORIZE EMAIL MESSAGE
4 ASSIGN TASK | 5 PRINT TASK | 6 CREATE AND USE NOTES

Sophia has three tasks to add regarding a project in her economics course to develop a new product plan. The first task is to research the information for a new product. Another task is to write the business plan for the new product. She also needs a task for editing and posting the new product assignment. Table 4–1 displays the business plan tasks with their due dates.

Table 4–1 Additional Tasks	
Subject	**Due Date**
Research the Information for a New Product	10/2/2017
Write the Business Plan for a New Product	10/9/2017
Edit and Post the New Product Assignment	10/16/2017

The following step creates the remaining tasks in the Task window. *Why? By adding academic tasks to your list, an item that requires attention will not be overlooked.*

- Click the New Task button (Home tab | New group) to display the Untitled – Task window.

- Enter the subject in the Subject text box for the first task in Table 4–1.

- Click the Due date Calendar button to display a calendar for the current month, and then select the due date for the task as shown in Table 4–1.

- Click the Save & Close button (Task tab | Actions group) to save the task and close the Task window.

- Repeat the actions in bullets 1 through 4 for the two remaining tasks in Table 4–1 (Figure 4–22).

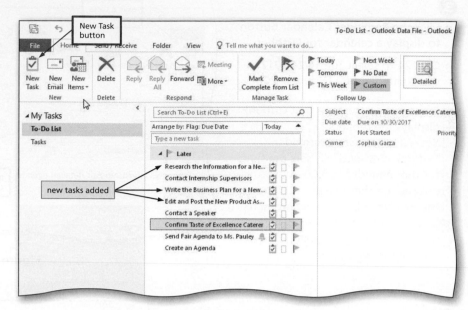

Figure 4–22

To Create a Recurring Task

1 CREATE NEW TASK | 2 CATEGORIZE TASK | 3 CATEGORIZE EMAIL MESSAGE
4 ASSIGN TASK | 5 PRINT TASK | 6 CREATE AND USE NOTES

When you create a task, you can specify it is a recurring task by selecting whether the task recurs daily, weekly, monthly, or yearly. For each of those options, you can provide specifics, such as the day of the month the task occurs. You can have the task recur indefinitely or you can specify the exact end date. Sophia has a weekly assignment due in her Math 121 course on Mondays from September 11 until December 11. The following steps add a recurring weekly task. **Why?** *When you have a task that occurs at regular intervals, you should set a recurring task to keep you informed.*

- Click the New Task button (Home tab | New group) to display the Untitled – Task window.

- Type `Math 121` in the Subject text box to enter a subject for the task.

- Type `Submit assignment online` in the task body area to enter a description for the task.

- Click the Start date Calendar button to display a calendar for the current month.

- Click the next or previous month arrow an appropriate number of times to display September 2017.

- Click 11 to select Mon 9/11/2017 as the start date (Figure 4–23).

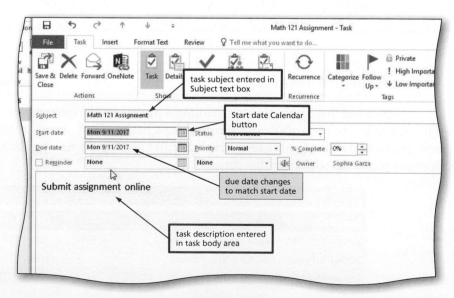

Figure 4–23

- Click the Recurrence button (Task tab | Recurrence group) to display the Task Recurrence dialog box (Figure 4–24).

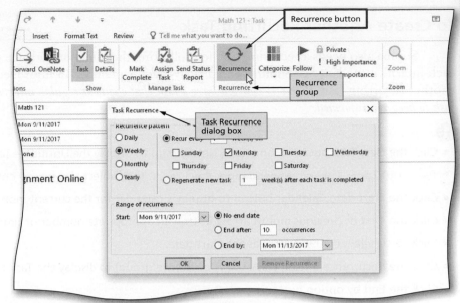

Figure 4–24

- Click the End by option button to select it.
- Click the End by box arrow to display a calendar.
- If necessary, click the next or previous month arrow an appropriate number of times to display December 2017.
- Click 11 to select Mon 12/11/2017 as the End by date (Figure 4–25).

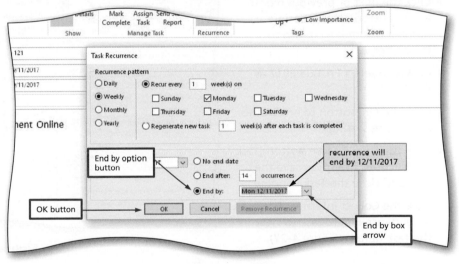

Figure 4–25

- Click the OK button (Task Recurrence dialog box) to accept the recurrence settings (Figure 4–26).

- Click the Save & Close button (Task tab | Actions group) to save the task and close the Task window.

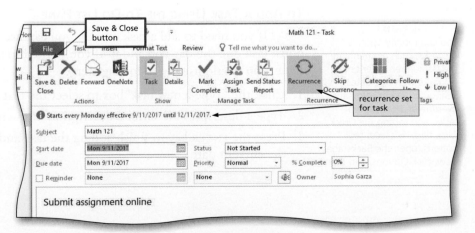

Figure 4–26

To Create Another Recurring Task

Sophia also needs a recurring task for collecting the intern attendance emails. The intern supervisors email each intern's attendance to Sophia every Friday from September 15 until December 8. The following step adds another recurring task. *Why? When you have a task that occurs at regular intervals, you should add it as a recurring task to keep you informed.*

- Click the New Task button (Home tab | New group) to display the Untitled – Task window.

- Type `Collect Intern Attendance Emails` in the Subject text box to enter a subject for the task.

- Click the Start date Calendar button to display a calendar for the current month.

- Click the next or previous month arrow button an appropriate number of times to display September 2017.

- Click 15 to select Fri 09/15/2017 as the start date.

- Click the Recurrence button (Task tab | Recurrence group) to display the Task Recurrence dialog box.

- Click the End by option button to select it.

- Click the End by box arrow to display a calendar.

- Click the next or previous month arrow button an appropriate number of times to return to December 2017.

- Click 8 to select Fri 12/8/2017 as the End by date.

- Click the OK button to accept the recurrence settings.

- Click the Save & Close button (Task tab | Actions group) to save the task and close the Task window.

- Click the Collect Intern Attendance Emails task to view the task details (Figure 4–27).

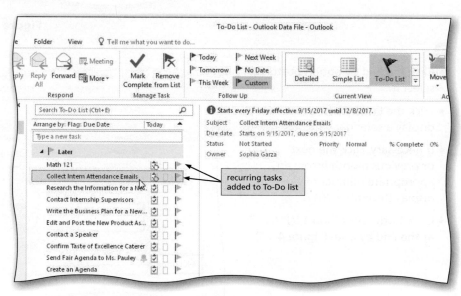

Figure 4–27

BTW
Task Options
You can modify options for tasks, such as changing the default reminder time for tasks with due dates, changing default colors for overdue and completed tasks, and setting the Quick Click flag. To access task options, open the Backstage view, click Options, and then click Tasks.

TO ADD A TASK USING THE TO-DO LIST PANE

If you need to add a task quickly, you can use the To-Do List Pane to create a quick task due the day you add it. If you wanted to add a task using the To-Do List Pane, you would use the following steps.

1. Click the 'Type a new task' box to select the text box.

2. Type a description to enter a description of the task.

3. Press the ENTER key to finish adding the task and display it in the To-Do list with the current date.

Categorizing Tasks

Outlook allows you to categorize email messages, contacts, tasks, and calendar items so that you can identify which ones are related to each other and quickly identify the items by their color. Module 2 used color categories to organize calendar items. In the same way, you can use color categories to organize tasks.

Six color categories are available by default, but you can also create your own categories and select one of 25 colors to associate with them. After you create a category, you can set it as a **Quick Click** category, which is applied by default when you click an item's category column in the To-Do list pane. For example, the default Quick Click category is the red category. If you click a task's category column in the To-Do list pane, the red category automatically is assigned to it.

To Create a New Category

1 CREATE NEW TASK | 2 CATEGORIZE TASK | 3 CATEGORIZE EMAIL MESSAGE
4 ASSIGN TASK | 5 PRINT TASK | 6 CREATE AND USE NOTES

Why? *Custom categories can organize tasks listed in Outlook.* The first category you want to create is the Pathways Internship Office category, which you can use for all tasks related to the internship program at Langford College. When you select a task and then create the category, Outlook applies the category to the selected task. After you create a category, apply it to other tasks as necessary. The following steps create a category and apply it to a task.

1

- Click the `Contact Internship Supervisors` task to select it.

- Click the Categorize button (Home tab | Tags group) to display the Categorize menu (Figure 4–28).

Q&A Why do I have to select the Contact Internship Supervisors task?
To activate the Categorize button, you first need to select a task or group of tasks.

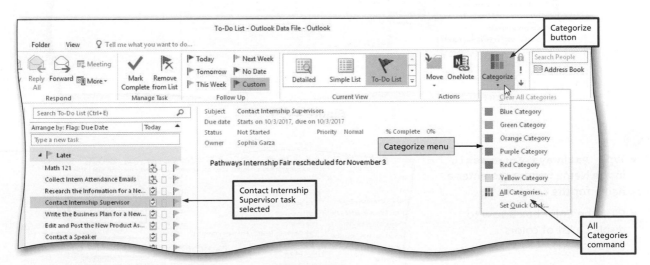

Figure 4–28

• Click All Categories to display the Color Categories dialog box (Figure 4–29).

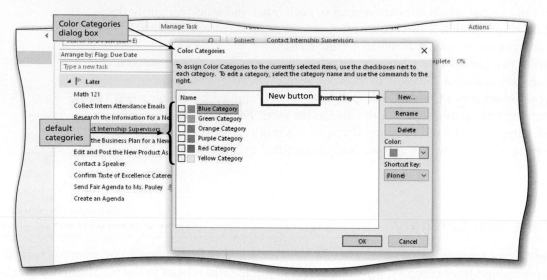

Figure 4–29

• Click the New button (Color Categories dialog box) to display the Add New Category dialog box (Figure 4–30).

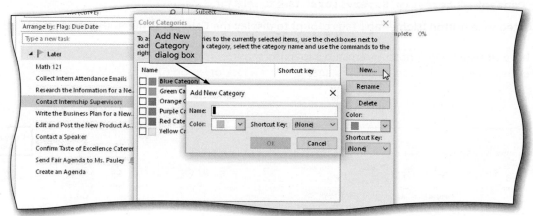

Figure 4–30

• Type **Pathways Internship** in the Name text box to enter a name for the category.

• Click the Color box arrow to display a list of colors (Figure 4–31).

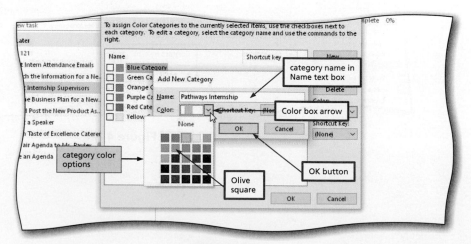

Figure 4–31

5

- Click the Olive square (column 2, row 2) to select a category color.
- Click the OK button (Add New Category dialog box) to create the new category and display it in the Color Categories dialog box (Figure 4–32).

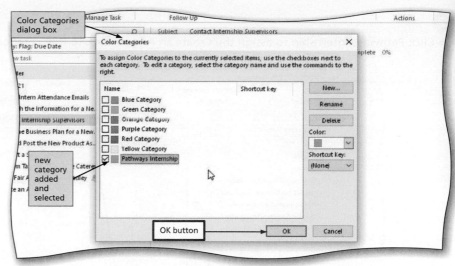

Figure 4–32

6

- Click the OK button (Color Categories dialog box) to assign the Contact Internship Supervisors task to the Pathways Internship category (Figure 4–33).

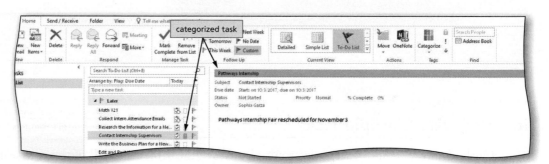

Figure 4–33

To Categorize a Task

1 CREATE NEW TASK | 2 CATEGORIZE TASK | 3 CATEGORIZE EMAIL MESSAGE
4 ASSIGN TASK | 5 PRINT TASK | 6 CREATE AND USE NOTES

After creating a category, you can apply other tasks that are related to that category. *Why? You can easily identify all the tasks for a specific category by using color categories.* The following steps assign a task to an existing color category.

1

- Click the Create an Agenda task to select it.
- Click the Categorize button (Home tab | Tags group) to display the Categorize menu (Figure 4–34).

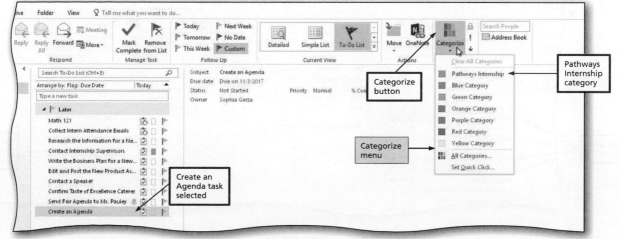

Figure 4–34

● Click Pathways Internship to assign the Create an Agenda task to that category (Figure 4–35).

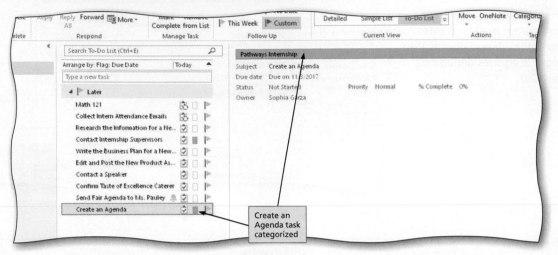

Figure 4–35

To Categorize Multiple Tasks

1 CREATE NEW TASK | 2 CATEGORIZE TASK | 3 CATEGORIZE EMAIL MESSAGE
4 ASSIGN TASK | 5 PRINT TASK | 6 CREATE AND USE NOTES

Outlook allows you to categorize multiple tasks at the same time. All of the course-related tasks can be assigned to a new category called Course Work, including the three new product assignments in the Economics class and the Math course task. The following steps create the Course Work category and apply it to the course-related tasks. *Why? As a student, you can view a single category to locate all of your assignments.*

● Select the Math 121, Research the Information for a New Product, Write the Business Plan for a New Product, and Edit and Post the New Product Assignment tasks.

● Click the Categorize button (Home tab | Tags group) to display the Categorize menu (Figure 4–36).

Q&A How do I select more than one task?
Click the first task, press and hold the CTRL key, and then click the other tasks to select them.

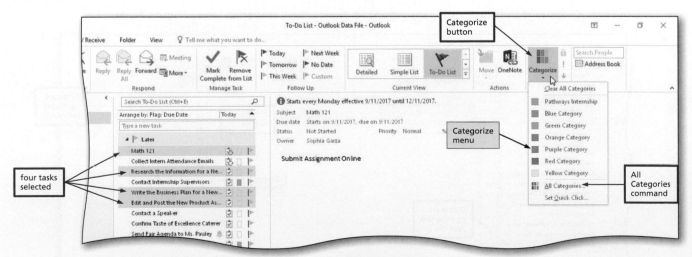

Figure 4–36

2

- Click All Categories to display the Color Categories dialog box.

- Click the New button (Color Categories dialog box) to display the Add New Category dialog box (Figure 4–37).

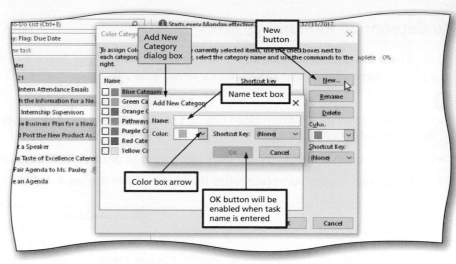

Figure 4–37

3

- Type `Course Work` in the Name text box to enter a name for the category.

- Click the Color box arrow to display a list of colors.

- Click the Dark Red square (column 1, row 4) to select the category color.

- Click the OK button (Add New Category dialog box) to create the Course Work category (Figure 4–38).

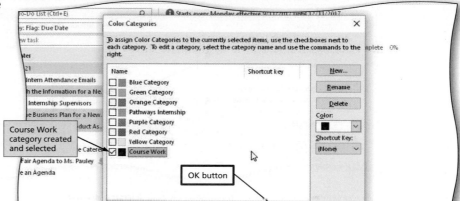

Figure 4–38

4

- Click the OK button (Color Categories dialog box) to assign the selected tasks to a category (Figure 4–39).

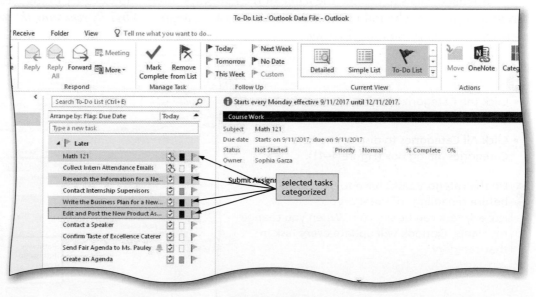

Figure 4–39

To Categorize Remaining Tasks

The following steps categorize the remaining tasks. *Why? When you sort by category, you will be able to view at a glance what tasks need completion in each facet of your life.*

- Select the Collect Intern Attendance Emails, Contact a Speaker, Confirm Taste of Excellence Caterer, and Send Fair Agenda to Ms. Pauley tasks.

- Click the Categorize button (Home tab | Tags group) to display the Categorize menu.

- Click Pathways Internship to categorize the selected tasks (Figure 4–40).

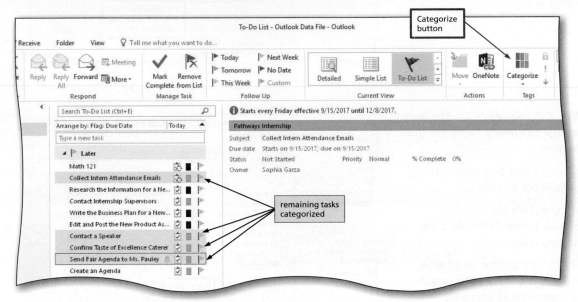

Figure 4–40

To Rename a Category

Sophia decides to change the name of the Pathways Internship category to the Pathways Internship Program category. The following steps rename a color category. *Why? By renaming the color categories, you can assign names that are meaningful to you.*

- Click the Categorize button (Home tab | Tags group) to display the Categorize menu.

- Click All Categories to display the Color Categories dialog box (Figure 4–41).

Q&A Do the category tasks have to be selected before renaming the category?
No, any task can be selected. When you change the name, Outlook will update every task in that category.

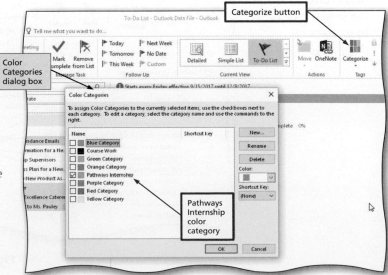

Figure 4–41

- Click the Pathways Internship category to select it.

- Click the Rename button (Color Categories dialog box) to select the category name for editing.

- Type **Pathways Internship Program** and then press the ENTER key to change the category name (Figure 4–42).

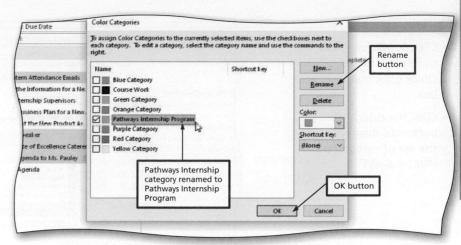

Figure 4–42

- Click the OK button (Color Categories dialog box) to apply the changes (Figure 4–43).

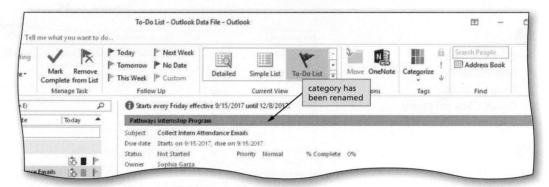

Figure 4–43

To Set a Quick Click

1 CREATE NEW TASK | 2 CATEGORIZE TASK | 3 CATEGORIZE EMAIL MESSAGE
4 ASSIGN TASK | 5 PRINT TASK | 6 CREATE AND USE NOTES

Instead of categorizing tasks using the Categorize menu options, you can assign a task to a category by clicking the category box for a task in the To-Do list pane. If you click the category box, the default category is applied. You can change the default category by setting one as a Quick Click. **Why?** *You can assign a frequently used color category (Quick Click category) by selecting it as your default color category.* Sophia realizes that most of her tasks are related to the Pathways Internship Program, so she decides to set the default category as the Pathways Internship Program category. The following steps assign the default category using a Quick Click.

- Click the Categorize button (Home tab | Tags group) to display the Categorize menu (Figure 4–44).

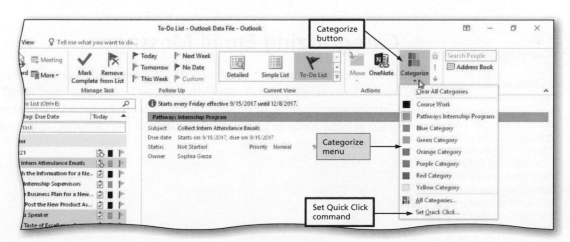

Figure 4–44

- Click Set Quick Click to display the Set Quick Click dialog box.

- Click the category button to display the list of categories (Figure 4–45).

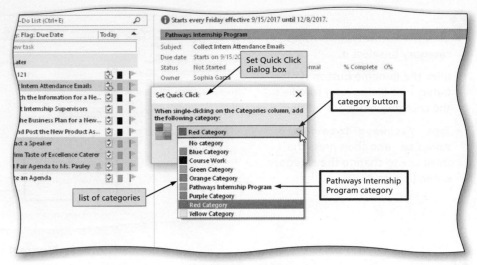

Figure 4–45

- Click Pathways Internship Program to set it as the Quick Click category (Figure 4–46).

- Click the OK button (Set Quick Click dialog box) to apply the changes.

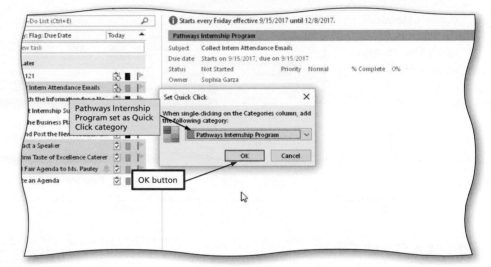

Figure 4–46

Break Point: If you wish to take a break, this is a good place to do so. To resume at a later time, continue to follow the steps from this location forward.

BTW
Copying and Moving Tasks
To move or copy a task to another folder, select the task, and then click the Move button (Home tab | Actions group). Click the Other Folder command to move the task; click the Copy to Folder command to copy the task. Select the folder to which you want to move or copy the task, and then click the OK button.

Categorizing Email Messages

Recall that you can use categories with email messages, contacts, tasks, and calendar items. Any category you create for a task can be used for your email messages. Categorizing your email messages allows you to create a link between them and other related items in Outlook. By looking at the category, you quickly can tell which Outlook items go together.

To Categorize an Email Message

1 CREATE NEW TASK | 2 CATEGORIZE TASK | 3 CATEGORIZE EMAIL MESSAGE
4 ASSIGN TASK | 5 PRINT TASK | 6 CREATE AND USE NOTES

Sophia received a couple of email messages from interns in the internship program. These email messages can be assigned to the Pathways Internship Program category. The following steps categorize email messages. *Why? Color categories can be assigned to email messages, enabling you to quickly identify them and associate them with related tasks.*

- Click the Mail button on the Navigation bar and open the Inbox folder to switch to your Inbox.
- Select the Zion Gibson and Yumi Mori email messages.
- Click the Categorize button (Home tab | Tags group) to display the Categorize menu (Figure 4–47).

Q&A What should I do if my Inbox email messages are not displayed?
Expand the Inbox folder in the Navigation Pane to view the messages.

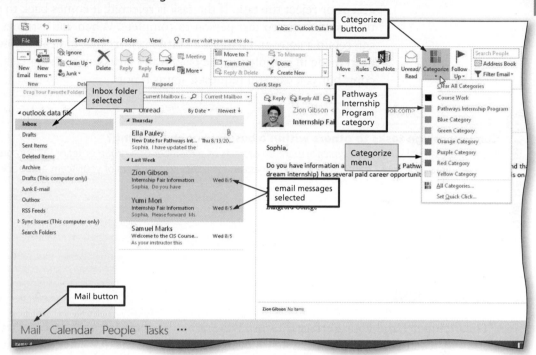

Figure 4–47

- Click Pathways Internship Program to assign the selected email messages to the Pathways Internship Program category (Figure 4–48).

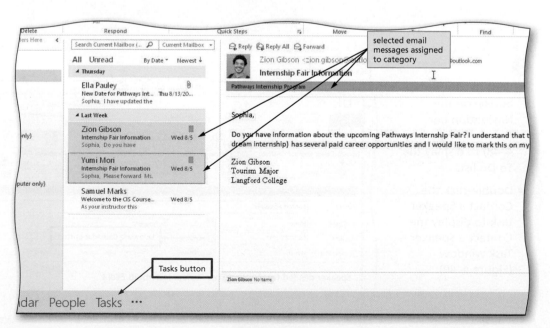

Figure 4–48

Managing Tasks

After creating one or more tasks in your To-Do list, you can manage them by marking tasks complete when you finish them, updating them, assigning some tasks to other people, adding attachments, and removing them. For example, when you email the agenda for the meeting to Ms. Pauley, mark the task as complete. That way, you will not have to remember later whether you completed the assignment.

When you are working on a project with others, you sometimes may want to assign tasks to them. Outlook allows you to assign tasks to other people and still monitor the tasks. When a task has been assigned to another person, that person can accept or reject the task. If the task is rejected, it comes back to you. If it is accepted, the task belongs to that person to complete. When you assign a nonrecurring task, you can retain a copy and request a **status report** that indicates how much progress has been made in completing the task. If the task is a recurring task, you cannot retain a copy, but you can still request a status report.

CONSIDER THIS

Can you assign tasks to others within a business or club setting?

In the professional world, you typically work on projects as a member of a group or team. As you organize the large and small tasks required to complete the project, you can assign each task to members of your team and track the progress of the entire project.

To Update a Task

1 CREATE NEW TASK | 2 CATEGORIZE TASK | 3 CATEGORIZE EMAIL MESSAGE
4 ASSIGN TASK | 5 PRINT TASK | 6 CREATE AND USE NOTES

The October Land Your Perfect Internship event has been moved so the Contact a Speaker task is due on October 24 instead of on October 27. The following steps change the due date for a task. *Why? As tasks change, be sure to update the due dates of your tasks.*

1

• Click the Tasks button on the Navigation bar (shown in Figure 4–48) to display the To-Do list.

• Double-click the Contact a Speaker task to display the Contact a Speaker – Task window (Figure 4–49).

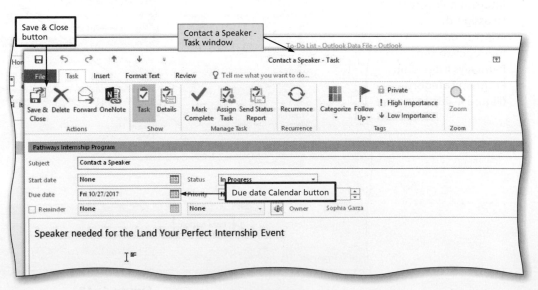

Figure 4–49

②

- Click the Due date Calendar button to display a calendar for October.

- Click 24 to select Tue 10/24/2017 as the due date.

- Click the Save & Close button (Task tab | Actions group) to save the changes (Figure 4–50).

Q&A

How do I change the task name only?

Click the task name in the task list to select it, and then click it again to edit the name.

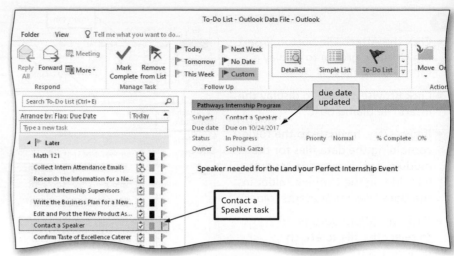

Figure 4–50

To Attach a File to a Task

1 CREATE NEW TASK | 2 CATEGORIZE TASK | 3 CATEGORIZE EMAIL MESSAGE
4 ASSIGN TASK | 5 PRINT TASK | 6 CREATE AND USE NOTES

Why? *Attaching a file to a task is helpful if you want quick access to information when you are looking at a task.* Ella Pauley has emailed you an updated Pathways Internship Fair flyer, which you already have saved to your computer. You decide that you should attach it to the Confirm Taste of Excellence Caterer task so that you can share the flyer with the catering staff for room and timing information. The following steps attach a document to a task.

①

- Double-click the Confirm Taste of Excellence Caterer task (shown in Figure 4–50) to display the Confirm Taste of Excellence Caterer - Task window.

- Click Insert on the ribbon to display the Insert tab (Figure 4–51).

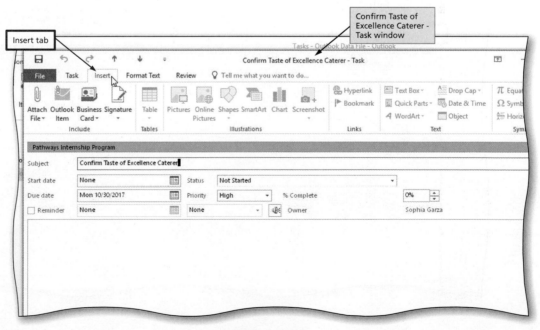

Figure 4–51

2

- Click the Attach File button (Insert tab | Include group) to display a list of recent files.
- Click Browse This PC to display the Insert File dialog box.
- If necessary, navigate to the folder containing the data files for this module (in this case, the Module 04 folder in the Outlook folder in the Data Files for Students folder).
- Click Fair (Word document) to select the file to attach (Figure 4–52).

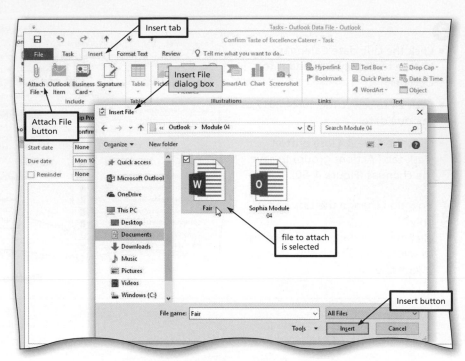

Figure 4–52

3

- Click the Insert button (Insert File dialog box) to attach the file (Figure 4–53).

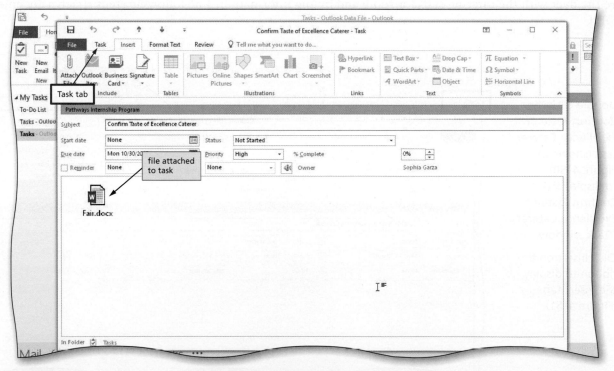

Figure 4–53

- Click Task on the ribbon to display the Task tab.
- Click the Save & Close button (Task tab | Actions group) to save the changes (Figure 4–54).

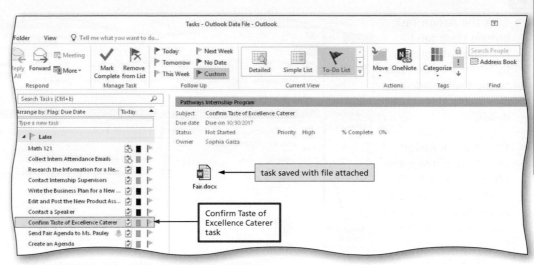

Figure 4–54

To Assign a Task

1 CREATE NEW TASK | 2 CATEGORIZE TASK | 3 CATEGORIZE EMAIL MESSAGE
4 ASSIGN TASK | 5 PRINT TASK | 6 CREATE AND USE NOTES

In addition to creating your own tasks, you can create tasks to assign to others. Yumi Mori, the Alumni Outreach coordinator, has volunteered to find a speaker for the Land Your Perfect Internship event. To assign a task, you first create the task, and then send it as a task request to someone. *Why? You can assign a task to someone else while ensuring that you retain a copy of the task and receive a status report once the task is completed.* The following steps assign a task.

- Double-click the Contact a Speaker task (shown in Figure 4–54) to reopen the Contact a Speaker - Task window (Figure 4–55).

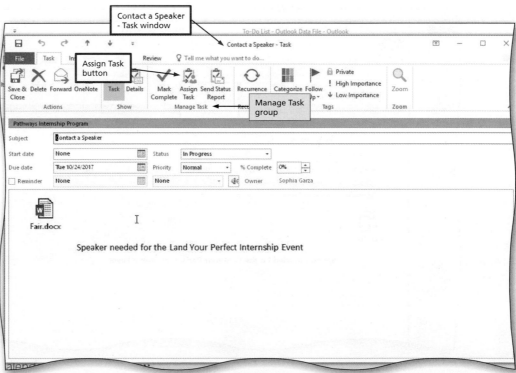

Figure 4–55

2

• Click the Assign Task button (Task tab | Manage Task group) to add the To text box to the task to add an email address (Figure 4–56).

Q&A Why did the Assign Task button disappear after it was clicked?
If you do not want to assign the task to an individual, click the Cancel Assignment button that replaced the Assign Task button.

Figure 4–56

3

• Type **yumi.mori@outlook.com** in the To text box to enter a recipient (Figure 4–57).

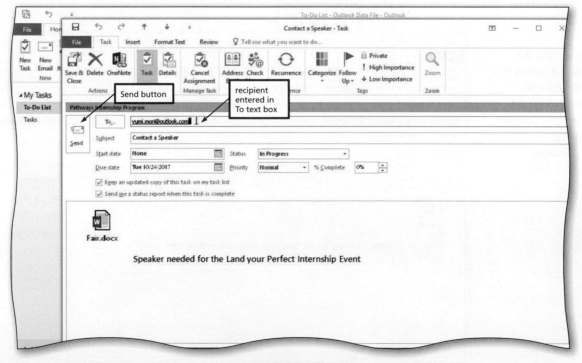

Figure 4–57

- Click the Send button (shown in Figure 4–57) to send the task to Yumi Mori (Figure 4–58).

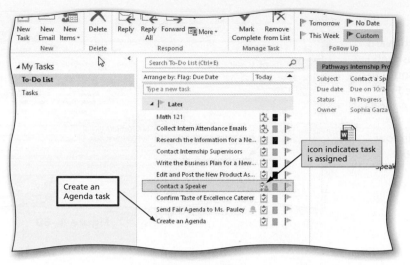

Figure 4–58

To Forward a Task

1 CREATE NEW TASK | 2 CATEGORIZE TASK | 3 CATEGORIZE EMAIL MESSAGE
4 ASSIGN TASK | 5 PRINT TASK | 6 CREATE AND USE NOTES

Why? *When you forward a task, you send a copy of the task to the person who can add it to their To-Do list for tracking.* Zion Gibson has agreed to assist you in creating the agenda for the Pathways Internship Fair. By forwarding the task to Zion, the task appears on his to-do list so he can track it on his own. The following steps forward a task.

- Double-click the Create an Agenda task (shown in Figure 4–58) to display the Create an Agenda – Task window (Figure 4–59).

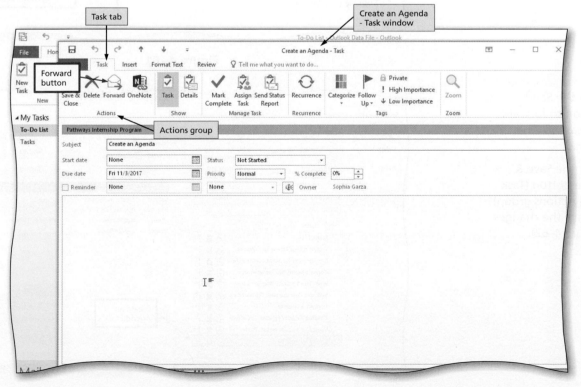

Figure 4–59

- Click the Forward button (Task tab | Actions group) to display the FW: Create an Agenda – Message (HTML) window (Figure 4–60).

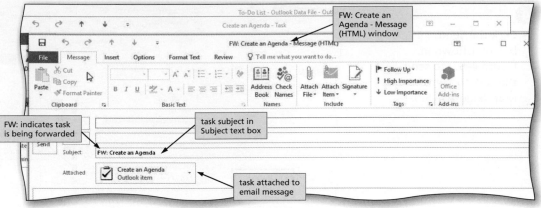

Figure 4–60

- Type `zion.gibson@ outlook.com` in the To text box to enter a recipient.

- Type `Attached is the agenda task for you to add to your to-do list.` in the message body area to enter a message.

- Press the ENTER key two times and then type `Sophia` to complete the message (Figure 4–61).

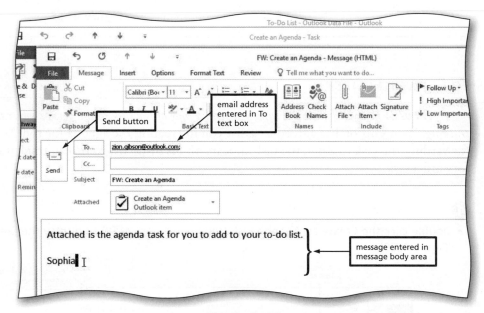

Figure 4–61

- Click the Send button to forward the task to Zion Gibson.

- Click the Save & Close button (Task tab | Actions group) to save the changes (Figure 4–62).

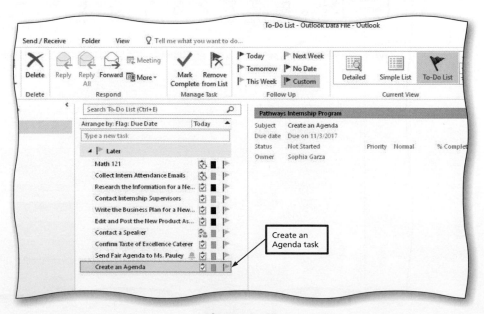

Figure 4–62

To Send a Status Report

While a task is in progress, you can send status reports to other people indicating the status and completion percentage of the task. Ms. Ella Pauley wants to be informed about the agenda for the November internship fair. Sophia has completed 25 percent of the work and wants to inform her that the task is in progress. The following steps create and send a status report. *Why? If you have been assigned a task, you can submit a status report before you complete the task to explain why the task has not been completed or why the task needs to be amended.*

- Double-click the Create an Agenda task to display the Create an Agenda - Task window.

- Click the Status box arrow to display a status list.

- Click In Progress to change the status of the task (Figure 4–63).

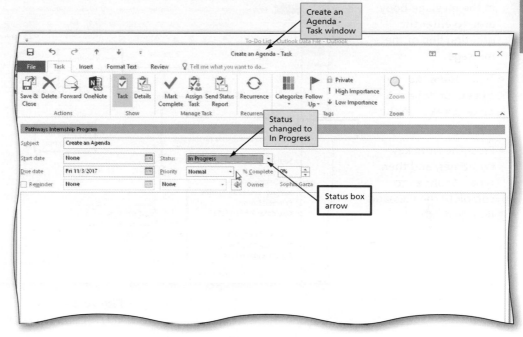

Figure 4–63

- Click the Up arrow to change the % Complete to 25% (Figure 4–64).

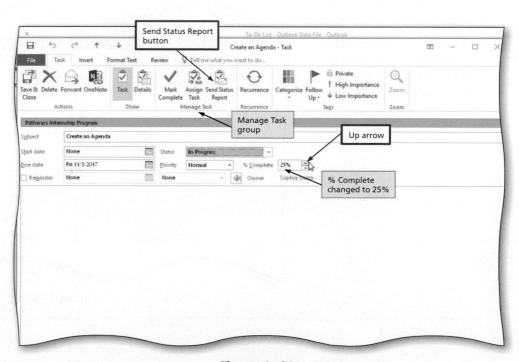

Figure 4–64

- Click the Send Status Report button (Task tab | Manage Task group) to display the Task Status Report: Create an Agenda - Message (Rich Text) window.

- Type `ella.pauley@outlook.com` in the To text box to enter a recipient.

- Type `Ms. Pauley,` and then press the ENTER key two times in the message body area to enter the greeting line of the message.

- Type `Here is my first update on this task.` in the message.

- Press the ENTER key two times, and then type `Sophia` to complete the message (Figure 4–65).

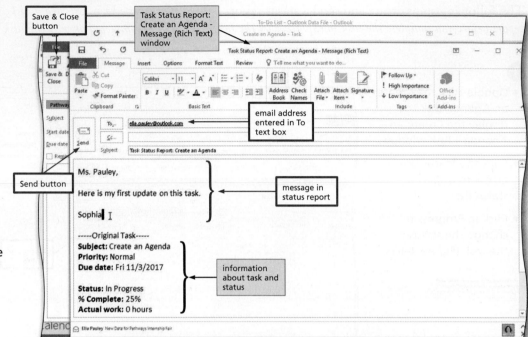

Figure 4–65

- Click the Send button to send the status report to Ella Pauley.

- Click the Save & Close button (Task tab | Actions group) to save the changes to the task (Figure 4–66).

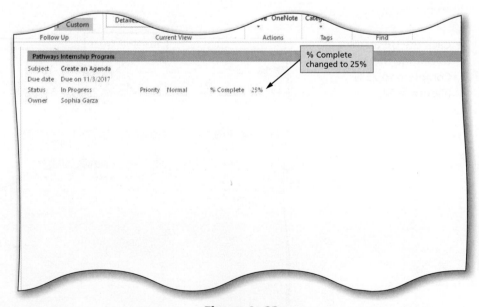

Figure 4–66

Outlook Module 4

To Mark a Task Complete

You have just completed the research for the new product assignment for your economics class, so you can mark it as complete. *Why? Mark a task as complete so that you know it is finished.* The following steps mark a task as complete.

1

• Click the Research the Information for a New Product task to select it (Figure 4–67).

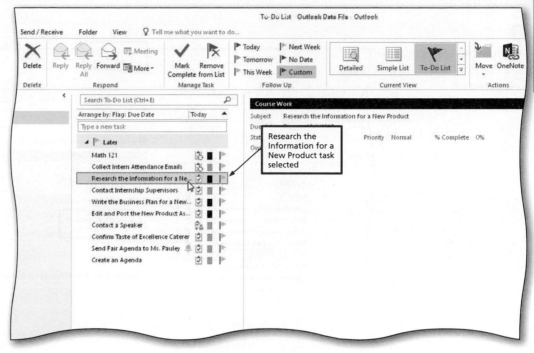

Figure 4–67

2

• Click the Mark Complete button (Home tab | Manage Task group) to mark the Research the Information for a New Product task as completed (Figure 4–68).

Q&A

Why was the Research the Information for a New Product task removed from the To-Do list? Once you mark a task as complete, Outlook removes it from the To-Do list and places it in the Completed list. You can see the Completed list by changing your view to Completed using the Change View button (Home tab | Current View group).

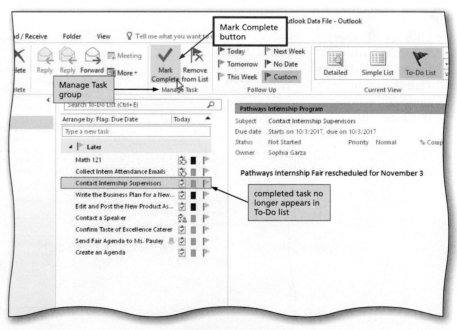

Figure 4–68

To Remove a Task

You sometimes may need to remove a task. *Why? When you remove a task, it is no longer displayed in your To-Do List.* The Pathways Internship Office has decided to remove the Contact Speaker for the Land Your Perfect Internship event task until the internship office has time to promote the event. The following steps remove a task.

• Click the Contact a Speaker task to select it (Figure 4–69).

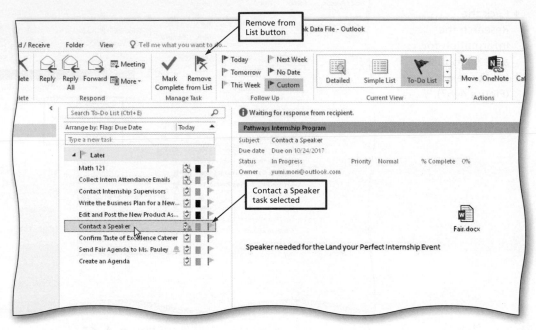

Figure 4–69

• Click the Remove from List button (Home tab | Manage Task group) to remove the task (Figure 4–70).

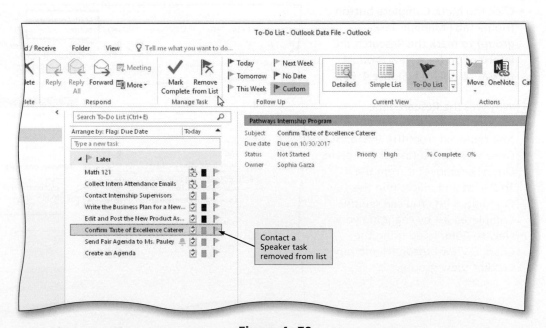

Figure 4–70

To Delete a Category

When you no longer need a category, you can delete it. Deleting a category removes it from the category list but not from the tasks that already have been assigned to it. If you wanted to delete a category, you would use the following steps.

1. Click a task within the category that you would like to delete.
2. Click the Categorize button (Home tab | Tags group) to display the Categorize menu.
3. Click All Categories to display the Color Categories dialog box.
4. Click the category that you want to delete to select it.
5. Click the Delete button (Color Categories dialog box) to delete the color category.
6. Click the Yes button (Microsoft Outlook dialog box) to confirm the deletion.
7. Click the OK button (Color Categories dialog box) to close the dialog box.

BTW
Touch Screen Differences
The Office and Windows interfaces may vary if you are using a touch screen. For this reason, you might notice that the function or appearance of your touch screen differs slightly from this module's presentation.

Choosing Display and Print Views

When working with tasks, you can change the view to view your tasks as a detailed list, simple list, priority list, or a complete list. Change the view of your tasks to fit your current needs. For example, if you want to see tasks listed according to their priority (High, Normal, or Low), you can display the tasks in the Prioritized view. You can also print tasks in a summarized list or include the details for each task.

To Change the Task View

Tasks can be displayed in different customized view layouts. By displaying tasks in Detailed view, you can view all tasks, including completed tasks. The following steps change the view to Detailed view. *Why? To see the total picture of what you have to accomplish, the Detailed view provides all the task details, including task subject, status, due date, and categories.*

1

• Click View on the ribbon to display the View tab.

• Click the Change View button (View tab | Current View group) to display the Change View gallery (Figure 4–71).

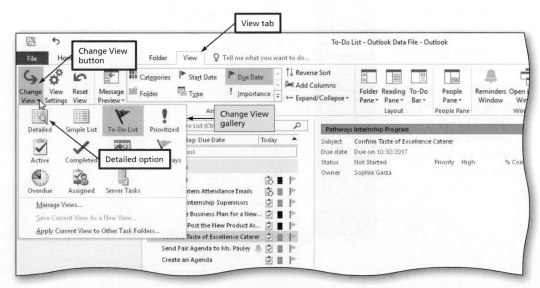

Figure 4–71

- Click Detailed to change the view (Figure 4–72).

Experiment

- Click the other views in the Current View gallery to view the tasks in other arrangements. When you are finished, click Detailed to return to Detailed view.

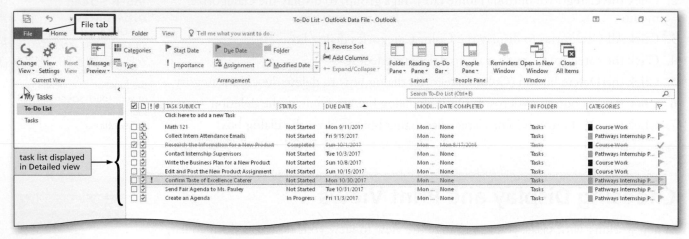

Figure 4–72

To Print Tasks

1 CREATE NEW TASK | 2 CATEGORIZE TASK | 3 CATEGORIZE EMAIL MESSAGE
4 ASSIGN TASK | 5 PRINT TASK | 6 CREATE AND USE NOTES

Outlook provides printing options based on the view and tasks you have selected. For example, in the To-Do List view, you can select a single task and print in Table Style or Menu Style. In Detailed view, which is the current view, you can print only in Table Style. The following steps print the tasks using Table Style. *Why? You might need a printed To-Do list to view when you are not working at your computer.*

- Click File on the ribbon to open the Backstage view.

- Click the Print tab in the Backstage view to display the Print gallery.

- If necessary, click Table Style in the Settings section to select a print format (Figure 4–73).

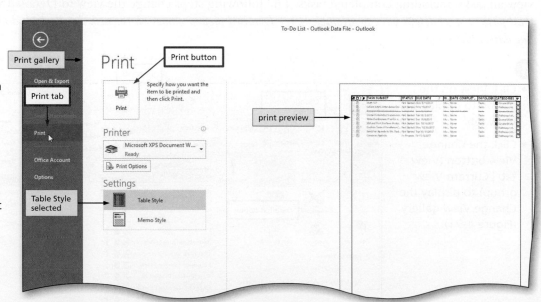

Figure 4–73

2
- Click the Print button to print the tasks in Table Style (Figure 4–74).

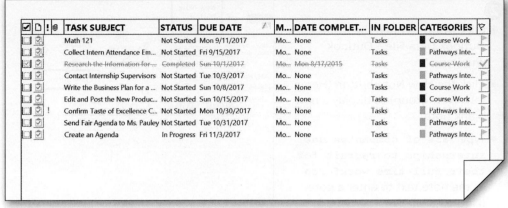

☑	◻	!	📎	TASK SUBJECT	STATUS	DUE DATE	M...	DATE COMPLET...	IN FOLDER	CATEGORIES	▽
◻	📋			Math 121	Not Started	Mon 9/11/2017	Mo...	None	Tasks	■ Course Work	
◻	📋			Collect Intern Attendance Em...	Not Started	Fri 9/15/2017	Mo...	None	Tasks	■ Pathways Inte...	
☑	📋			~~Research the Information for ...~~	~~Completed~~	~~Sun 10/1/2017~~	~~Mo...~~	~~Mon 8/17/2015~~	~~Tasks~~	~~■ Course Work~~	✓
◻	📋			Contact Internship Supervisors	Not Started	Tue 10/3/2017	Mo...	None	Tasks	■ Pathways Inte...	
◻	📋			Write the Business Plan for a ...	Not Started	Sun 10/8/2017	Mo...	None	Tasks	■ Course Work	
◻	📋			Edit and Post the New Produc...	Not Started	Sun 10/15/2017	Mo...	None	Tasks	■ Course Work	
◻	📋	!		Confirm Taste of Excellence C...	Not Started	Mon 10/30/2017	Mo...	None	Tasks	▮ Pathways Inte...	▷
◻	📋			Send Fair Agenda to Ms. Pauley	Not Started	Tue 10/31/2017	Mo...	None	Tasks	▮ Pathways Inte...	▷
◻	📋			Create an Agenda	In Progress	Fri 11/3/2017	Mo...	None	Tasks	▮ Pathways Inte...	▷

Figure 4–74

Using Notes

Outlook allows you to create the equivalent of paper notes using the Notes feature. Use notes to record ideas, spur-of-the-moment questions, and even words that you would like to recall or use at a later time. You can leave notes open on the screen while you continue using Outlook, or you can close them and view them in the Notes window. The Notes window contains the Navigation Pane and Notes Pane.

Can I use the Outlook Notes as sticky notes?

Notes are the electronic equivalent of yellow paper sticky notes. You can jot down notes for the directions that you find online to your interview, for example, or write questions that you want to remember to ask.

CONSIDER THIS

To Create a Note

1 CREATE NEW TASK | 2 CATEGORIZE TASK | 3 CATEGORIZE EMAIL MESSAGE
4 ASSIGN TASK | 5 PRINT TASK | 6 CREATE AND USE NOTES

Why? *A note can be a reminder from a phone conversation, information you find online for future reference, or even a grocery list.* When you enter text into a note, Outlook saves with the last modified date shown at the bottom of the note; you do not have to click a Save button. As Sophia was surfing the web, she found information that she wants to share with the interns. The following steps create a note reminder.

1
- Click the Navigation Options button (three dots) on the Navigation bar to display the Navigation Options menu (Figure 4–75).

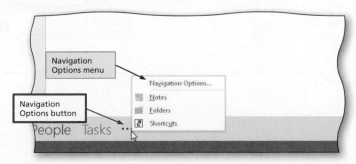

Figure 4–75

2

- Click Notes to open the Notes – Outlook Data File – Outlook window.

- Click the New Note button (Home tab | New group) to display a new blank note.

- Type `85% of companies use internships to recruit for their full-time workforce` as the note text to enter a note (Figure 4–76).

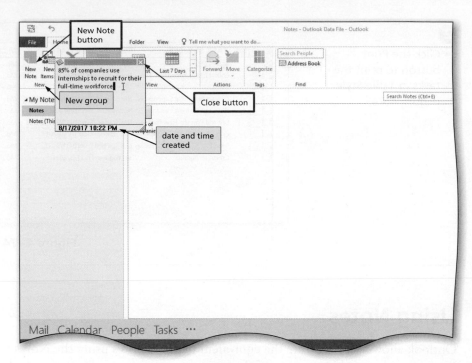

Figure 4–76

3

- Click the Close button to save and close the note (Figure 4–77).

Q&A

Why is my Notes view different from Figure 4–77?
There are three basic Notes views: Icon, Notes List, and Last 7 Days. Figure 4–77 displays the note in Icon view. To switch to Icon view, click the Icon button (Home tab | Current View group).

Can I print notes?
Yes. First, select the note(s) you want to print. To select multiple notes, hold the CTRL key while clicking the notes to print. Next, click the File tab to open the Backstage view, click the Print tab, and then click the Print button.

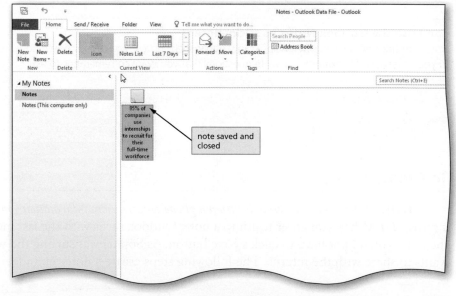

Figure 4–77

Other Ways

1. Press CTRL+SHIFT+N

To Change the Notes View

Why? *You would like to display your notes as a list instead of in the sticky note layout.* You decide to change your notes view to Notes List. The following step changes the view to Notes List view.

1

- Click the Notes List button (Home tab | Current View group) to change the view to Notes List (Figure 4–78).

🔍 **Experiment**

- Click the other views in the Current View group to view the notes in other arrangements. When you are finished, click Notes List to return to Notes List view.

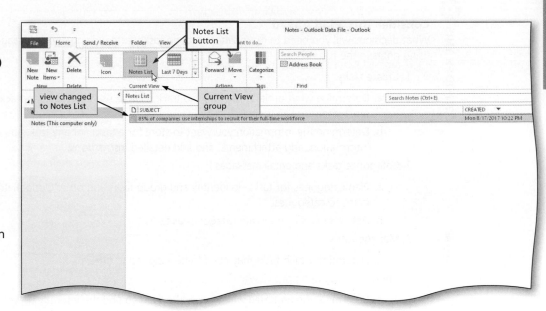

Figure 4–78

To Delete a Note

Why? *When you no longer need a note, you should delete it.* After sharing the note about recruiting interns for full-time positions, you decide to delete the note because you no longer need it. The following steps delete a note and close Outlook.

1

- If necessary, click the note about companies use of internships to select it.

- Click the Delete button (Home tab | Delete group) to delete the note (Figure 4–79).

2

- Close Outlook.

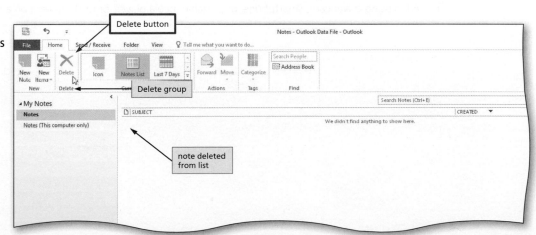

Figure 4–79

Summary

In this module, you have learned how to use Outlook to create tasks, categorize tasks, categorize email messages, manage tasks, print tasks, create notes, and print notes.

CONSIDER THIS

Consider This: Plan Ahead

What decisions will you need to make when creating tasks, categorizing email messages, choosing views, and using notes in the future?

1. Create tasks.

    a. Determine what projects you want to track. People use tasks to keep track of the projects that are most important to them.

    b. Determine the information you want to store for a task. For any task, you can store basic information, add attachments, and add detailed instructions.

2. Categorize tasks and email messages.

    a. Plan categories for tasks. To identify and group tasks and other Outlook items easily, assign the items to categories.

    b. Assign emails to the same categories as tasks.

3. Manage tasks.

    a. Determine which tasks may need to be assigned to others.

4. Choose display and print views.

    a. Determine the preferred way to view the tasks to find the information you are seeking.

    b. Determine how you want to view your tasks.

5. Use notes.

    a. Determine what reminder notes would assist you.

How should you submit solutions to questions in the assignments identified with a ✹ symbol?

Every assignment in this book contains one or more questions with a ✹ symbol. These questions require you to think beyond the assigned file. Present your solutions to the question in the format required by your instructor. Possible formats may include one or more of these options: write the answer; create a document that contains the answer; present your answer to the class; discuss your answer in a group; record the answer as audio or video using a webcam, smartphone, or portable media player; or post answers on a blog, wiki, or website.

Apply Your Knowledge

Reinforce the skills and apply the concepts you learned in this module.

Note: To complete this assignment, you will be required to use the Data Files. Please contact your instructor for information about accessing the Data Files.

Editing a Task List

Instructions: Run Outlook. Import the Apply Your Knowledge 4-1 Youth in Politics Tasks file from the Data Files folder into Outlook. This file contains tasks for Shea Padilla, a student leader of the Youth in Politics Club on campus. Many of the tasks have changed and some are incomplete. You need to revise the tasks and then create categories for her. Then, you will print the resulting task list (Figure 4–80).

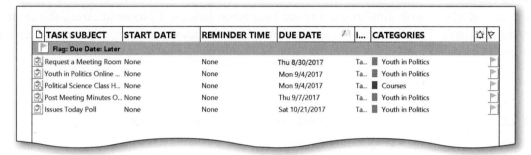

	TASK SUBJECT	START DATE	REMINDER TIME	DUE DATE	I...	CATEGORIES	
	Flag: Due Date: Later						
	Request a Meeting Room	None	None	Thu 8/30/2017	Ta...	Youth in Politics	
	Youth in Politics Online ...	None	None	Mon 9/4/2017	Ta...	Youth in Politics	
	Political Science Class H...	None	None	Mon 9/4/2017	Ta...	Courses	
	Post Meeting Minutes O...	None	None	Thu 9/7/2017	Ta...	Youth in Politics	
	Issues Today Poll	None	None	Sat 10/21/2017	Ta...	Youth in Politics	

Figure 4–80

Perform the following tasks:

1. Display the Apply Your Knowledge 4-1 Youth in Politics Tasks folder in the Outlook Tasks window as a To-Do List.

2. Change the due date of the Youth in Politics Online Newsletter task to September 4, 2017. Change the % Complete to 75%.

3. Change the task name of Post Minutes Online to Post Meeting Minutes Online. Configure the task as a recurring task that occurs every Thursday from September 7, 2017, until December 7, 2017.

4. Make Request a Meeting Room a recurring task that occurs every Wednesday from August 30, 2017, until December 6, 2017. Change the status to Waiting on Someone Else.

5. Change the due date of the Issues Today Poll task to October 21, 2017. In the Task body, type **Create an online poll with 10 questions gauging which issues are important to our student population.**

6. Make Political Science Class Homework a recurring task that occurs every Monday, Wednesday, and Saturday from September 4, 2017, until December 15, 2017.

7. Create two color categories. Name the first one Youth in Politics and the second one Courses. Use the colors of your choice. Categorize each task accordingly.

8. Print the final task list in Table Style, as shown in Figure 4–80, and then submit it in the format specified by your instructor.

Continued >

Apply Your Knowledge *continued*

9. Export the Apply Your Knowledge 4-1 Tasks folder to a USB flash drive and then delete the folder from the hard disk. Submit the .pst file in the format specified by your instructor.

10. ✳ What task categories would you create to categorize the tasks in your personal life? Name at least five categories.

Extend Your Knowledge

Extend the skills you learned in this module and experiment with new skills. You may need to use Help to complete the assignment.

Creating Notes

Instructions: Run Outlook. Import the Extend Your Knowledge 4-1 Notes file from the Data Files folder into Outlook. This file has no notes, so you will create notes, categorize them, and then print the notes.

Perform the following tasks:

1. Use Help to learn about customizing notes.

2. Display the Extend Your Knowledge 4-1 Notes folder in the Outlook Notes window.

3. Create the following notes for a landscaper:
   - Send an email message to Lila Lucas about the mulch delivery time.
   - Pick up seasonal flowers for Layton job.
   - Order irrigation system for Poplar Forest Golf Course.
   - Create a snow removal contract for Liberty Public School System.
   - Create a formal bid for a landscape design for Tracey Thompson.
   - Advertise our snow removal services on website.

4. Select the Irrigation system task, and then create a color category named ASAP. Use a color of your choosing.

5. Categorize the notes about snow removal with a new "Snow Removal" category. Use a color of your choosing.

6. Categorize the remaining notes using a new "Complete This Week" category. Use a color of your choosing.

7. Replace "Tracey Thompson" in the "Create a formal bid for a landscape design for Tracey Thompson." note with the name of your favorite teacher.

8. Change the view to Notes List. Print the notes in Table Style, as shown in Figure 4–81, and then submit them in the format specified by your instructor.

9. Export the Extend Your Knowledge 4-1 Notes folder to a USB flash drive and then submit the file in the format specified by your instructor.

10. ✳ When is it appropriate to create a note instead of creating a task?

□	SUBJECT	CREATED ▽	CATEGORIES
	Advertise our snow removal services on website.	Fri 8/21/2018 10:24 AM	■ Snow Removal
	Create a formal bid for a landscape design for Tracey Thompson.	Fri 8/21/2018 10:24 AM	■ Complete This Week
	Create a snow removal contract for Liberty Public School System.	Fri 8/21/2018 10:23 AM	■ Snow Removal
	Order irrigation system for Poplar Forest Golf Course.	Fri 8/21/2018 10:23 AM	■ ASAP
	Pick up seasonal flowers for Layton job.	Fri 8/21/2018 10:20 AM	■ Complete This Week
	Send an email message to Lila Lucas about the mulch delivery time.	Fri 8/21/2018 10:20 AM	■ Complete This Week

Figure 4–81

Expand Your World: Cloud and Web Technologies

Creating an Outlook.com Web-Based Task List Online

Create a solution that uses cloud or web technologies by learning and investigating on your own from general guidance.

Instructions: Outlook.com allows you to enter and maintain a task list from any computer with a web browser and an Internet connection. You are to use Outlook.com to create a task list for Bravo Tapas Café using the information in Table 4–2. You have five events coming up in the next month and want to create the tasks along with the reminders for them.

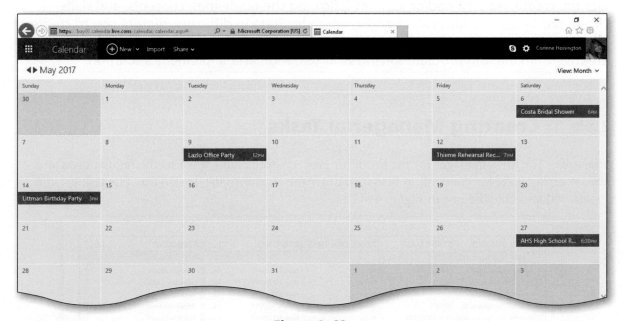

Figure 4–82

Continued >

Expand Your World: Cloud and Web Technologies *continued*

Perform the following tasks:

1. Start your web browser and navigate to outlook.com.

2. Sign in to outlook.com. If necessary, sign up for a Microsoft account.

3. View the calendar.

4. Create the tasks shown in Table 4–2.

Table 4–2 Bravo Tapas Cafe Tasks				
Event	Due Date	Time	Reminder Time	How Long
Costa Bridal Shower	May 6, 2017	6:00 PM	2 days before	2 hours
Lazlo Office Party	May 9, 2017	12:00 PM	2 weeks before	1.5 hours
Thieme Rehearsal Dinner	May 12, 2017	7:00 PM	1 week before	3 hours
Littman Birthday Party	May 14, 2017	3:00 PM	1 hour before	2 hours
AHS High School Reunion	May 27, 2017	6:30 PM	1 week before	4.5 hours

5. When you finish adding the tasks, share the calendar with your instructor. Your instructor should be able to view the details on your calendar but should not be able to edit anything. If you have additional items on your calendar that you do not want to share with your instructor, contact your instructor and determine an alternate way to submit this assignment.

6. ✳ When would you want to add your tasks to Outlook.com instead of using Microsoft Outlook? Is there a way to automatically get your tasks in Microsoft Outlook to appear in your Outlook.com account?

In the Labs

Design, create, modify, and/or use files following the guidelines, concepts, and skills presented in this module. Labs 1 and 2, which increase in difficulty, require you to create solutions based on what you learned in the module; Lab 3 requires you to apply your creative thinking and problem-solving skills to design and implement a solution.

Lab 1: **Creating Managerial Tasks**

Problem: You are a manager for the Fresh Air grocery store. Table 4–3 lists the regular tasks and the recurring tasks for your role as manager. Enter the tasks into the To-Do list. The task list you create will look like the one in Figure 4–83.

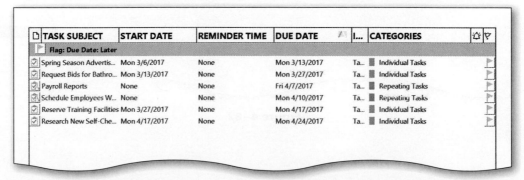

	TASK SUBJECT	START DATE	REMINDER TIME	DUE DATE		I...	CATEGORIES		
⚑	**Flag: Due Date: Later**								
✓	Spring Season Advertis...	Mon 3/6/2017	None	Mon 3/13/2017		Ta...	■ Individual Tasks		⚑
✓	Request Bids for Bathro...	Mon 3/13/2017	None	Mon 3/27/2017		Ta...	■ Individual Tasks		⚑
✓	Payroll Reports	None	None	Fri 4/7/2017		Ta...	■ Repeating Tasks		⚑
✓	Schedule Employees W...	None	None	Mon 4/10/2017		Ta...	■ Repeating Tasks		⚑
✓	Reserve Training Facilities	Mon 3/27/2017	None	Mon 4/17/2017		Ta...	■ Individual Tasks		⚑
✓	Research New Self-Che...	Mon 4/17/2017	None	Mon 4/24/2017		Ta...	■ Individual Tasks		⚑

Figure 4–83

Perform the following tasks:

1. Create an Outlook Data File named Lab 4-1 Fresh Air Grocery Store.

2. Create a Tasks folder named Lab 4-1 Tasks.

3. Create the regular tasks in the Lab 4-1 Tasks folder using the information listed in Table 4–3.

Table 4–3 Fresh Air Grocery Story Managerial Tasks				
Task	**Start Date**	**Due Date**	**Status**	**Priority**
Spring Season Advertisements	3/6/2017	3/13/2017	In Progress	Normal
Request Bids for Bathroom Update	3/13/2017	3/27/2017		Normal
Reserve Training Facilities	3/27/2017	4/17/2017		High
Research New Self-Checkout System	4/17/2017	4/24/2017		High

4. Create the recurring tasks in the Lab 4-1 Tasks folder using the information listed in Table 4–4.

Table 4–4 Fresh Air Grocery Store Managerial Recurring Tasks			
Task	**Start Date**	**Due Date**	**Recurrence**
Schedule Employees Work Hours	4/10/2017	end of year	Monthly, second Monday
Payroll Reports	4/7/2017	20 occurrences	Weekly, Fridays

5. Open the Schedule Employees Work Hours task and add the detail in the task body that **Noah Cunningham cannot work on Monday or Wednesday due to college classes**.

6. Create a color category called Individual Tasks, using a color of your choice. Categorize the tasks in Table 4–3.

7. Create a color category called Repeating Tasks, using a color of your choice. Categorize all tasks with this category in Table 4–4.

8. Print the Lab 4-1 Tasks list in Table Style, and then submit it in a format specified by your instructor (Figure 4–83).

9. Export the Lab 4-1 Tasks folder to your USB flash drive and then delete the folder from the hard disk.

10. ✸ Why is it a good idea to include as much detail as possible in each task?

Lab 2: **Creating a Car Maintenance Task List**

Problem: You are the owner of a Toyota Prius and decide to enter the recommended car maintenance checklist into Outlook. You need to create a list of all the tasks and categorize them appropriately (Figure 4–84).

Continued >

In the Labs *continued*

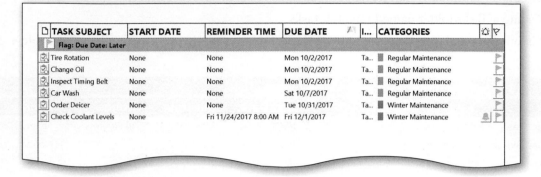

Figure 4–84

Perform the following tasks:

1. Create an Outlook Data File named Lab 4-2 Car Maintenance Tasks.
2. Create the tasks using the information listed in Table 4–5.

Table 4–5   Car Maintenance Tasks

Task	Task Body	Due Date	Status	Priority	Reminder
Check Coolant Levels	Complete before first freeze	12/1/2017		High	11/24/2017
Order Deicer	Sale on Amazon	10/31/2017	In Progress	Low	

3. Create the recurring tasks using the information listed in Table 4–6.

Table 4–6   Car Maintenance Recurring Tasks

Task	Due Date	Task Body	Recurrence
Tire Rotation	10/2/2017	Request wheel alignment	Yearly, No End Date
Change Oil	10/2/2017	Replace oil filter	First Monday of Each Month, Every 2 Months, No End Date
Inspect Timing Belt	10/2/2017	Replace as needed	Yearly, No End Date
Car Wash	10/7/2017	Exterior and interior	Weekly, Saturday, No End Date

4. Categorize the Winter tasks as Winter Maintenance by creating a new color category.
5. Categorize the remaining tasks as Regular Maintenance by creating a new color category.
6. Add a note **A Toyota Prius battery replacement costs approximately $2500**.
7. Print the tasks in Table Style, and then submit the task list in the format specified by your instructor.
8. Export the Lab 4-2 Car Maintenance Tasks to a USB flash drive and then submit the file in the format specified by your instructor.
9. ✸ Why is it a good idea to update the status of a task as it changes?

Lab 3: **Creating and Assigning Tasks**

Research and Collaboration

Part 1:   Your Western Civilization History instructor has assigned a term paper to be completed by a team of three people. Each person in the team is responsible for researching one aspect of the topic "Class Struggles in European History." The three subtopics are Feudalism, Immigration, and Industrial Revolution. After you perform adequate research and write your part of the paper, send it to another team member for a peer review. After all team members have performed a peer review, finalize the content, compile into one document, and prepare it for submission. Using Outlook, each team member should create tasks for the work they have to perform on the term paper (for example, research, writing the first draft, sending for peer review, performing a peer review, finalizing content, compiling into one master document, preparing for submission, and submitting the paper). Add as much information to the tasks as possible, such as the start date, due date, priority, status, and percent complete. Categorize the tasks appropriately. Assign the peer review task to the team member who will review your content. Finally, send a status report to all team members showing how much of each task you currently have completed. Submit the task list in a format specified by your instructor.

Part 2:   ✹ You have made several decisions while creating the task list in this assignment, such as which tasks to create, what details to add to each task, and how to categorize each task. What was the rationale behind each of these decisions?

Inbox - Outlook Data File - Outlook
Microsoft Outlook 2016

File   Home   Send / Receive   Folder   View   Q Tell me what you want to do...

5 | Customizing Outlook

Objectives

You will have mastered the material in this module when you can:

- Add another email account
- Insert Quick Parts in email messages
- Insert hyperlinks in email messages
- Insert images in email messages
- Create a search folder
- Set the default message format
- Create an email signature
- Format a signature

- Assign signatures
- Customize personal stationery
- Configure junk email options
- Create rules
- Configure AutoArchive settings
- Adjust calendar settings
- Subscribe to a news feed

This module covers features and functions common to customizing Outlook 2016.

Roadmap

In this module, you will learn how to perform basic customizing tasks. The following roadmap identifies general activities you will perform as you progress through this module:

1. CUSTOMIZE EMAIL MESSAGES
2. CUSTOMIZE SIGNATURES and STATIONERY
3. MANAGE JUNK EMAIL FILTERS
4. CONFIGURE RULES
5. CHANGE CALENDAR OPTIONS
6. ADD a NEWS FEED

At the beginning of step instructions throughout the module, you will see an abbreviated form of this roadmap. The abbreviated roadmap uses colors to indicate module progress: gray means the module is beyond that activity, blue means the task being shown is covered in that activity, and black means that activity is yet to be covered. For example, the following abbreviated roadmap indicates the section would be about managing junk email filters.

1 CUSTOMIZE EMAIL MESSAGES | 2 CUSTOMIZE SIGNATURES & STATIONERY | 3 MANAGE JUNK EMAIL FILTERS
4 CONFIGURE RULES | 5 CHANGE CALENDAR OPTIONS | 6 ADD NEWS FEED

Use the abbreviated roadmap as a progress guide while you read or step through the instructions in this module.

Microsoft Outlook 2016

Inbox - Outlook Data File - Outlook

File   Home   Send / Receive   Folder   View   ♀ Tell me what you want to do...

Introduction to Customizing Outlook

Outlook provides many options for customizing your experience when working with email messages, calendars, and other items. From creating custom email signatures to adjusting how the workweek is displayed in your calendar, you can make Outlook fit your requirements so that you can use it more efficiently. For example, a rule is a command that tells Outlook how to process an email message. Using rules, you quickly can categorize or flag your email messages as they arrive so that you can identify at a glance which ones you first want to address. You can change the fonts and colors that are used by default as well. Outlook's customization options can help you become more productive.

Project — Adding a New Email Account and Customizing Options

People often have more than one email account. In fact, some people have more than they can remember. Outlook allows you to manage multiple email accounts. That way, you can read your email messages from all accounts without needing to use several email programs such as one for a Microsoft email account, another for a Gmail account, and a third for a school or work email account.

The project in this module follows general guidelines and uses Outlook to add a new email account and customize Outlook options, as shown in Figure 5–1.

(a) New Email Account

(b) Signature

© iStock.com/Alex Belomlinsky

(c) Customized Calendar

(d) Email Rules

Figure 5–1

Adding New Email Accounts

As you learned in Module 1, when setting up an email account, you need to know basic information such as the email address and password. For example, in Figure 5–2, the first mailbox is displayed as Outlook Data File (Sophia Module 5.pst). The second mailbox displayed in Figure 5–2 is an additional Internet-based email account named sophiagarza99@hotmail.com.

BTW
**The Ribbon and
Screen Resolution**
Outlook may change how
the groups and buttons
within the groups appear
on the ribbon, depending
on the computer or mobile
device's screen resolution.
Thus, your ribbon may look
different from the ones in
this book if you are using a
screen resolution other than
1366 × 768.

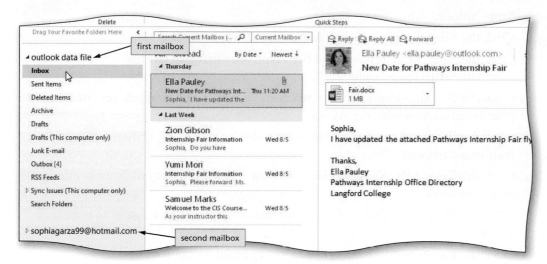

Figure 5–2

After you install Outlook, the Auto Account Setup feature runs and helps you to set up the first email account that Outlook manages. You can add another account and then use Outlook to manage two or more mailboxes.

Depending on your instructor's preferences and your email services, you can perform the steps in this module by opening an Outlook data file provided with the book and by adding a new email account to Outlook. Before you can add a new email account in Outlook, you must have an account set up with an email service provider that is different from any other account already set up in Outlook. For example, you might have a Microsoft account that provides email service. If you have not configured this account in Outlook, you can complete the steps in this module to do so.

To add a new account, you use the Add Account option in the Backstage view, which lets you add an account using the Add Account dialog box. If you want to add an account and change advanced settings, you should use the Account Settings dialog box instead.

My work email address requires additional information to set up my account. Where do I place this server information?

For the work email account you plan to add, make sure you know the account properties and settings before you start to add the account. Gather the following information: type of account, such as email, text messaging, or fax mail; your name, email address, and password; and the server information, including account type and the addresses of incoming and outgoing mail servers. You typically receive the server information from the IT staff at your place of employment. If additional server information is needed, click Manual setup or additional server types when you create an account to add this information.

CONSIDER THIS

To Add an Email Account

Sophia has a second email address that she dedicates to mailing lists. Sophia uses a second email account (sophiagarza99@hotmail.com) within Outlook so that she can manage both her primary and secondary email accounts. To follow all the steps within this module, an additional email account is necessary.

If you choose to add an email account to Outlook, you would use the following steps. If you are performing these steps on your computer, enter the name, email address, and password for an email account you own but have not yet added to Outlook.

1. Run Outlook.
2. Click the File tab and then click Add Account.
3. Click the Your Name text box and then type your first and last name to associate your name with the account.
4. Click the E-mail Address text box and then type your full email address to associate your email address with the account.
5. Click the Password text box and then type your password to verify the password to your email account.
6. Click the Retype Password text box and then type your password again to confirm your password.
7. Click the Next button to configure your account settings and sign in to your mail server.
8. Click the Finish button to add the secondary email account.
9. Click the new email account to select it.

BTW
Multiple Email Accounts
If you have multiple email accounts configured in Outlook, you can decide which email account to use each time you compose and send a new email message. To select the account from which to send the email message, click the From button in the Untitled - Message window, and then click the desired email account.

BTW
Touch Screen Differences
The Office and Windows interfaces may vary if you are using a touch screen. For this reason, you might notice that the function or appearance of your touch screen differs slightly from this module's presentation.

Customizing Email Messages

No matter what type of message you are composing in Outlook, whether business or personal, you always can find a way to add your unique style. With a variety of features such as background colors, graphics, designs, hyperlinks, and custom signatures, your email message starts as a blank, generic canvas and becomes an attractive, memorable communication.

To Add a Hyperlink to an Email Message

1 CUSTOMIZE EMAIL MESSAGES | 2 CUSTOMIZE SIGNATURES & STATIONERY | 3 MANAGE JUNK EMAIL FILTERS
4 CONFIGURE RULES | 5 CHANGE CALENDAR OPTIONS | 6 ADD NEWS FEED

Zion Gibson asked Sophia to send him the web address of the Kennedy Center internship site. Zion is hoping to land an internship at the Kennedy Center and wants to check the webpage for more information. Sophia can send him the web address as a hyperlink in an email message. *Why? Outlook automatically formats hyperlinks so that recipients can use them to access a website directly.* To follow the link, the recipient can hold down the CTRL key and click the hyperlink, which is formatted as blue, underlined text by default. The following steps add a hyperlink within an email message.

- If the Sophia Module 5.pst Outlook Data File is not open in Outlook, click outlook data file in the Navigation Pane to display its contents.
- Click the Inbox folder to display the mailbox.
- Click the New Email button (Home tab | New group) to open the Untitled - Message (HTML) window.
- Type `zion.gibson@outlook.com` in the To text box to enter the email address of the recipient.

- Click the Subject text box, and then type `Kennedy Center Internship` to enter the subject line.

- Press the TAB key to move the insertion point into the message area (Figure 5–3).

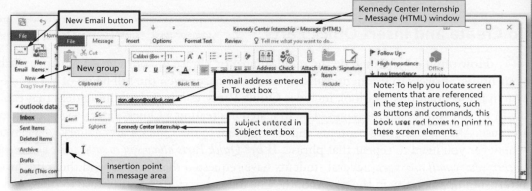

Figure 5–3

2

- Type `Zion,` as the greeting line and then press the ENTER key to insert a new line.

- Type `Per your request, the Kennedy Center internship site can be found at` and then press the SPACEBAR to enter the message text.

- Click Insert on the ribbon to display the Insert tab (Figure 5–4).

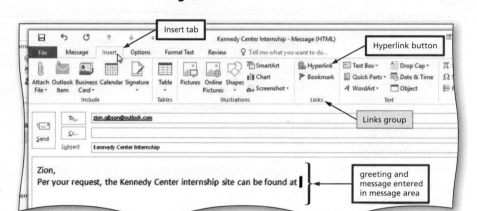

Figure 5–4

3

- Click the Hyperlink button (Insert tab | Links group) to display the Insert Hyperlink dialog box.

- In the Address box, type `kennedy-center.org/education/internships` to enter a hyperlink to a web address (Figure 5–5).

 Why do I not have to type the http:// part of the web address?
When you insert a hyperlink, Outlook does not require the hypertext transfer protocol (http) portion of the address.

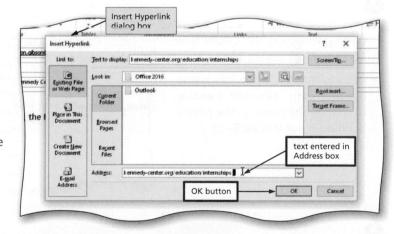

Figure 5–5

4

- Click the OK button to insert the hyperlink in the message body (Figure 5–6).

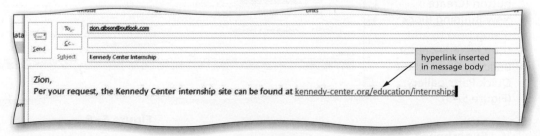

Figure 5–6

Other Ways

1. Press CTRL + K

To Create and Insert Quick Parts

How often do you include the same snippet or phrase in your correspondence, such as directions to your home, answers to frequently answered questions, or even the full name of a school or business? To assist you in these situations, Outlook includes **Quick Parts**, common building blocks that can be recycled and used again within your email messages. The first step in creating a Quick Part is to select the content that you want to reuse. After naming the contents and saving them to the Quick Parts gallery, you can use the Quick Part whenever you need to repeat that phrase. *Why? Quick Parts allow you to save pieces of content to reuse them easily within your email messages.* Several students have requested that Sophia send them the link to the Kennedy Center internship opportunity in the past month. The following steps save a phrase to the Quick Parts gallery.

- Select the phrase 'Per your request, the Kennedy Internship site can be found at kennedy-center.org/education/internships'.

- Click the Quick Parts button (Insert tab | Text group) to display the Quick Parts list of options (Figure 5–7).

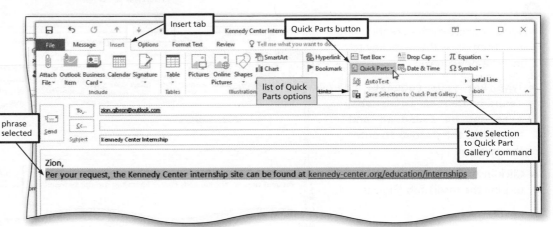

Figure 5–7

- Click 'Save Selection to Quick Part Gallery' to display the Create New Building Block dialog box.

- Replace the text in the Name text box by typing `Kennedy Center` to change the name of the new building block (Figure 5–8).

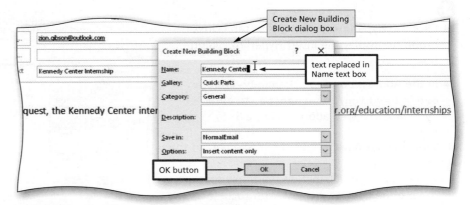

Figure 5–8

❸

- Click the OK button (Create New Building Block dialog box) to add the Kennedy Center Building Block to the Quick Parts gallery (Figure 5–9).

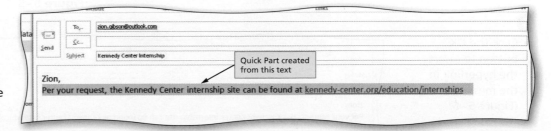

Figure 5–9

Experiment

- Click the Quick Parts button (Insert tab | Text group) to display a list of Quick Parts options. Click Kennedy Center to insert the building block into the email message. When you are finished, click the Undo button on the Quick Access Toolbar to remove the Kennedy Center internship text.

To Insert an Image into an Email Message

1 CUSTOMIZE EMAIL MESSAGES | 2 CUSTOMIZE SIGNATURES & STATIONERY | 3 MANAGE JUNK EMAIL FILTERS
4 CONFIGURE RULES | 5 CHANGE CALENDAR OPTIONS | 6 ADD NEWS FEED

As you learned in Module 1, you can attach files to an email message, including image files. Outlook also provides the ability to insert an image directly within the message body of an email message. *Why? The recipient can quickly view the image without downloading an attachment or saving the picture on their computer.* Sophia would like to add a recent picture taken by one of their interns of the Kennedy Center. The picture is available with the Data Files for Module 05. The following steps insert an image into an email message.

- Click after the kennedy-center.org/ education/internships web address, and then press the ENTER key twice to move the insertion point to a new line.

- Click the Pictures button (Insert tab | Illustrations group) to display the Insert Picture dialog box.

- Navigate to the file location, in this case, the Module 05 folder in the Outlook folder provided with the Data Files.

- Click Kennedy to select the photo of the Kennedy Center (Figure 5–10).

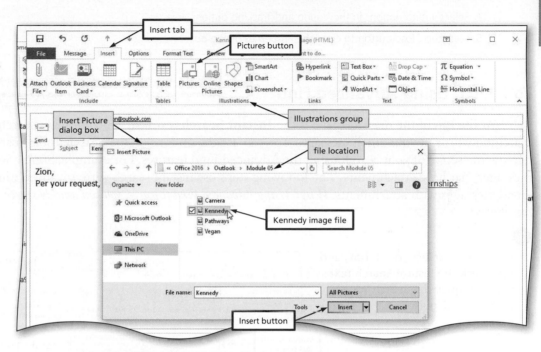

Figure 5–10

- Click the Insert button (shown in Figure 5–10) to add an image to the message body (Figure 5–11).

- Click the Save button on the Quick Access Toolbar to save the email message in the Drafts folder.

- Close the Kennedy Center Internship - Message (HTML) window.

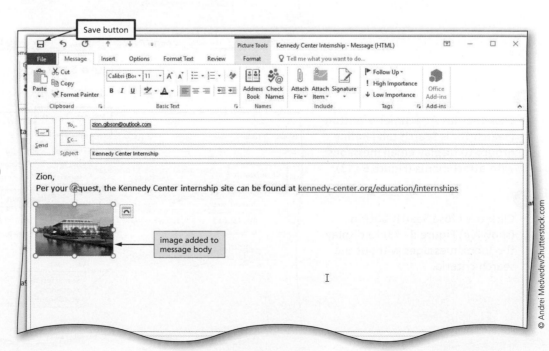

Figure 5–11

CONSIDER THIS

Can I use Outlook to allow a message recipient to vote, such as when I want to poll club members for their preferred speaker for our next event?

When composing a message, you can configure voting options by using the Properties dialog box. For example, you can choose to use voting buttons as well as request delivery and read receipts. To configure voting options:

1. While composing a message, click Options on the ribbon to display the Options tab.

2. Click the Use Voting Buttons button (Options tab | Tracking group) to display a list of options.

3. Click Custom to display the Properties dialog box.

4. Select voting options in the Voting and Tracking options area.

5. Click the Close button to close the Properties dialog box.

To Search Using Advanced Find

1 CUSTOMIZE EMAIL MESSAGES | 2 CUSTOMIZE SIGNATURES & STATIONERY | 3 MANAGE JUNK EMAIL FILTERS
4 CONFIGURE RULES | 5 CHANGE CALENDAR OPTIONS | 6 ADD NEWS FEED

At the top of the message pane is the **Instant Search** text box, which displays search results based on any matching words in your email messages. You can use the options on the Search Tools Search tab to broaden or narrow the scope of your search using the Advanced Find features. For example, Sophia would like to search for messages that have attachments. The following steps use instant search with Advanced Find features to locate email messages with attachments. *Why? Using Advanced Find features, you can quickly search for an email with an attachment.*

- If necessary, select your Inbox, and then click the Instant Search text box to display the Search Tools Search tab (Figure 5–12).

Figure 5–12

- Click the Has Attachments button (Search Tools Search tab | Refine group) to display email messages with attachments (Figure 5–13).

- Click the Close Search button (shown in Figure 5–13) to display the Inbox messages without the search criteria.

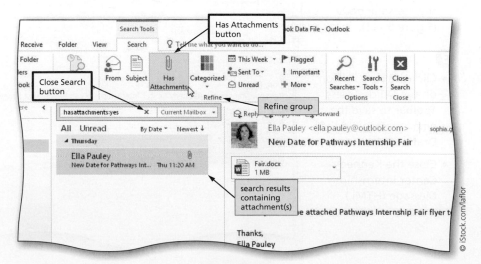

Figure 5–13

To Create a New Search Folder

Use search folders to gather email messages and other items into a folder based on search criteria. For example, Sophia wants to place messages with attachments into a separate search folder. You might want to create other search folders to view all messages that you have not read yet or to combine messages from a specific person. The following steps create a new search folder for email messages with attachments. *Why?* *By using search folders, you can better manage large amounts of email.*

1

- Click Folder on the ribbon to display the Folder tab.

- Click the New Search Folder button (Folder tab | New group) to display the New Search Folder dialog box (Figure 5–14).

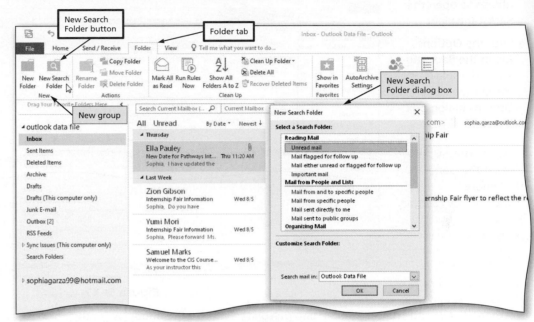

Figure 5–14

2

- Scroll down to view the Organizing Mail category.

- Click 'Mail with attachments' (New Search Folder dialog box) to select the type of email to store in a search folder (Figure 5–15).

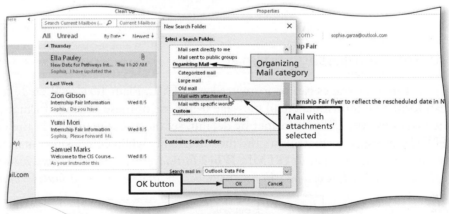

Figure 5–15

3

- Click the OK button (New Search Folder dialog box) to create a new search folder that searches for and collects email messages with attachments (Figure 5–16).

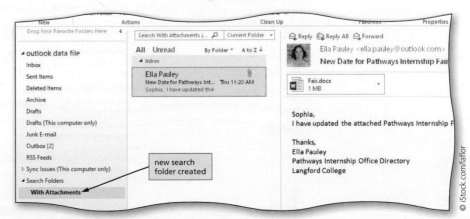

Figure 5–16

Outlook Module 5

To Display Outlook Options

Why? *To customize your Outlook email with default settings such as the message format, you use the Outlook Options dialog box.* The following step displays the Outlook Options dialog box.

- Click File on the ribbon to open the Backstage view.

- Click the Options tab in the Backstage view to display the Outlook Options dialog box (Figure 5–17).

Q&A

What options can I set in the General category?
The General category allows you to customize the user interface by enabling the Mini Toolbar and Live Preview, and by changing the

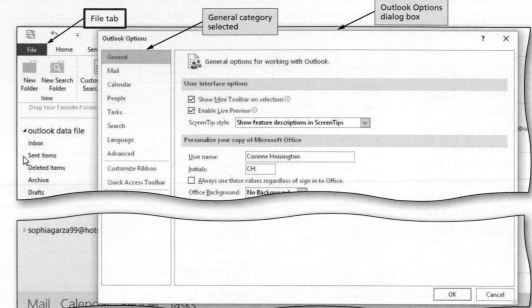

Figure 5–17

ScreenTip style and Theme. You can also personalize Microsoft Outlook by specifying your user name and initials. The Start up options allow you to specify whether Outlook should be the default program for email, contacts, and calendar.

To Set the Message Format

Email messages can be formatted as HTML, Plain Text, or Rich Text. As you learned in Module 1, you can format an individual email message using one of these message formats. To make sure that all your email messages use the HTML format by default, set the message format in the Outlook Options dialog box. The HTML message format allows the most flexibility when composing email messages. The following steps set the default message format to HTML. *Why?* *Instead of changing each email message to a different format, you can set a default in the Outlook options. All new messages are displayed in the default format.*

- Click Mail in the Category list to display the Mail options (Figure 5–18).

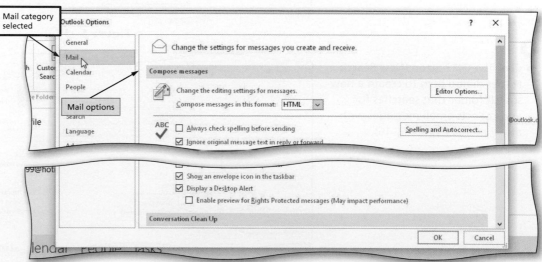

Figure 5–18

2

• Click the 'Compose messages in this format' box arrow to display a list of formatting options (Figure 5–19).

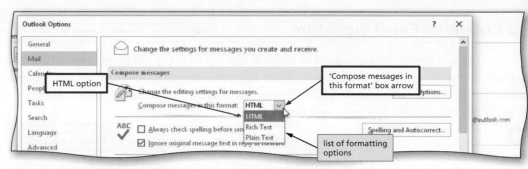

Figure 5–19

3

• If necessary, click HTML to set the default message format to HTML (Figure 5–20).

Q&A

What if HTML already is selected as the default message format?
Depending on who set up Outlook, the default message format already might be HTML. In that case, you can skip Step 3.

What if I want to choose a different format?
When you display the available message formats, choose the type you want to use. For example, if you want all new email messages to be in the Plain Text format, click the Plain Text option.

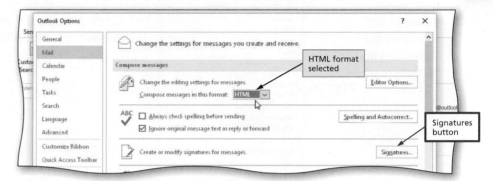

Figure 5–20

Can I sort my email messages by conversation instead of by date, which is the default setting?

Yes, you can sort by conversation if you prefer to sort your email messages by their subject field grouped by conversation. To sort by conversation:

1. Click View on the ribbon to display the View tab.

2. Click the Show as Conversations check box (View tab | Messages group) to select Show as Conversations.

Your Inbox is re-sorted, linking email messages in the same conversation together. Individual messages that do not belong to a conversation will look the same as before, while those involved in conversations will have a white triangle on the upper-left part of the message header.

Creating Signatures and Stationery

You can configure Outlook to add signatures to your email messages automatically. A **signature** is similar to a closing set of lines in a formal letter. It can include your full name, job title, email address, phone number, company information, and logo. You even can include business cards in your signature.

If you have more than one email account, you need to select the account for which you want to create the signature. You can create the signature while you are creating an email message or you can use the Outlook Options dialog box at any other time. If you create the signature while writing an email message, you have to apply the signature to the email message, because Outlook will not insert it automatically. If you create a signature using the Outlook Options dialog box, it is added automatically to all subsequent messages.

Besides adding signatures to your email messages, you can customize the **stationery**, which determines the appearance of your email messages, including background, fonts, and colors. You can pick fonts to use in the email message text, or you can select a theme or stationery design and apply that to your email messages.

To Create an Email Signature

An email signature provides a consistent closing to every email message without requiring you to retype signature lines repeatedly. Sophia would like to create an email signature named Work that includes her name, office name, and email address. The following steps create an email signature. *Why? An email signature provides your contact information in a condensed format, typically two to four lines.*

- Click the Signatures button (Outlook Options dialog box) (shown in Figure 5–20) to display the Signatures and Stationery dialog box (Figure 5–21).

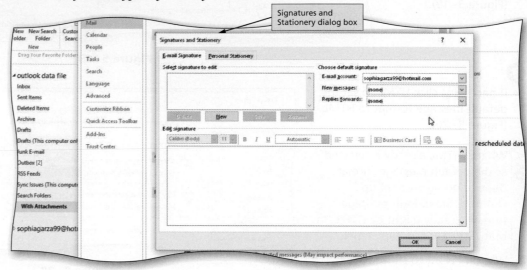

Figure 5–21

- Click the New button (Signatures and Stationery dialog box) to display the New Signature dialog box (Figure 5–22).

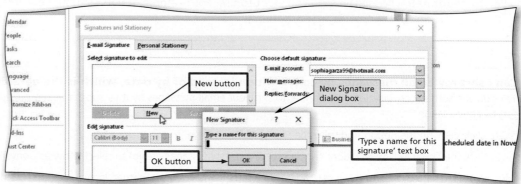

Figure 5–22

❸

- Type `Work` in the 'Type a name for this signature' text box to enter a name for the signature.

- Click the OK button (shown in Figure 5–22) to name the signature (Figure 5–23).

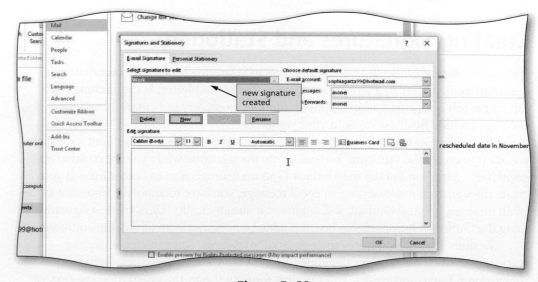

Figure 5–23

To Format an Email Signature

The email message signature will include Sophia's name, office name, and email address. In addition, she wants to use a format that suits her style. The format of the signature should be attractive, but maintain a professional, clean appearance. The following steps format and add the text for the signature. *Why? An email signature should convey the impression you are trying to make. A company might require employees to use a certain email signature when communicating with customers to create a consistent look.*

- Click the Font box arrow (Signatures and Stationery dialog box) to display a list of fonts (Figure 5–24).

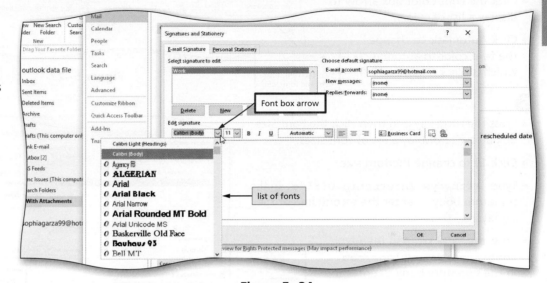

Figure 5–24

- Scroll down until Garamond is visible, and then click Garamond to select the font.
- Click the Font Size box arrow to display a list of font sizes (Figure 5–25).

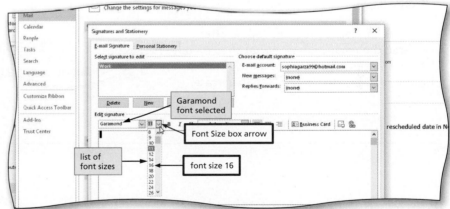

Figure 5–25

- Click 16 to change the font size.
- Click the Bold button to change the font to bold.
- Click the Font Color box arrow to display a list of colors (Figure 5–26).

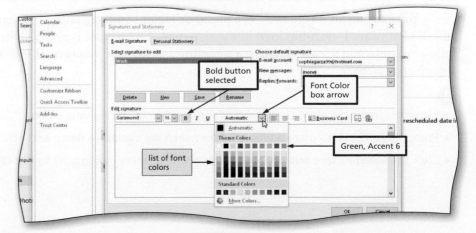

Figure 5–26

- Click Green, Accent 6 (first row, last column) to change the font color.

- Type `Sophia Garza` in the signature body to enter the first line of the signature.

- Click the Font Color box arrow to display a list of colors.

- Click Automatic to change the font color to automatic, which is black (Figure 5–27).

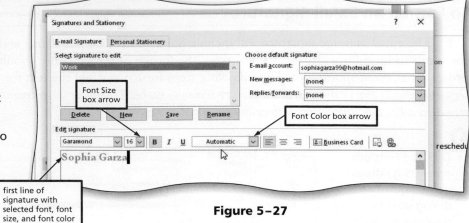

Figure 5–27

- Press the ENTER key and then click the Font Size box arrow to display a list of font sizes.

- Click 12 to change the font size.

- Type `Pathways Internship Office` in the signature body to enter the second line of the signature.

- Press the ENTER key and then type `sophia.garza@outlook.com` in the signature body to enter the third line of the signature (Figure 5–28).

Q&A Outlook capitalized the S in Sophia after I entered the email address. What should I do?
If you want the signature to match the figures in this module, change the S to lowercase.

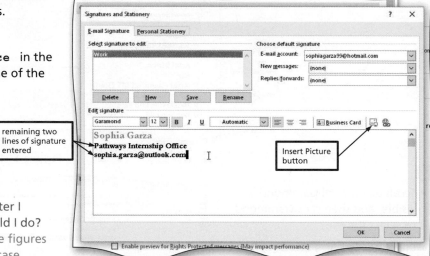

Figure 5–28

To Add an Image to an Email Signature

1 CUSTOMIZE EMAIL MESSAGES | 2 CUSTOMIZE SIGNATURES & STATIONERY | 3 MANAGE JUNK EMAIL FILTERS
4 CONFIGURE RULES | 5 CHANGE CALENDAR OPTIONS | 6 ADD NEWS FEED

You can add an image such as a photo or logo to your signature to create visual appeal. Sophia wants to add the Pathways Internship logo in the signature. The picture is available in the Data Files for Module 05. The following steps add a logo image to a signature and save the changes. *Why? Adding a logo can promote brand or organization identity.*

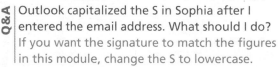

- Move the insertion point to the end of the first line of the signature text.

- Press the ENTER key to place a blank line between the signature name and office name.

- Click the Insert Picture button (Signatures and Stationery dialog box) to display the Insert Picture dialog box.

- Navigate to the file location, in this case, the Module 05 folder in the Outlook folder provided with the Data Files.

- Click Pathways to select the Pathways Internship logo (Figure 5–29).

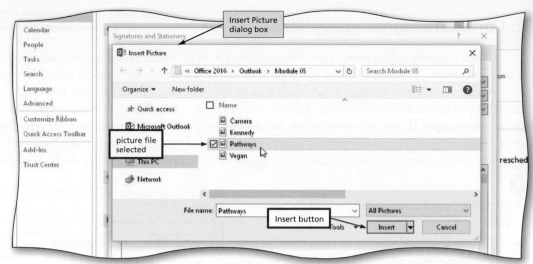

Figure 5–29

2

- Click the Insert button (Insert Picture dialog box) (shown in Figure 5–29) to insert the image into the signature (Figure 5–30).

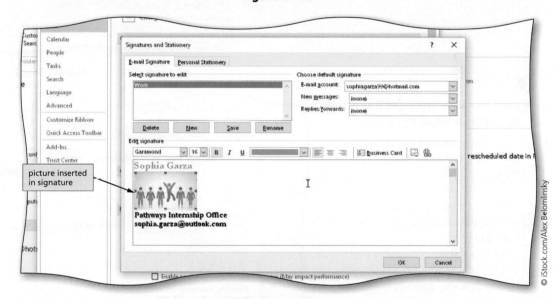

© iStock.com/Alex Belomlinsky

Figure 5–30

3

- Click the Save button (Signatures and Stationery dialog box) to save the changes to the signature (Figure 5–31).

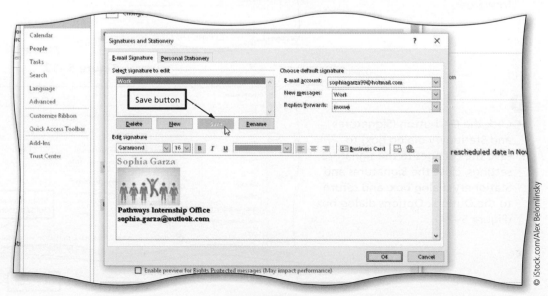

© iStock.com/Alex Belomlinsky

Figure 5–31

To Configure Signature Options

After creating a signature, you need to assign it to an email account. You can associate the signature with as many accounts as you want. You can set two default signatures for a single account: one for new messages and one for replies and forwards. Sophia wants to apply her signature for new messages to her email account named sophiagarza99@hotmail.com (select your own account). The following steps set the default signature for new messages. If you are completing these steps on a personal computer, your email account must be set up in Outlook (see Module 1) to be able to select an email account to apply the signature. ***Why?*** *By associating a signature with a particular email account, your signature automatically appears at the bottom of new messages.*

1

- Click the E-mail account box arrow to display a list of accounts.

- Click your email account, in this case sophiagarza99@hotmail.com, to select the email account (Figure 5–32).

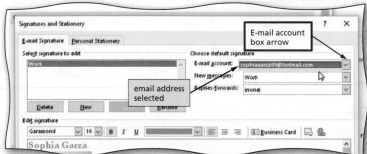

Figure 5–32

2

- Click the New messages box arrow to display a list of signatures.

- Click Work to make it the default signature for new messages (Figure 5–33).

Q&A How do I place a signature in all messages including replies and forwards?
Click the Replies/forwards box arrow and then click a signature to make it the default signature for all message replies and forwards.

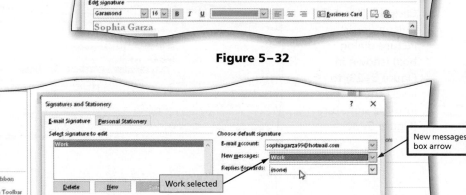

Figure 5–33

3

- Click the OK button (Signatures and Stationery dialog box) to save the changes to the signature settings, close the Signatures and Stationery dialog box, and return to the Outlook Options dialog box (Figure 5–34).

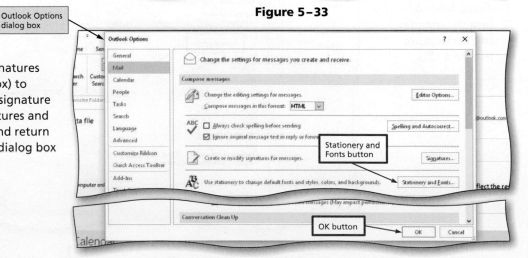

Figure 5–34

To Customize Stationery

Outlook provides backgrounds and patterns for email message stationery and offers themes, which are sets of unified design elements, such as fonts, bullets, colors, and effects that you can apply to messages. Sophia decides to use a stationery named Edge, which provides a professional, stylish design. The following steps customize the email message stationery. *Why? Stationery provides a distinctive look for your email messages.*

1
- Click the Stationery and Fonts button (Outlook Options dialog box) to display the Signatures and Stationery dialog box (Figure 5–35).

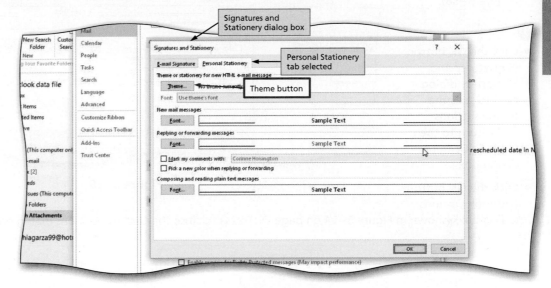

Figure 5–35

2
- Click the Theme button (Signatures and Stationery dialog box) to display the Theme or Stationery dialog box (Figure 5–36).

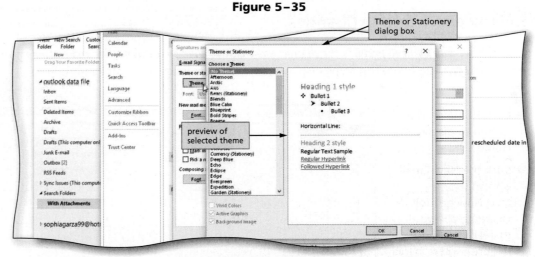

Figure 5–36

3
- Click Edge to select it and display a preview of its formats (Figure 5–37).

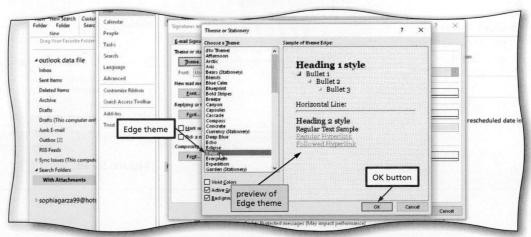

Figure 5–37

● Click the OK button (Theme or Stationery dialog box) to apply the theme to the stationery (Figure 5–38).

● Click the OK button (Signatures and Stationery dialog box) to save the theme settings and return to the Outlook Options dialog box.

● Click the OK button (Outlook Options dialog box) (shown in Figure 5–34 on page OUT 224) to close the Outlook Options dialog box.

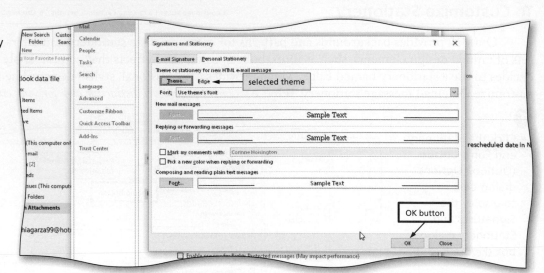

Figure 5–38

To Preview Message Changes

1 CUSTOMIZE EMAIL MESSAGES | 2 CUSTOMIZE SIGNATURES & STATIONERY | 3 MANAGE JUNK EMAIL FILTERS
4 CONFIGURE RULES | 5 CHANGE CALENDAR OPTIONS | 6 ADD NEWS FEED

Why? *You want to preview the changes you made to your email signature and stationery and see how they look in an email message.* The following steps display a new email message without sending it.

● Click Home on the ribbon to display the Home tab.

● Click the New Email button (Home tab | New group) to create a new email message (Figure 5–39).

● Close the email message without sending it.

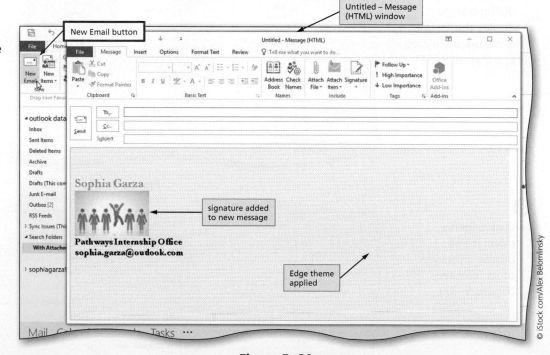

Figure 5–39

© iStock.com/Alex Belomlinsky

To Assign Signatures to a Single Email Message

If you use multiple email accounts, you can set a signature for each account or you can apply a signature to an individual email message. Sophia still needs to send the email about the Kennedy Center internship link to Zion and wants to apply the Work signature to that message, which is now stored in the Drafts folder. *Why? Instead of assigning your email address to one signature, you may want to create different signatures and apply a signature to individual email messages before you send them.* The following steps assign a signature to a single email message.

1

- Click the Drafts folder in the Navigation Pane to display the message header for the Kennedy Center Internship email message in the message list.

- Double-click the Kennedy Center Internship message header in the messages pane to open the Kennedy Center Internship - Message (HTML) window (Figure 5–40).

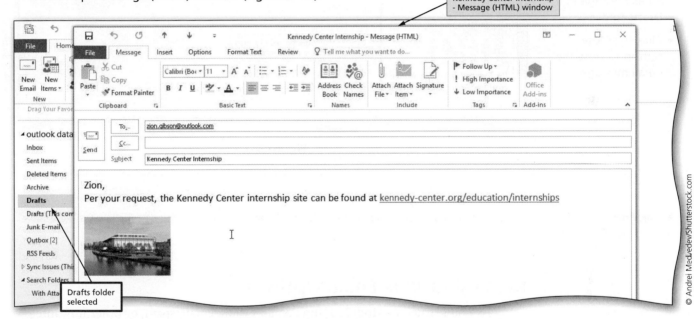

© Andrei Medvedev/Shutterstock.com

Figure 5–40

2

- Place the insertion point to the right of the Kennedy Center image and then press the ENTER key to move to the next line.

- Click Insert on the ribbon to display the Insert tab.

- Click the Signature button (Insert tab | Include group) to display a list of signatures (Figure 5–41).

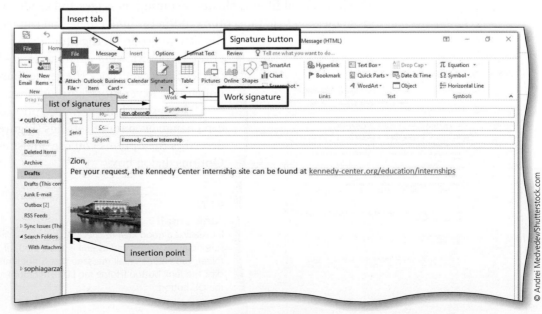

© Andrei Medvedev/Shutterstock.com

Figure 5–41

3

• Click Work to add the Work signature to the email message body.

• Scroll down to view the full signature (Figure 5–42).

4

• Click the Save button on the Quick Access Toolbar to save the email message in the Drafts folder.

• Click the Close button to close the email message.

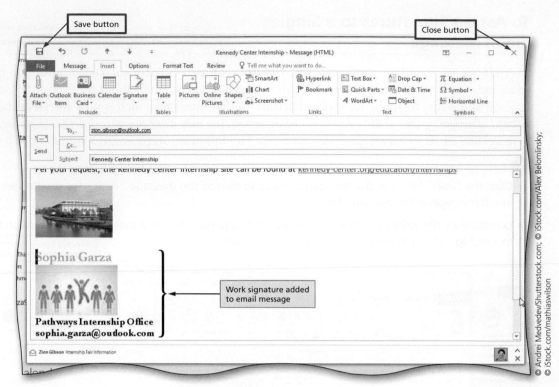

Figure 5–42

Break Point: If you wish to take a break, this is a good place to do so. To resume at a later time, continue to follow the steps from this location forward.

Managing Junk Email Options

As you learned in Module 1, junk email is bulk email, spam, or other unwanted email messages. Outlook uses a filter to control the amount of junk email you receive. The junk email filter evaluates incoming messages and sends to the Junk E-mail folder those messages that meet the criteria for junk email. You can use the Junk button in the Delete group on the Home tab to override the default criteria when viewing email messages by deciding to block the sender, never block the sender, never block the sender's domain, or never block a group or mailing list.

Using the Junk E-mail Options dialog box, you can change even more settings (Figure 5–43). Table 5–1 describes the options you can adjust using the Junk E-mail Options dialog box.

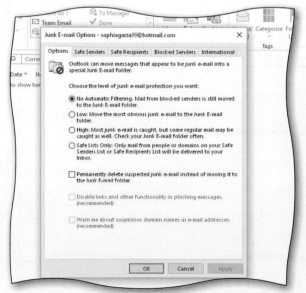

BTW
Junk Email
It usually is a good idea to check your Junk E-mail folder regularly to make sure no items are labeled as junk inadvertently. If, after clicking the Junk E-mail folder, you find an email message that is not junk, select the email message, click the Junk button (Home tab | Delete group), click Not Junk, and then click the OK button.

Figure 5–43

Table 5–1	Junk E-mail Options
Tab	**Description**
Options	Allows you to choose the level of protection (No Automatic Filtering, Low, High, Safe Lists Only), as well as set whether junk email is deleted, links are disabled in phishing messages, and warnings are provided for suspicious domain names.
Safe Senders	Permits the specification of safe email addresses and domains. Email messages from the listed email addresses and domains will not be treated as junk email.
Safe Recipients	Specifies that email messages sent to email addresses or domains in the safe recipient list will not be treated as junk email.
Blocked Senders	Allows you to manage your list of blocked email addresses and domains.
International	Manages which domains and encodings you would like to block based on languages used.

To Add a Domain to the Safe Senders List

1 CUSTOMIZE EMAIL MESSAGES | 2 CUSTOMIZE SIGNATURES & STATIONERY | 3 MANAGE JUNK EMAIL FILTERS
4 CONFIGURE RULES | 5 CHANGE CALENDAR OPTIONS | 6 ADD NEWS FEED

The junk email filter in Outlook is turned on by default, providing a protection level that is set to Low. This level is designed to catch only the most obvious junk email messages. Sophia feels that too many incoming messages from Microsoft are being sent to her Junk E-mail folder. Microsoft.com can be added to the Safe Senders list, which adjusts the filter sensitivity of Outlook, so the Microsoft messages are sent to the Inbox instead of the Junk E-mail folder. If you are completing these steps on a personal computer, your email account must be set up in Outlook (see Module 1) to be able to select an email account to configure the junk email options. The following steps configure the junk email options for an email account. *Why? The Junk E-mail folder helps to sort out relevant email messages from junk mail.*

- Click your personal email account (in this case, sophiagarza99@hotmail.com) in the Navigation Pane to select the mailbox (Figure 5–44).

Q&A Why did I have to select the email account?
To change junk email options for an account, the account first should be selected. If you selected a different mailbox, you would have changed junk email settings for that account.

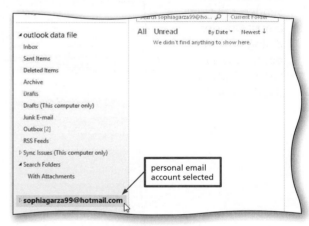

Figure 5–44

- Click the Junk button (Home tab | Delete group) to display the Junk options (Figure 5–45).

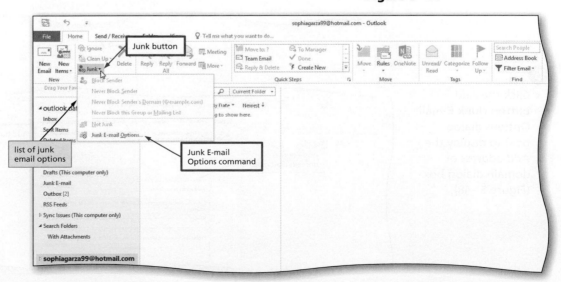

Figure 5–45

• Click Junk E-mail
Options to display
the Junk E-mail
Options dialog box
(Figure 5–46).

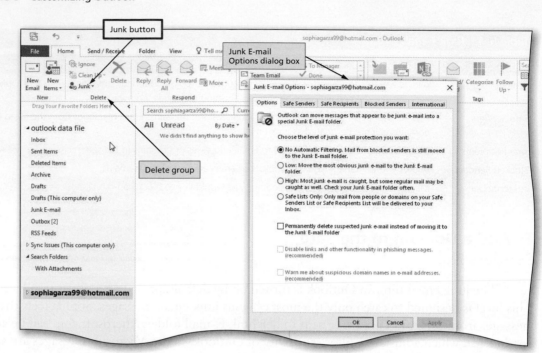

Figure 5–46

• Click the Safe
Senders tab (Junk
E-mail Options
dialog box) to
display the Safe
Senders options
(Figure 5–47).

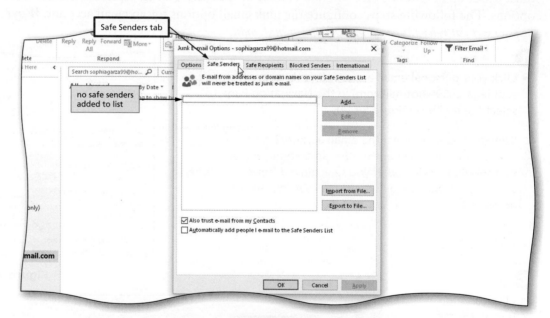

Figure 5–47

• Click the Add
button (Junk E-mail
Options dialog
box) to display the
Add address or
domain dialog box
(Figure 5–48).

Figure 5–48

• Type **@Microsoft.com** in the text box to enter a domain name to add to the Safe Senders list (Figure 5–49).

Q&A
Do I have to type the @ symbol?
Although Outlook recommends that you type the @ symbol to indicate a domain name, you can omit the symbol. In that case, you leave it up to Outlook to determine if your entry is a domain name or email address. Most of the time, Outlook interprets the entry correctly; however, to be certain, type the @ symbol.

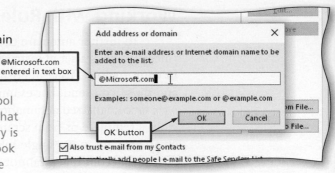

Figure 5–49

• Click the OK button (Add address or domain dialog box) to add the domain to the Safe Senders List (Figure 5–50).

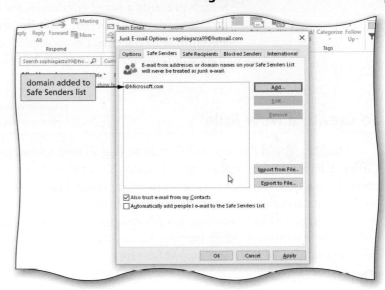

BTW

Using the Clutter Feature
If you have an Office 365 subscription, a feature called **Clutter** assists in filtering low-priority email, saving you time to focus on important emails. If you turn on Clutter, the Office 365 Exchange server automatically keeps track of the email messages you read and the email messages that you ignore. Office 365 moves the ignored messages to a folder in your Inbox called the Clutter items folder.

Figure 5–50

To Block a Specific Email Address

1 CUSTOMIZE EMAIL MESSAGES | 2 CUSTOMIZE SIGNATURES & STATIONERY | 3 MANAGE JUNK EMAIL FILTERS
4 CONFIGURE RULES | 5 CHANGE CALENDAR OPTIONS | 6 ADD NEWS FEED

Why? *You may want to block a specific email address or domain to prevent people or companies from sending you messages you do not want to receive.* Sophia has received multiple unwanted emails from the following email address: getrich2@live.com. She considers these messages as junk email. The following steps block a specific email address using the junk filters.

• Click the Blocked Senders tab (Junk E-mail Options dialog box) to display the Blocked Senders options.

• Click the Add button (Junk E-mail Options dialog box) to display the Add address or domain dialog box.

• Type **getrich2@live.com** in the text box to enter the domain name to add to the Blocked Senders list (Figure 5–51).

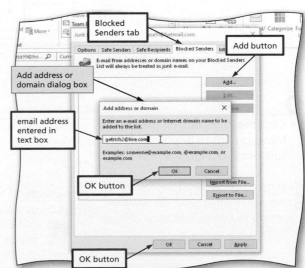

2

• Click the OK button (Add address or domain dialog box) to add the domain to the Blocked Senders List.

• Click the OK button (Junk E-mail Options dialog box) to close the Junk E-mail Options dialog box.

Figure 5–51

Working with Rules

To further automate the processing of email messages in Outlook, you can create rules. A **rule** is a set of instructions that tells Outlook how to handle email messages in your mailbox. You can create rules that apply to email messages you have received and those you send. For example, you can specify that email messages from a particular user be categorized automatically or placed in a specified folder. You can create rules from a template or from scratch based on conditions you specify. Rules apply to an email account, not a single folder or file. If you are working with a data file instead of an email account, you cannot create rules.

To simplify the process of creating rules, Outlook provides a Rules Wizard, which presents a list of conditions for selecting an email message and then lists actions to take with messages that meet the conditions. If necessary, you can also specify exceptions to the rule. For example, you can move certain messages to a specified folder unless they are sent with high importance.

To Create a New Rule

Sophia would like to create a rule to flag all email messages from the director of the Pathways Internship Office, Ella Pauley, for follow-up. This way, she easily can remember to follow up with Ms. Pauley on important tasks. If you are completing these steps on a personal computer, your email account must be set up in Outlook so that you can select an email account to create a rule. The following steps create a rule that automatically flags email messages. *Why? Rules help you file and follow up on email messages. For example, your instructor can create a rule for messages from a specific course section, such as CIS 101. You can set CIS 101 in the Subject line to be flagged for follow-up and moved to a folder named Literacy.*

- Click the outlook data file Inbox to display the Inbox messages.
- If necessary, click the Ella Pauley email message to select it (Figure 5–52).

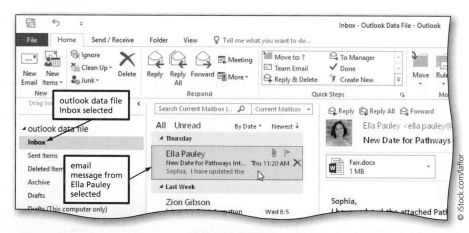

Figure 5–52

- Click the Rules button (Home tab | Move group) to display a list of rule options (Figure 5–53).

Q&A | Why is my Rules button missing?
An active email address must be set up in Outlook to view the Rules button.

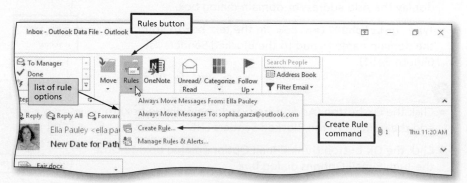

Figure 5–53

3

- Click the Create Rule command to display the Create Rule dialog box (Figure 5–54).

Figure 5–54

4

- Click the 'From Ella Pauley' check box to select it (Figure 5–55).

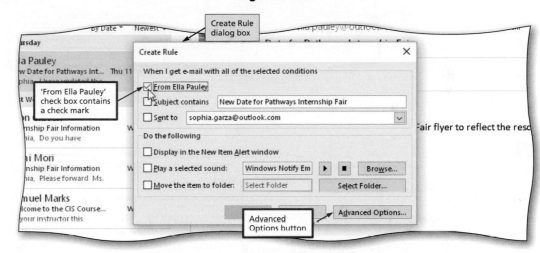

Figure 5–55

5

- Click the Advanced Options button (Create Rule dialog box) to display the Rules Wizard dialog box (Figure 5–56).

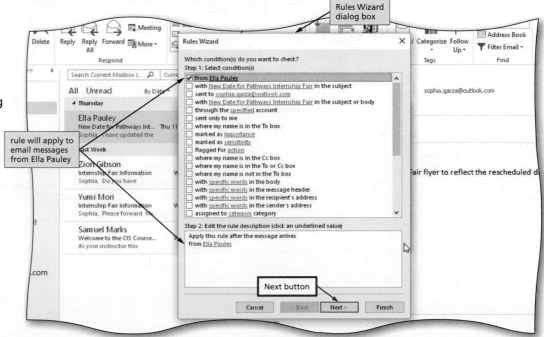

Figure 5–56

6

- Click the Next button (Rules Wizard dialog box) to continue to the next step, where you specify one or more actions to take with a selected message (Figure 5–57).

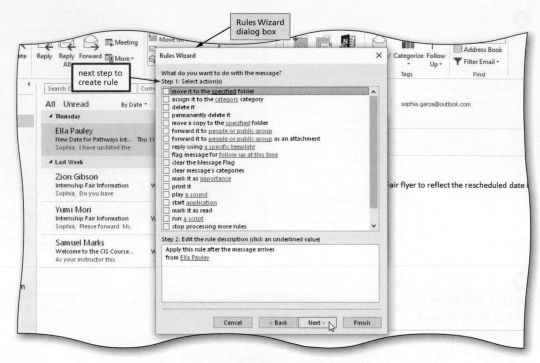

Figure 5–57

7

- Click the 'flag message for follow up at this time' check box to select it.

- If necessary, click the Yes button if a dialog box opens informing you that the rule you are creating can never be edited in previous versions of Outlook (Figure 5–58).

Q&A What is the effect of selecting the 'flag message for follow up at this time' check box?
Messages that meet the conditions you specify, in this case, messages from Ella Pauley, appear in the message list with a flag icon to indicate they need to be followed up.

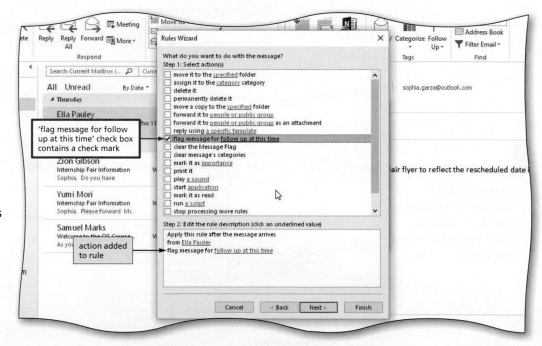

Figure 5–58

8

- Click the 'follow up at this time' link in the Step 2 area to display the Flag Message dialog box (Figure 5–59).

 For what purposes can I use the Flag Message dialog box? You can flag a message for follow up (the default) or for other options, including For Your Information, No Response Necessary, and Reply. You can also specify when to follow up: Today (the default), Tomorrow, This Week, Next Week, No Date, or Complete.

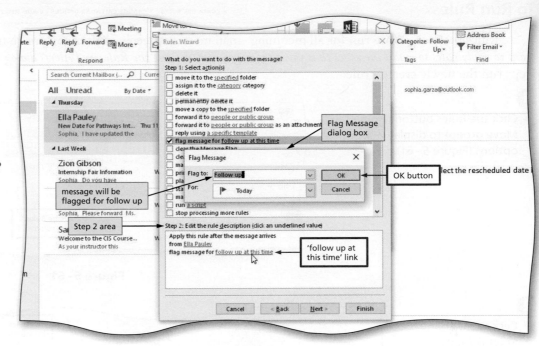

Figure 5–59

9

- Click the OK button (Flag Message dialog box) to accept the default settings and return to the Rules Wizard dialog box (Figure 5–60).

10

- Click the Finish button (Rules Wizard dialog box) to save the rule.

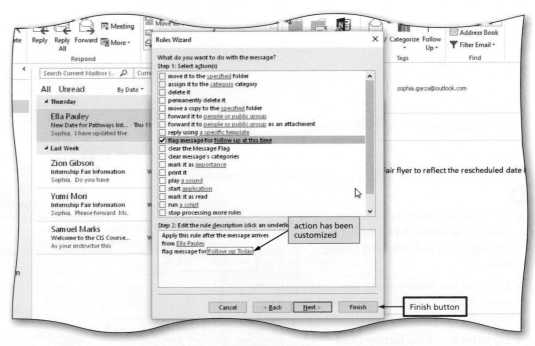

Figure 5–60

To Run Rules

Rules that you create run for all incoming email messages received after you create the rule. *Why? If you want to apply rules to email messages that you already received, you use the Rules and Alerts dialog box.* The following steps run the newly created rule.

1

- Click the Rules button (Home tab | Move group) to display a list of rule options (Figure 5–61).

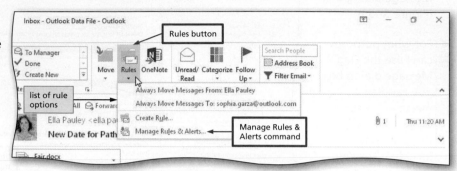

Figure 5–61

2

- Click the Manage Rules & Alerts command to display the Rules and Alerts dialog box (Figure 5–62).

Q&A

After I create a rule, can I modify it?
Yes. To modify an existing rule, select the rule you want to modify, click the Change Rule button, and then click the Edit Rule Settings command. Next, make the desired changes in the Rules Wizard. Click the Finish button after making all necessary changes.

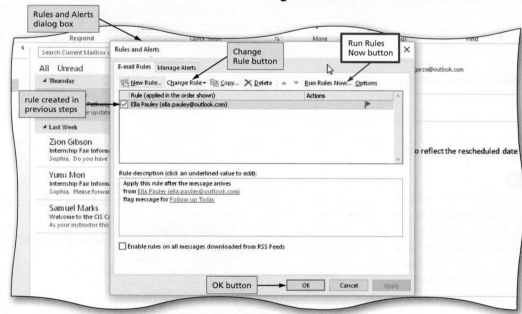

Figure 5–62

3

- Click the Run Rules Now button (Rules and Alerts dialog box) to display the Run Rules Now dialog box.

- Click the Ella Pauley check box to select it and specify the rule that will run.

- Click the Run Now button (Run Rules Now dialog box) to run the rule (Figure 5–63).

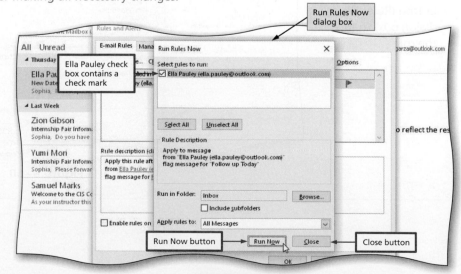

Figure 5–63

④
- Click the Close button (Run Rules Now dialog box) to close the Run Rules Now dialog box.

- Click the OK button (Rules and Alerts dialog box) (shown in Figure 5–62) to close the Rules and Alerts dialog box (Figure 5–64).

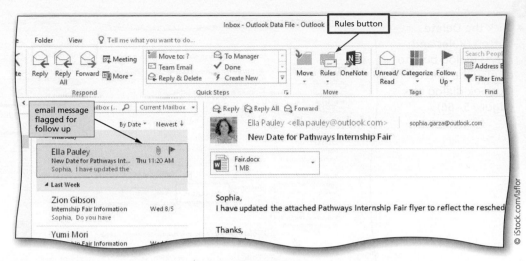

Figure 5–64

1 CUSTOMIZE EMAIL MESSAGES | 2 CUSTOMIZE SIGNATURES & STATIONERY | 3 MANAGE JUNK EMAIL FILTERS
4 CONFIGURE RULES | 5 CHANGE CALENDAR OPTIONS | 6 ADD NEWS FEED

To Delete a Rule

Why? When you no longer need a rule, you should delete it. After further consideration, you decide that you do not need to flag all email messages from your faculty advisor; therefore, you decide to delete the rule. The following steps delete a rule.

- Click the Rules button (Home tab | Move group) (shown in Figure 5–64) to display a list of rule options.

- Click the Manage Rules & Alerts command to display the Rules and Alerts dialog box (Figure 5–65).

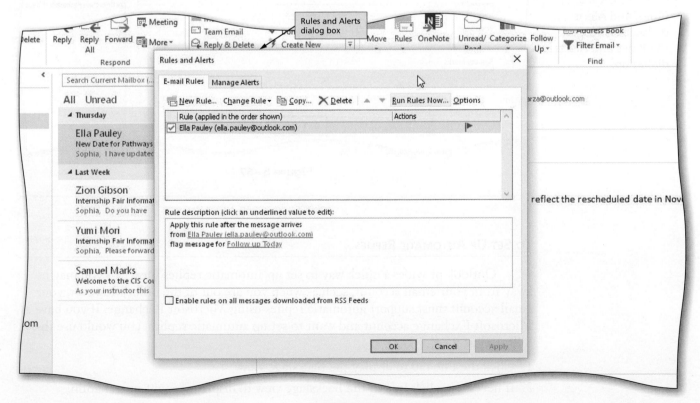

Figure 5–65

● Click the Delete
button (Rules and
Alerts dialog box) to
display the Microsoft
Outlook dialog box
(Figure 5–66).

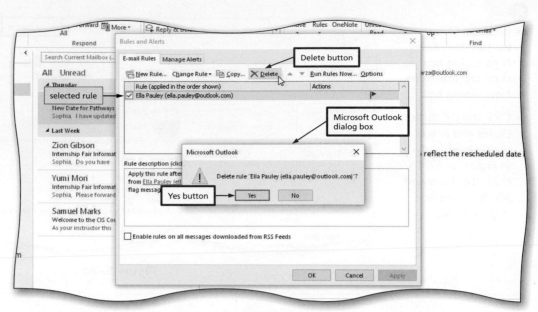

Figure 5–66

● Click the Yes button
(Microsoft Outlook
dialog box) to delete
the Ella Pauley rule
(Figure 5–67).

● Click the OK button
(Rules and Alerts
dialog box) to close
the Rules and Alerts
dialog box.

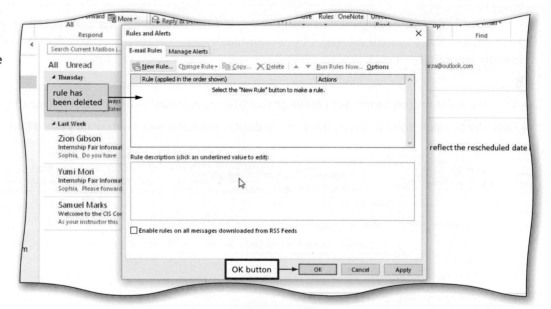

Figure 5–67

TO SET UP AUTOMATIC REPLIES

Outlook provides a quick way to set up automatic replies for when you may be
away from your email account, such as when you are out of the office; however, your
email account must support automatic replies using Microsoft Exchange. If you have a
Microsoft Exchange account and want to set up automatic replies, you would use the
following steps.

1. Click the File tab to display the Backstage view.

2. If necessary, click Info in the Backstage view to display account information.

3. Click Automatic Replies to display the Automatic Replies dialog box.

4. Click 'Send automatic replies' to turn on automatic replies.

5. Change the Start time to select the day and time for the automatic replies to start.

6. Change the End time to select the day and time for the automatic replies to stop.

7. Select Inside My Organization and enter an email message for email messages to be sent inside your organization.

8. Select Outside My Organization and enter an email message for email messages to be sent outside your organization.

9. Click OK to save the rule for automatic replies.

BTW

Cleanup Tools
In addition to archiving email messages, Outlook provides cleanup tools to help control the size of your mailbox. To access the various cleanup tools, display the Backstage view, click the Info tab, If necessary, click the Cleanup Tools button, and then click the desired cleanup tool you want to access.

---

1 CUSTOMIZE EMAIL MESSAGES | 2 CUSTOMIZE SIGNATURES & STATIONERY | 3 MANAGE JUNK EMAIL FILTERS

To Set AutoArchive Settings

4 CONFIGURE RULES | 5 CHANGE CALENDAR OPTIONS | 6 ADD NEWS FEED

Why? *You can have Outlook transfer old items to a storage file. Items are only considered old after a certain number of days that you specify.* Sophia decides that she should back up the email messages in her email account. By default, when AutoArchive is turned on, Outlook archives messages every 14 days. The following steps turn on AutoArchive.

• Click the File tab to display the Backstage view.

• Click Options in the Backstage view to display the Outlook Options dialog box.

• Click Advanced in the Category list to display the Advanced options (Figure 5–68).

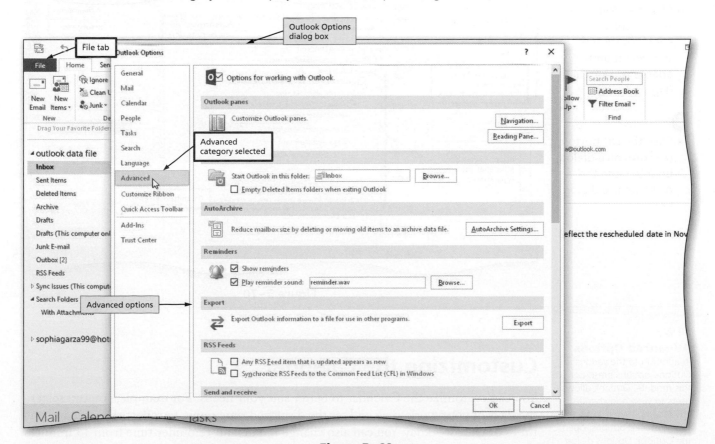

Figure 5–68

• Click the AutoArchive Settings button (Outlook Options dialog box) to display the AutoArchive dialog box (Figure 5–69).

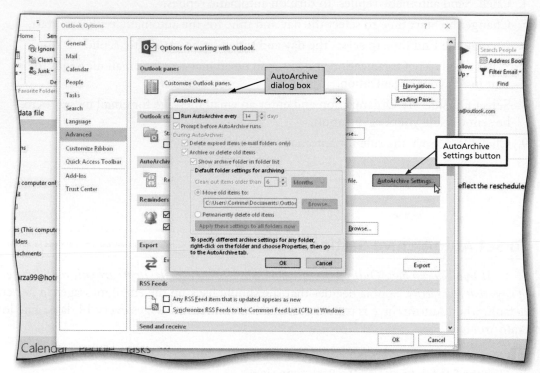

Figure 5–69

• Click the 'Run AutoArchive every' check box to select it and enable AutoArchive (Figure 5–70).

• Click the OK button (AutoArchive dialog box) to close the AutoArchive dialog box.

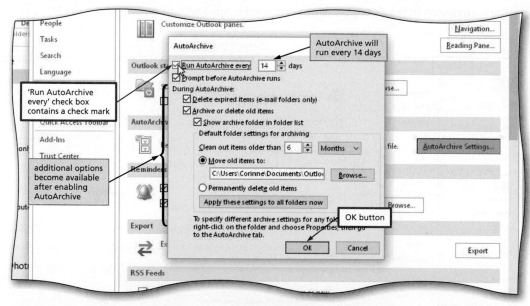

Figure 5–70

BTW
Advanced Options
In addition to the various Outlook options presented in this module, Outlook allows users to view and change advanced options. To access the advanced options, open the Outlook Options dialog box and then click Advanced in the Category list.

Customizing the Calendar

You can customize the Calendar to better suit your needs. For example, you can select the days of your work week and set the displayed time range to reflect the start and end times of your workday. You can also change the default reminder time from 15 minutes to any other interval, such as five minutes or a half-hour. Other Calendar options you can customize include the calendar font and current time zone.

To Change the Work Time on the Calendar

Sophia would like to customize the work time on the Calendar so that it reflects her work schedule. She normally works from 9:00 AM to 4:30 PM on Mondays, Wednesdays, Fridays, and Saturdays. The following steps change the Calendar settings to match the work schedule and make Monday the first day of the week. *Why? By default, the Calendar Work Week is set for Monday through Friday, but you can select which days comprise your work week.*

- Click Calendar in the Category list in the Outlook Options dialog box to display the Calendar options (Figure 5–71).

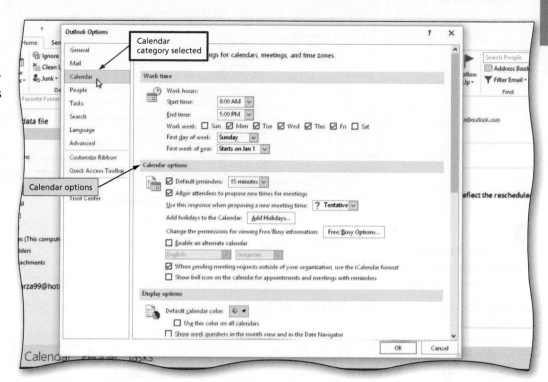

Figure 5–71

2

- Click the Start time box arrow to display a list of start times.

- Select 9:00 AM to change the start time.

- Click the End time box arrow to display a list of end times.

- Select 4:30 PM to change the end time (Figure 5–72).

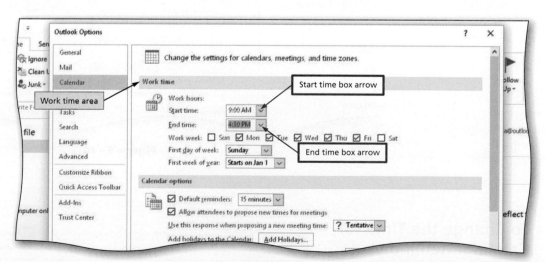

Figure 5–72

- Click the Tue check box to deselect it.
- Click the Thu check box to deselect it.
- Click the Sat check box to select it (Figure 5–73).

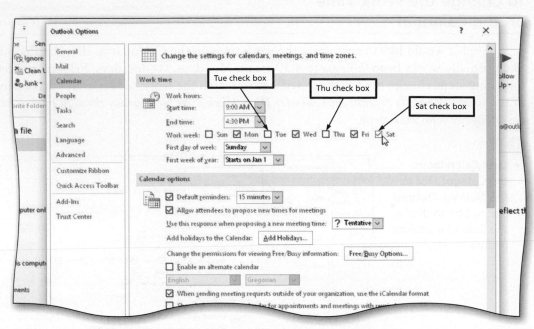

Figure 5–73

- Click the 'First day of week' box arrow to display a list of days.
- Click Monday to change the first day of the week to Monday (Figure 5–74).

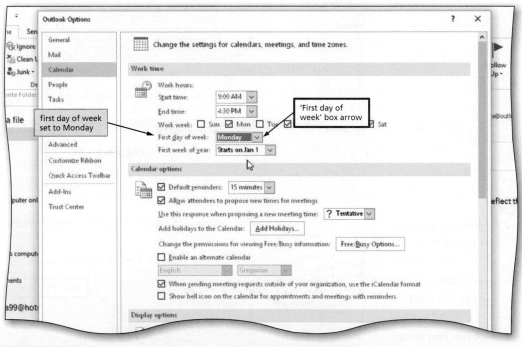

Figure 5–74

To Change the Time for Calendar Reminders

1 CUSTOMIZE EMAIL MESSAGES | 2 CUSTOMIZE SIGNATURES & STATIONERY | 3 MANAGE JUNK EMAIL FILTERS
4 CONFIGURE RULES | 5 CHANGE CALENDAR OPTIONS | 6 ADD NEWS FEED

To further customize the Outlook calendar, Sophia would like to increase the time for reminders to 30 minutes. The following step changes the time for reminders. *Why? By default, the Calendar reminders are set for 15 minutes prior to an appointment or meeting.*

- Click the Default reminders box arrow to display a list of times.

- Click 30 minutes to select it as the default time for reminders (Figure 5–75).

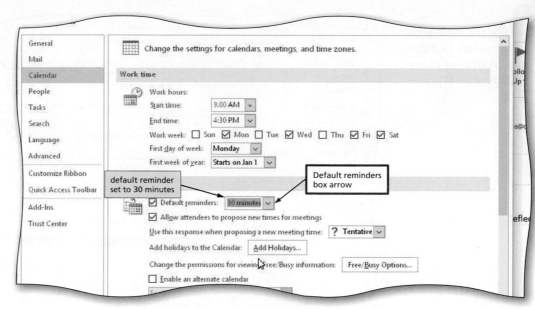

Figure 5–75

To Change the Time Zone Setting

1 CUSTOMIZE EMAIL MESSAGES | 2 CUSTOMIZE SIGNATURES & STATIONERY | 3 MANAGE JUNK EMAIL FILTERS
4 CONFIGURE RULES | 5 CHANGE CALENDAR OPTIONS | 6 ADD NEWS FEED

Why? *When you travel, your time zone may change and your calendar should be updated. If you change the time zone setting in Calendar, Outlook updates your appointments to display the new time zone when you arrive.* Sophia is participating in an internship summit this summer with the director, Ms. Pauley in Honolulu, Hawaii, and needs to change the time zones accordingly. The following steps change the time zone.

- Scroll down until the Time zones settings are visible in the Outlook Options dialog box (Figure 5–76).

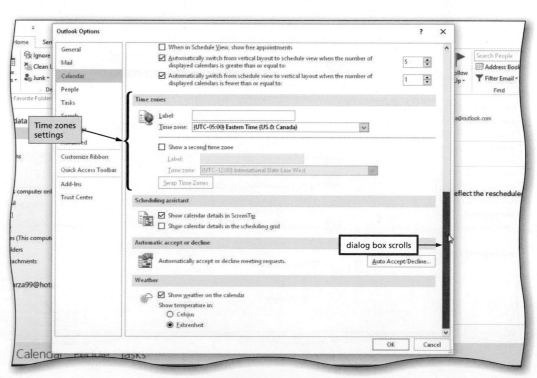

Figure 5–76

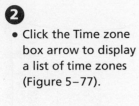

- Click the Time zone box arrow to display a list of time zones (Figure 5–77).

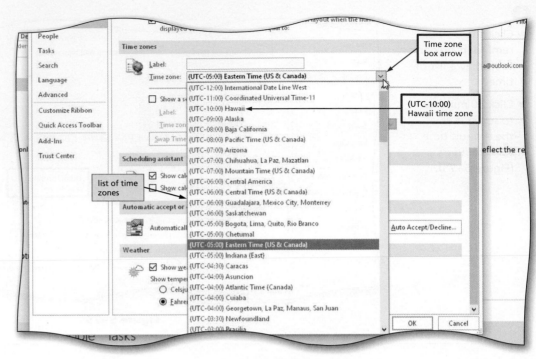

Figure 5–77

❸

- Scroll and then click (UTC-10:00) Hawaii to select the time zone (Figure 5–78).

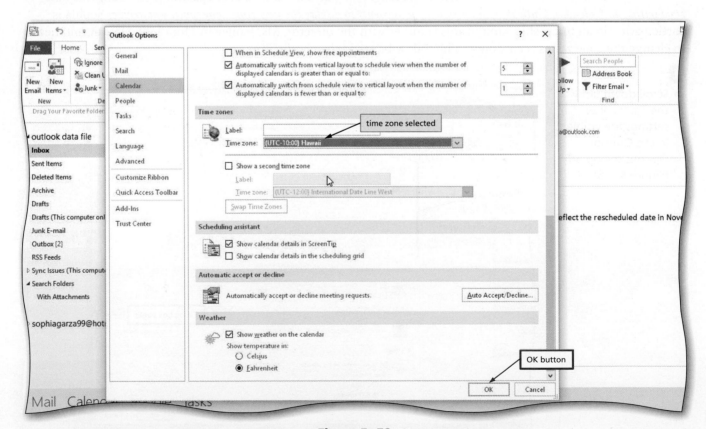

Figure 5–78

4

- Click the OK button (Outlook Options dialog box) to close the Outlook Options dialog box.

- Click the Calendar button in the Navigation Bar to display the Calendar to view the changes (Figure 5–79).

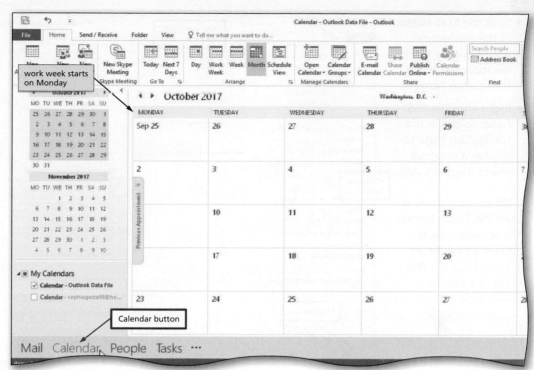

Figure 5–79

Working with RSS Feeds

Really Simple Syndication (RSS) is a way for content publishers to make news, blogs, and other content available to subscribers. RSS feeds typically are found on news websites, political discussion boards, educational blogs, and other sites that frequently update their content. For example, the PBS website contains an RSS feed on the Frontline webpage that allow people to view recent news stories in one convenient location. If you frequently visit websites that offer RSS feeds, you quickly can review the feed content of all the websites in a simple list in your browser by subscribing to their RSS feeds, without having to first navigate to each individual site.

If you want to use Outlook to read the feed, you can add the RSS feed to your account using the Account Settings dialog box. Outlook creates an easy way to manage and work with your RSS feed. Some accounts let you access the feeds from your web browser if they are using a common feeds folder; however, not all accounts allow for this.

To Subscribe to an RSS Feed

1 CUSTOMIZE EMAIL MESSAGES | 2 CUSTOMIZE SIGNATURES & STATIONERY | 3 MANAGE JUNK EMAIL FILTERS
4 CONFIGURE RULES | 5 CHANGE CALENDAR OPTIONS | **6 ADD NEWS FEED**

Sophia subscribes to several RSS feeds in her web browser. To view the feed using Outlook, she needs to set up an RSS feed from http://www.nirmaltv.com/feed/. The following steps subscribe to an RSS feed and display the messages. **Why?** *The benefit of displaying an RSS feed in Outlook is the ability to combine feeds from multiple web sources in one place. You no longer have to visit different websites for news, weather, blogs, and other information.*

1

- Click the Mail button in the Navigation Bar to display the mailboxes in the Navigation Pane.

- Right-click the RSS Feeds folder in the Navigation Pane to display a shortcut menu (Figure 5–80).

Q&A What should I do if an RSS Feeds folder does not appear in Sophia's mailbox? Right-click the RSS Feeds folder in a different mailbox on your computer.

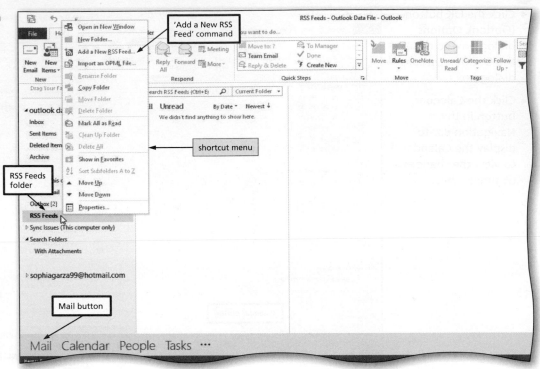

Figure 5–80

2

- Click the Add a New RSS Feed command to display the New RSS Feed dialog box (Figure 5–81).

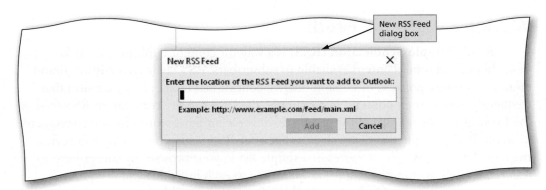

Figure 5–81

3

- Type http://www.nirmaltv.com/feed/ in the text box to enter the address of an RSS feed (Figure 5–82).

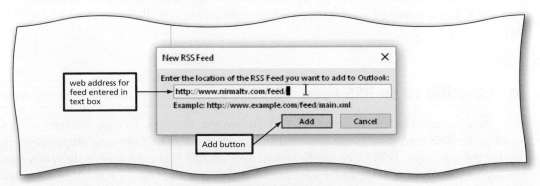

Figure 5–82

4

- Click the Add button (New RSS Feed dialog box) to add the RSS feed to the RSS Feeds folder.
- Click the Yes button (Microsoft Outlook dialog box) to confirm you want to add the RSS feed (Figure 5–83).

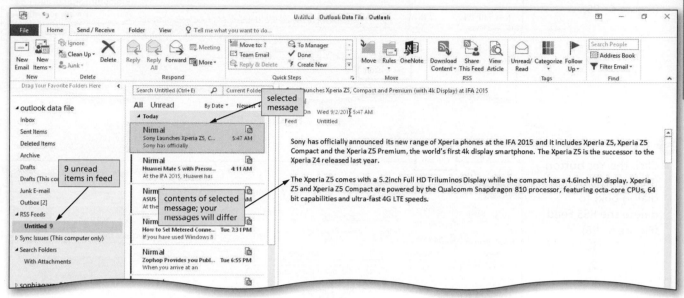

Figure 5–83

Experiment

- Click the different messages to see what has been posted in the RSS Feeds folder.

To Delete an RSS Feed

1 CUSTOMIZE EMAIL MESSAGES | 2 CUSTOMIZE SIGNATURES & STATIONERY | 3 MANAGE JUNK EMAIL FILTERS
4 CONFIGURE RULES | 5 CHANGE CALENDAR OPTIONS | **6 ADD NEWS FEED**

Why? *When you no longer need to use an RSS feed, you should delete it so that you do not have unwanted messages in your account.* The following steps delete an RSS feed.

1

- Right-click the Untitled folder below the RSS Feeds folder in the Navigation Pane to display a shortcut menu (Figure 5–84).

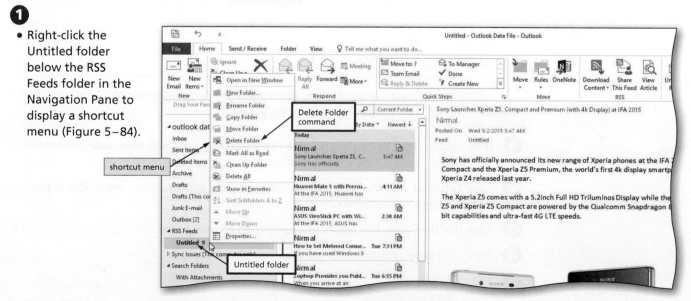

Figure 5–84

- Click the Delete Folder command to display the Microsoft Outlook dialog box (Figure 5–85).

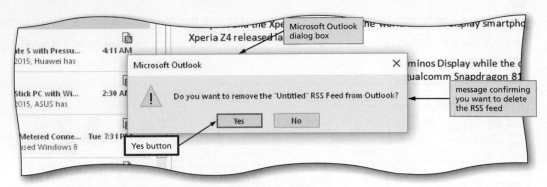

Figure 5–85

- Click the Yes button (Microsoft Outlook dialog box) to delete the RSS Feed (Figure 5–86).

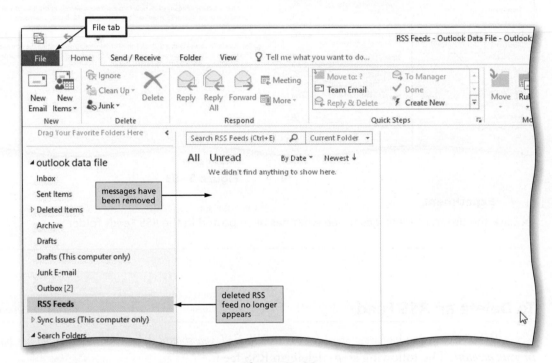

Figure 5–86

To Reset the Time Zone Setting

Why? You should change the time zone back to your original time zone before quitting *Outlook*. The following steps reset the time zone.

1. If necessary, click the File tab to open the Backstage view, and then click Options to display the Outlook Options dialog box.

2. Click Calendar, and then scroll down until the Time zones settings are visible in the Outlook Options dialog box.

3. Click the Time zone box arrow to display a list of time zones.

4. Click your time zone to select the time zone.

5. Exit Outlook.

Summary

In this module, you have learned how to add another email account, customize Outlook options, add signatures and stationery, manage the junk email filter, create rules, customize calendar options, and add RSS Feeds.

What future decisions will you need to make when customizing email messages, adding signatures and stationery, managing junk email options, working with rules, customizing the calendar, and adding RSS feeds?

    1. Customize Email Messages.

        a) Determine which options you want to customize.

        b) Determine the information to include in your signature.

        c) Determine the layout that you would like for stationery.

    2. Managing Junk Email Options.

        a) Determine which domains should be placed on the Safe Senders list.

        b) Determine which specific email addresses should be placed on the Blocked Senders list.

    3. Working with Rules.

        a) Plan rules to use with your email messages.

        b) Determine how you would like your email messages to be processed.

    4. Customizing the Calendar.

        a) Determine the calendar settings you need.

    5. Adding RSS Feeds.

        a) Determine what news feeds you would like to use.

CONSIDER THIS: PLAN AHEAD

How should you submit solutions to questions in the assignments identified with a symbol?

Every assignment in this book contains one or more questions with a symbol. These questions require you to think beyond the assigned file. Present your solutions to the question in the format required by your instructor. Possible formats may include one or more of these options: write the answer; create a document that contains the answer; present your answer to the class; discuss your answer in a group; record the answer as audio or video using a webcam, smartphone, or portable media player; or post answers on a blog, wiki, or website.

CONSIDER THIS

Apply Your Knowledge

Reinforce the skills and apply the concepts you learned in this module.

Note: To complete this assignment, you will be required to use the Data Files. Please contact your instructor for information about accessing the Data Files.

Creating a Personalized Signature

Instructions: Run Outlook. You will use the Signatures and Stationery dialog box (Figure 5–87) to create a personalized signature to use when you send email messages to others.

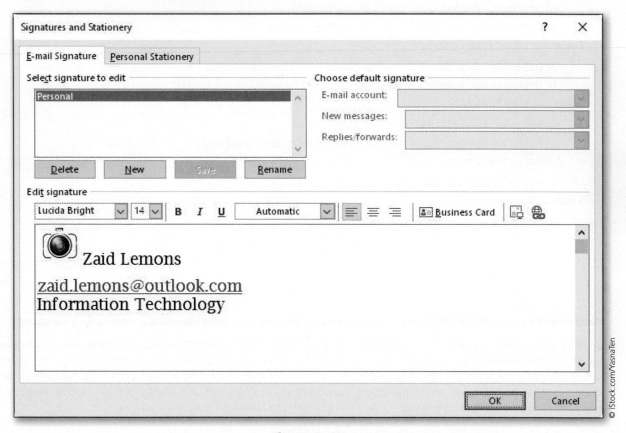

Figure 5–87

Perform the following tasks:

1. Display the Outlook Options dialog box, and then display the Signatures and Stationery dialog box.
2. Create a signature using **Personal** as the name of the signature.
3. From the Data Files, add the image named Camera to the signature.
4. Change the font to Lucida Bright and the font size to 14.
5. On three lines, enter the following information: your name, your email address, and your major.
6. Set the signature to apply to new messages, replies, and forwards.

7. Select the Profile theme as your stationery.

8. Accept the changes in the dialog boxes and then create a new email message addressed to your instructor to display your new signature and stationery.

9. Submit the email message in the format specified by your instructor.

10. ✸ Why is it a good idea to configure Outlook to include a signature in outgoing email messages?

Extend Your Knowledge

Extend the skills you learned in this module and experiment with new skills. You may need to use Help to complete the assignment.

Adding a Second Email Account to Microsoft Outlook

Instructions: Run Outlook. You are going to add a second email account to Microsoft Outlook so that you can send and receive email messages from two accounts. If you do not already have another email account to add to Microsoft Outlook, sign up for a free account using a service such as Outlook.com, Gmail, or Yahoo!. Once you create the account, you will add the email account to Outlook using the Add Account Wizard shown in Figure 5–88, and then send an email to your instructor.

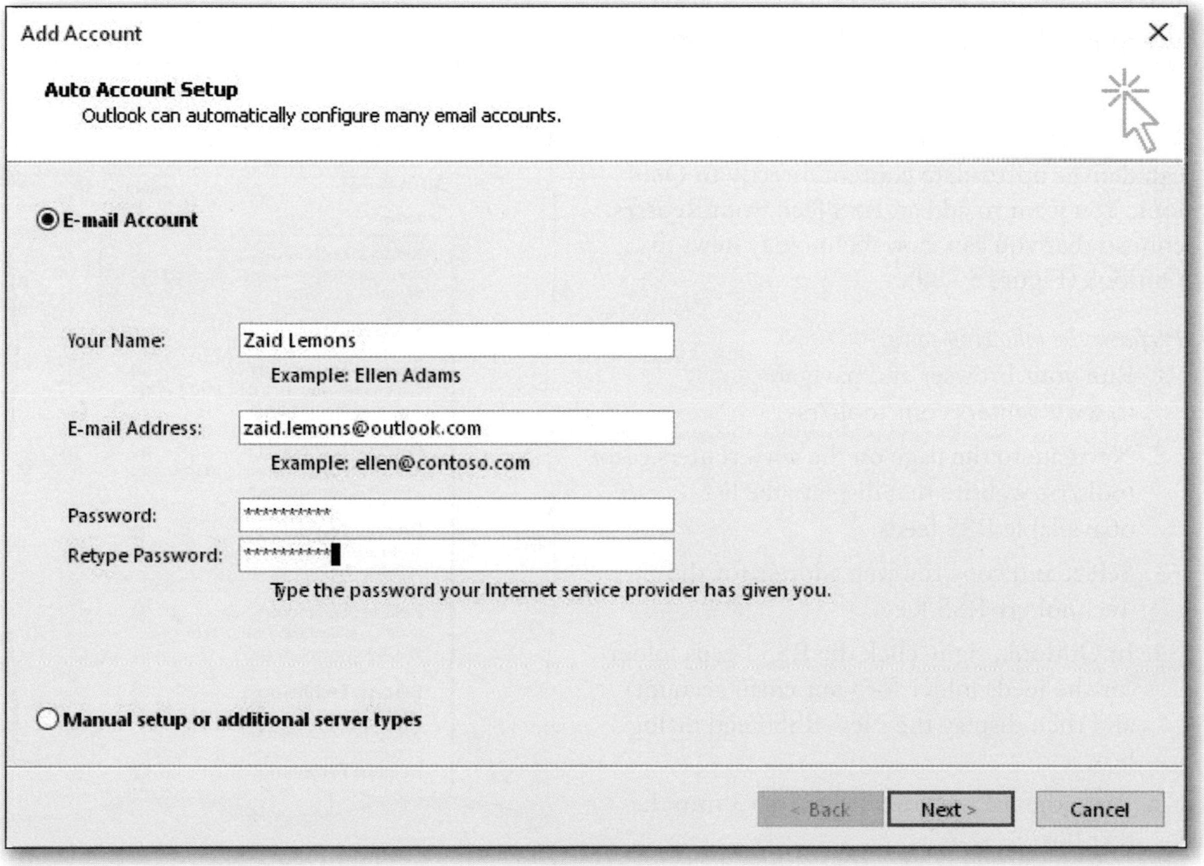

Figure 5–88

Continued >

Extend Your Knowledge *continued*

Perform the following tasks:

1. If necessary, navigate to a free email service and sign up for a free email account.

2. Start Outlook and display the Backstage view.

3. If necessary, click the Info tab to display the Info gallery.

4. Click the Add Account button to display the first dialog box in the Add Account Wizard.

5. Enter the desired information for the email account you are adding, including your name, email address, and password.

6. Click the Next button to instruct Outlook to automatically configure the account. If Outlook is unable to configure the account automatically, you may need to manually configure the account settings.

7. When the account has been configured successfully, click the Finish button.

8. Open a new email message addressed to your instructor stating that you have configured a new email account in Outlook. Send the email message to your instructor using the account you have just configured.

9. ✴ In what circumstances is it helpful to have multiple email accounts configured in Microsoft Outlook?

Expand Your World: Cloud and Web Technologies

Viewing a Tech News RSS Feed in Outlook

Problem: RSS feeds are web technologies that can deliver up-to-date content directly to Outlook. You want to add an RSS feed from Reuters.com so that you can view technology news in Outlook (Figure 5–89).

Perform the following tasks:

1. Run your browser and navigate to www.reuters.com/tools/rss.

2. Navigate to the page on the www.reuters.com/tools/rss website that displays the list of available RSS feeds.

3. Select and copy the web address for the Technology RSS feed.

4. In Outlook, right-click the RSS Feeds folder (or the feeds folder for your email account) and then display the New RSS Feed dialog box.

5. Paste the web address from Step 3 into the text box.

6. Add the feed to Outlook.

7. Open the first RSS message.

8. Print the message and then submit it in the format specified by your instructor.

9. ✴ What other RSS feeds might you find useful to include in Microsoft Outlook?

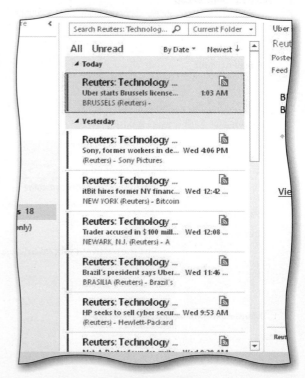

Figure 5–89

In the Labs

Design, create, modify, and/or use files following the guidelines, concepts, and skills presented in this module. Labs 1 and 2, which increase in difficulty, require you to create solutions based on what you learned in the module; Lab 3 requires you to apply your creative thinking and problem-solving skills to design and implement a solution.

Lab 1: **Creating Multiple Signatures**

Problem: You communicate with both instructors and other students via email. Your professors ask students to clearly identify themselves in email messages, but you do not want to include the same information in email messages you send to your friends. Instead, you want to include your nickname and cell phone number in your email signature. You will create two signatures: one to use when you send email messages to your instructors, and another for email messages you send to friends. You will use the Signatures and Stationery dialog box to create the signatures (Figure 5–90).

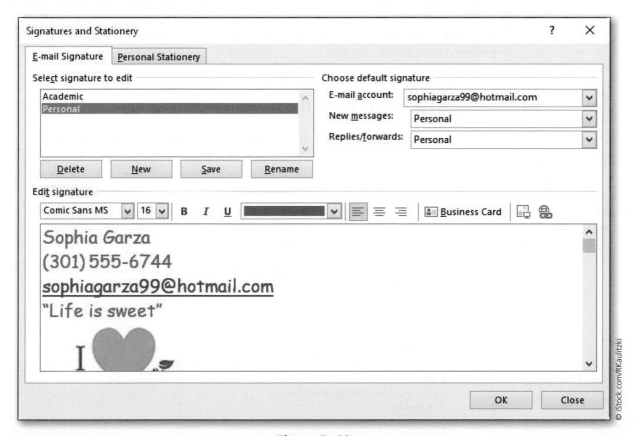

Figure 5–90

Perform the following tasks:

1. Display the Outlook Options dialog box, and then display the Signatures and Stationery dialog box.

2. Create a signature using **Academic** as the name of the signature.

3. Change the font to Cooper Black and the font size to 16.

Continued >

In the Labs *continued*

4. On three lines, enter the following information: your name, the name of your school, and your email address.

5. Using the Academic signature, send an email message to your instructor. The email message should specify that the signature is the Academic signature.

6. Create another signature using `Personal` as the name of the signature.

7. Change the font to Comic Sans MS, the font size to 16, and the font color to one of your choosing.

8. On four lines, enter the following information: your name, your phone number, your email address, and a life quote in quotation marks.

9. From the Data Files, add the image named Vegan in your signature file or add your own photo for your personal signature.

10. Select a Theme for your Personal signature.

11. Using the Personal signature, send an email message to a friend and a copy to your instructor to tell them what you are learning in this class. The email message should specify that the signature is the Personal signature.

12. ✳ Do you think it is easier to switch back and forth between different signatures or manually type signature information individually into each email message? Why?

Lab 2: **Configuring Junk Email**

Problem: You occasionally find email messages you want to read in the Junk E-mail folder for your Outlook email account. You also receive spam from a certain email address. You want to use the Junk E-mail Options dialog box to make sure you receive email messages from some senders, while blocking email messages from another sender. Set up a rule as shown in Figure 5-91. This lab requires that you capture screen shots during the following steps. Your instructor will provide instructions for how to create a screen shot using the Microsoft Word Screenshot tool or the Microsoft Windows Snipping Tool.

Figure 5–91

Perform the following tasks:

1. In Outlook, display the Junk E-mail Options dialog box.

2. Add @yahoo.com to the Safe Senders list. Take a screen shot of what is displayed in the Safe Senders list.

3. Add eblue179@gmail.com to the Safe Recipients list. Take a screen shot of what is displayed in the Safe Recipients list.

4. Add @worldgames.net to the Blocked Senders list. Take a screen shot of what is displayed in the Blocked Senders list.

5. Create a new rule that flags messages for follow-up from ctirrell@live.com. Flag the message for follow-up today. Take a screen shot of what is displayed in the Rules Wizard setup dialog box after you set up the rule as shown in Figure 5–91.

6. Submit the screen shots in the format specified by your instructor.

7. ✳ What other domains and email addresses might you add to the Safe Senders list? What are some examples of other domains and email addresses you might add to the Blocked Senders list?

Lab 3: **Consider This: Your Turn**

Apply your creative thinking and problem solving skills to design and implement a solution.

Creating Rules for Email

Problem: This semester you will be receiving emails from many different instructors. To stay organized, create the following folders and rules. This lab requires that you capture screen shots during the following steps. Your instructor will provide instructions for how to create a screen shot using the Microsoft Word Screenshot tool or the Microsoft Windows Snipping Tool.

Part 1: For four of the classes you are currently taking, create email folders for each class and take a screen shot of the four folders. Create four rules to move messages related to the classes to the appropriate class email folder and take a screen shot of each completed rule. Write a rule for the fourth class that flags messages for follow-up for today. Submit the screen shots in the format specified by your instructor.

Part 2: ✳ You made several decisions when creating the rules in this exercise, such as which folders to create and how to set up the rule to identify to which class an email message belongs. What was the rationale behind each of these decisions?

Microsoft® Office 365™
OUTLOOK® 2016

Microsoft® Office 365™
OUTLOOK® 2016

INTERMEDIATE

HOISINGTON

CENGAGE
Learning·

SHELLY CASHMAN SERIES®

Australia • Brazil • Japan • Korea • Mexico • Singapore • Spain • United Kingdom • United States

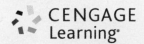

**Shelly Cashman Microsoft Office 365 &
Outlook 2016: Intermediate**
Corinne Hoisington

SVP, GM Skills & Global Product Management:
 Dawn Gerrain

Product Director: Kathleen McMahon

Senior Product Team Manager: Lauren Murphy

Product Team Manager: Andrea Topping

Associate Product Manager: Melissa Stehler

Senior Director, Development: Marah
 Bellegarde

Product Development Manager: Leigh Hefferon

Senior Content Developer: Alyssa Pratt

Developmental Editor: Lisa Ruffolo

Product Assistant: Erica Chapman

Manuscript Quality Assurance Project Leader:
 Jeffrey Schwartz

Senior Production Director: Wendy Troeger

Production Director: Patty Stephan

Content Project Manager: Arul Joseph Raj,
 Lumina

Manufacturing Planner: Julio Esperas

Designer: Diana Graham

Text Design: Joel Sadagursky

Cover Template Designer: Diana Graham

Cover images: Mario7/Shutterstock.com; Mrs.
 Opossum/Shutterstock.com

Compositor: Lumina Datamatics

Vice President, Marketing: Brian Joyner

Marketing Director: Michele McTighe

Marketing Manager: Stephanie Albracht

For product information and technology assistance, contact us at
Cengage Learning Customer & Sales Support, 1-800-354-9706

For permission to use material from this text or product,
submit all requests online at www.cengage.com/permissions.
Further permissions questions can be e-mailed to
permissionrequest@cengage.com

Library of Congress Control Number: 2015957838

ISBN: 978-1-305-87114-4

Cengage Learning
20 Channel Center Street
Boston, MA 02210
USA

Cengage Learning is a leading provider of customized learning solutions with
employees residing in nearly 40 different countries and sales in more than 125
countries around the world. Find your local representative at
www.cengage.com.

Cengage Learning products are represented in Canada by Nelson Education, Ltd.

To learn more about Cengage Learning, visit **www.cengage.com**

Purchase any of our products at your local college store or at our preferred
online store **www.cengagebrain.com**

Printed in the United States of America
Print Number: 01   Print Year: 2016

Productivity Apps for School and Work

Corinne Hoisington

Lochlan keeps track of his class notes, football plays, and internship meetings with OneNote.

Zoe is using the annotation features of Microsoft Edge to take and save web notes for her research paper.

Nori is creating a Sway site to highlight this year's activities for the Student Government Association.

Hunter is adding interactive videos and screen recordings to his PowerPoint resume.

© Rawpixel/Shutterstock.com

Being computer literate no longer means mastery of only Word, Excel, PowerPoint, Outlook, and Access. To become technology power users, Hunter, Nori, Zoe, and Lochlan are exploring Microsoft OneNote, Sway, Mix, and Edge in Office 2016 and Windows 10.

In this Module

Introduction to OneNote 2016 2
Introduction to Sway 6
Introduction to Office Mix 10
Introduction to Microsoft Edge 14

Learn to use productivity apps!
Links to companion **Sways**, featuring **videos** with hands-on instructions, are located on www.cengagebrain.com.

Introduction to OneNote 2016

notebook | section tab | To Do tag | screen clipping | note | template | Microsoft OneNote Mobile app | sync | drawing canvas | inked handwriting | Ink to Text

As you glance around any classroom, you invariably see paper notebooks and notepads on each desk. Because deciphering and sharing handwritten notes can be a challenge, Microsoft OneNote 2016 replaces physical notebooks, binders, and paper notes with a searchable, digital notebook. OneNote captures your ideas and schoolwork on any device so you can stay organized, share notes, and work with others on projects. Whether you are a student taking class notes as shown in **Figure 1** or an employee taking notes in company meetings, OneNote is the one place to keep notes for all of your projects.

Bottom Line
- OneNote is a note-taking app for your academic and professional life.
- Use OneNote to get organized by gathering your ideas, sketches, webpages, photos, videos, and notes in one place.

Figure 1: OneNote 2016 notebook

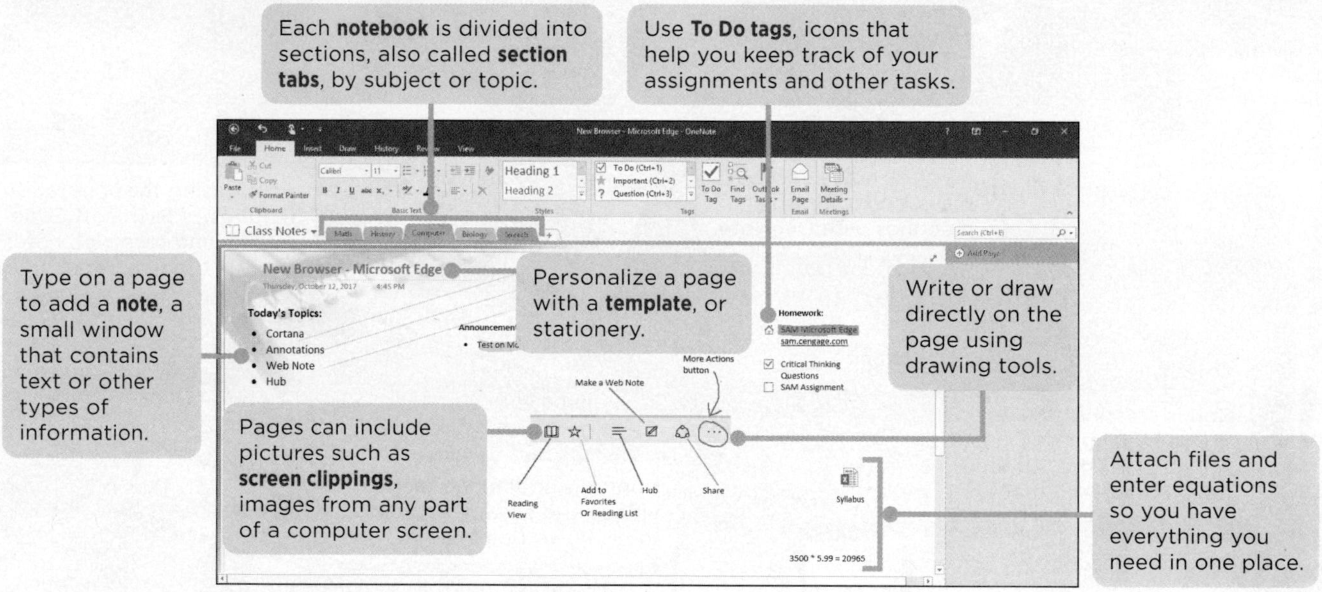

Each **notebook** is divided into sections, also called **section tabs**, by subject or topic.

Use **To Do tags**, icons that help you keep track of your assignments and other tasks.

Type on a page to add a **note**, a small window that contains text or other types of information.

Personalize a page with a **template**, or stationery.

Write or draw directly on the page using drawing tools.

Pages can include pictures such as **screen clippings**, images from any part of a computer screen.

Attach files and enter equations so you have everything you need in one place.

Creating a OneNote Notebook

OneNote is divided into sections similar to those in a spiral-bound notebook. Each OneNote notebook contains sections, pages, and other notebooks. You can use One-Note for school, business, and personal projects. Store information for each type of project in different notebooks to keep your tasks separate, or use any other organization that suits you. OneNote is flexible enough to adapt to the way you want to work.

When you create a notebook, it contains a blank page with a plain white background by default, though you can use templates, or stationery, to apply designs in categories such as Academic, Business, Decorative, and Planners. Start typing or use the buttons on the Insert tab to insert notes, which are small resizable windows that can contain text, equations, tables, on-screen writing, images, audio and video recordings, to-do lists, file attachments, and file printouts. Add as many notes as you need to each page.

Learn to use OneNote!
Links to companion **Sways**, featuring **videos** with hands-on instructions, are located on www.cengagebrain.com.

Syncing a Notebook to the Cloud

OneNote saves your notes every time you make a change in a notebook. To make sure you can access your notebooks with a laptop, tablet, or smartphone wherever you are, OneNote uses cloud-based storage, such as OneDrive or SharePoint. **Microsoft OneNote Mobile app**, a lightweight version of OneNote 2016 shown in **Figure 2**, is available for free in the Windows Store, Google Play for Android devices, and the AppStore for iOS devices.

If you have a Microsoft account, OneNote saves your notes on OneDrive automatically for all your mobile devices and computers, which is called **syncing**. For example, you can use OneNote to take notes on your laptop during class, and then open OneNote on your phone to study later. To use a notebook stored on your computer with your OneNote Mobile app, move the notebook to OneDrive. You can quickly share notebook content with other people using OneDrive.

Figure 2: Microsoft OneNote Mobile app

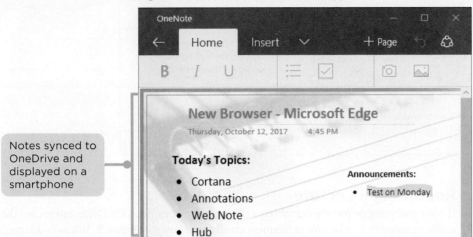

Notes synced to OneDrive and displayed on a smartphone

Taking Notes

Use OneNote pages to organize your notes by class and topic or lecture. Beyond simple typed notes, OneNote stores drawings, converts handwriting to searchable text and mathematical sketches to equations, and records audio and video.

OneNote includes drawing tools that let you sketch freehand drawings such as biological cell diagrams and financial supply-and-demand charts. As shown in **Figure 3**, the Draw tab on the ribbon provides these drawing tools along with shapes so you can insert diagrams and other illustrations to represent your ideas. When you draw on a page, OneNote creates a **drawing canvas**, which is a container for shapes and lines.

On the Job Now

OneNote is ideal for taking notes during meetings, whether you are recording minutes, documenting a discussion, sketching product diagrams, or listing follow-up items. Use a meeting template to add pages with content appropriate for meetings.

Figure 3: Tools on the Draw tab

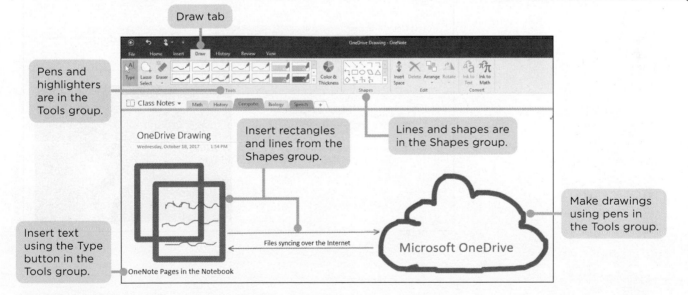

Draw tab

Pens and highlighters are in the Tools group.

Insert rectangles and lines from the Shapes group.

Lines and shapes are in the Shapes group.

Make drawings using pens in the Tools group.

Insert text using the Type button in the Tools group.

Converting Handwriting to Text

When you use a pen tool to write on a notebook page, the text you enter is called **inked handwriting**. OneNote can convert inked handwriting to typed text when you use the **Ink to Text** button in the Convert group on the Draw tab, as shown in **Figure 4**. After OneNote converts the handwriting to text, you can use the Search box to find terms in the converted text or any other note in your notebooks.

Figure 4: Converting handwriting to text

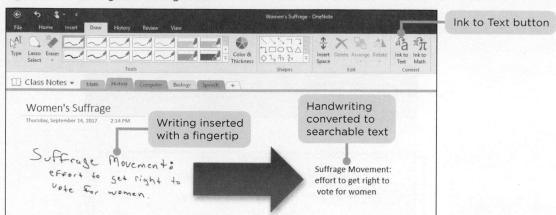

Ink to Text button

Women's Suffrage
Thursday, September 14, 2017   2:14 PM

Writing inserted with a fingertip

Suffrage Movement: effort to get right to vote for women.

Handwriting converted to searchable text

Suffrage Movement: effort to get right to vote for women

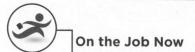
Recording a Lecture

If your computer or mobile device has a microphone or camera, OneNote can record the audio or video from a lecture or business meeting as shown in **Figure 5**. When you record a lecture (with your instructor's permission), you can follow along, take regular notes at your own pace, and review the video recording later. You can control the start, pause, and stop motions of the recording when you play back the recording of your notes.

Figure 5: Video inserted in a notebook

Record Video button

Audio & Video Recording tab

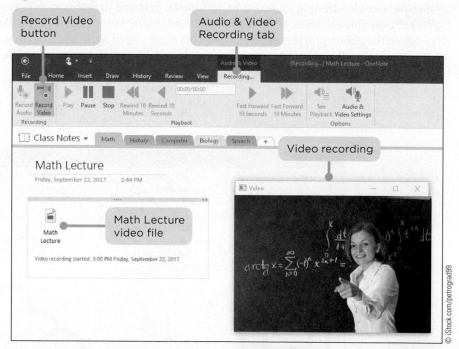

Video recording

Math Lecture
Friday, September 22, 2017   2:44 PM

Math Lecture video file

Video recording started: 3:00 PM Friday, September 22, 2017

© iStock.com/petrograd99

Try This Now

1: Taking Notes for a Week

As a student, you can get organized by using OneNote to take detailed notes in your classes. Perform the following tasks:

    a. Create a new OneNote notebook on your Microsoft OneDrive account (the default location for new notebooks). Name the notebook with your first name followed by "Notes," as in **Caleb Notes**.

    b. Create four section tabs, each with a different class name.

    c. Take detailed notes in those classes for one week. Be sure to include notes, drawings, and other types of content.

    d. Sync your notes with your OneDrive. Submit your assignment in the format specified by your instructor.

> **Learn to use OneNote!**
> Links to companion **Sways**, featuring **videos** with hands-on instructions, are located on www.cengagebrain.com.

2: Using OneNote to Organize a Research Paper

You have a research paper due on the topic of three habits of successful students. Use OneNote to organize your research. Perform the following tasks:

    a. Create a new OneNote notebook on your Microsoft OneDrive account. Name the notebook **Success Research**.

    b. Create three section tabs with the following names:

- **Take Detailed Notes**
- **Be Respectful in Class**
- **Come to Class Prepared**

    c. On the web, research the topics and find three sources for each section. Copy a sentence from each source and paste the sentence into the appropriate section. When you paste the sentence, OneNote inserts it in a note with a link to the source.

    d. Sync your notes with your OneDrive. Submit your assignment in the format specified by your instructor.

3: Planning Your Career

Note: This activity requires a webcam or built-in video camera on any type of device.

Consider an occupation that interests you. Using OneNote, examine the responsibilities, education requirements, potential salary, and employment outlook of a specific career. Perform the following tasks:

    a. Create a new OneNote notebook on your Microsoft OneDrive account. Name the notebook with your first name followed by a career title, such as **Kara - App Developer**.

    b. Create four section tabs with the names **Responsibilities, Education Requirements, Median Salary**, and **Employment Outlook**.

    c. Research the responsibilities of your career path. Using OneNote, record a short video (approximately 30 seconds) of yourself explaining the responsibilities of your career path. Place the video in the Responsibilities section.

    d. On the web, research the educational requirements for your career path and find two appropriate sources. Copy a paragraph from each source and paste them into the appropriate section. When you paste a paragraph, OneNote inserts it in a note with a link to the source.

    e. Research the median salary for a single year for this career. Create a mathematical equation in the Median Salary section that multiplies the amount of the median salary times 20 years to calculate how much you will possibly earn.

    f. For the Employment Outlook section, research the outlook for your career path. Take at least four notes about what you find when researching the topic.

    g. Sync your notes with your OneDrive. Submit your assignment in the format specified by your instructor.

Introduction to Sway

Sway site | responsive design | Storyline | card | Creative Commons license | animation emphasis effects | Docs.com

Expressing your ideas in a presentation typically means creating PowerPoint slides or a Word document. Microsoft Sway gives you another way to engage an audience. Sway is a free Microsoft tool available at Sway.com or as an app in Office 365. Using Sway, you can combine text, images, videos, and social media in a website called a **Sway site** that you can share and display on any device. To get started, you create a digital story on a web-based canvas without borders, slides, cells, or page breaks. A Sway site organizes the text, images, and video into a **responsive design**, which means your content adapts perfectly to any screen size as shown in **Figure 6**. You store a Sway site in the cloud on OneDrive using a free Microsoft account.

Figure 6: Sway site with responsive design

You can display a Sway presentation in a web browser.

Sway uses responsive design to make sure pages fit perfectly on any device.

© iStock.com/marinello, © iStock.com/marekuliasz

Creating a Sway Presentation
You can use Sway to build a digital flyer, a club newsletter, a vacation blog, an informational site, a digital art portfolio, or a new product rollout. After you select your topic and sign into Sway with your Microsoft account, a **Storyline** opens, providing tools and a work area for composing your digital story. See **Figure 7**. Each story can include text, images, and videos. You create a Sway by adding text and media content into a Storyline section, or **card**. To add pictures, videos, or documents, select a card in the left pane and then select the Insert Content button. The first card in a Sway presentation contains a title and background image.

Figure 7: Creating a Sway site

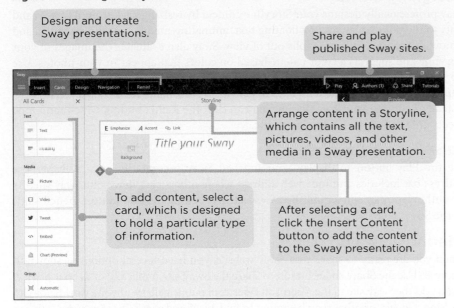

Design and create Sway presentations.

Share and play published Sway sites.

Arrange content in a Storyline, which contains all the text, pictures, videos, and other media in a Sway presentation.

To add content, select a card, which is designed to hold a particular type of information.

After selecting a card, click the Insert Content button to add the content to the Sway presentation.

Adding Content to Build a Story

As you work, Sway searches the Internet to help you find relevant images, videos, tweets, and other content from online sources such as Bing, YouTube, Twitter, and Facebook. You can drag content from the search results right into the Storyline. In addition, you can upload your own images and videos directly in the presentation. For example, if you are creating a Sway presentation about the market for commercial drones, Sway suggests content to incorporate into the presentation by displaying it in the left pane as search results. The search results include drone images tagged with a **Creative Commons license** at online sources as shown in **Figure 8**. A Creative Commons license is a public copyright license that allows the free distribution of an otherwise copyrighted work. In addition, you can specify the source of the media. For example, you can add your own Facebook or OneNote pictures and videos in Sway without leaving the app.

On the Job Now

If you have a Microsoft Word document containing an outline of your business content, drag the outline into Sway to create a card for each topic.

Figure 8: Images in Sway search results

Select the source of media objects

Information about Creative Commons licenses

Storyline title

The Market for Commercial Drones

Drag an image to the picture placeholder box

Suggested images in the search results

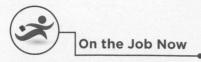
Designing a Sway

Sway professionally designs your Storyline content by resizing background images and fonts to fit your display, and by floating text, animating media, embedding video, and removing images as a page scrolls out of view. Sway also evaluates the images in your Storyline and suggests a color palette based on colors that appear in your photos. Use the Design button to display tools including color palettes, font choices, **animation emphasis effects**, and style templates to provide a personality for a Sway presentation. Instead of creating your own design, you can click the Remix button, which randomly selects unique designs for your Sway site.

Publishing a Sway

Use the Play button to display your finished Sway presentation as a website. The Address bar includes a unique web address where others can view your Sway site. As the author, you can edit a published Sway site by clicking the Edit button (pencil icon) on the Sway toolbar.

Sharing a Sway

When you are ready to share your Sway website, you have several options as shown in **Figure 9**. Use the Share slider button to share the Sway site publically or keep it private. If you add the Sway site to the Microsoft **Docs.com** public gallery, anyone worldwide can use Bing, Google, or other search engines to find, view, and share your Sway site. You can also share your Sway site using Facebook, Twitter, Google+, Yammer, and other social media sites. Link your presentation to any webpage or email the link to your audience. Sway can also generate a code for embedding the link within another webpage.

Figure 9: Sharing a Sway site

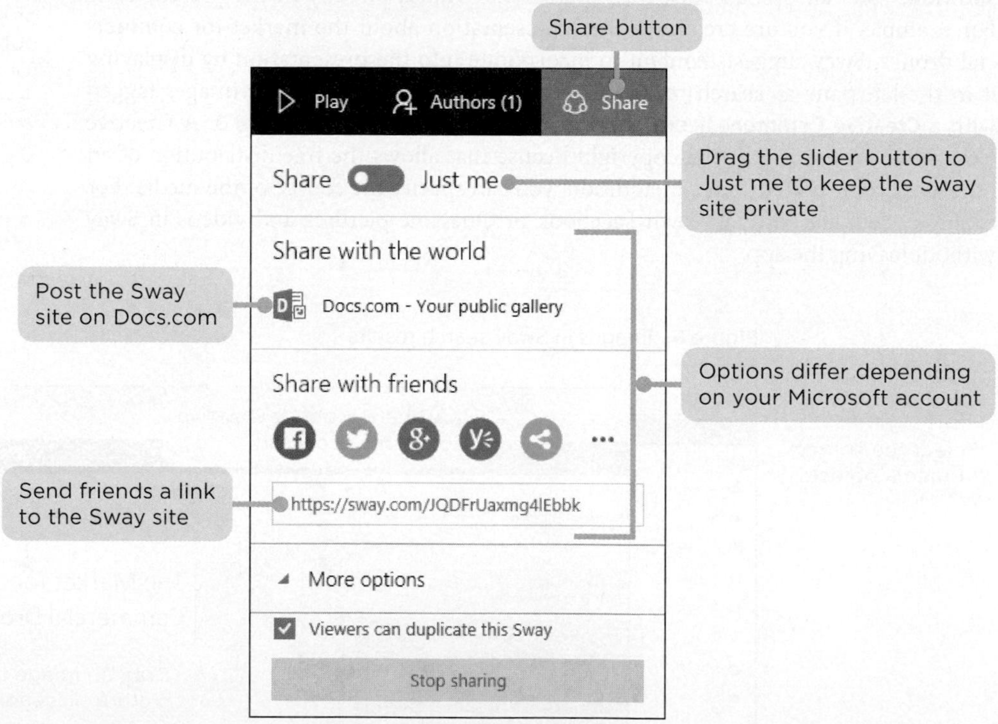

Try This Now

Learn to use Sway!
Links to companion **Sways**, featuring **videos** with hands-on instructions, are located on www.cengagebrain.com.

1: Creating a Sway Resume

Sway is a digital storytelling app. Create a Sway resume to share the skills, job experiences, and achievements you have that match the requirements of a future job interest. Perform the following tasks:

    a. Create a new presentation in Sway to use as a digital resume. Title the Sway Storyline with your full name and then select a background image.

    b. Create three separate sections titled **Academic Background, Work Experience**, and **Skills**, and insert text, a picture, and a paragraph or bulleted points in each section. Be sure to include your own picture.

    c. Add a fourth section that includes a video about your school that you find online.

    d. Customize the design of your presentation.

    e. Submit your assignment link in the format specified by your instructor.

2: Creating an Online Sway Newsletter

Newsletters are designed to capture the attention of their target audience. Using Sway, create a newsletter for a club, organization, or your favorite music group. Perform the following tasks:

    a. Create a new presentation in Sway to use as a digital newsletter for a club, organization, or your favorite music group. Provide a title for the Sway Storyline and select an appropriate background image.

    b. Select three separate sections with appropriate titles, such as Upcoming Events. In each section, insert text, a picture, and a paragraph or bulleted points.

    c. Add a fourth section that includes a video about your selected topic.

    d. Customize the design of your presentation.

    e. Submit your assignment link in the format specified by your instructor.

3: Creating and Sharing a Technology Presentation

To place a Sway presentation in the hands of your entire audience, you can share a link to the Sway presentation. Create a Sway presentation on a new technology and share it with your class. Perform the following tasks:

    a. Create a new presentation in Sway about a cutting-edge technology topic. Provide a title for the Sway Storyline and select a background image.

    b. Create four separate sections about your topic, and include text, a picture, and a paragraph in each section.

    c. Add a fifth section that includes a video about your topic.

    d. Customize the design of your presentation.

    e. Share the link to your Sway with your classmates and submit your assignment link in the format specified by your instructor.

Introduction to Office Mix

add-in | clip | slide recording | Slide Notes | screen recording | free-response quiz

To enliven business meetings and lectures, Microsoft adds a new dimension to presentations with a powerful toolset called Office Mix, a free add-in for PowerPoint. (An **add-in** is software that works with an installed app to extend its features.) Using Office Mix, you can record yourself on video, capture still and moving images on your desktop, and insert interactive elements such as quizzes and live webpages directly into PowerPoint slides. When you post the finished presentation to OneDrive, Office Mix provides a link you can share with friends and colleagues. Anyone with an Internet connection and a web browser can watch a published Office Mix presentation, such as the one in **Figure 10**, on a computer or mobile device.

Figure 10: Office Mix presentation

Adding Office Mix to PowerPoint

To get started, you create an Office Mix account at the website mix.office.com using an email address or a Facebook or Google account. Next, you download and install the Office Mix add-in (see **Figure 11**). Office Mix appears as a new tab named Mix on the PowerPoint ribbon in versions of Office 2013 and Office 2016 running on personal computers (PCs).

Figure 11: Getting started with Office Mix

Capturing Video Clips

A **clip** is a short segment of audio, such as music, or video. After finishing the content on a PowerPoint slide, you can use Office Mix to add a video clip to animate or illustrate the content. Office Mix creates video clips in two ways: by recording live action on a webcam and by capturing screen images and movements. If your computer has a webcam, you can record yourself and annotate the slide to create a **slide recording** as shown in **Figure 12**.

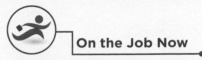

On the Job Now

Companies are using Office Mix to train employees about new products, to explain benefit packages to new workers, and to educate interns about office procedures.

Figure 12: Making a slide recording

Record your voice; also record video if your computer has a camera.

Use the Slide Notes button to display notes for your narration.

For best results, look directly at your webcam while recording video.

Use inking tools to write and draw on the slide as you record.

Choose a video and audio device to record images and sound.

When you are making a slide recording, you can record your spoken narration at the same time. The **Slide Notes** feature works like a teleprompter to help you focus on your presentation content instead of memorizing your narration. Use the Inking tools to make annotations or add highlighting using different pen types and colors. After finishing a recording, edit the video in PowerPoint to trim the length or set playback options.

The second way to create a video is to capture on-screen images and actions with or without a voiceover. This method is ideal if you want to show how to use your favorite website or demonstrate an app such as OneNote. To share your screen with an audience, select the part of the screen you want to show in the video. Office Mix captures everything that happens in that area to create a **screen recording**, as shown in **Figure 13**. Office Mix inserts the screen recording as a video in the slide.

On the Job Now

To make your video recordings accessible to people with hearing impairments, use the Office Mix closed-captioning tools. You can also use closed captions to supplement audio that is difficult to understand and to provide an aid for those learning to read.

Figure 13: Making a screen recording

Record the action on the screen within the red dashed outline.

Select Area button

Record audio while capturing your on-screen actions.

Inserting Quizzes, Live Webpages, and Apps

To enhance and assess audience understanding, make your slides interactive by adding quizzes, live webpages, and apps. Quizzes give immediate feedback to the user as shown in **Figure 14**. Office Mix supports several quiz formats, including a **free-response quiz** similar to a short answer quiz, and true/false, multiple-choice, and multiple-response formats.

Figure 14: Creating an interactive quiz

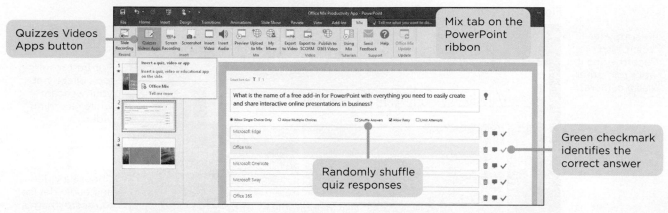

Sharing an Office Mix Presentation

When you complete your work with Office Mix, upload the presentation to your personal Office Mix dashboard as shown in **Figure 15**. Users of PCs, Macs, iOS devices, and Android devices can access and play Office Mix presentations. The Office Mix dashboard displays built-in analytics that include the quiz results and how much time viewers spent on each slide. You can play completed Office Mix presentations online or download them as movies.

Figure 15: Sharing an Office Mix presentation

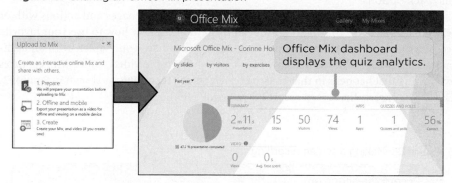

Try This Now

1: Creating an Office Mix Tutorial for OneNote

Note: This activity requires a microphone on your computer.

Office Mix makes it easy to record screens and their contents. Create PowerPoint slides with an Office Mix screen recording to show OneNote 2016 features. Perform the following tasks:

  a. Create a PowerPoint presentation with the Ion Boardroom template. Create an opening slide with the title **My Favorite OneNote Features** and enter your name in the subtitle.
  b. Create three additional slides, each titled with a new feature of OneNote. Open OneNote and use the Mix tab in PowerPoint to capture three separate screen recordings that teach your favorite features.
  c. Add a fifth slide that quizzes the user with a multiple-choice question about OneNote and includes four responses. Be sure to insert a checkmark indicating the correct response.
  d. Upload the completed presentation to your Office Mix dashboard and share the link with your instructor.
  e. Submit your assignment link in the format specified by your instructor.

2: Teaching Augmented Reality with Office Mix

Note: This activity requires a webcam or built-in video camera on your computer.

A local elementary school has asked you to teach augmented reality to its students using Office Mix. Perform the following tasks:

  a. Research augmented reality using your favorite online search tools.
  b. Create a PowerPoint presentation with the Frame template. Create an opening slide with the title **Augmented Reality** and enter your name in the subtitle.
  c. Create a slide with four bullets summarizing your research of augmented reality. Create a 20-second slide recording of yourself providing a quick overview of augmented reality.
  d. Create another slide with a 30-second screen recording of a video about augmented reality from a site such as YouTube or another video-sharing site.
  e. Add a final slide that quizzes the user with a true/false question about augmented reality. Be sure to insert a checkmark indicating the correct response.
  f. Upload the completed presentation to your Office Mix dashboard and share the link with your instructor.
  g. Submit your assignment link in the format specified by your instructor.

3: Marketing a Travel Destination with Office Mix

Note: This activity requires a webcam or built-in video camera on your computer.

To convince your audience to travel to a particular city, create a slide presentation marketing any city in the world using a slide recording, screen recording, and a quiz. Perform the following tasks:

  a. Create a PowerPoint presentation with any template. Create an opening slide with the title of the city you are marketing as a travel destination and your name in the subtitle.
  b. Create a slide with four bullets about the featured city. Create a 30-second slide recording of yourself explaining why this city is the perfect vacation destination.
  c. Create another slide with a 20-second screen recording of a travel video about the city from a site such as YouTube or another video-sharing site.
  d. Add a final slide that quizzes the user with a multiple-choice question about the featured city with five responses. Be sure to include a checkmark indicating the correct response.
  e. Upload the completed presentation to your Office Mix dashboard and share your link with your instructor.
  f. Submit your assignment link in the format specified by your instructor.

Introduction to Microsoft Edge

Reading view | Hub | Cortana | Web Note | Inking | sandbox

Microsoft Edge is the default web browser developed for the Windows 10 operating system as a replacement for Internet Explorer. Unlike its predecessor, Edge lets you write on webpages, read webpages without advertisements and other distractions, and search for information using a virtual personal assistant. The Edge interface is clean and basic, as shown in **Figure 16**, meaning you can pay more attention to the webpage content.

Figure 16: Microsoft Edge tools

- Forward button
- New tab button
- Web address in the Address bar
- Add to favorites or reading list button
- Back button
- Reading view button
- More button
- Share Web Note button
- Refresh (F5) button
- Hub (Favorites, reading list, history, and downloads) button
- Make a Web Note button

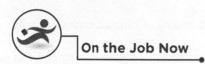

Browsing the Web with Microsoft Edge

One of the fastest browsers available, Edge allows you to type search text directly in the Address bar. As you view the resulting webpage, you can switch to **Reading view**, which is available for most news and research sites, to eliminate distracting advertisements. For example, if you are catching up on technology news online, the webpage might be difficult to read due to a busy layout cluttered with ads. Switch to Reading view to refresh the page and remove the original page formatting, ads, and menu sidebars to read the article distraction-free.

Consider the **Hub** in Microsoft Edge as providing one-stop access to all the things you collect on the web, such as your favorite websites, reading list, surfing history, and downloaded files.

Locating Information with Cortana

Cortana, the Windows 10 virtual assistant, plays an important role in Microsoft Edge. After you turn on Cortana, it appears as an animated circle in the Address bar when you might need assistance, as shown in the restaurant website in **Figure 17**. When you click the Cortana icon, a pane slides in from the right of the browser window to display detailed information about the restaurant, including maps and reviews. Cortana can also assist you in defining words, finding the weather, suggesting coupons for shopping, updating stock market information, and calculating math.

Figure 17: Cortana providing restaurant information

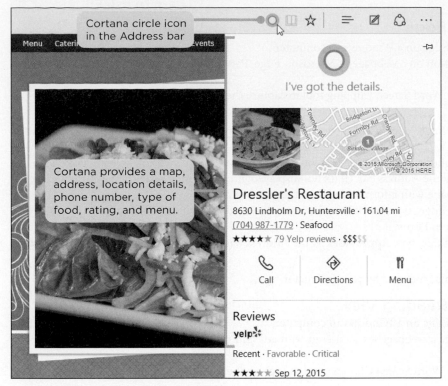

Cortana circle icon in the Address bar

Cortana provides a map, address, location details, phone number, type of food, rating, and menu.

I've got the details.

Dressler's Restaurant
8630 Lindholm Dr, Huntersville · 161.04 mi
(704) 987-1779 · Seafood
★★★★☆ 79 Yelp reviews · $$$$$

📞 Call   ◈ Directions   🍴 Menu

Reviews
yelp⁂
Recent · Favorable · Critical
★★★☆☆ Sep 12, 2015

Annotating Webpages

One of the most impressive Microsoft Edge features are the **Web Note** tools, which you use to write on a webpage or to highlight text. When you click the Make a Web Note button, an **Inking** toolbar appears, as shown in **Figure 18**, that provides writing and drawing tools. These tools include an eraser, a pen, and a highlighter with different colors. You can also insert a typed note and copy a screen image (called a screen clipping). You can draw with a pointing device, fingertip, or stylus using different pen colors. Whether you add notes to a recipe, annotate sources for a research paper, or select a product while shopping online, the Web Note tools can enhance your productivity. After you complete your notes, click the Save button to save the annotations to OneNote, your Favorites list, or your Reading list. You can share the inked page with others using the Share Web Note button.

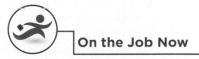

On the Job Now

To enhance security, Microsoft Edge runs in a partial sandbox, an arrangement that prevents attackers from gaining control of your computer. Browsing within the **sandbox** protects computer resources and information from hackers.

Figure 18: Web Note tools in Microsoft Edge

Inking toolbar with Web Note tools for making annotations

Writing and drawing created with the Pen tool

Highlighted text

Save a copy of the webpage with annotations

Typed note

Try This Now

Learn to use Edge!

Links to companion **Sways**, featuring **videos** with hands-on instructions, are located on www.cengagebrain.com.

1: Using Cortana in Microsoft Edge

Note: This activity requires using Microsoft Edge on a Windows 10 computer.

   Cortana can assist you in finding information on a webpage in Microsoft Edge. Perform the following tasks:

   a. Create a Word document using the Word Screen Clipping tool to capture the following screenshots.

   - Screenshot A—Using Microsoft Edge, open a webpage with a technology news article. Right-click a term in the article and ask Cortana to define it.
   - Screenshot B—Using Microsoft Edge, open the website of a fancy restaurant in a city near you. Make sure the Cortana circle icon is displayed in the Address bar. (If it's not displayed, find a different restaurant website.) Click the Cortana circle icon to display a pane with information about the restaurant.
   - Screenshot C—Using Microsoft Edge, type **10 USD to Euros** in the Address bar without pressing the Enter key. Cortana converts the U.S. dollars to Euros.
   - Screenshot D—Using Microsoft Edge, type **Apple stock** in the Address bar without pressing the Enter key. Cortana displays the current stock quote.

   b. Submit your assignment in the format specified by your instructor.

2: Viewing Online News with Reading View

Note: This activity requires using Microsoft Edge on a Windows 10 computer.

   Reading view in Microsoft Edge can make a webpage less cluttered with ads and other distractions. Perform the following tasks:

   a. Create a Word document using the Word Screen Clipping tool to capture the following screenshots.

   - Screenshot A—Using Microsoft Edge, open the website **mashable.com**. Open a technology article. Click the Reading view button to display an ad-free page that uses only basic text formatting.
   - Screenshot B—Using Microsoft Edge, open the website **bbc.com**. Open any news article. Click the Reading view button to display an ad-free page that uses only basic text formatting.
   - Screenshot C—Make three types of annotations (Pen, Highlighter, and Add a typed note) on the BBC article page displayed in Reading view.

   b. Submit your assignment in the format specified by your instructor.

3: Inking with Microsoft Edge

Note: This activity requires using Microsoft Edge on a Windows 10 computer.

   Microsoft Edge provides many annotation options to record your ideas. Perform the following tasks:

   a. Open the website **wolframalpha.com** in the Microsoft Edge browser. Wolfram Alpha is a well-respected academic search engine. Type **US$100 1965 dollars in 2015** in the Wolfram Alpha search text box and press the Enter key.

   b. Click the Make a Web Note button to display the Web Note tools. Using the Pen tool, draw a circle around the result on the webpage. Save the page to OneNote.

   c. In the Wolfram Alpha search text box, type the name of the city closest to where you live and press the Enter key. Using the Highlighter tool, highlight at least three interesting results. Add a note and then type a sentence about what you learned about this city. Save the page to OneNote. Share your OneNote notebook with your instructor.

   d. Submit your assignment link in the format specified by your instructor.

Office 2016 and Windows 10: Essential Concepts and Skills

Objectives

You will have mastered the material in this module when you can:

- Use a touch screen
- Perform basic mouse operations
- Start Windows and sign in to an account
- Identify the objects on the Windows 10 desktop
- Identify the apps in and versions of Microsoft Office 2016
- Run an app
- Identify the components of the Microsoft Office ribbon

- Create folders
- Save files
- Change screen resolution
- Perform basic tasks in Microsoft Office apps
- Manage files
- Use Microsoft Office Help and Windows Help

This introductory module covers features and functions common to Office 2016 apps, as well as the basics of Windows 10.

Roadmap

In this module, you will learn how to perform basic tasks in Windows and the Office apps. The following roadmap identifies general activities you will perform as you progress through this module:

1. SIGN IN to an account
2. USE WINDOWS
3. USE Office APPS
4. FILE and Folder MANAGEMENT
5. SWITCH between APPS

6. SAVE and Manage FILES

7. CHANGE SCREEN RESOLUTION

8. EXIT Office APPS

9. USE ADDITIONAL Office APPS

10. USE Office and Windows HELP

At the beginning of the step instructions throughout each module, you will see an abbreviated form of this roadmap. The abbreviated roadmap uses colors to indicate module progress: gray means the module is beyond that activity, blue means the task being shown is covered in that activity, and black means that activity is yet to be covered. For example, the following abbreviated roadmap indicates the module would be showing a task in the USE APPS activity.

1 SIGN IN | 2 USE WINDOWS | 3 USE APPS | 4 FILE MANAGEMENT | 5 SWITCH APPS | 6 SAVE FILES
7 CHANGE SCREEN RESOLUTION | 8 EXIT APPS | 9 USE ADDITIONAL APPS | 10 USE HELP

Use the abbreviated roadmap as a progress guide while you read or step through the instructions in this module.

Introduction to the Windows 10 Operating System

Windows 10 is the newest version of Microsoft Windows, which is a popular and widely used operating system (Figure 1). An **operating system (OS)** is a set of programs that coordinate all the activities among computer or mobile device hardware.

Windows 10 desktop

Figure 1

The Windows operating system simplifies the process of working with documents and apps by organizing the manner in which you interact with the computer. Windows is used to run apps. An application, or **app**, consists of programs designed to make users more productive and/or assist them with personal tasks, such as word processing or browsing the web.

OFF 2

Using a Touch Screen and a Mouse

Windows users who have computers or devices with touch screen capability can interact with the screen using gestures. A **gesture** is a motion you make on a touch screen with the tip of one or more fingers or your hand. Touch screens are convenient because they do not require a separate device for input. Table 1 presents common ways to interact with a touch screen.

If you are using your finger on a touch screen and are having difficulty completing the steps in this module, consider using a stylus. Many people find it easier to be precise with a stylus than with a finger. In addition, with a stylus you see the pointer. If you still are having trouble completing the steps with a stylus, try using a mouse.

Table 1 Touch Screen Gestures			
Motion	**Description**	**Common Uses**	**Equivalent Mouse Operation**
Tap	Quickly touch and release one finger one time.	Activate a link (built-in connection). Press a button. Run a program or an app.	Click
Double-tap	Quickly touch and release one finger two times.	Run a program or an app. Zoom in (show a smaller area on the screen, so that contents appear larger) at the location of the double-tap.	Double-click
Press and hold	Press and hold one finger to cause an action to occur, or until an action occurs.	Display a shortcut menu (immediate access to allowable actions). Activate a mode enabling you to move an item with one finger to a new location.	Right-click
Drag, or slide	Press and hold one finger on an object and then move the finger to the new location.	Move an item around the screen. Scroll.	Drag
Swipe	Press and hold one finger and then move the finger horizontally or vertically on the screen.	Select an object. Swipe from edge to display a bar such as the Action Center, Apps bar, and Navigation bar (all discussed later).	Drag
Stretch	Move two fingers apart.	Zoom in (show a smaller area on the screen, so that contents appear larger).	None
Pinch	Move two fingers together.	Zoom out (show a larger area on the screen, so that contents appear smaller).	None

Will your screen look different if you are using a touch screen?
The Windows and Microsoft Office interfaces vary slightly if you are using a touch screen. For this reason, you might notice that your screen looks slightly different from the screens in the module.

CONSIDER THIS

Windows users who do not have touch screen capabilities typically work with a mouse that has at least two buttons. For a right-handed user, the left button usually is

BTW
Pointer
If you are using a touch screen, the pointer may not appear on the screen as you perform touch gestures. The pointer will reappear when you begin using the mouse.

the primary mouse button, and the right mouse button is the secondary mouse button. Left-handed people, however, can reverse the function of these buttons.

Table 2 explains how to perform a variety of mouse operations. Some apps also use keys in combination with the mouse to perform certain actions. For example, when you hold down the CTRL key while rolling the mouse wheel, text on the screen may become larger or smaller based on the direction you roll the wheel. The function of the mouse buttons and the wheel varies depending on the app.

Table 2 Mouse Operations

Operation	Mouse Action	Example*	Equivalent Touch Gesture
Point	Move the mouse until the pointer on the desktop is positioned on the item of choice.	Position the pointer on the screen.	None
Click	Press and release the primary mouse button, which usually is the left mouse button.	Select or deselect items on the screen or run an app or app feature.	Tap
Right-click	Press and release the secondary mouse button, which usually is the right mouse button.	Display a shortcut menu.	Press and hold
Double-click	Quickly press and release the primary mouse button twice without moving the mouse.	Run an app or app feature.	Double-tap
Triple-click	Quickly press and release the primary mouse button three times without moving the mouse.	Select a paragraph.	Triple-tap
Drag	Point to an item, hold down the primary mouse button, move the item to the desired location on the screen, and then release the mouse button.	Move an object from one location to another or draw pictures.	Drag or slide
Right-drag	Point to an item, hold down the right mouse button, move the item to the desired location on the screen, and then release the right mouse button.	Display a shortcut menu after moving an object from one location to another.	Press and hold, then drag
Rotate wheel	Roll the wheel forward or backward.	Scroll vertically (up and down).	Swipe
Free-spin wheel	Whirl the wheel forward or backward so that it spins freely on its own.	Scroll through many pages in seconds.	Swipe
Press wheel	Press the wheel button while moving the mouse.	Scroll continuously.	None
Tilt wheel	Press the wheel toward the right or left.	Scroll horizontally (left and right).	None
Press thumb button	Press the button on the side of the mouse with your thumb.	Move forward or backward through webpages and/or control media, games, etc.	None

© 2015 Cengage Learning

*Note: The examples presented in this column are discussed as they are demonstrated in this chapter.

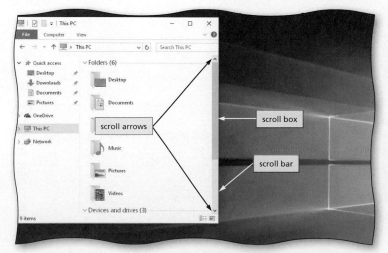

Figure 2

Scrolling

A **scroll bar** is a horizontal or vertical bar that appears when the contents of an area may not be visible completely on the screen (Figure 2). A scroll bar contains **scroll arrows** and a **scroll box** that enable you to view areas that currently cannot be seen on the screen. Clicking the up and down scroll arrows moves the screen content up or down one line. You also can click above or below the scroll box to move up or down a section, or drag the scroll box up or down to move to a specific location.

Keyboard Shortcuts

In many cases, you can use the keyboard instead of the mouse to accomplish a task. To perform tasks using the keyboard, you press one or more keyboard keys, sometimes identified as a **keyboard shortcut**. Some keyboard shortcuts consist of a single key, such as the F1 key. For example, to obtain help in many apps, you can press the F1 key. Other keyboard shortcuts consist of multiple keys, in which case a plus sign separates the key names, such as CTRL+ESC. This notation means to press and hold down the first key listed, press one or more additional keys, and then release all keys. For example, to display the Start menu, press CTRL+ESC, that is, hold down the CTRL key, press the ESC key, and then release both keys.

Starting Windows

It is not unusual for multiple people to use the same computer in a work, educational, recreational, or home setting. Windows enables each user to establish a **user account**, which identifies to Windows the resources, such as apps and storage locations, a user can access when working with the computer.

Each user account has a user name and may have a password and an icon, as well. A **user name** is a unique combination of letters or numbers that identifies a specific user to Windows. A **password** is a private combination of letters, numbers, and special characters associated with the user name that allows access to a user's account resources. An icon is a small image that represents an object; thus, a **user icon** is a picture associated with a user name.

When you turn on a computer, Windows starts and displays a **lock screen** consisting of the time and date (Figure 3). To unlock the screen, click the lock screen. Depending on your computer's settings, Windows may or may not display a sign-in screen that shows the user names and user icons for users who have accounts on the computer. This **sign-in screen** enables you to sign in to your user account and makes the computer available for use. Clicking the user icon begins the process of signing in, also called logging on, to your user account.

BTW
Minimize Wrist Injury
Computer users frequently switch between the keyboard and the mouse during a word processing session; such switching strains the wrist. To help prevent wrist injury, minimize switching. For instance, if your fingers already are on the keyboard, use keyboard keys to scroll. If your hand already is on the mouse, use the mouse to scroll. If your hand is on the touch screen, use touch gestures to scroll.

lock screen

current date and time

2:57
Wednesday, September 23

Figure 3

At the bottom of the sign-in screen is the 'Connect to Internet' button, 'Ease of access' button, and a Shut down button. Clicking the 'Connect to Internet' button displays a list of each network connection and its status. You also can connect to or disconnect from a network. Clicking the 'Ease of access' button displays the Ease of access menu, which provides tools to optimize a computer to accommodate the needs of the mobility, hearing, and vision impaired users. Clicking the Shut down button displays a menu containing commands related to putting the computer or mobile device in a low-power state, shutting it down, and restarting the computer or mobile device. The commands available on your computer or mobile device may differ.

- The Sleep command saves your work, turns off the computer fans and hard drive, and places the computer in a lower-power state. To wake the computer from sleep mode, press the power button or lift a laptop's cover, and sign in to your account.
- The Shut down command exits running apps, shuts down Windows, and then turns off the computer.
- The Restart command exits running apps, shuts down Windows, and then restarts Windows.

To Sign In to an Account

1 SIGN IN | 2 USE WINDOWS | 3 USE APPS | 4 FILE MANAGEMENT | 5 SWITCH APPS | 6 SAVE FILES
7 CHANGE SCREEN RESOLUTION | 8 EXIT APPS | 9 USE ADDITIONAL APPS | 10 USE HELP

The following steps, which use SCSeries as the user name, sign in to an account based on a typical Windows installation. *Why? After starting Windows, you might be required to sign in to an account to access the computer or mobile device's resources.* You may need to ask your instructor how to sign in to your account.

- Click the lock screen (shown in Figure 3) to display a sign-in screen.
- Click the user icon (for SCSeries, in this case) on the sign-in screen, which depending on settings, either will display a second sign-in screen that contains a Password text box (Figure 4) or will display the Windows desktop (Figure 5).

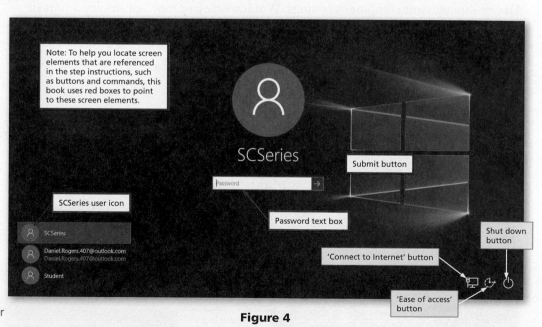

Note: To help you locate screen elements that are referenced in the step instructions, such as buttons and commands, this book uses red boxes to point to these screen elements.

SCSeries

Submit button

Password

Password text box

SCSeries user icon

SCSeries

Daniel.Rogers.407@outlook.com
Daniel.Rogers.407@outlook.com

Student

Shut down button

'Connect to Internet' button

'Ease of access' button

Figure 4

Q&A

Why do I not see a user icon?
Your computer may require you to type a user name instead of clicking an icon.

What is a text box?
A text box is a rectangular box in which you type text.

Why does my screen not show a Password text box?
Your account does not require a password.

- If Windows displays a sign-in screen with a Password text box, type your password in the text box.

2

- Click the Submit button (shown in Figure 4) to sign in to your account and display the Windows desktop (Figure 5).

Q&A

Why does my desktop look different from the one in Figure 5?

The Windows desktop is customizable, and your school or employer may have modified the desktop to meet its needs. Also, your screen resolution, which affects the size of the elements on the screen, may differ from the screen resolution used in this book. Later in this module, you learn how to change screen resolution.

How do I type if my tablet has no keyboard?

You can use your fingers to press keys on a keyboard that appears on the screen, called an on-screen keyboard, or you can purchase a separate physical keyboard that attaches to or wirelessly communicates with the tablet.

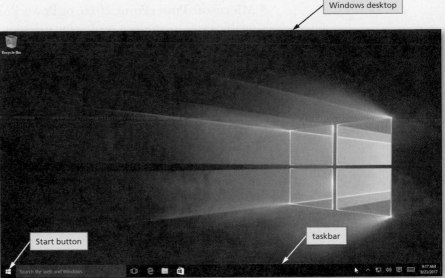

Figure 5

The Windows Desktop

The Windows 10 desktop (Figure 5) and the objects on the desktop emulate a work area in an office. Think of the Windows desktop as an electronic version of the top of your desk. You can perform tasks such as placing objects on the desktop, moving the objects around the desktop, and removing items from the desktop.

When you run an app in Windows 10, it appears on the desktop. Some icons also may be displayed on the desktop. For instance, the icon for the **Recycle Bin**, the location of files that have been deleted, appears on the desktop by default. A **file** is a named unit of storage. Files can contain text, images, audio, and video. You can customize your desktop so that icons representing programs and files you use often appear on your desktop.

Introduction to Microsoft Office 2016

Microsoft Office 2016 is the newest version of Microsoft Office, offering features that provide users with better functionality and easier ways to work with the various files they create. This version of Office also is designed to work more optimally on mobile devices and online.

Microsoft Office 2016 Apps

Microsoft Office 2016 includes a wide variety of apps, such as Word, PowerPoint, Excel, Access, Outlook, Publisher, and OneNote:

- **Microsoft Word 2016**, or Word, is a full-featured word processing app that allows you to create professional-looking documents and revise them easily.

- **Microsoft PowerPoint 2016**, or PowerPoint, is a complete presentation app that enables you to produce professional-looking presentations and then deliver them to an audience.

- **Microsoft Excel 2016**, or Excel, is a powerful spreadsheet app that allows you to organize data, complete calculations, make decisions, graph data, develop professional-looking reports, publish organized data to the web, and access real-time data from websites.

- **Microsoft Access 2016**, or Access, is a database management system that enables you to create a database; add, change, and delete data in the database; ask questions concerning the data in the database; and create forms and reports using the data in the database.

- **Microsoft Outlook 2016**, or Outlook, is a communications and scheduling app that allows you to manage email accounts, calendars, contacts, and access to other Internet content.

- **Microsoft Publisher 2016**, or Publisher, is a desktop publishing app that helps you create professional-quality publications and marketing materials that can be shared easily.

- **Microsoft OneNote 2016**, or OneNote, is a note taking app that allows you to store and share information in notebooks with other people.

Microsoft Office 2016 Suites

A **suite** is a collection of individual apps available together as a unit. Microsoft offers a variety of Office suites, including a stand-alone desktop app, Microsoft Office 365, and Microsoft Office Online. **Microsoft Office 365**, or Office 365, provides plans that allow organizations to use Office in a mobile setting while also being able to communicate and share files, depending upon the type of plan selected by the organization. **Microsoft Office Online** includes apps that allow you to edit and share files on the web using the familiar Office interface.

During the Office 365 installation, you select a plan, and depending on your plan, you receive different apps and services. Office Online apps do not require a local installation and can be accessed through OneDrive and your browser. **OneDrive** is a cloud storage service that provides storage and other services, such as Office Online, to computer users.

Apps in a suite, such as Microsoft Office, typically use a similar interface and share features. Once you are comfortable working with the elements and the interface and performing tasks in one app, the similarity can help you apply the knowledge and skills you have learned to another app(s) in the suite. For example, the process for saving a file in Word is the same in PowerPoint, Excel, and some of the other Office apps. While briefly showing how to use several Office apps, this module illustrates some of the common functions across the apps and identifies the characteristics unique to these apps.

Running and Using an App

To use an app, you must instruct the operating system to run the app. Windows provides many different ways to run an app, one of which is presented in this section (other ways to run an app are presented throughout this module). After an app is running, you can use it to perform a variety of tasks. The following pages use Word to discuss some elements of the Office interface and to perform tasks that are common to other Office apps.

Word

Word is a full-featured word processing app that allows you to create many types of personal and business documents, including flyers, letters, memos, resumes, reports, fax cover sheets, mailing labels, and newsletters. Word also provides tools that enable you to create webpages and save these webpages directly on a web server. Word has many features designed to simplify the production of documents and add visual appeal. Using Word, you easily can change the shape, size, and color of text. You also can include borders, shading, tables, images, pictures, charts, and web addresses in documents.

To Run an App Using the Start Menu and Create a Blank Document

1 SIGN IN | 2 USE WINDOWS | 3 USE APPS | 4 FILE MANAGEMENT | 5 SWITCH APPS | 6 SAVE FILES
7 CHANGE SCREEN RESOLUTION | 8 EXIT APPS | 9 USE ADDITIONAL APPS | 10 USE HELP

Across the bottom of the Windows 10 desktop is the taskbar. The taskbar contains the **Start button**, which you use to access apps, files, folders, and settings. A **folder** is a named location on a storage medium that usually contains related documents.

Clicking the Start button displays the Start menu. The **Start menu** allows you to access programs, folders, and files on the computer or mobile device and contains commands that allow you to start programs, store and search for documents, customize the computer or mobile device, and sign out of a user account or shut down the computer or mobile device. A **menu** is a list of related items, including folders, programs, and commands. Each **command** on a menu performs a specific action, such as saving a file or obtaining help. *Why? When you install an app, for example, the app's name will be added to the All apps list on the Start menu.*

The following steps, which assume Windows is running, use the Start menu to run an Office app and create a blank document based on a typical installation. You may need to ask your instructor how to run an Office app on your computer. Although the steps illustrate running the Word app, the steps to run any Office app are similar.

- Click the Start button on the Windows 10 taskbar to display the Start menu (Figure 6).

Figure 6

2

- Click All apps at the bottom of the left pane of the Start menu to display a list of apps installed on the computer or mobile device. If necessary, scroll to display the app you wish to run (Figure 7).

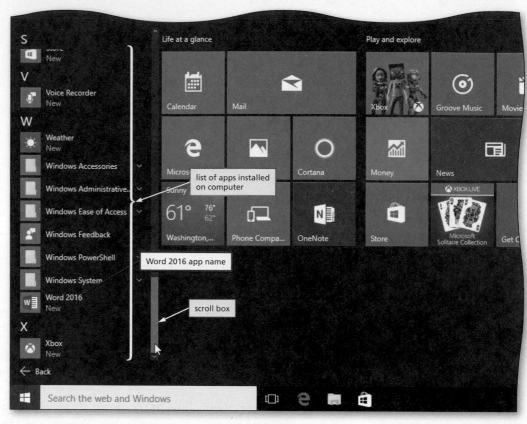

Figure 7

3

- If the app you wish to run is located in a folder, click or scroll to and then click the folder in the All apps list to display a list of the folder's contents.
- Click, or scroll to and then click, the program name (Microsoft Word 2016, in this case) in the list to run the selected program (Figure 8).

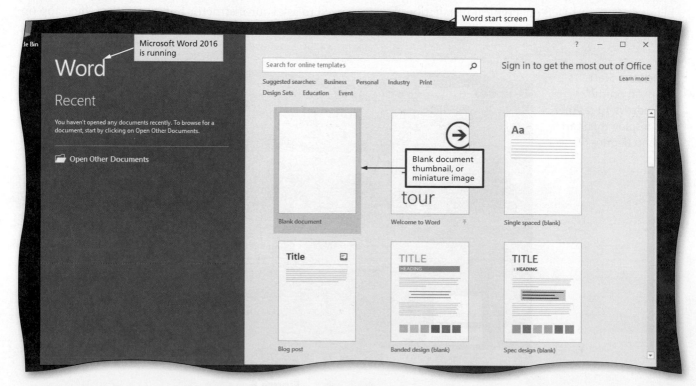

Figure 8

4

- Click the Blank document thumbnail on the Word start screen to create a blank Word document in the Word window (Figure 9).

Q&A What happens when you run an app?
Some apps provide a means for you to create a blank document, as shown in Figure 8; others immediately display a blank document in an app window, such as the Word window shown in Figure 9. A **window** is a rectangular area that displays data and information. The top of a window has a **title bar**, which is a horizontal space that contains the window's name.

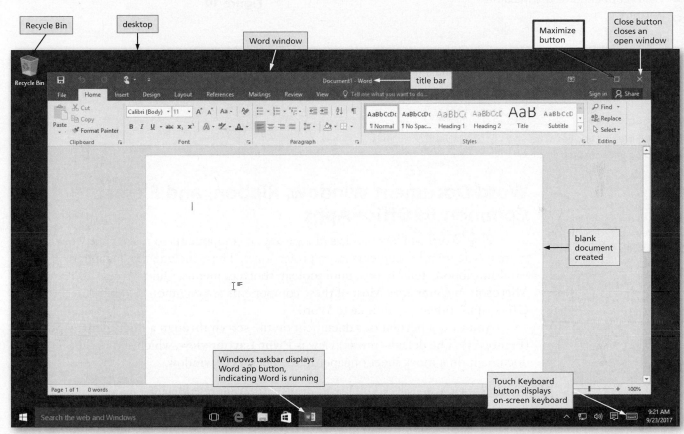

Figure 9

Other Ways

1. Type app name in search box, click app name in results list
2. Double-click file created in app you want to run

1 SIGN IN | 2 USE WINDOWS | 3 USE APPS | 4 FILE MANAGEMENT | 5 SWITCH APPS | 6 SAVE FILES
7 CHANGE SCREEN RESOLUTION | 8 EXIT APPS | 9 USE ADDITIONAL APPS | 10 USE HELP

To Maximize a Window

Sometimes content is not visible completely in a window. One method of displaying the entire contents of a window is to **maximize** it, or enlarge the window so that it fills the entire screen. The following step maximizes the Word window; however, any Office app's window can be maximized using this step. *Why? A maximized window provides the most space available for using the app.*

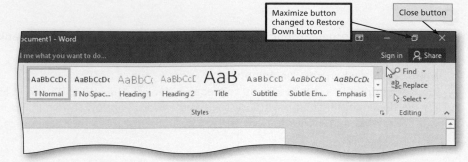

Figure 10

- If the app window is not maximized already, click the Maximize button (shown in Figure 9) next to the Close button on the window's title bar (the Word window title bar, in this case) to maximize the window (Figure 10).

Q&A

What happened to the Maximize button?
It changed to a Restore Down button, which you can use to return a window to its size and location before you maximized it.

How do I know whether a window is maximized?
A window is maximized if it fills the entire display area and the Restore Down button is displayed on the title bar.

Other Ways

1. Double-click title bar
2. Drag title bar to top of screen

BTW

Touch Keyboard
To display the on-screen touch keyboard, click the Touch Keyboard button on the Windows taskbar. When finished using the touch keyboard, click the X button on the touch keyboard to close the keyboard.

Word Document Window, Ribbon, and Elements Common to Office Apps

The Word window consists of a variety of components to make your work more efficient and documents more professional. These include the document window, ribbon, Tell Me box, mini toolbar, shortcut menus, Quick Access Toolbar, and Microsoft Account area. Most of these components are common to other Microsoft Office apps; others are unique to Word.

You view a portion of a document on the screen through a **document window** (Figure 11). The default (preset) view is **Print Layout view**, which shows the document on a mock sheet of paper in the document window.

Scroll Bars   You use a scroll bar to display different portions of a document in the document window. At the right edge of the document window is a vertical scroll bar. If a document is too wide to fit in the document window, a horizontal scroll bar also appears at the bottom of the document window. On a scroll bar, the position of the scroll box reflects the location of the portion of the document that is displayed in the document window.

Status Bar   The **status bar**, located at the bottom of the document window above the Windows taskbar, presents information about the document, the progress of current tasks, and the status of certain commands and keys; it also provides controls for viewing the document. As you type text or perform certain tasks, various indicators and buttons may appear on the status bar.

The left side of the status bar in Figure 11 shows the current page followed by the total number of pages in the document, the number of words in the document, and an icon to check spelling and grammar. The right side of the status bar includes buttons and controls you can use to change the view of a document and adjust the size of the displayed document.

Ribbon   The ribbon, located near the top of the window below the title bar, is the control center in Word and other Office apps (Figure 12). The ribbon provides easy, central access to the tasks you perform while creating a document. The ribbon consists

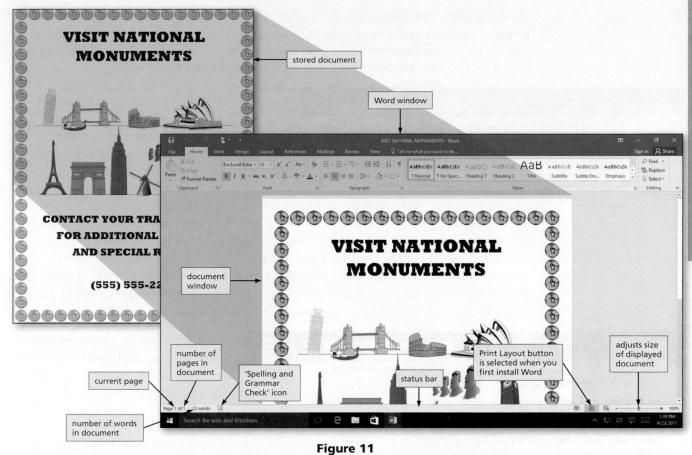

Figure 11

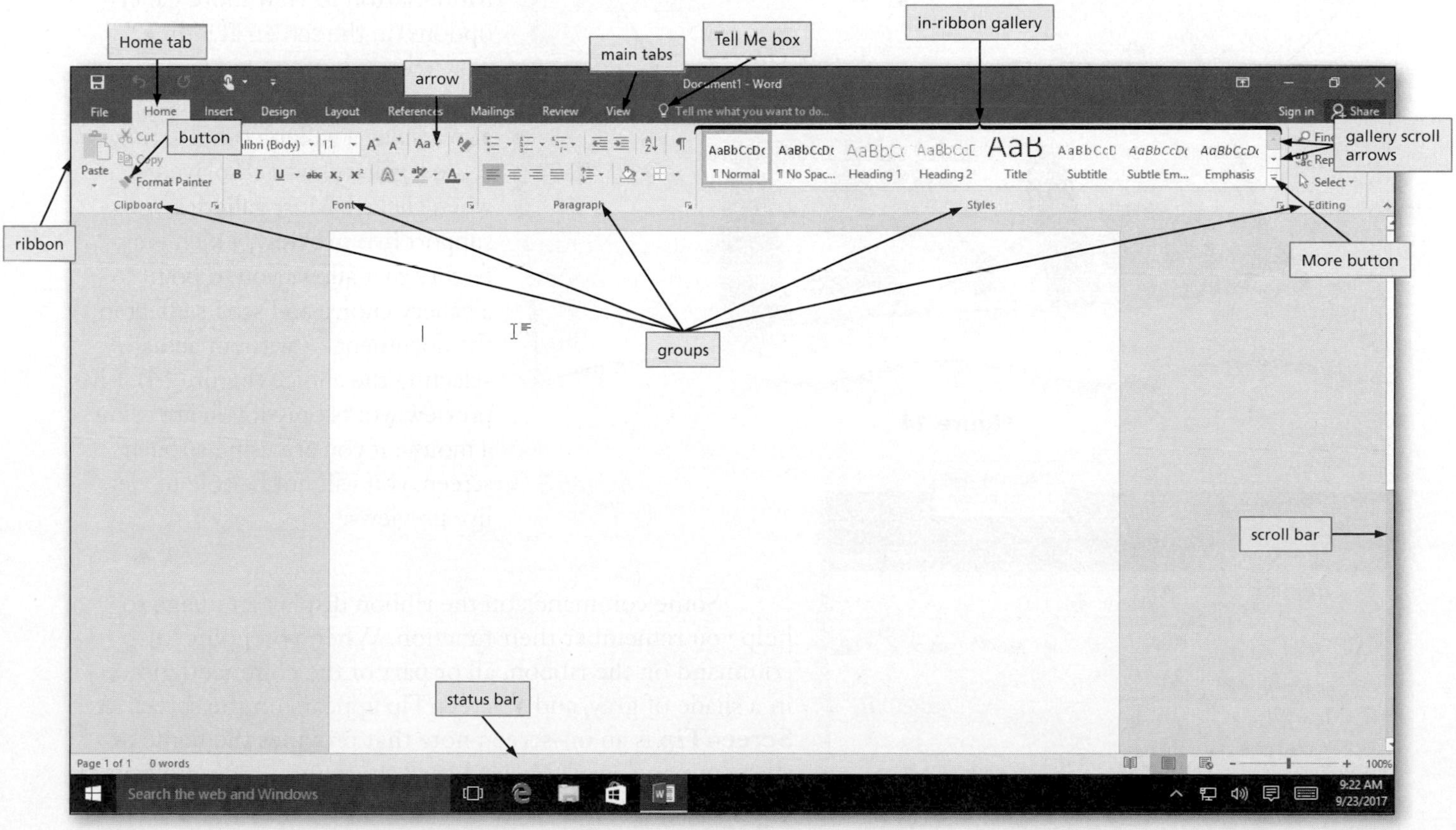

Figure 12

of tabs, groups, and commands. Each **tab** contains a collection of groups, and each **group** contains related commands. When you run an Office app, such as Word, it initially displays several main tabs, also called default or top-level tabs. All Office apps have a Home tab, which contains the more frequently used commands.

Figure 13

In addition to the main tabs, the Office apps display **tool tabs**, also called contextual tabs (Figure 13), when you perform certain tasks or work with objects such as pictures or tables. If you insert a picture in a Word document, for example, the Picture Tools tab and its related subordinate Format tab appear, collectively referred to as the Picture Tools Format tab. When you are finished working with the picture, the Picture Tools Format tab disappears from the ribbon. Word and other Office apps determine when tool tabs should appear and disappear based on tasks you perform. Some tool tabs, such as the Table Tools tab, have more than one related subordinate tab.

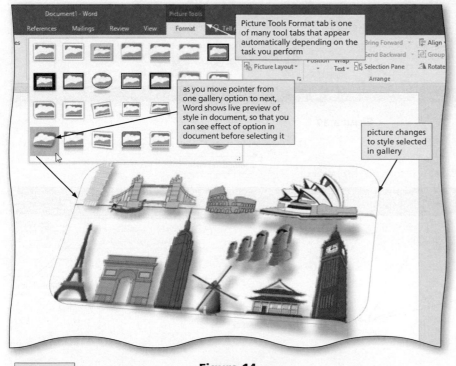

Figure 14

Items on the ribbon include buttons, boxes, and galleries (shown in Figure 12). A **gallery** is a set of choices, often graphical, arranged in a grid or in a list. You can scroll through choices in an in-ribbon gallery by clicking the gallery's scroll arrows. Or, you can click a gallery's More button to view more gallery options on the screen at a time.

Some buttons and boxes have arrows that, when clicked, also display a gallery; others always cause a gallery to be displayed when clicked. Most galleries support **live preview**, which is a feature that allows you to point to a gallery choice and see its effect in the document — without actually selecting the choice (Figure 14). Live preview works only if you are using a mouse; if you are using a touch screen, you will not be able to view live previews.

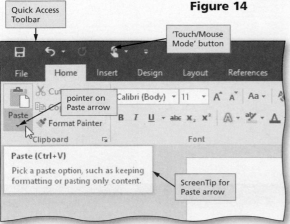

Figure 15

Some commands on the ribbon display an image to help you remember their function. When you point to a command on the ribbon, all or part of the command glows in a shade of gray, and a ScreenTip appears on the screen. A **ScreenTip** is an on-screen note that provides the name of the command, available keyboard shortcut(s), a description of the command, and sometimes instructions for how to obtain help about the command (Figure 15).

Some groups on the ribbon have a small arrow in the lower-right corner, called a **Dialog Box Launcher**, that when clicked, displays a dialog box or a task pane with additional options for the group (Figure 16). When presented with a dialog box, you make selections and must close the dialog box before returning to the document. A **task pane**, in contrast to a dialog box, is a window that can remain open and visible while you work in the document.

BTW
Touch Mode
The Office and Windows interfaces may vary if you are using touch mode. For this reason, you might notice that the function or appearance of your touch screen differs slightly from this module's presentation.

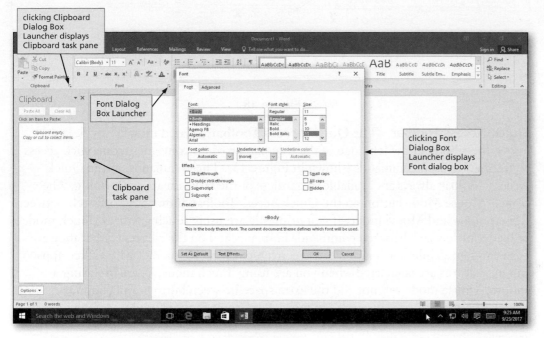

Figure 16

Tell Me Box   The **Tell Me box**, which appears to the right of the tabs on the ribbon, is a type of search box that helps you to perform specific tasks in an Office app (Figure 17). As you type in the Tell Me box, the word-wheeling feature displays search results that are refined as you type. For example, if you want to center text in a document, you can type "center" in the Tell Me box and then select the appropriate command. The Tell Me box also lists the last five commands accessed from the box.

Mini Toolbar   The **mini toolbar**, which appears automatically based on tasks you perform, contains commands related to changing the appearance of text in a document (Figure 18). If you do not use the mini toolbar, it disappears from the screen. The buttons, arrows, and boxes on the mini toolbar vary, depending on whether you are using Touch mode versus Mouse mode. If you right-click an item in the document window, Word displays both the mini toolbar and a shortcut menu, which is discussed in a later section in this module.

All commands on the mini toolbar also exist on the ribbon. The purpose of the mini toolbar is to minimize hand or mouse movement.

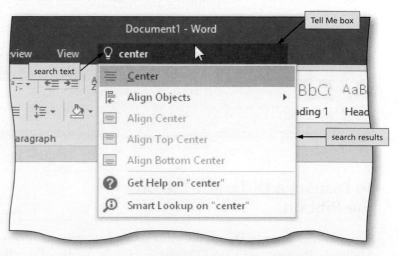

Figure 17

BTW
Turning Off the Mini Toolbar
If you do not want the mini toolbar to appear, click File on the ribbon to open the Backstage view, click the Options tab in the Backstage view, if necessary, click General (Options dialog box), remove the check mark from the 'Show Mini Toolbar on selection' check box, and then click the OK button.

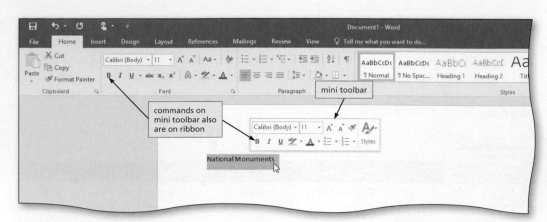

Figure 18

Quick Access Toolbar   The **Quick Access Toolbar**, located initially (by default) above the ribbon at the left edge of the title bar, provides convenient, one-click access to frequently used commands (shown in Figure 15). The commands on the Quick Access Toolbar always are available, regardless of the task you are performing. The Touch/Mouse Mode button on the Quick Access Toolbar allows you to switch between Touch mode and Mouse mode. If you primarily are using touch gestures, Touch mode will add more space between commands in menus and on the ribbon so that they are easier to tap. While touch gestures are convenient ways to interact with Office apps, not all features are supported when you are using Touch mode. If you are using a mouse, Mouse mode will not add the extra space between buttons and commands. The Quick Access Toolbar is discussed in more depth later in the module.

KeyTips   If you prefer using the keyboard instead of the mouse, you can press the ALT key on the keyboard to display **KeyTips**, or keyboard code icons, for certain commands (Figure 19). To select a command using the keyboard, press the letter or number displayed in the KeyTip, which may cause additional KeyTips related to the selected command to appear. To remove KeyTips from the screen, press the ALT key or the ESC key until all KeyTips disappear, or click anywhere in the app window.

Microsoft Account Area   In this area, you can use the Sign in link to sign in to your Microsoft account. Once signed in, you will see your account information, as well as a picture if you have included one in your Microsoft account.

Figure 19

To Display a Different Tab on the Ribbon

1 SIGN IN | 2 USE WINDOWS | 3 USE APPS | 4 FILE MANAGEMENT | 5 SWITCH APPS | 6 SAVE FILES
7 CHANGE SCREEN RESOLUTION | 8 EXIT APPS | 9 USE ADDITIONAL APPS | 10 USE HELP

When you run Word, the ribbon displays nine main tabs: File, Home, Insert, Design, Layout, References, Mailings, Review, and View. The tab currently displayed is called the **active tab**.

The following step displays the Insert tab, that is, makes it the active tab. *Why? When working with an Office app, you may need to switch tabs to access other options for working with a document.*

- Click Insert on the ribbon to display the Insert tab (Figure 20).

Experiment

- Click the other tabs on the ribbon to view their contents. When you are finished, click Insert on the ribbon to redisplay the Insert tab.

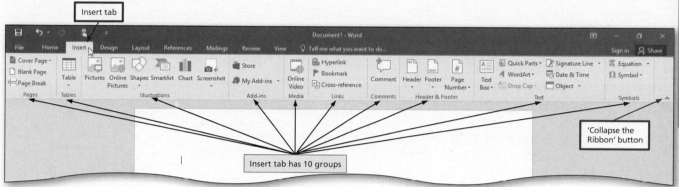

Figure 20

Other Ways

1. Press ALT, press letter corresponding to tab to display
2. Press ALT, press LEFT ARROW or RIGHT ARROW until desired tab is displayed

To Collapse and Expand the Ribbon and Use Full Screen Mode

1 SIGN IN | 2 USE WINDOWS | **3 USE APPS** | 4 FILE MANAGEMENT | 5 SWITCH APPS | 6 SAVE FILES
7 CHANGE SCREEN RESOLUTION | 8 EXIT APPS | 9 USE ADDITIONAL APPS | 10 USE HELP

To display more of a document or other item in the window of an Office app, some users prefer to collapse the ribbon, which hides the groups on the ribbon and displays only the main tabs, or to use **Full Screen mode**, which hides all the commands and just displays the document. Each time you run an Office app, the ribbon appears the same way it did the last time you used that Office app. The modules in this book, however, begin with the ribbon appearing as it did at the initial installation of the software.

The following steps collapse, expand, and restore the ribbon in an Office app and then switch to Full Screen mode. *Why? If you need more space on the screen to work with your document, you may consider collapsing the ribbon or switching to Full Screen mode to gain additional workspace.*

- Click the 'Collapse the Ribbon' button on the ribbon (shown in Figure 20) to collapse the ribbon (Figure 21).

Q&A What happened to the 'Collapse the Ribbon' button?
The 'Pin the ribbon' button replaces the 'Collapse the Ribbon' button when the ribbon is collapsed. You will see the 'Pin the ribbon' button only when you expand a ribbon by clicking a tab.

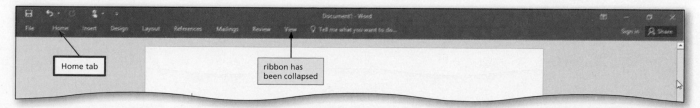

Figure 21

● Click Home on the ribbon to expand the Home tab (Figure 22).

Q&A | Why would I click the Home tab?
If you want to use a command on a collapsed ribbon, click the main tab to display the groups for that tab. After you select a command on the ribbon and resume working in the document, the groups will be collapsed once again. If you decide not to use a command on the ribbon, you can collapse the groups by clicking the same main tab or clicking in the app window.

🔎 Experiment

● Click Home on the ribbon to collapse the groups again. Click Home on the ribbon to expand the Home tab.

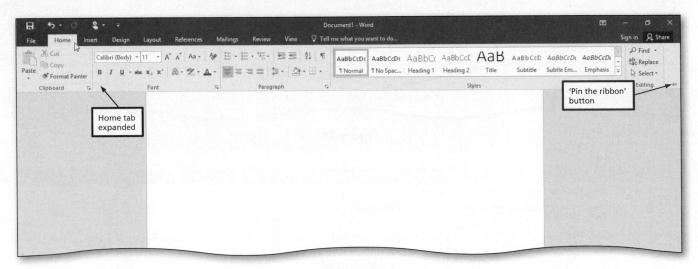

Figure 22

❸

● Click the 'Pin the ribbon' button on the expanded Home tab to restore the ribbon.
● Click the 'Ribbon Display Options' button to display the Ribbon Display Options menu (Figure 23).

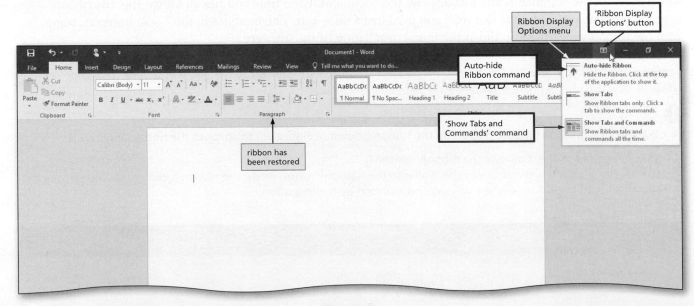

Figure 23

- Click Auto-hide Ribbon to hide all the commands from the screen (Figure 24).
- Click the ellipsis to temporarily display the ribbon.
- Click the 'Ribbon Display Options' button to display the Ribbon Display Options menu (shown in Figure 23).
- Click 'Show Tabs and Commands' to exit Full Screen mode.

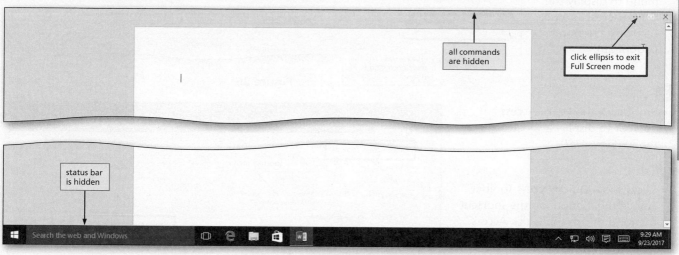

Figure 24

Other Ways

1. Double-click a main tab on the ribbon
2. Press CTRL+F1

To Use a Shortcut Menu to Relocate the Quick Access Toolbar

1 SIGN IN | 2 USE WINDOWS | 3 USE APPS | 4 FILE MANAGEMENT | 5 SWITCH APPS | 6 SAVE FILES
7 CHANGE SCREEN RESOLUTION | 8 EXIT APPS | 9 USE ADDITIONAL APPS | 10 USE HELP

When you right-click certain areas of the Word and other Office app windows, a shortcut menu will appear. A **shortcut menu** is a list of frequently used commands that relate to an object. *Why? You can use shortcut menus to access common commands quickly.* When you right-click the status bar, for example, a shortcut menu appears with commands related to the status bar. When you right-click the Quick Access Toolbar, a shortcut menu appears with commands related to the Quick Access Toolbar. The following steps use a shortcut menu to move the Quick Access Toolbar, which by default is located on the title bar.

- Right-click the Quick Access Toolbar to display a shortcut menu that presents a list of commands related to the Quick Access Toolbar (Figure 25).

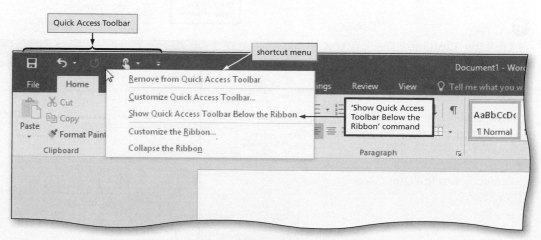

Figure 25

- Click 'Show Quick Access Toolbar Below the Ribbon' on the shortcut menu to display the Quick Access Toolbar below the ribbon (Figure 26).

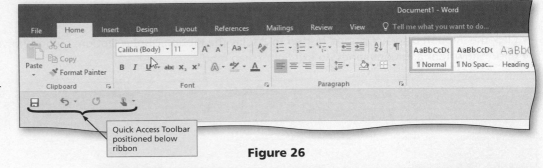

Figure 26

- Right-click the Quick Access Toolbar to display a shortcut menu (Figure 27).

- Click 'Show Quick Access Toolbar Above the Ribbon' on the shortcut menu to return the Quick Access Toolbar to its original position (shown in Figure 25).

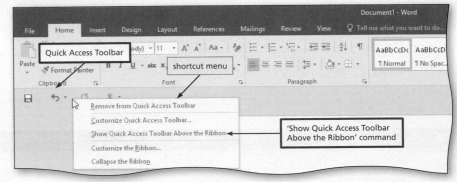

Figure 27

Other Ways

1. Click 'Customize Quick Access Toolbar' button on Quick Access Toolbar, click 'Show Below the Ribbon' or 'Show Above the Ribbon'

To Customize the Quick Access Toolbar

1 SIGN IN | 2 USE WINDOWS | 3 USE APPS | 4 FILE MANAGEMENT | 5 SWITCH APPS | 6 SAVE FILES
7 CHANGE SCREEN RESOLUTION | 8 EXIT APPS | 9 USE ADDITIONAL APPS | 10 USE HELP

The Quick Access Toolbar provides easy access to some of the more frequently used commands in the Office apps. By default, the Quick Access Toolbar contains buttons for the Save, Undo, and Redo commands. If your computer or mobile device has a touch screen, the Quick Access Toolbar also might display the Touch/ Mouse Mode button. You can customize the Quick Access Toolbar by changing its location in the window, as shown in the previous steps, and by adding more buttons to reflect commands you would like to access easily. The following steps add the Quick Print button to the Quick Access Toolbar. *Why? Adding the Quick Print button to the Quick Access Toolbar speeds up the process of printing.*

- Click the 'Customize Quick Access Toolbar' button to display the Customize Quick Access Toolbar menu (Figure 28).

Q&A
Which commands are listed on the Customize Quick Access Toolbar menu?
It lists commands that commonly are added to the Quick Access Toolbar.

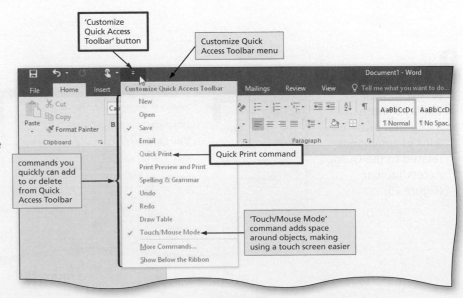

Figure 28

2

- Click Quick Print on the Customize Quick Access Toolbar menu to add the Quick Print button to the Quick Access Toolbar (Figure 29).

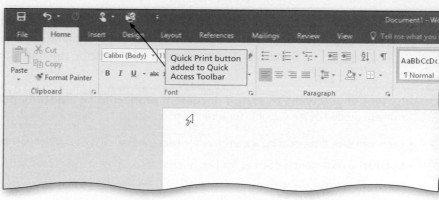

Figure 29

 How would I remove a button from the Quick Access Toolbar?
You would right-click the button you wish to remove and then click 'Remove from Quick Access Toolbar' on the shortcut menu or click the 'Customize Quick Access Toolbar' button on the Quick Access Toolbar and then click the button name in the Customize Quick Access Toolbar menu to remove the check mark.

To Enter Text in a Document

1 SIGN IN | 2 USE WINDOWS | **3 USE APPS** | 4 FILE MANAGEMENT | 5 SWITCH APPS | 6 SAVE FILES
7 CHANGE SCREEN RESOLUTION | 8 EXIT APPS | 9 USE ADDITIONAL APPS | 10 USE HELP

The first step in creating a document is to enter its text by typing on the keyboard. By default, Word positions text at the left margin as you type. The following steps type this first line of a flyer. *Why? To begin creating a flyer, for example, you type the headline in the document window.*

1

- Type **VISIT NATIONAL MONUMENTS** as the text (Figure 30).

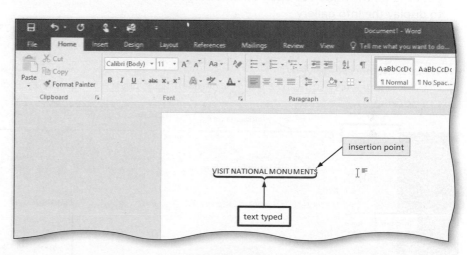

Figure 30

 What is the blinking vertical bar to the right of the text?
The blinking bar is the insertion point, which indicates where text, graphics, and other items will be inserted in the document. As you type, the insertion point moves to the right, and when you reach the end of a line, it moves down to the beginning of the next line.

What if I make an error while typing?
You can press the BACKSPACE key until you have deleted the text in error and then retype the text correctly.

2

- Press the ENTER key to move the insertion point to the beginning of the next line (Figure 31).

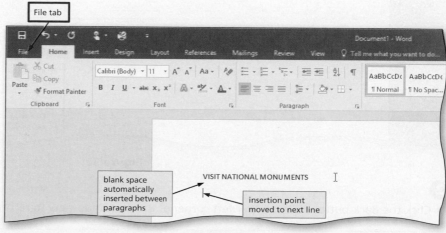

Figure 31

Why did blank space appear between the entered text and the insertion point?
Each time you press the ENTER key, Word creates a new paragraph and inserts blank space between the two paragraphs. Depending on your settings, Office may or may not insert a blank space between the two paragraphs.

Document Properties

You can organize and identify your files by using **document properties**, which are the details about a file, such as the project author, title, and subject. For example, a class name or document topic can describe the file's purpose or content.

CONSIDER THIS

Why would you want to assign document properties to a document?

Document properties are valuable for a variety of reasons:

- Users can save time locating a particular file because they can view a file's document properties without opening the file.

- By creating consistent properties for files having similar content, users can better organize their files.

- Some organizations require users to add document properties so that other employees can view details about these files.

To Change Document Properties

1 SIGN IN | 2 USE WINDOWS | 3 USE APPS | 4 FILE MANAGEMENT | 5 SWITCH APPS | 6 SAVE FILES
7 CHANGE SCREEN RESOLUTION | 8 EXIT APPS | 9 USE ADDITIONAL APPS | 10 USE HELP

You can change the document properties while working with the file in an Office app. When you save the file, the Office app (Word, in this case) will save the document properties with the file. The following steps change document properties. *Why? Adding document properties will help you identify characteristics of the file without opening it.*

1

- Click File on the ribbon to open the Backstage view and then, if necessary, click the Info tab in the Backstage view to display the Info gallery.
- Click to the right of the Comments property in the Properties list, and type `CIS 101 Assignment` in the text box (Figure 32).

Q&A
What is the Backstage view?
The **Backstage view** contains a set of commands that enable you to manage documents and provides data about the documents.

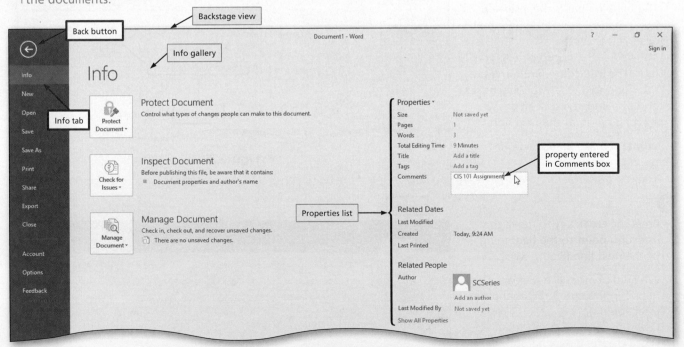

Figure 32

2

- Click the Back button in the upper-left corner of the Backstage view to return to the document window.

Printing, Saving, and Organizing Files

BTW
File Type
Depending on your Windows settings, the file type .docx may be displayed immediately to the right of the file name after you save the file. The file type .docx is a Word 2016 document.

While you are creating a document, the computer or mobile device stores it in memory. When you save a document, the computer or mobile device places it on a storage medium, such as a hard disk, solid state drive (SSD), USB flash drive, or optical disc. The storage medium can be permanent in your computer, may be portable where you remove it from your computer, or may be on a web server you access through a network or the Internet.

A saved document is referred to as a file. A **file name** is the name assigned to a file when it is saved. When saving files, you should organize them so that you easily can find them later. Windows provides tools to help you organize files.

Printing a Document

After creating a document, you may want to print it. Printing a document enables you to distribute it to others in a form that can be read or viewed but typically not edited.

CONSIDER THIS

What is the best method for distributing a document?

The traditional method of distributing a document uses a printer to produce a hard copy. A **hard copy** or **printout** is information that exists on a physical medium, such as paper. Hard copies can be useful for the following reasons:

- Some people prefer proofreading a hard copy of a document rather than viewing it on the screen to check for errors and readability.

- Hard copies can serve as a backup reference if your storage medium is lost or becomes corrupted and you need to recreate the document.

Instead of distributing a hard copy of a document, users can distribute the document as an electronic image that mirrors the original document's appearance. The electronic image of the document can be sent as an email attachment, posted on a website, or copied to a portable storage medium, such as a USB flash drive. Two popular electronic image formats, sometimes called fixed formats, are PDF by Adobe Systems and XPS by Microsoft. In Word, you can create electronic image files through the Save As dialog box and the Export, Share, and Print tabs in the Backstage view. Electronic images of documents, such as PDF and XPS, can be useful for the following reasons:

- Users can view electronic images of documents without the software that created the original document (e.g., Word). For example, to view a PDF file you use a program called Adobe Reader, which can be downloaded free from Adobe's website.

- Sending electronic documents saves paper and printer supplies. Society encourages users to contribute to **green computing**, which involves reducing the electricity consumed and environmental waste generated when using computers, mobile devices, and related technologies.

To Print a Document

1 SIGN IN | 2 USE WINDOWS | 3 USE APPS | 4 FILE MANAGEMENT | 5 SWITCH APPS | 6 SAVE FILES
7 CHANGE SCREEN RESOLUTION | 8 EXIT APPS | 9 USE ADDITIONAL APPS | 10 USE HELP

With the document opened, you may want to print it. *Why? Because you want to see how the text will appear on paper; you want to print a hard copy on a printer.* The following steps print a hard copy of the contents of the document.

1
- Click File on the ribbon to open the Backstage view.
- Click the Print tab in the Backstage view to display the Print gallery (Figure 33).

Q&A How can I print multiple copies of my document?
Increase the number in the Copies box in the Print gallery.

What if I decide not to print the document at this time?
Click the Back button in the upper-left corner of the Backstage view to return to the document window.

• Verify that the selected printer will print a hard copy of the document. If necessary, click the Printer Status button to display a list of available printer options and then click the desired printer to change the currently selected printer.

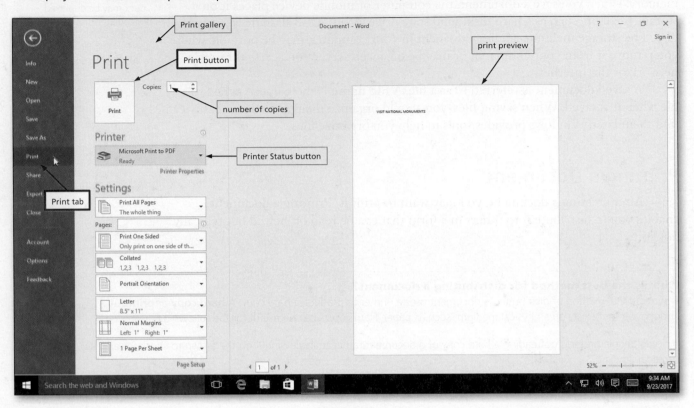

Figure 33

• Click the Print button in the Print gallery to print the document on the currently selected printer.

• When the printer stops, retrieve the hard copy (Figure 34).

Q&A
What if I want to print an electronic image of a document instead of a hard copy?

You would click the Printer Status button in the Print gallery and then select the desired electronic image option, such as Microsoft XPS Document Writer, which would create an XPS file.

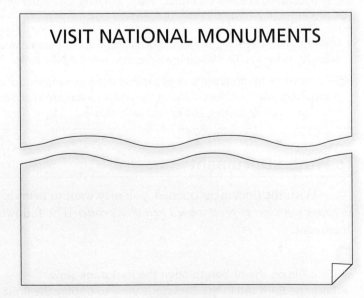

VISIT NATIONAL MONUMENTS

Figure 34

Other Ways

1. Press CTRL+P

Organizing Files and Folders

A file contains data. This data can range from a research paper to an accounting spreadsheet to an electronic math quiz. You should organize and store files in folders to avoid misplacing a file and to help you find a file quickly.

If you are taking an introductory computer class (CIS 101, for example), you may want to design a series of folders for the different subjects covered in the class. To accomplish this, you can arrange the folders in a hierarchy for the class, as shown in Figure 35.

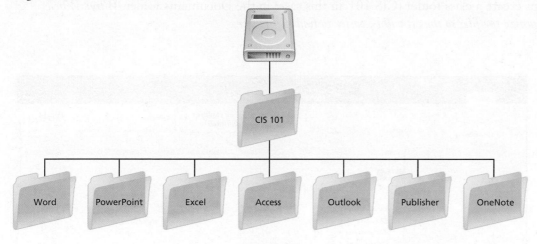

Figure 35

The hierarchy contains three levels. The first level contains the storage medium, such as a hard drive. The second level contains the class folder (CIS 101, in this case), and the third level contains seven folders, one each for a different Office app that will be covered in the class (Word, PowerPoint, Excel, Access, Outlook, Publisher, and OneNote).

When the hierarchy in Figure 35 is created, the storage medium is said to contain the CIS 101 folder, and the CIS 101 folder is said to contain the separate Office folders (i.e., Word, PowerPoint, Excel, etc.). In addition, this hierarchy easily can be expanded to include folders from other classes taken during additional semesters.

The vertical and horizontal lines in Figure 35 form a pathway that allows you to navigate to a drive or folder on a computer or network. A **path** consists of a drive letter (preceded by a drive name when necessary) and colon, to identify the storage device, and one or more folder names. A hard disk typically has a drive letter of C. Each drive or folder in the hierarchy has a corresponding path.

By default, Windows saves documents in the Documents folder, music in the Music folder, photos in the Pictures folder, videos in the Videos folder, and downloads in the Downloads folder.

The following pages illustrate the steps to organize the folders for this class and save a file in one of those folders:

1. Create the folder identifying your class.
2. Create the Word folder in the folder identifying your class.
3. Create the remaining folders in the folder identifying your class (one each for PowerPoint, Excel, Access, Outlook, Publisher, and OneNote).
4. Save a file in the Word folder.
5. Verify the location of the saved file.

To Create a Folder

When you create a folder, such as the CIS 101 folder shown in Figure 35, you must name the folder. A folder name should describe the folder and its contents. A folder name can contain spaces and any uppercase or lowercase characters, except a backslash (\), slash (/), colon (:), asterisk (*), question mark (?), quotation marks ("), less than symbol (<), greater than symbol (>), or vertical bar (|). Folder names cannot be CON, AUX, COM1, COM2, COM3, COM4, LPT1, LPT2, LPT3, PRN, or NUL. The same rules for naming folders also apply to naming files.

The following steps create a class folder (CIS 101, in this case) in the Documents folder. *Why? When storing files, you should organize the files so that it will be easier to find them later.*

- Click the File Explorer button on the taskbar to run the File Explorer.
- If necessary, double-click This PC in the navigation pane to expand the contents of your computer.
- Click the Documents folder in the navigation pane to display the contents of the Documents folder in the file list (Figure 36).

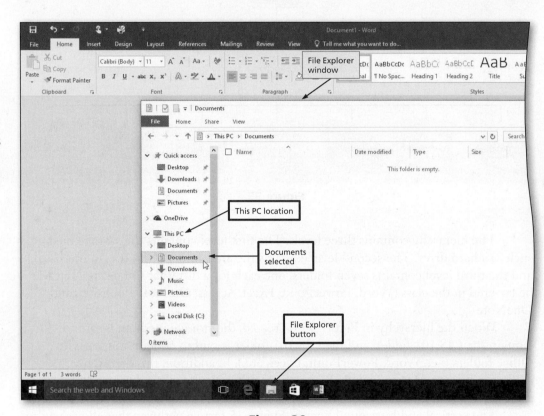

Figure 36

- Click the New folder button on the Quick Access Toolbar to create a new folder with the name, New folder, selected in a text box (Figure 37).

Q&A
Why is the folder icon displayed differently on my computer or mobile device?
Windows might be configured to display contents differently on your computer or mobile device.

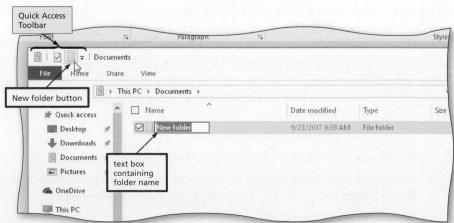

Figure 37

- Type CIS 101 (or your class code) in the text box as the new folder name.
- If requested by your instructor, add your last name to the end of the folder name.
- Press the ENTER key to change the folder name from New folder to a folder name identifying your class (Figure 38).

Q&A What happens when I press the ENTER key?

The class folder (CIS 101, in this case) is displayed in the file list, which contains the folder name, date modified, type, and size.

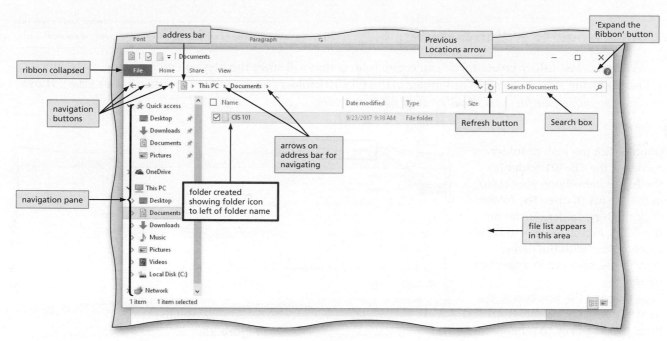

Figure 38

Other Ways

1. Press CTRL+SHIFT+N
2. Click the New folder button (Home tab | New group)

Folder Windows

The File Explorer window (shown in Figure 38) is called a folder window. Recall that a folder is a specific named location on a storage medium that contains related files. Most users rely on **folder windows** for finding, viewing, and managing information on their computers. Folder windows have common design elements, including the following (shown in Figure 38).

- The **address bar** provides quick navigation options. The arrows on the address bar allow you to visit different locations on the computer or mobile device.
- The buttons to the left of the address bar allow you to navigate the contents of the navigation pane and view recent pages.
- The **Previous Locations arrow** displays the locations you have visited.
- The **Refresh button** on the right side of the address bar refreshes the contents of the folder list.
- The **Search box** contains the dimmed words, Search Documents. You can type a term in the search box for a list of files, folders, shortcuts, and elements containing that term within the location you are searching.

- The **ribbon** contains four tabs used to accomplish various tasks on the computer related to organizing and managing the contents of the open window. This ribbon works similarly to the ribbon in the Office apps.
- The **navigation pane** on the left contains the Quick access area, the OneDrive area, the This PC area, and the Network area.
- The **Quick Access area** shows locations you access frequently. By default, this list contains links only to your Desktop, Downloads, Documents, and Pictures.

To Create a Folder within a Folder

1 SIGN IN | 2 USE WINDOWS | 3 USE APPS | **4 FILE MANAGEMENT** | 5 SWITCH APPS | 6 SAVE FILES
7 CHANGE SCREEN RESOLUTION | 8 EXIT APPS | 9 USE ADDITIONAL APPS | 10 USE HELP

With the class folder created, you can create folders that will store the files you create using each Office app. The following step creates a Word folder in the CIS 101 folder (or the folder identifying your class). *Why? To be able to organize your files, you should create a folder structure.*

1

- Double-click the icon or folder name for the CIS 101 folder (or the folder identifying your class) in the file list to open the folder.
- Click the New folder button on the Quick Access Toolbar to create a new folder with the name, New folder, selected in a text box folder.
- Type **Word** in the text box as the new folder name.
- Press the ENTER key to rename the folder (Figure 39).

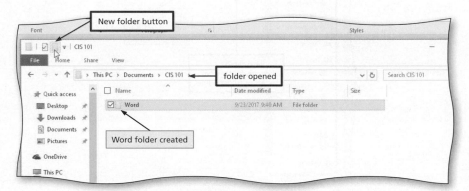

Figure 39

Other Ways

1. Press CTRL+SHIFT+N
2. Click the New folder button (Home tab | New group)

To Create the Remaining Folders

The following steps create the remaining folders in the folder identifying your class (in this case, CIS 101).

1 Click the New folder button on the Quick Access Toolbar to create a new folder with the name, New folder, selected in a text box.

2 Type **PowerPoint** in the text box as the new folder name.

3 Press the ENTER key to rename the folder.

4 Repeat Steps 1 through 3 to create each of the remaining folders, using Excel, Access, Outlook, Publisher, and OneNote as the folder names (Figure 40).

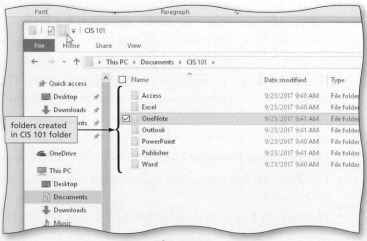

Figure 40

To Expand a Folder, Scroll through Folder Contents, and Collapse a Folder

1 SIGN IN | 2 USE WINDOWS | 3 USE APPS | 4 FILE MANAGEMENT | 5 SWITCH APPS | 6 SAVE FILES
7 CHANGE SCREEN RESOLUTION | 8 EXIT APPS | 9 USE ADDITIONAL APPS | 10 USE HELP

Folder windows display the hierarchy of items and the contents of drives and folders in the file list. You might want to expand a folder in the navigation pane to view its contents, scroll through its contents, and collapse it when you are finished viewing its contents. *Why? When a folder is expanded, you can see all the folders it contains. By contrast, a collapsed folder hides the folders it contains.* The following steps expand, scroll through, and then collapse the folder identifying your class (CIS 101, in this case).

- Double-click the Documents folder in the This PC area of the navigation pane, which expands the folder to display its contents and displays a black arrow to the left of the Documents folder icon (Figure 41).

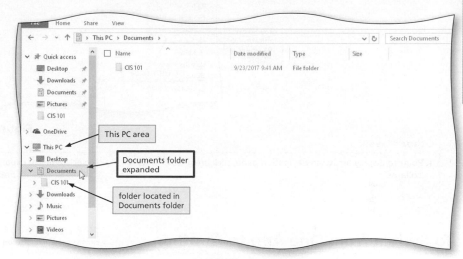

Figure 41

- Double-click the CIS 101 folder, which expands the folder to display its contents and displays a black arrow to the left of the folder icon (Figure 42).

Experiment

- Drag the scroll box down or click the down scroll arrow on the vertical scroll bar to display additional folders at the bottom of the navigation pane. Drag the scroll box up or click the scroll bar above the scroll box to move the scroll box to the top of the navigation pane. Drag the scroll box down the scroll bar until the scroll box is halfway down the scroll bar.

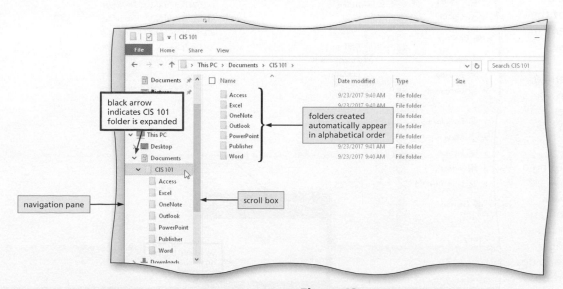

Figure 42

③

- Double-click the folder identifying your class (CIS 101, in this case) to collapse the folder (Figure 43).

Q&A Why are some folders indented below others?
A folder contains the indented folders below it.

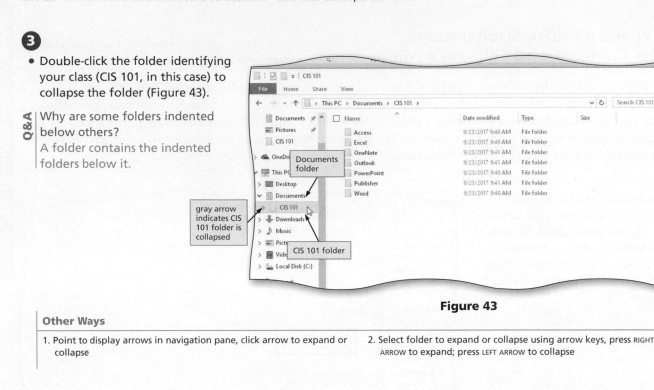

Figure 43

Other Ways

1. Point to display arrows in navigation pane, click arrow to expand or collapse
2. Select folder to expand or collapse using arrow keys, press RIGHT ARROW to expand; press LEFT ARROW to collapse

To Switch from One App to Another

1 SIGN IN | 2 USE WINDOWS | 3 USE APPS | 4 FILE MANAGEMENT | 5 SWITCH APPS | 6 SAVE FILES
7 CHANGE SCREEN RESOLUTION | 8 EXIT APPS | 9 USE ADDITIONAL APPS | 10 USE HELP

The next step is to save the Word file containing the headline you typed earlier. Word, however, currently is not the active window. You can use the button on the taskbar and live preview to switch to Word and then save the document in the Word document window.

Why? By clicking the appropriate app button on the taskbar, you can switch to the open app you want to use. The steps below switch to the Word window; however, the steps are the same for any active Office app currently displayed as a button on the taskbar.

①

- Point to the Word app button on the taskbar to see a live preview of the open document(s) or the window title(s) of the open document(s), depending on your computer's configuration (Figure 44).

Q&A What if I am using a touch screen?
Live preview will not work if you are using a touch screen. If you are using a touch screen and do not have a mouse, proceed to Step 2.

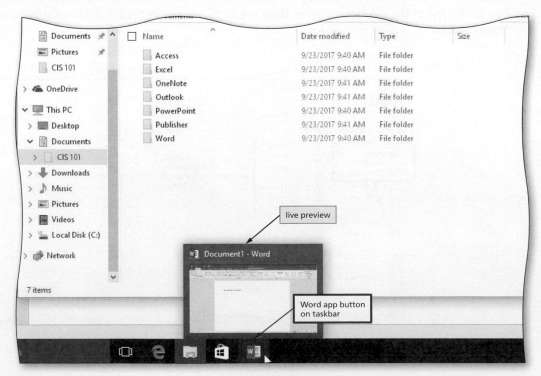

Figure 44

2

- Click the button or the live preview to make the app associated with the app button the active window (Figure 45).

Q&A | What if multiple documents are open in an app?
Click the desired live preview to switch to the window you want to use.

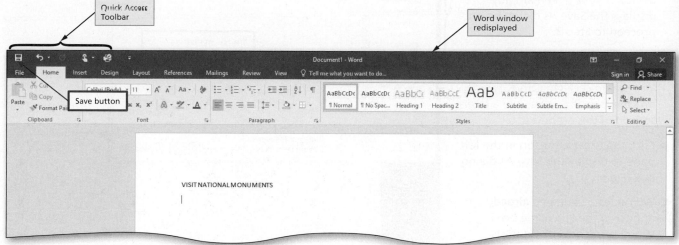

Figure 45

Other Ways

1. Press ALT+TAB until app you wish to display is selected

To Save a File in a Folder

1 SIGN IN | 2 USE WINDOWS | 3 USE APPS | 4 FILE MANAGEMENT | 5 SWITCH APPS | 6 SAVE FILES
7 CHANGE SCREEN RESOLUTION | 8 EXIT APPS | 9 USE ADDITIONAL APPS | 10 USE HELP

With the folders for storing your files created, you can save the Word document. *Why? Without saving a file, you may lose all the work you have done and will be unable to reuse or share it with others later.* The following steps save a file in the Word folder contained in your class folder (CIS 101, in this case) using the file name, National Monuments.

1

- Click the Save button (shown in Figure 45) on the Quick Access Toolbar, which depending on settings, will display either the Save As gallery in the Backstage view (Figure 46) or the Save As dialog box (Figure 47).

Q&A | What if the Save As gallery is not displayed in the Backstage view?
Click the Save As tab to display the Save As gallery.

How do I close the Backstage view?
Click the Back button in the upper-left corner of the Backstage view to return to the app window.

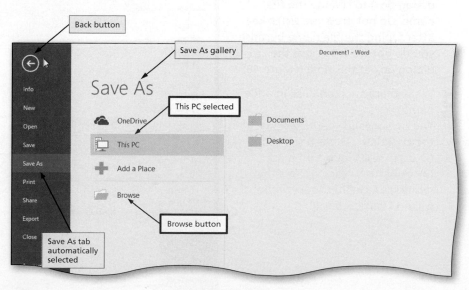

Figure 46

2

- If your screen displays the Backstage view, click This PC, if necessary, to display options in the right pane related to saving on your computer or mobile device; if your screen already displays the Save As dialog box, proceed to Step 3.

Q&A | What if I wanted to save on OneDrive instead?
You would click OneDrive. Saving on OneDrive is discussed in a later section in this module.

- Click the Browse button in the left pane to display the Save As dialog box (Figure 47).

Q&A | Why does a file name already appear in the File name box?
Word automatically suggests a file name the first time you save a document. The file name normally consists of the first few words contained in the document. Because the suggested file name is selected, you do not need to delete it; as soon as you begin typing, the new file name replaces the selected text.

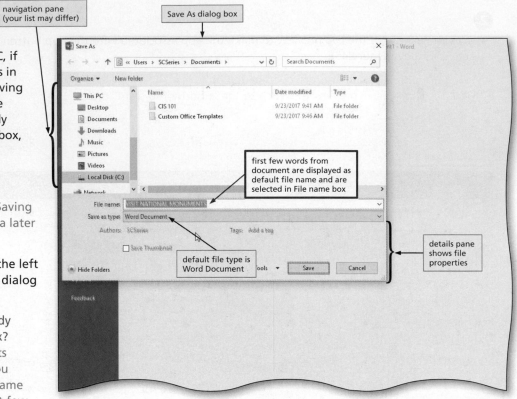

Figure 47

3

- Type **National Monuments** in the File name box (Save As dialog box) to change the file name. Do not press the ENTER key after typing the file name because you do not want to close the dialog box at this time (Figure 48).

Q&A | What characters can I use in a file name?
The only invalid characters are the backslash (\), slash (/), colon (:), asterisk (*), question mark (?), quotation mark ("), less than symbol (<), greater than symbol (>), and vertical bar (|).

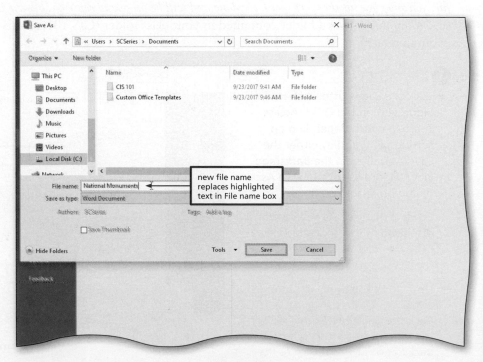

Figure 48

4

- Navigate to the desired save location (in this case, the Word folder in the CIS 101 folder [or your class folder] in the Documents folder) by performing the tasks in Steps 4a and 4b.

4a

- If the Documents folder is not displayed in the navigation pane, drag the scroll bar in the navigation pane until Documents appears.

- If the Documents folder is not expanded in the navigation pane, double-click Documents to display its folders in the navigation pane.

- If your class folder (CIS 101, in this case) is not expanded, double-click the CIS 101 folder to select the folder and display its contents in the navigation pane (Figure 49).

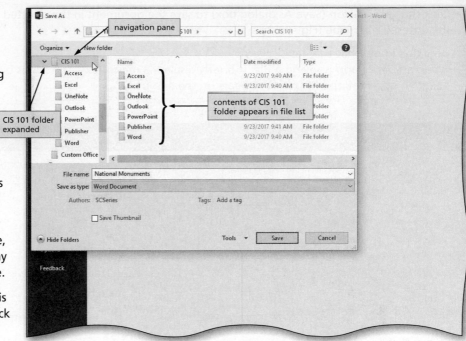

Figure 49

Q&A What if I do not want to save in a folder?

Although storing files in folders is an effective technique for organizing files, some users prefer not to store files in folders. If you prefer not to save this file in a folder, select the storage device on which you wish to save the file and then proceed to Step 5.

4b

- Click the Word folder in the navigation pane to select it as the new save location and display its contents in the file list (Figure 50).

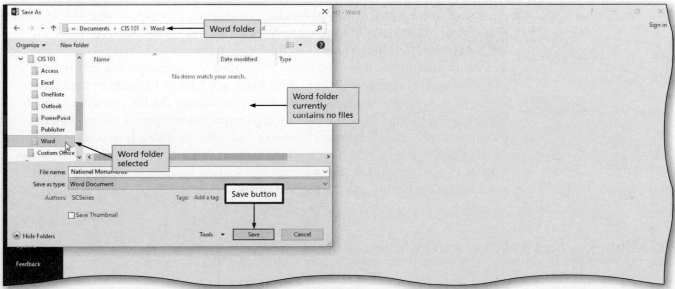

Figure 50

- Click the Save button (Save As dialog box) to save the document in the selected folder in the selected location with the entered file name (Figure 51).

Q&A | How do I know that the file is saved?

While an Office app is saving a file, it briefly displays a message on the status bar indicating the amount of the file saved. In addition, the file name appears on the title bar.

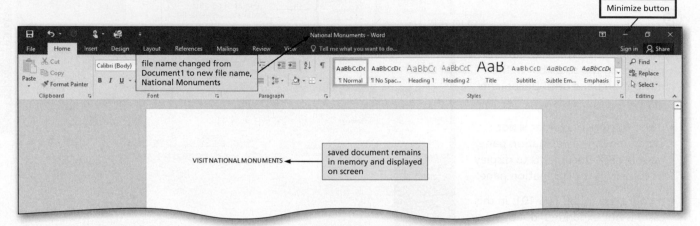

Figure 51

Other Ways

1. Click File on ribbon, click Save As in Backstage view, click This PC, click Browse button, type file name (Save As dialog box), navigate to desired save location, click Save button

2. Press F12, type file name (Save As dialog box), navigate to desired save location, click Save button

CONSIDER THIS

How often should you save a document?

It is important to save a document frequently for the following reasons:

- The document in memory might be lost if the computer is turned off or you lose electrical power while an app is running.

- If you run out of time before completing a project, you may finish it at a future time without starting over.

Navigating in Dialog Boxes

Navigating is the process of finding a location on a storage device. While saving the National Monuments file, for example, Steps 4a and 4b navigated to the Word folder located in the CIS 101 folder in the Documents folder. When performing certain functions in Windows apps, such as saving a file, opening a file, or inserting a picture in an existing document, you most likely will have to navigate to the location where you want to save the file or to the folder containing the file you want to open or insert. Most dialog boxes in Windows apps requiring navigation follow a similar procedure; that is, the way you navigate to a folder in one dialog box, such as the Save As dialog box, is similar to how you might navigate in another dialog box, such as the Open dialog box. If you chose to navigate to a specific location in a dialog box, you would follow the instructions in Steps 4a and 4b.

To Minimize and Restore a Window

1 SIGN IN | **2 USE WINDOWS** | 3 USE APPS | 4 FILE MANAGEMENT | 5 SWITCH APPS | 6 SAVE FILES
7 CHANGE SCREEN RESOLUTION | 8 EXIT APPS | 9 USE ADDITIONAL APPS | 10 USE HELP

Before continuing, you can verify that the Word file was saved properly. To do this, you will minimize the Word window and then open the CIS 101 window so that you can verify the file is stored in the CIS 101 folder on the hard drive. A **minimized window** is an open window that is hidden from view but can be displayed quickly by clicking the window's button on the taskbar.

In the following example, Word is used to illustrate minimizing and restoring windows; however, you would follow the same steps regardless of the Office app you are using. *Why? Before closing an app, you should make sure your file saved correctly so that you can find it later.*

The following steps minimize the Word window, verify that the file is saved, and then restore the minimized window.

1

- Click the Minimize button on the app's title bar (shown in Figure 51) to minimize the window (Figure 52).

Q&A Is the minimized window still available?

The minimized window, Word in this case, remains available but no longer is the active window. It is minimized as a button on the taskbar.

- If the File Explorer window is not open on the screen, click the File Explorer button on the taskbar to make the File Explorer window the active window.

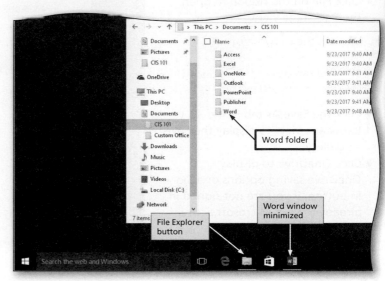

Figure 52

2

- Double-click the Word folder in the file list to select the folder and display its contents (Figure 53).

Q&A Why does the File Explorer button on the taskbar change?

A selected app button indicates that the app is active on the screen. When the button is not selected, the app is running but not active.

3

- After viewing the contents of the selected folder, click the Word button on the taskbar to restore the minimized window (as shown in Figure 51).

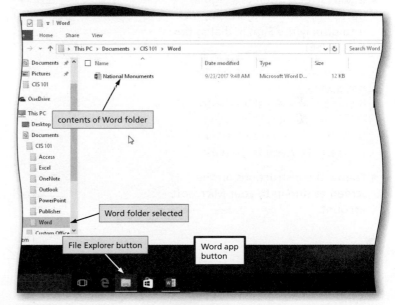

Figure 53

Other Ways

1. Right-click title bar, click Minimize on shortcut menu, click taskbar button in taskbar button area
2. Press WINDOWS+M, press WINDOWS+SHIFT+M
3. Click Word app button on taskbar to minimize window. Click Word app button again to restore window.

1 SIGN IN | 2 USE WINDOWS | 3 USE APPS | 4 FILE MANAGEMENT | 5 SWITCH APPS | 6 SAVE FILES
7 CHANGE SCREEN RESOLUTION | 8 EXIT APPS | 9 USE ADDITIONAL APPS | 10 USE HELP

To Save a File on OneDrive

One of the features of Office is the capability to save files on OneDrive so that you can use the files on multiple computers or mobile devices without having to use an external storage device, such as a USB flash drive. Storing files on OneDrive also enables you to share files more efficiently with others, such as when using Office Online and Office 365.

In the following example, Word is used to save a file on OneDrive. *Why? Storing files on OneDrive provides more portability options than are available from storing files in the Documents folder.*

You can save files directly on OneDrive from within an Office app. The following steps save the current Word file on OneDrive. These steps require you have a Microsoft account and an Internet connection.

- Click File on the ribbon to open the Backstage view.

Q&A What is the purpose of the File tab?
The File tab opens the Backstage view for each Office app.

- Click the Save As tab in the Backstage view to display the Save As gallery.
- Click OneDrive to display OneDrive saving options or a Sign In button, if you are not signed in already to your Microsoft account (Figure 54).

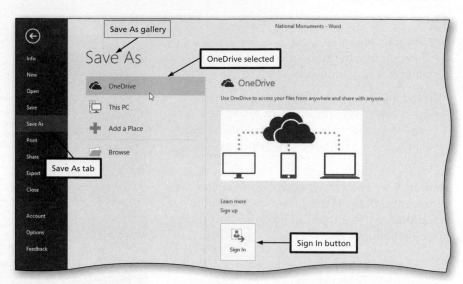

Figure 54

- If your screen displays a Sign In button (shown in Figure 54), click it to display the Sign in dialog box (Figure 55).

Q&A What if the Sign In button does not appear?
If you already are signed into your Microsoft account, the Sign In button will not be displayed. In this case, proceed to Step 3.

- Follow the instructions on the screen to sign in to your Microsoft account.

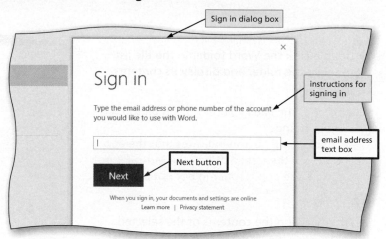

Figure 55

- If necessary, click OneDrive in the left pane.
- In the Backstage view, click the Documents folder in the right pane to display the Save As dialog box (Figure 56).

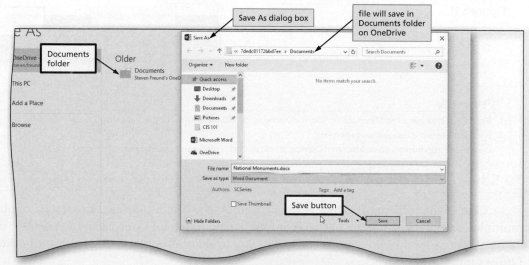

- Click the Save button (Save As dialog box) to save the file on OneDrive.

Figure 56

To Sign Out of a Microsoft Account

If you are using a public computer or otherwise wish to sign out of your Microsoft account, you should sign out of the account from the Accounts gallery in the Backstage view. Signing out of the account is the safest way to make sure that nobody else can access online files or settings stored in your Microsoft account. *Why? For security reasons, you should sign out of your Microsoft account when you are finished using a public or shared computer. Staying signed in to your Microsoft account might enable others to access your files.*

The following steps sign out of a Microsoft account from Word. You would use the same steps in any Office app. If you do not wish to sign out of your Microsoft account, read these steps without performing them.

1 Click File on the ribbon to open the Backstage view.

2 Click the Account tab to display the Account gallery (Figure 57).

3 Click the Sign out link, which displays the Remove Account dialog box. If a Can't remove Windows accounts dialog box appears instead of the Remove Account dialog box, click the OK button and skip the remaining steps.

Q&A Why does a Can't remove Windows accounts dialog box appear?
If you signed in to Windows using your Microsoft account, then you also must sign out from Windows, rather than signing out from within Word. When you are finished using Windows, be sure to sign out at that time.

4 Click the Yes button (Remove Account dialog box) to sign out of your Microsoft account on this computer.

Q&A Should I sign out of Windows after removing my Microsoft account?
When you are finished using the computer, you should sign out of Windows for maximum security.

5 Click the Back button in the upper-left corner of the Backstage view to return to the document.

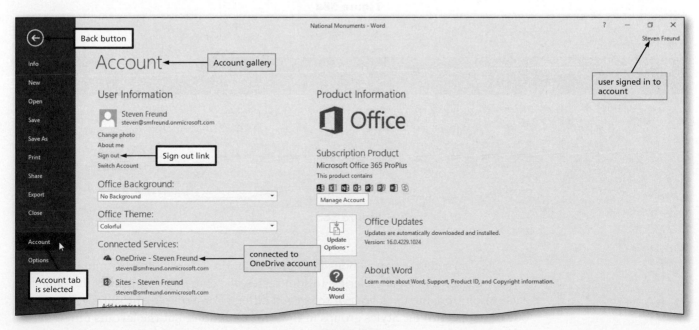

Figure 57

Screen Resolution

Screen resolution indicates the number of pixels (dots) that the computer uses to display the letters, numbers, graphics, and background you see on the screen. When you increase the screen resolution, Windows displays more information on the screen, but the information decreases in size. The reverse also is true: as you decrease the screen resolution, Windows displays less information on the screen, but the information increases in size.

Screen resolution usually is stated as the product of two numbers, such as 1366 × 768 (pronounced "thirteen sixty-six by seven sixty-eight"). A 1366 × 768 screen resolution results in a display of 1366 distinct pixels on each of 768 lines, or about 1,050,624 pixels. Changing the screen resolution affects how the ribbon appears in Office apps and some Windows dialog boxes. Figure 58 shows the Word ribbon at screen resolutions of 1366 × 768 and 1024 × 768. All of the same commands are available regardless of screen resolution. The app (Word, in this case), however, makes changes to the groups and the buttons within the groups to accommodate the various screen resolutions. The result is that certain commands may need to be accessed differently depending on the resolution chosen. A command that is visible on the ribbon and available by clicking a button at one resolution may not be visible and may need to be accessed using its Dialog Box Launcher at a different resolution.

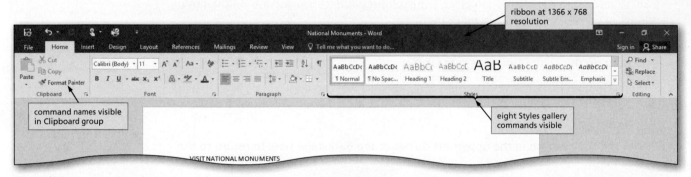

Figure 58a

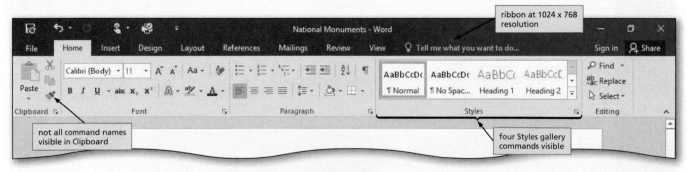

Figure 58b

Comparing the two ribbons in Figure 58, notice the changes in content and layout of the groups and galleries. In some cases, the content of a group is the same in each resolution, but the layout of the group differs. For example, the same gallery and buttons appear in the Styles groups in the two resolutions, but the layouts differ. In other cases, the content and layout are the same across the resolution, but the level of detail differs with the resolution.

To Change the Screen Resolution

If you are using a computer to step through the modules in this book and you want your screen to match the figures, you may need to change your screen's resolution. *Why? The figures in this book use a screen resolution of 1366 × 768.* The following steps change the screen resolution to 1366 × 768. Your computer already may be set to 1366 × 768. Keep in mind that many computer labs prevent users from changing the screen resolution; in that case, read the following steps for illustration purposes.

1

- Click the Show desktop button, which is located at the far-right edge of the taskbar, to display the Windows desktop.

- Right-click an empty area on the Windows desktop to display a shortcut menu that contains a list of commands related to the desktop (Figure 59).

Q&A Why does my shortcut menu display different commands? Depending on your computer's hardware and configuration, different commands might appear on the shortcut menu.

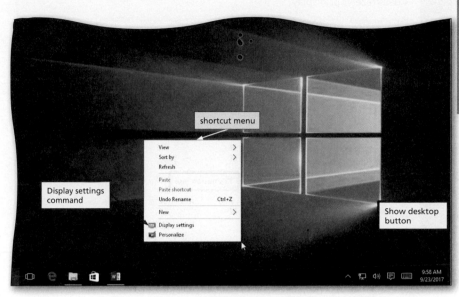

Figure 59

2

- Click Display settings on the shortcut menu to open the Settings app window. If necessary, scroll to display the 'Advanced display settings' link (Figure 60).

Figure 60

3

- Click 'Advanced display settings' in the Settings window to display the advanced display settings.
- If necessary, scroll to display the Resolution box (Figure 61).

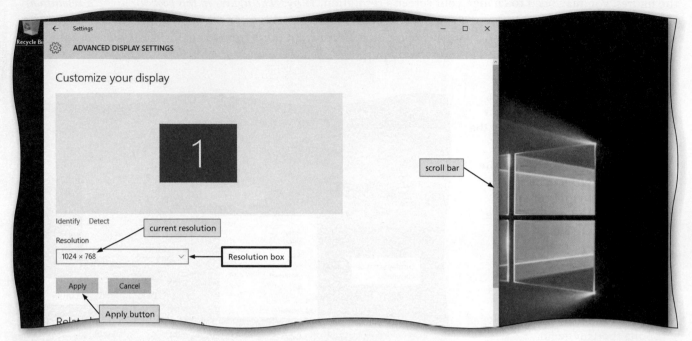

Figure 61

4

- Click the Resolution box to display a list of available screen resolutions (Figure 62).
- If necessary, scroll to and then click 1366 × 768 to select the screen resolution.

Q&A What if my computer does not support the 1366 × 768 resolution?
Some computers do not support the 1366 × 768 resolution. In this case, select a resolution that is close to the 1366 × 768 resolution.

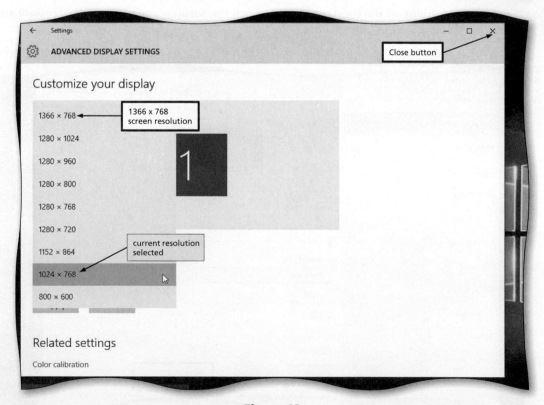

Figure 62

5

- Click the Apply button (Advanced Display Settings window) (shown in Figure 61) to change the screen resolution and display a confirmation message (Figure 63).
- Click the Keep changes button to accept the new screen resolution.
- Click the Close button (shown in Figure 62) to close the Settings app window.

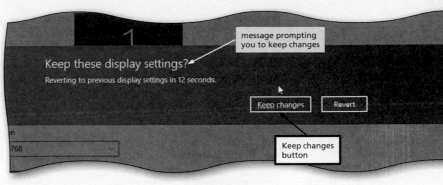

Figure 63

Other Ways

1. Click Start button, click Settings, click System, click Display, click 'Advanced display settings,' select desired resolution in Resolution box, click Apply button, click Keep changes button

2. Type `screen resolution` in search box, click 'Change the screen resolution,' select desired resolution in Resolution box, click Apply, click Keep changes

To Exit an Office App with One Document Open

1 SIGN IN | 2 USE WINDOWS | 3 USE APPS | 4 FILE MANAGEMENT | 5 SWITCH APPS | 6 SAVE FILES
7 CHANGE SCREEN RESOLUTION | 8 EXIT APPS | 9 USE ADDITIONAL APPS | 10 USE HELP

When you exit an Office app, such as Word, if you have made changes to a file since the last time the file was saved, the Office app displays a dialog box asking if you want to save the changes you made to the file before it closes the app window. *Why? The dialog box contains three buttons with these resulting actions: the Save button saves the changes and then exits the Office app, the Don't Save button exits the Office app without saving changes, and the Cancel button closes the dialog box and redisplays the file without saving the changes.*

If no changes have been made to an open document since the last time the file was saved, the Office app will close the window without displaying a dialog box.

The following steps exit an Office app. In the following example, Word is used to illustrate exiting an Office app; however, you would follow the same steps regardless of the Office app you were using.

1

- If necessary, click the Word app button on the taskbar to display the Word window on the desktop (Figure 64).

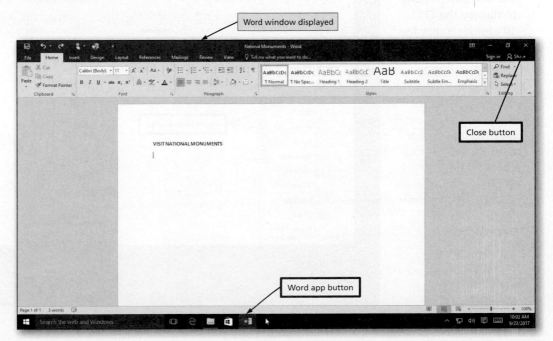

Figure 64

- Click the Close button to close the document and exit Word. If a Microsoft Word dialog box appears, click the Save button to save any changes made to the document since the last save.

Q&A What if I have more than one document open in an Office app?

You could click the Close button for each open document. When you click the last open document's Close button, you also exit the Office app. As an alternative that is more efficient, you could right-click the app button on the taskbar and then click 'Close all windows' on the shortcut menu, or press ALT+F4 to close all open documents and exit the Office app.

Other Ways

1. Right-click the Office app button on Windows taskbar, click Close window on shortcut menu
2. Press ALT+F4

To Copy a Folder to OneDrive

1 SIGN IN | 2 USE WINDOWS | 3 USE APPS | **4 FILE MANAGEMENT** | 5 SWITCH APPS | 6 SAVE FILES
7 CHANGE SCREEN RESOLUTION | 8 EXIT APPS | **9 USE ADDITIONAL APPS** | **10 USE HELP**

To back up your files or easily make them available on another computer or mobile device, you can copy them to OneDrive. The following steps copy your CIS 101 folder to OneDrive. If you do not have access to a OneDrive account, read the following steps without performing them. *Why? It often is good practice to have a backup of your files so that they are available in case something happens to your original copies.*

- Click the File Explorer button on the taskbar to make the folder window the active window.
- Click Documents in the This PC area of the navigation pane to display the CIS 101 folder in the file list.

Q&A What if my CIS 101 folder is stored in a different location?

Use the navigation pane to navigate to the location of your CIS 101 folder. The CIS 101 folder should be displayed in the file list once you have located it.

- Click the CIS 101 folder in the file list to select it (Figure 65).

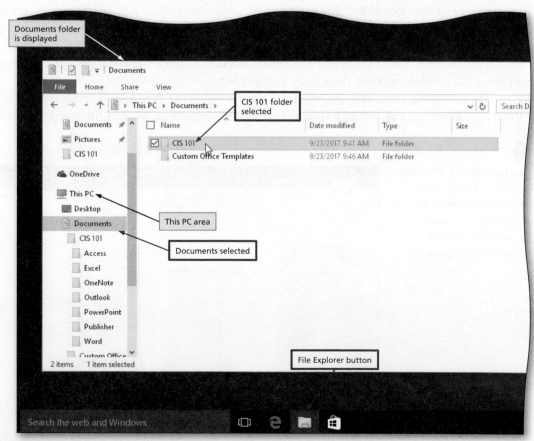

Figure 65

②

- Click Home on the ribbon to display the Home tab.
- Click the Copy to button (Home tab | Organize group) to display the Copy to menu (Figure 66).

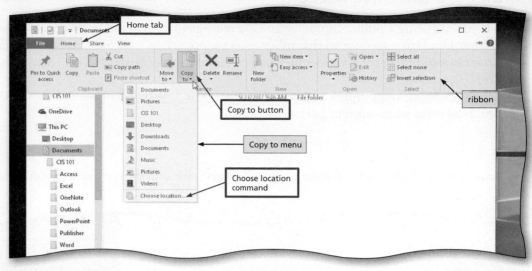

Figure 66

③

- Click Choose location on the Copy to menu to display the Copy Items dialog box.
- Click OneDrive (Copy Items dialog box) to select it (Figure 67).

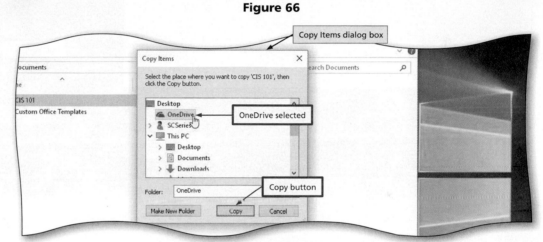

Figure 67

④

- Click the Copy button (Copy Items dialog box) to copy the selected folder to OneDrive.
- Click OneDrive in the navigation pane to verify the CIS 101 folder displays in the file list (Figure 68).

Q&A Why does a Microsoft OneDrive dialog box display when I click OneDrive in the navigation pane?
If you are not currently signed in to Windows using a Microsoft account, you will manually need to sign in to a Microsoft account to save files to OneDrive. Follow the instructions on the screen to sign in to your Microsoft account.

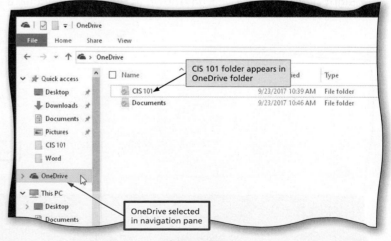

Figure 68

Other Ways

1. In File Explorer, select folder to copy, click Copy button (Home tab | Clipboard group), display contents of OneDrive in file list, click Paste button (Home tab | Clipboard group)

2. In File Explorer, select folder to copy, press CTRL+C, display contents of OneDrive in file list, press CTRL+V

3. Drag folder to copy to OneDrive in navigation pane

To Unlink a OneDrive Account

If you are using a public computer and are not signed in to Windows with a Microsoft account, you should unlink your OneDrive account so that other users cannot access it. **Why?** *If you do not unlink your OneDrive account, other people using the same user account on the computer will be able to view, remove, and add to files stored in your OneDrive account.*

The following steps unlink your OneDrive account. If you do not wish to sign out of your Microsoft account, read these steps without performing them.

- Click the 'Show hidden icons' button on the Windows taskbar to show a menu of hidden icons (Figure 69).

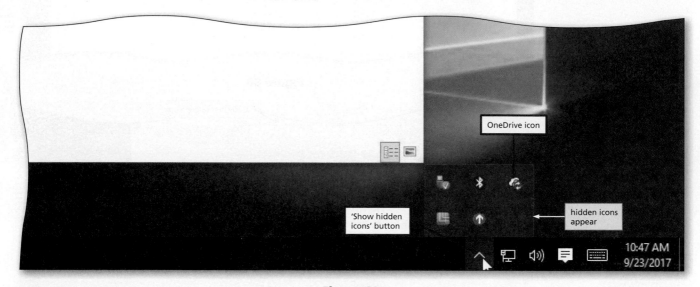

Figure 69

2

- Right click the OneDrive icon (shown in Figure 69) to display a shortcut menu (Figure 70).

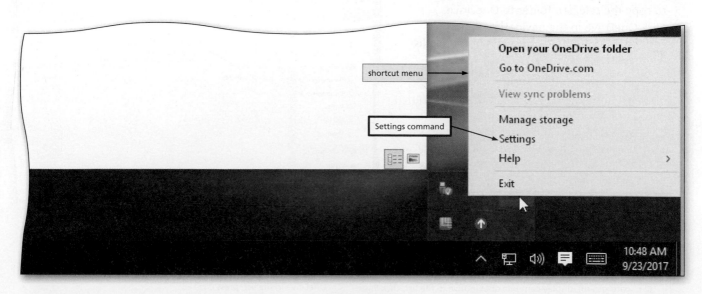

Figure 70

3

- Click Settings on the shortcut menu to display the Microsoft OneDrive dialog box (Figure 71).

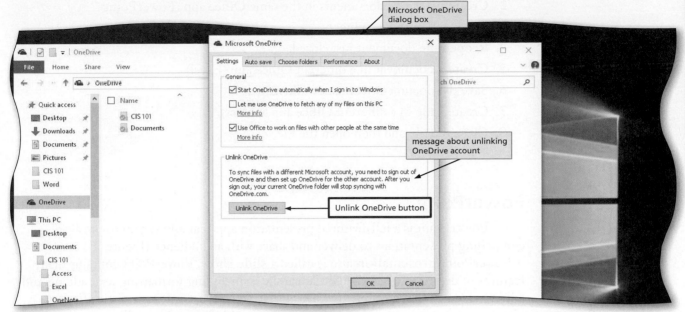

Figure 71

4

- If necessary, click the Settings tab.
- Click the Unlink OneDrive button (Microsoft OneDrive dialog box) to unlink the OneDrive account (Figure 72).
- When the Microsoft OneDrive dialog box appears with a Welcome to OneDrive message, click the Close button.
- Minimize the File Explorer window.

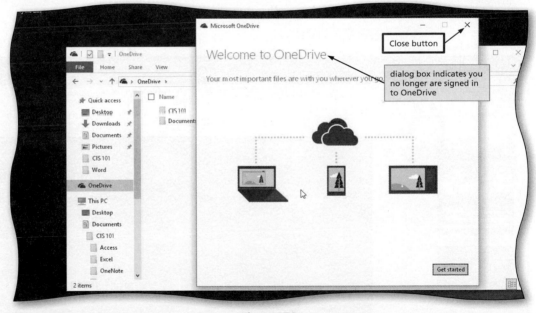

Figure 72

Break Point: If you wish to take a break, this is a good place to do so. To resume at a later time, continue to follow the steps from this location forward.

Additional Microsoft Office Apps

The previous section used Word to illustrate common features of Office and some basic elements unique to Word. The following sections present elements unique to PowerPoint, Excel, and Access, as well as illustrate additional common features of Office.

In the following pages, you will learn how to do the following:

1. Run an Office app (PowerPoint) using the search box.
2. Create two small documents in the same Office app (PowerPoint).
3. Close one of the documents.
4. Reopen the document just closed.
5. Create a document in a different Office app (Excel).
6. Save the document with a new file name.
7. Create a file in a different Office app (Access).
8. Close the file and then open the file.

PowerPoint

PowerPoint is a full-featured presentation app that allows you to produce compelling presentations to deliver and share with an audience (Figure 73). A PowerPoint **presentation** also is called a **slide show**. PowerPoint contains many features to design, develop, and organize slides, including formatting text, adding and editing video and audio clips, creating tables and charts, applying artistic effects to pictures, animating graphics, and collaborating with friends and colleagues. You then can turn your presentation into a video, broadcast your slide show on the web, or create a photo album.

Figure 73

To Run an App Using the Search Box

The following steps, which assume Windows is running, use the search box to run the PowerPoint app based on a typical installation; however, you would follow similar steps to run any Office app. *Why? Some people prefer to use the search box to locate and run an app, as opposed to searching through a list of all apps on the Start menu.* You may need to ask your instructor how to run apps for your computer.

1

- Type **PowerPoint 2016** as the search text in the search box and watch the search results appear in the search results (Figure 74).

Q&A

Do I need to type the complete app name or use correct capitalization?
No, you need to type just enough characters of the app name for it to appear in the search results. For example, you may be able to type PowerPoint or powerpoint, instead of PowerPoint 2016.

2

- Click the app name, PowerPoint 2016 in this case, in the search results to run PowerPoint (Figure 75).

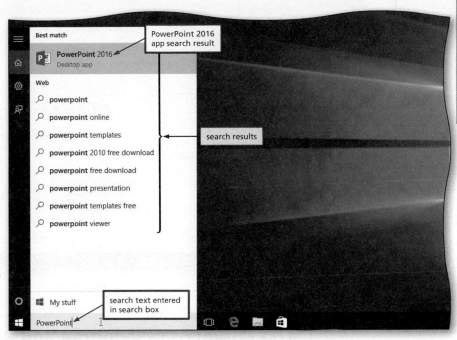

Figure 74

Figure 75

• Click the Blank Presentation thumbnail to create a blank presentation and display it in the PowerPoint window.

• If the app window is not maximized, click the Maximize button on its title bar to maximize the window (Figure 76).

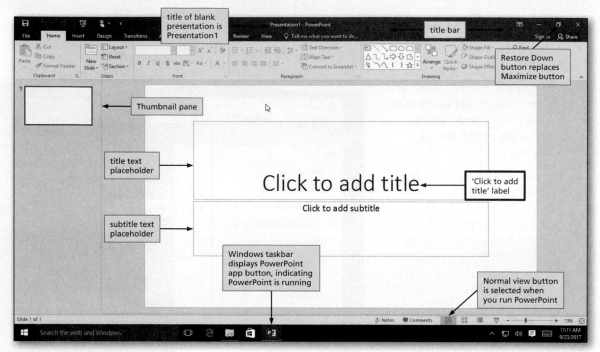

Figure 76

The PowerPoint Window and Ribbon

The PowerPoint window consists of a variety of components to make your work more efficient and documents more professional: the window, ribbon, mini toolbar, shortcut menus, Quick Access Toolbar, and Microsoft Account area. Many of these components are common to other Office apps and have been discussed earlier in this module. Other components, discussed in the following paragraphs and later in subsequent modules, are unique to PowerPoint.

The basic unit of a PowerPoint presentation is a **slide**. A slide may contain text and objects, such as graphics, tables, charts, and drawings. **Layouts** are used to position this content on the slide. When you create a new presentation, the default **Title Slide** layout appears (shown in Figure 76). The purpose of this layout is to introduce the presentation to the audience. PowerPoint includes several other built-in standard layouts.

The default slide layouts are set up in **landscape orientation**, where the slide width is greater than its height. In landscape orientation, the slide size is preset to 13.3 inches wide and 7.5 inches high when printed on a standard sheet of paper measuring 11 inches wide and 8.5 inches high.

Placeholders   **Placeholders** are boxes with dashed or solid borders that are displayed when you create a new slide. All layouts except the Blank slide layout contain placeholders. Depending on the particular slide layout selected, title and subtitle placeholders are displayed for the slide title and subtitle; a content placeholder is displayed for text or a table, chart, picture, graphic, or movie. The title slide in Figure 76 has two text placeholders for the main heading, or title, and the subtitle.

Ribbon   The ribbon in PowerPoint is similar to the one in Word and the other Microsoft Office apps. When you run PowerPoint, the ribbon displays nine main tabs: File, Home, Insert, Design, Transitions, Animations, Slide Show, Review, and View.

To Enter Content in a Title Slide

With the exception of a blank slide, PowerPoint assumes every new slide has a title. Many of PowerPoint's layouts have both a title text placeholder and at least one content placeholder. To make creating a presentation easier, any text you type after a new slide appears becomes title text in the title text placeholder. As you begin typing text in the title text placeholder, the title text also is displayed in the Slide 1 thumbnail in the Thumbnail pane. The title for this presentation is Mara's Marbles. The following step enters a presentation title on the title slide. *Why? In general, every presentation should have a title to describe what the presentation will be covering.*

1

- Click the 'Click to add title' label located inside the title text placeholder (shown in Figure 76) to select the placeholder.

- Type **Mara's Marbles** in the title text placeholder. Do not press the ENTER key because you do not want to create a new line of text (Figure 77).

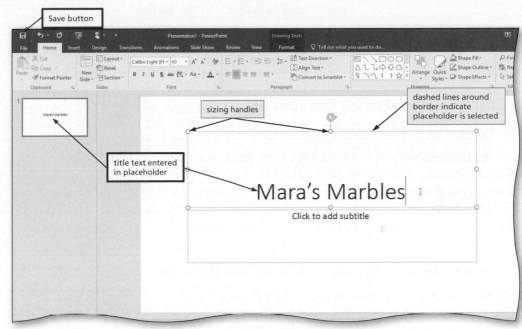

Figure 77

To Save a File in a Folder

The following steps save the presentation in the PowerPoint folder in the class folder (CIS 101, in this case) in the Documents folder using the file name, Mara's Marbles.

1 Click the Save button on the Quick Access Toolbar (shown in Figure 77), which depending on settings will display either the Save As gallery in the Backstage view or the Save As dialog box.

2 If your screen displays the Backstage view, click This PC, if necessary, to display options in the right pane related to saving on your computer; if your screen already displays the Save As dialog box, proceed to Step 4.

3 Click the Browse button in the left pane to display the Save As dialog box.

4 If necessary, type **Mara's Marbles** in the File name box (Save As dialog box) to change the file name. Do not press the ENTER key after typing the file name because you do not want to close the dialog box at this time.

5 Navigate to the desired save location (in this case, the PowerPoint folder in the CIS 101 folder [or your class folder] in the Documents folder). For specific instructions, perform the tasks in Steps 5a through 5e.

5a If the Documents folder is not displayed in the navigation pane, slide to scroll or drag the scroll bar in the navigation pane until Documents appears.

5b If the Documents folder is not expanded in the navigation pane, double-click Documents to display its folders in the navigation pane.

5c If the Documents folder is not expanded in the navigation pane, double-click Documents to display its folders in the navigation pane.

5d If your class folder (CIS 101, in this case) is not expanded, double-click the CIS 101 folder to select the folder and display its contents in the navigation pane.

5e Click the PowerPoint folder in the navigation pane to select it as the new save location and display its contents in the file list.

6 Click the Save button (Save As dialog box) to save the presentation in the selected folder in the selected location with the entered file name.

To Create a New Office Document from the Backstage View

1 SIGN IN | 2 USE WINDOWS | 3 USE APPS | 4 FILE MANAGEMENT | 5 SWITCH APPS | 6 SAVE FILES
7 CHANGE SCREEN RESOLUTION | 8 EXIT APPS | 9 USE ADDITIONAL APPS | 10 USE HELP

As discussed earlier, the Backstage view contains a set of commands that enable you to manage documents and data about the documents. *Why? From the Backstage view in PowerPoint, for example, you can create, open, print, and save presentations. You also can share documents, manage versions, set permissions, and modify document properties. In other Office 2016 apps, the Backstage view may contain features specific to those apps.* The following steps create a file, a blank presentation in this case, from the Backstage view.

1

• Click File on the ribbon to open the Backstage view (Figure 78).

Q&A What is the purpose of the Info tab in the Backstage view?
The Info tab, which is selected by default when you click File on the ribbon, allows you to protect your document, inspect your document, and manage versions of your document as well as view all the file properties, such as when the file was created.

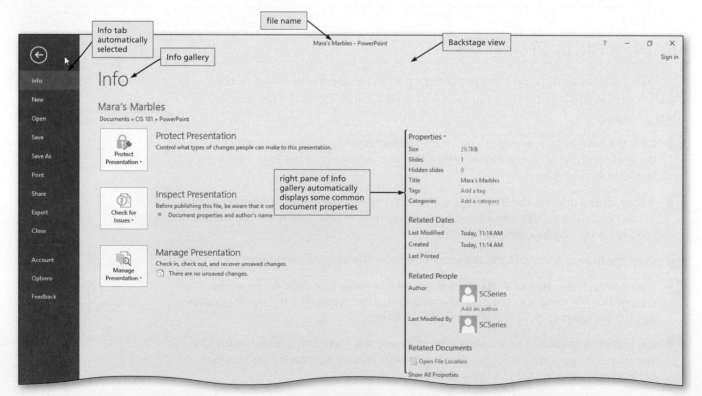

Figure 78

2
- Click the New tab in the Backstage view to display the New gallery (Figure 79).

Q&A Can I create documents through the Backstage view in other Office apps? Yes. If the Office app has a New tab in the Backstage view, the New gallery displays various options for creating a new file.

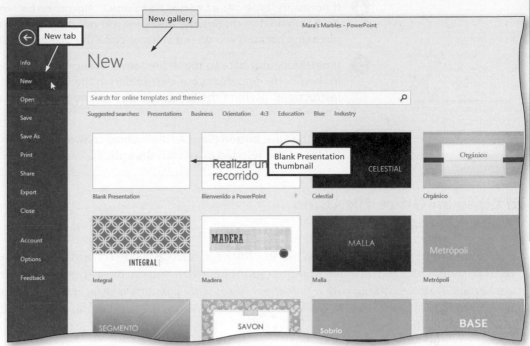

Figure 79

3
- Click the Blank Presentation thumbnail in the New gallery to create a new presentation.

Other Ways
1. Press CTRL+N

To Enter Content in a Title Slide of a Second PowerPoint Presentation

The presentation title for this presentation is Visiting National Monuments. The following steps enter a presentation title on the title slide.

1 Click the title text placeholder to select it.

2 Type **Visiting National Monuments** in the title text placeholder. Do not press the ENTER key.

To Save a File in a Folder

The following steps save the second presentation in the PowerPoint folder in the class folder (CIS 101, in this case) in the Documents folder using the file name, Visiting National Monuments.

1 Click the Save button on the Quick Access Toolbar, which depending on settings will display either the Save As gallery in the Backstage view or the Save As dialog box.

2 If your screen displays the Backstage view, click This PC, if necessary, to display options in the right pane related to saving on your computer; if your screen already displays the Save As dialog box, proceed to Step 4.

3 Click the Browse button in the left pane to display the Save As dialog box.

4 If necessary, type `Visiting National Monuments` in the File name box (Save As dialog box) to change the file name. Do not press the ENTER key after typing the file name because you do not want to close the dialog box at this time.

5 If necessary, navigate to the desired save location (in this case, the PowerPoint folder in the CIS 101 folder [or your class folder] in the Documents folder). For specific instructions, perform the tasks in Steps 5a through 5e in the previous section titled To Save a File in a Folder.

6 Click the Save button (Save As dialog box) to save the presentation in the selected folder on the selected drive with the entered file name.

To Close an Office File Using the Backstage View

1 SIGN IN | 2 USE WINDOWS | 3 USE APPS | 4 FILE MANAGEMENT | 5 SWITCH APPS | 6 SAVE FILES
7 CHANGE SCREEN RESOLUTION | 8 EXIT APPS | 9 USE ADDITIONAL APPS | 10 USE HELP

Sometimes, you may want to close an Office file, such as a PowerPoint presentation, entirely and start over with a new file. You also may want to close a file when you are done working with it. *Why? You should close a file when you are done working with it so that you do not make inadvertent changes to it.* The following steps close the current active Office file, that is, the Visiting National Monuments presentation, without exiting the active app (PowerPoint, in this case).

- Click File on the ribbon to open the Backstage view (Figure 80).

- Click Close in the Backstage view to close the open file (Visiting National Monuments, in this case) without exiting the active app.

Q&A

What if the Office app displays a dialog box about saving?
Click the Save button if you want to save the changes, click the Don't Save button if you want to ignore the changes since the last time you saved, and click the Cancel button if you do not want to close the document.

Can I use the Backstage view to close an open file in other Office apps, such as Word and Excel?
Yes.

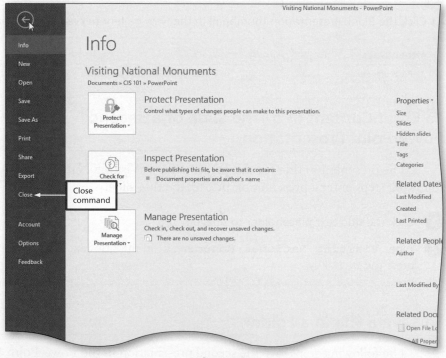

Figure 80

Other Ways

1. Press CTRL+F4

To Open a Recent Office File Using the Backstage View

1 SIGN IN | 2 USE WINDOWS | 3 USE APPS | 4 FILE MANAGEMENT | 5 SWITCH APPS | 6 SAVE FILES
7 CHANGE SCREEN RESOLUTION | 8 EXIT APPS | 9 USE ADDITIONAL APPS | 10 USE HELP

You sometimes need to open a file that you recently modified. *Why? You may have more changes to make, such as adding more content or correcting errors.* The Backstage view allows you to access recent files easily. The following steps reopen the Visiting National Monuments file just closed.

1
- Click File on the ribbon to open the Backstage view.
- Click the Open tab in the Backstage view to display the Open gallery (Figure 81).

2
- Click the desired file name in the Recent list, Visiting National Monuments in this case, to open the file.

Q&A
Can I use the Backstage view to open a recent file in other Office apps, such as Word and Excel?

Yes, as long as the file name appears in the list of recent files.

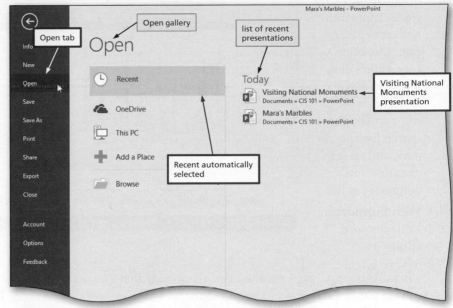

Figure 81

Other Ways

1. Click File on ribbon, click Open in Backstage view, click This PC, click Browse button, navigate to file (Open dialog box), click Open button

To Exit an Office App

You are finished using PowerPoint. Thus, you should exit this Office app. The following steps exit PowerPoint.

1 If you have one Office document open, click the Close button on the right side of the title bar to close the document and exit the Office app; or if you have multiple Office documents open, right-click the app button on the taskbar and then click 'Close all windows' on the shortcut menu, or press ALT+F4 to close all open documents and exit the Office app.

Q&A
If I am using a touch screen, could I press and hold the Close button until all windows close and the app exits?

Yes.

2 If a dialog box appears, click the Save button to save any changes made to the document since the last save.

Excel

Excel is a powerful spreadsheet app that allows users to organize data, complete calculations, make decisions, graph data, develop professional-looking reports (Figure 82), publish organized data to the web, and access real-time data from websites. The four major parts of Excel are:

- **Workbooks and Worksheets:** A **workbook** is like a notebook. Inside the workbook are sheets, each of which is called a **worksheet**. Thus, a workbook is a collection of worksheets. Worksheets allow users to enter, calculate, manipulate, and analyze data, such as numbers and text. The terms worksheet and spreadsheet are interchangeable.
- **Charts:** Excel can draw a variety of charts, such as column charts and pie charts.

• **Tables:** Tables organize and store data within worksheets. For example, once a user enters data into a worksheet, an Excel table can sort the data, search for specific data, and select data that satisfies defined criteria.

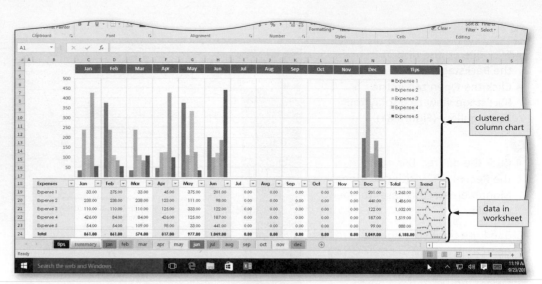

Figure 82

• **Web Support:** Web support allows users to save Excel worksheets or parts of a worksheet in a format that a user can view in a browser, so that a user can view and manipulate the worksheet using a browser. Excel web support also provides access to real-time data, such as stock quotes, using web queries.

To Create a New Blank Office Document from File Explorer

1 SIGN IN | 2 USE WINDOWS | 3 USE APPS | 4 FILE MANAGEMENT | 5 SWITCH APPS | 6 SAVE FILES
7 CHANGE SCREEN RESOLUTION | 8 EXIT APPS | 9 USE ADDITIONAL APPS | 10 USE HELP

File Explorer provides a means to create a blank Office document without running an Office app. The following steps use File Explorer to create a blank Excel document. *Why? Sometimes you might need to create a blank document and then return to it later for editing.*

• If necessary, click the File Explorer button on the taskbar to make the folder window the active window.
• If necessary, double-click the Documents folder in the navigation pane to expand the Documents folder.
• If necessary, double-click your class folder (CIS 101, in this case) in the navigation pane to expand the folder.
• Click the Excel folder in the navigation pane to display its contents in the file list.
• With the Excel folder selected, right-click an open area in the file list to display a shortcut menu.
• Point to New on the shortcut menu to display the New submenu (Figure 83).

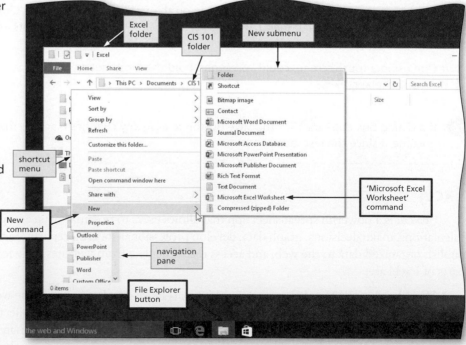

Figure 83

Office 2016 and Windows 10 Module

- Click 'Microsoft Excel Worksheet' on the New submenu to display an icon and text box for a new file in the current folder window with the file name, New Microsoft Excel Worksheet, selected (Figure 84).

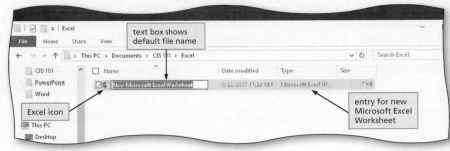

Figure 84

- Type **Silver Sky Hardware** in the text box and then press the ENTER key to assign a new file name to the new file in the current folder (Figure 85).

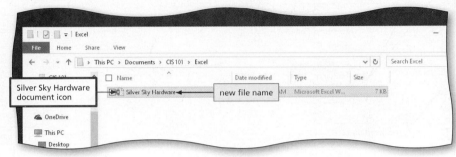

Figure 85

To Run an App from File Explorer and Open a File

1 SIGN IN | 2 USE WINDOWS | 3 USE APPS | 4 FILE MANAGEMENT | 5 SWITCH APPS | 6 SAVE FILES
7 CHANGE SCREEN RESOLUTION | 8 EXIT APPS | 9 USE ADDITIONAL APPS | 10 USE HELP

Previously, you learned how to run an Office app using the Start menu and the search box. The following steps, which assume Windows is running, use File Explorer to run the Excel app based on a typical installation. *Why? Another way to run an Office app is to open an existing file from File Explorer, which causes the app in which the file was created to run and then open the selected file.* You may need to ask your instructor how to run Office apps for your computer.

- If necessary, display the file to open in the folder window in File Explorer (shown in Figure 85).
- Right-click the file icon or file name (Silver Sky Hardware, in this case) to display a shortcut menu (Figure 86).

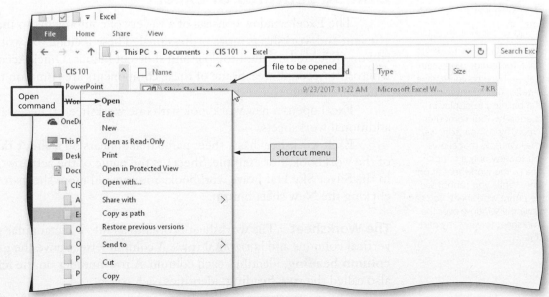

Figure 86

- Click Open on the shortcut menu to open the selected file in the app used to create the file, Excel in this case (Figure 87).
- If the window is not maximized, click the Maximize button on the title bar to maximize the window.

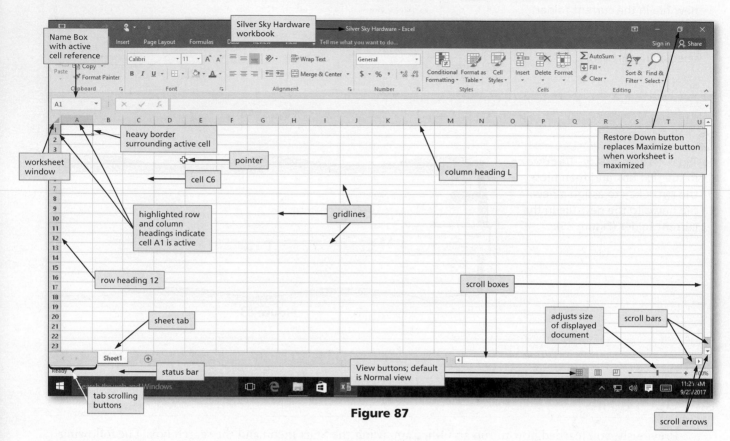

Figure 87

Q&A Instead of using File Explorer, can I run Excel using the same method shown previously for Word and PowerPoint?
Yes, you can use any method of running an Office app to run Excel.

BTW

The Worksheet Size and Window

The 16,384 columns and 1,048,576 rows in Excel make for a huge worksheet that — if you could imagine — takes up the entire side of a building to display in its entirety. Your computer screen, by comparison, is a small window that allows you to view only a minute area of the worksheet at one time. While you cannot see the entire worksheet, you can move the window over the worksheet to view any part of it.

Unique Features of Excel

The Excel window consists of a variety of components to make your work more efficient and worksheets more professional. These include the worksheet window, ribbon, Tell Me box, mini toolbar and shortcut menus, Quick Access Toolbar, and Microsoft Account area. Some of these components are common to other Office apps; others are unique to Excel.

Excel opens a new workbook with one worksheet. If necessary, you can add additional worksheets.

Each worksheet has a sheet name that appears on a **sheet tab** at the bottom of the workbook. For example, Sheet1 is the name of the active worksheet displayed in the Silver Sky Hardware workbook. You can add more sheets to the workbook by clicking the New sheet button.

The Worksheet The worksheet is organized into a rectangular grid containing vertical columns and horizontal rows. A column letter above the grid, also called the **column heading**, identifies each column. A row number on the left side of the grid, also called the **row heading**, identifies each row.

The intersection of each column and row is a cell. A **cell** is the basic unit of a worksheet into which you enter data. Each worksheet in a workbook has 16,384 columns and 1,048,576 rows for a total of 17,179,869,184 cells. Only a small fraction of the active worksheet appears on the screen at one time.

A cell is referred to by its unique address, or **cell reference**, which is the coordinates of the intersection of a column and a row. To identify a cell, specify the column letter first, followed by the row number. For example, cell reference C6 refers to the cell located at the intersection of column C and row 6 (Figure 87).

One cell on the worksheet, designated the **active cell**, is the one into which you can enter data. The active cell in Figure 87 is A1. The active cell is identified in three ways. First, a heavy border surrounds the cell; second, the active cell reference shows immediately above column A in the Name box; and third, the column heading A and row heading 1 are highlighted so that it is easy to see which cell is active (Figure 87).

The horizontal and vertical lines on the worksheet itself are called **gridlines**. Gridlines make it easier to see and identify each cell in the worksheet. If desired, you can turn the gridlines off so that they do not show on the worksheet. While learning Excel, gridlines help you to understand the structure of the worksheet.

The pointer in Figure 87 has the shape of a block plus sign. The pointer appears as a block plus sign whenever it is located in a cell on the worksheet. Another common shape of the pointer is the block arrow. The pointer turns into the block arrow when you move it outside the worksheet or when you drag cell contents between rows or columns.

Ribbon   When you run Excel, the ribbon displays eight main tabs: File, Home, Insert, Page Layout, Formulas, Data, Review, and View. The Formulas and Data tabs are specific to Excel. The Formulas tab allows you to work with Excel formulas, and the Data tab allows you to work with data processing features such as importing and sorting data.

Formula Bar   As you type, Excel displays the entry in the **formula bar**, which appears below the ribbon (Figure 88). You can make the formula bar larger by dragging the sizing handle at the bottom of the formula bar or clicking the expand button to the right of the formula bar. Excel also displays the active cell reference in the **Name box** on the left side of the formula bar.

BTW

Customizing the Ribbon
In addition to customizing the Quick Access Toolbar, you can add items to and remove items from the ribbon. To customize the ribbon, click File on the ribbon to open the Backstage view, click the Options tab in the Backstage view, and then click Customize Ribbon in the left pane of the Options dialog box. More information about customizing the ribbon is presented in a later module.

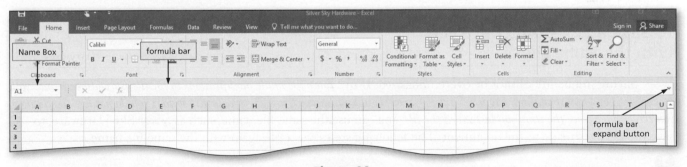

Figure 88

To Enter a Worksheet Title

1 SIGN IN | 2 USE WINDOWS | 3 USE APPS | 4 FILE MANAGEMENT | 5 SWITCH APPS | 6 SAVE FILES
7 CHANGE SCREEN RESOLUTION | 8 EXIT APPS | 9 USE ADDITIONAL APPS | 10 USE HELP

To enter data into a cell, you first must select it. The easiest way to select a cell (make it active) is to use the mouse to move the block plus sign pointer to the cell and then click. An alternative method is to use the arrow keys that are located just to the right of the typewriter keys on the keyboard. An arrow key selects the cell adjacent to the active cell in the direction of the arrow on the key.

In Excel, any set of characters containing a letter, hyphen (as in a telephone number), or space is considered text. **Text** is used to place titles, such as worksheet titles, column titles, and row titles, on the worksheet. The following steps enter the worksheet title in cell A1. *Why? A title informs others as to the contents of the worksheet, such as information regarding a company.*

1

- If it is not already the active cell, click cell A1 to make it the active cell.
- Type Silver Sky Hardware in cell A1 (Figure 89).

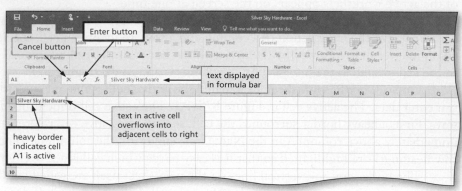

Figure 89

2

- Click the Enter button to complete the entry and enter the worksheet title in cell A1 (Figure 90).

Q&A Why do some commands on the ribbon appear dimmed?
Excel dims the commands that are unavailable for use at the current time.

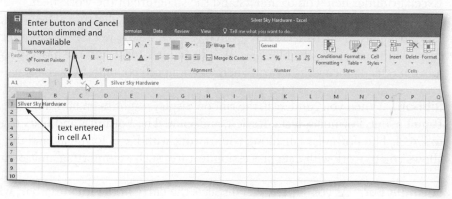

Figure 90

Other Ways

1. To complete entry, click any cell other than active cell

2. To complete entry, press ENTER, HOME, PAGE UP, PAGE DOWN, END, UP ARROW, DOWN ARROW, LEFT ARROW, or RIGHT ARROW

To Save an Existing Office File with the Same File Name

1 SIGN IN | 2 USE WINDOWS | 3 USE APPS | 4 FILE MANAGEMENT | 5 SWITCH APPS | 6 SAVE FILES
7 CHANGE SCREEN RESOLUTION | 8 EXIT APPS | 9 USE ADDITIONAL APPS | 10 USE HELP

Saving frequently cannot be overemphasized. *Why? You have made modifications to the file (spreadsheet) since you created it. Thus, you should save again. Similarly, you should continue saving files frequently so that you do not lose the changes you have made since the time you last saved the file.* You can use the same file name, such as Silver Sky Hardware, to save the changes made to the document. The following step saves a file again with the same file name.

1

- Click the Save button on the Quick Access Toolbar to overwrite the previously saved file (Silver Sky Hardware, in this case) in the Excel folder (Figure 91).

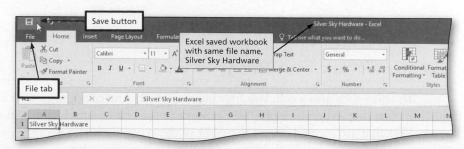

Figure 91

Other Ways

1. Press CTRL+S

2. Press SHIFT+F12

To Save a File with a New File Name

You might want to save a file with a different file name or to a different location. For example, you might start a homework assignment with a data file and then save it with a final file name for submission to your instructor, saving it to a location designated by your instructor. The following steps save a file with a different file name.

1 Click the File tab to open the Backstage view.

2 Click the Save As tab to display the Save As gallery.

3 If necessary, click This PC to display options in the right pane related to saving on your computer.

4 Click the Browse button in the left pane to display the Save As dialog box.

5 Type `Silver Sky Hardware Sales Summary` in the File name box (Save As dialog box) to change the file name. Do not press the ENTER key after typing the file name because you do not want to close the dialog box at this time.

6 If necessary, navigate to the desired save location (in this case, the Excel folder in the CIS 101 folder [or your class folder] in the Documents folder). For specific instructions, perform the tasks in Steps 5a through 5e in the previous section titled To Save a File in a Folder, replacing the PowerPoint folder with the Excel folder.

7 Click the Save button (Save As dialog box) to save the worksheet in the selected folder on the selected drive with the entered file name.

To Exit an Office App

You are finished using Excel. The following steps exit Excel.

1 If you have one Office document open, click the Close button on the right side of the title bar to close the document and exit the Office app; or if you have multiple Office documents open, right-click the app button on the taskbar and then click 'Close all windows' on the shortcut menu, or press ALT+F4 to close all open documents and exit the Office app.

2 If a dialog box appears, click the Save button to save any changes made to the file since the last save.

Access

The term **database** describes a collection of data organized in a manner that allows access, retrieval, and use of that data. **Access** is a database management system. A **database management system** is software that allows you to use a computer to create a database; add, change, and delete data in the database; create queries that allow you to ask questions concerning the data in the database; and create forms and reports using the data in the database.

To Run an App

The following steps, which assume Windows is running, run the Access app based on a typical installation. You may need to ask your instructor how to run apps for your computer.

① Type `Access 2016` as the search text in the search box and watch the search results appear in the search results.

② Click the app name, Access 2016 in this case, in the search results to run Access.

③ If the window is not maximized, click the Maximize button on its title bar to maximize the window (Figure 92).

Q&A

Do I have to run Access using these steps?

No. You can use any previously discussed method of running an Office app to run Access.

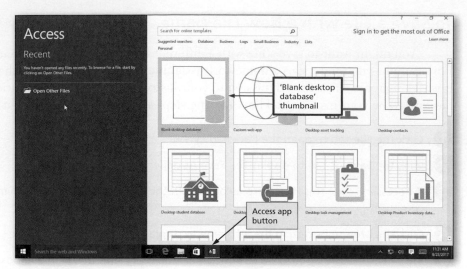

Figure 92

Unique Elements in Access

You work on objects such as tables, forms, and reports in the **Access work area**. Figure 93 shows a work area with multiple objects open. **Object tabs** for the open objects appear at the top of the work area. You select an open object by clicking its tab. In the figure, the Customer List table is the selected object. To the left of the work area is the Navigation Pane, which contains a list of all the objects in the database. You use this pane to open an object. You also can customize the way objects are displayed in the Navigation Pane.

Because the Navigation Pane can take up space in the window, you may not have as much open space for working as you would with Word or Excel. You can use the 'Shutter Bar Open/Close Button' to minimize the Navigation Pane when you are not using it, which allows more space to work with tables, forms, reports, and other database elements.

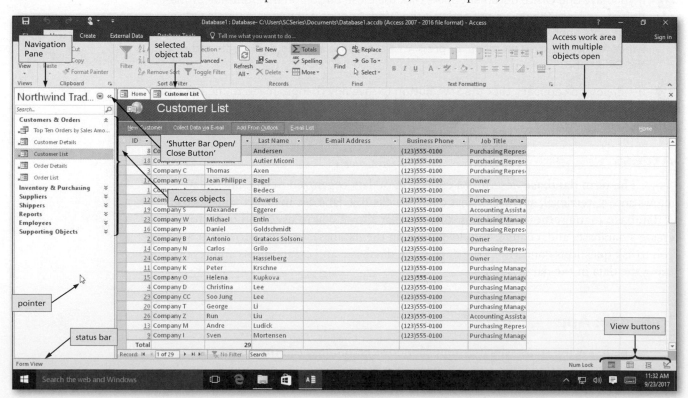

Figure 93

Ribbon   When you run Access, the ribbon displays five main tabs: File, Home, Create, External Data, and Database Tools. Access has unique groupings such as Sort & Filter and Records that are designed specifically for working with databases. Many of the formatting options are reserved for the tool tabs that appear when you are working with forms and reports.

To Create an Access Database

1 SIGN IN | 2 USE WINDOWS | 3 USE APPS | 4 FILE MANAGEMENT | 5 SWITCH APPS | 6 SAVE FILES
7 CHANGE SCREEN RESOLUTION | 8 EXIT APPS | 9 USE ADDITIONAL APPS | 10 USE HELP

Unlike the other Office apps, Access saves a database when you first create it. When working in Access, you will add data to an Access database. As you add data to a database, Access automatically saves your changes rather than waiting until you manually save the database or exit Access. Recall that in Word and Excel, you entered the data first and then saved it.

Because Access automatically saves the database as you add and change data, you do not always have to click the Save button on the Quick Access Toolbar. Instead, the Save button in Access is used for saving the objects (including tables, queries, forms, reports, and other database objects) a database contains. You can use either the 'Blank desktop database' option or a template to create a new database. If you already know the organization of your database, you would use the 'Blank desktop database' option. If not, you can use a template. Templates can guide you by suggesting some commonly used database organizations.

The following steps use the 'Blank desktop database' option to create a database named Rimitoein Electronics in the Access folder in the class folder (CIS 101, in this case) in the Documents folder. *Why? You have decided to use Microsoft Access to maintain large amounts of data.*

1
- Click the 'Blank desktop database' thumbnail (shown in Figure 92) to select the database type.
- Type **Rimitoein Electronics** in the File Name text box (Blank desktop database dialog box) to enter the new file name. Do not press the ENTER key after typing the file name because you do not want to create the database at this time (Figure 94).

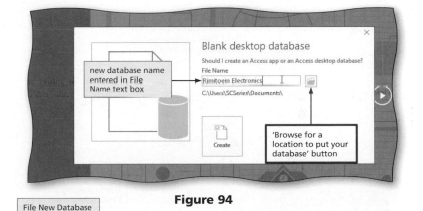

Figure 94

2
- Click the 'Browse for a location to put your database' button to display the File New Database dialog box.
- Navigate to the location for the database, that is, the Documents folder, then to the folder identifying your class (CIS 101, in this case), and then to the Access folder (Figure 95). For specific instructions, perform the tasks in Steps 5a through 5e in the previous section titled To Save a File in a Folder, replacing the PowerPoint folder with the Access folder.

Q&A Why does the 'Save as type' box say Microsoft Access 2007-2016 Databases?
Microsoft Access database formats change with some new versions of Microsoft Access. The most recent format is the Microsoft Access 2007-2016 Databases format, which was released with Access 2007.

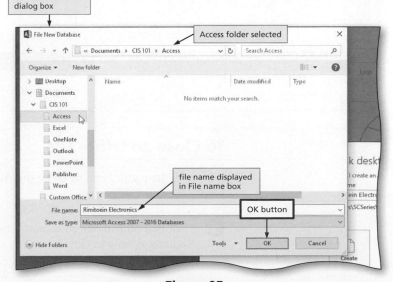

Figure 95

• Click the OK button (File New Database dialog box) to select the Access folder as the location for the database and close the dialog box (Figure 96).

• Click the Create button (Blank desktop database dialog box) to create the database on the selected drive in the selected folder with the file name, Rimitoein Electronics (Figure 97).

Q&A How do I know that the Rimitoein Electronics database is created?

The file name of the database appears on the title bar.

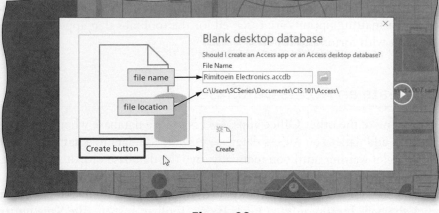

Figure 96

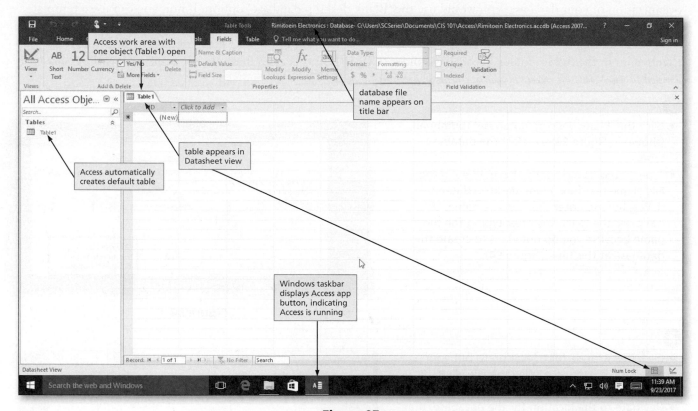

Figure 97

To Close an Office File

Assume you need to close the Access database and return to it later. The following step closes an Office file.

1 Click File on the ribbon to open the Backstage view and then click Close in the Backstage view to close the open file (Rimitoein Electronics, in this case) without exiting the active app.

Q&A Why is Access still on the screen?

When you close a database, the app remains running.

To Open an Existing Office File

Assume you wish to continue working on an existing file, that is, a file you previously saved. Earlier in this module, you learned how to open a recently used file through the Backstage view. The following step opens a database, specifically the Rimitoein Electronics database, that recently was saved. *Why? Because the file has been created already, you just need to reopen it.*

- Click File on the ribbon to open the Backstage view and then click Open in the Backstage view to display the Open gallery in the Backstage view.
- Click This PC to display recent folders accessed on your computer.
- Click the Browse button to display the Open dialog box.
- If necessary, navigate to the location of the file to open.
- Click the file to open, Rimitoein Electronics in this case, to select the file (Figure 98).
- Click the Open button (Open dialog box) to open the file. If necessary, click the Enable Content button.

Q&A
Why did the Security Warning appear?
The Security Warning appears when you open an Office file that might contain harmful content. The files you create in this module are not harmful, but you should be cautious when opening files from other people.

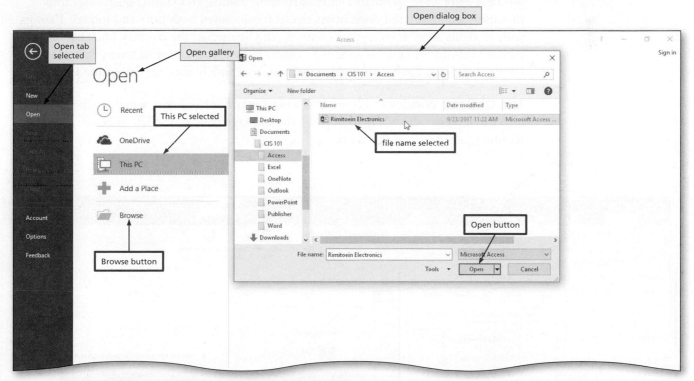

Figure 98

Other Ways

1. Press CTRL+O   2. Navigate to file in File Explorer window, double-click file name

To Exit an Office App

You are finished using Access. The following step exits Access.

1 Click the Close button on the right side of the title bar to close the file and exit the Office app.

Office 2016 and Windows 10 Module

Other Office Apps

In addition to the Office apps discussed thus far, three other apps are useful when collaborating and communicating with others: Outlook, Publisher, and OneNote.

Outlook

Outlook is a powerful communications and scheduling app that helps you communicate with others, keep track of contacts, and organize your calendar. Apps such as Outlook provide a way for individuals and workgroups to organize, find, view, and share information easily. Outlook allows you to send and receive email messages and provides a means to organize contacts. Users can track email messages, meetings, and notes related to a particular contact. Outlook's Calendar, People, Tasks, and Notes components aid in this organization. Contact information readily is available from the Outlook Calendar, Mail, People, and Tasks components by accessing the Search Contacts feature.

Email is the transmission of messages and files over a computer network. Email has become an important means of exchanging information and files between business associates, classmates and instructors, friends, and family. Businesses find that using email to send documents electronically saves both time and money. Parents with students away at college or relatives who live across the country find that communicating by email is an inexpensive and easy way to stay in touch with their family members. Exchanging email messages is a widely used service of the Internet.

The Outlook Window Figure 99 shows an Outlook window, which is divided into three panes: the Navigation pane, the message pane to the left of center, and the Reading pane to the right of center.

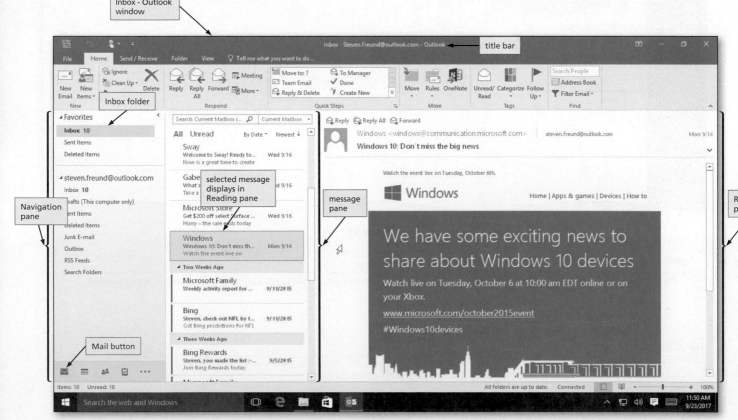

Figure 99

When an email message is open in Outlook, it is displayed in a Message window (Figure 100). When you open a message, the Message tab on the ribbon appears, which contains the more frequently used commands.

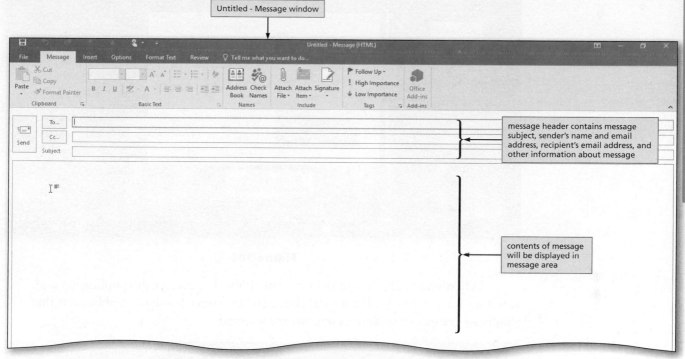

Untitled - Message window

message header contains message subject, sender's name and email address, recipient's email address, and other information about message

contents of message will be displayed in message area

Figure 100

Publisher

Publisher is a powerful desktop publishing (DTP) app that assists you in designing and producing professional-quality documents that combine text, graphics, illustrations, and photos. DTP software provides additional tools beyond those typically found in word processing apps, including design templates, graphic manipulation tools, color schemes or libraries, advanced layout and printing tools, and web components. For large jobs, businesses use DTP software to design publications that are camera ready, which means the files are suitable for outside commercial printing. In addition, DTP software can be used to create webpages and interactive web forms.

Publisher is used by people who regularly produce high-quality color publications, such as newsletters, brochures, flyers, logos, signs, catalogs, cards, and business forms. Publisher has many features designed to simplify production and make publications visually appealing. Using Publisher, you easily can change the shape, size, and color of text and graphics. You can include many kinds of graphical objects, including mastheads, borders, tables, images, pictures, charts, and web objects in publications, as well as integrate spreadsheets and databases.

The Publisher Window   Publisher initially displays a list of publication types. **Publication types** are typical publications used by desktop publishers. The more popular types are displayed in the center of the window.

Once you select a publication type, a dialog box is displayed to allow you to create the publication (Figure 101). Some templates are installed with Publisher, and others are available online. In Figure 101, the Business newsletter publication dialog box is displayed.

BTW
Running Publisher
When you first run Publisher, the New templates gallery usually is displayed in the Backstage view. If it is not displayed, click File on the ribbon, click the Options tab in the Backstage view, click General (Publisher Options dialog box), and then click 'Show the New template gallery when starting Publisher' to select the check box in the right pane.

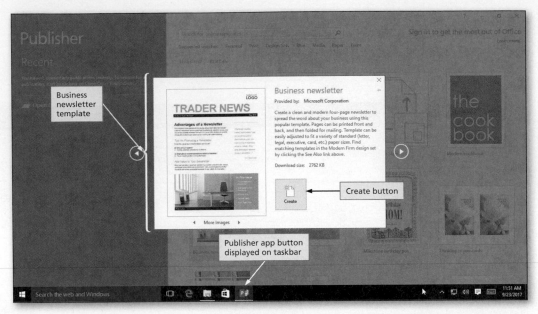

Figure 101

When you select the desired template, Publisher creates the publication and sets it up for you to edit. Figure 102 shows the Business newsletter publication that Publisher creates when default options are selected.

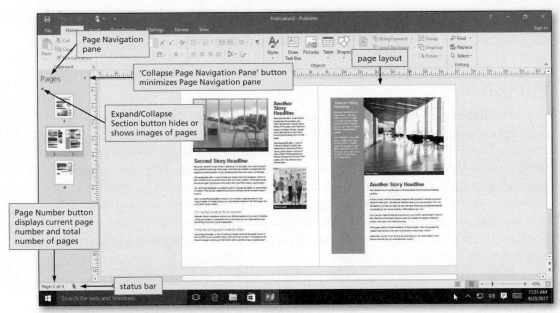

Figure 102

OneNote

OneNote is a note taking app that assists you in entering, saving, organizing, searching, and using notes. It enables you to create pages, which are organized in sections, just as in a physical notebook. In OneNote, you can type notes anywhere on a page and then easily move the notes around on the page. You can create lists and outlines, use handwriting to enter notes, and create drawings. If you use a tablet to add handwritten notes to a document, OneNote can convert the handwriting to text. It also can perform searches on the handwritten entries. Pictures and data from other apps easily are incorporated in your notes.

In addition to typing and handwriting, you can take audio notes. For example, you could record conversations during a meeting or lecture. As you record, you can take additional notes. When you play back the audio notes, you can synchronize the additional notes you took; that is, OneNote will show you during playback the exact points at which you added the notes. A variety of note flags, which are symbols that call your attention to notes on a page, enable you to flag notes as being important. You then can use the Note Flags summary to view the flagged notes, which can be sorted in a variety of ways.

OneNote includes tools to assist you with organizing a notebook and navigating its contents. It also includes a search feature, making it easy to find the specific notes in which you are interested. For short notes that you always want to have available readily, you can use Side Notes, which are used much like the sticky notes that you might use in a physical notebook.

OneNote Window   All activity in OneNote takes place in the **notebook** (Figure 103). Like a physical notebook, the OneNote notebook consists of notes that are placed on **pages**. The pages are grouped into **sections**, which can be further grouped into **folders**. (No folders are shown in the notebook in the figure.) You can use the Search box to search for specific text in your notes.

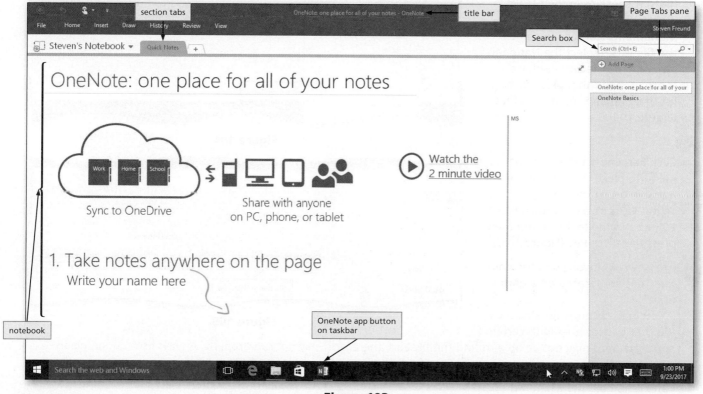

Figure 103

You can add pages to the notebook using the Add Page button in the Page Tabs pane. If page tabs are displayed, you can switch to a page by clicking its tab. Figure 103 shows the Quick Notes page being displayed for the notebook.

> **Break Point:** If you wish to take a break, this is a good place to do so. To resume at a later time, continue to follow the steps from this location forward.

Renaming, Moving, and Deleting Files

Earlier in this module, you learned how to organize files in folders, which is part of a process known as **file management**. The following sections cover additional file management topics including renaming, moving, and deleting files.

To Rename a File

In some circumstances, you may want to change the name of, or rename, a file or a folder. *Why? You may want to distinguish a file in one folder or drive from a copy of a similar file, or you may decide to rename a file to better identify its contents.* The following steps change the name of the National Monuments file in the Word folder to National Monuments Flyer.

- If necessary, click the File Explorer button on the taskbar to make the folder window the active window.
- Navigate to the location of the file to be renamed (in this case, the Word folder in the CIS 101 [or your class folder] folder in the Documents folder) to display the file(s) it contains in the file list.
- Right-click the National Monuments icon or file name in the file list to select the National Monuments file and display a shortcut menu that presents a list of commands related to files (Figure 104).

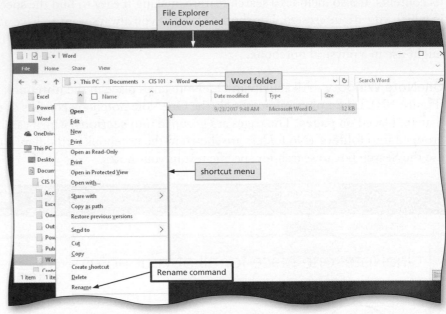

Figure 104

- Click Rename on the shortcut menu to place the current file name in a text box.
- Type `National Monuments Flyer` in the text box and then press the ENTER key (Figure 105).

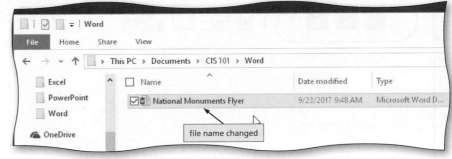

Figure 105

Q&A

Are any risks involved in renaming files that are located on a hard drive?

If you inadvertently rename a file that is associated with certain apps, the apps may not be able to find the file and, therefore, may not run properly. Always use caution when renaming files.

Can I rename a file when it is open?

No, a file must be closed to change the file name.

Other Ways

1. Select file, press F2, type new file name, press ENTER   2. Select file, click Rename (Home tab | Organize group), type new file name, press ENTER

To Move a File

Why? At some time, you may want to move a file from one folder, called the source folder, to another, called the destination folder. When you move a file, it no longer appears in the original folder. If the destination and the source folders are on the same media, you can move a file by dragging it. If the folders are on different media, then you will need to right-drag the file, and then click Move here on the shortcut menu. The following step moves the Silver Sky Hardware Sales Summary file from the Excel folder to the OneNote folder.

- In File Explorer, navigate to the location of the file to be moved (in this case, the Excel folder in the CIS 101 folder [or your class folder] in the Documents folder).
- Click the Excel folder in the navigation pane to display the files it contains in the right pane (Figure 106).
- Drag the Silver Sky Hardware Sales Summary file in the right pane to the OneNote folder in the navigation pane.

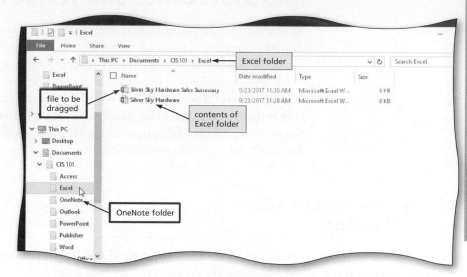

Figure 106

Other Ways

1. Right-click file to move, click Cut on shortcut menu, right-click destination folder, click Paste on shortcut menu

2. Select file to move, press CTRL+X, select destination folder, press CTRL+V

To Delete a File

A final task you may want to perform is to delete a file. Exercise extreme caution when deleting a file or files. When you delete a file from a hard drive, the deleted file is stored in the Recycle Bin where you can recover it until you empty the Recycle Bin. If you delete a file from removable media, such as a USB flash drive, the file is deleted permanently. The next steps delete the Visiting National Monuments file from the PowerPoint folder. *Why? When a file no longer is needed, you can delete it to conserve space on your storage location.*

- In File Explorer, navigate to the location of the file to be deleted (in this case, the PowerPoint folder in the CIS 101 folder [or your class folder] in the Documents folder).
- Click the Visiting National Monuments icon or file name in the right pane to select the file.
- Right-click the selected file to display a shortcut menu (Figure 107).

- Click Delete on the shortcut menu to delete the file.
- If a dialog box appears, click the Yes button to delete the file.

Q&A Can I use this same technique to delete a folder?

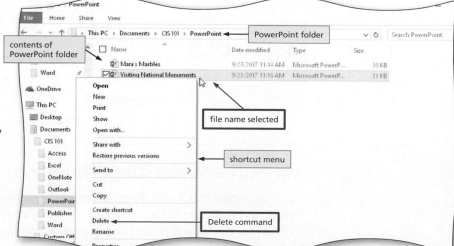

Figure 107

Yes. Right-click the folder and then click Delete on the shortcut menu. When you delete a folder, all of the files and folders contained in the folder you are deleting, together with any files and folders on lower hierarchical levels, are deleted as well. For example, if you delete the CIS 101 folder, you will delete all folders and files inside the CIS 101 folder.

Other Ways

1. Select file, press DELETE

Microsoft Office and Windows Help

At any time while you are using one of the Office apps, you can use Office Help to display information about all topics associated with the app. To illustrate the use of Office Help, this section uses Word. Help in other Office apps operates in a similar fashion.

In Office, Help is presented in a window that has browser-style navigation buttons. Each Office app has its own Help home page, which is the starting Help page that is displayed in the Help window. If your computer is connected to the Internet, the contents of the Help page reflect both the local help files installed on the computer and material from Microsoft's website.

To Open the Help Window in an Office App

1 SIGN IN | 2 USE WINDOWS | 3 USE APPS | 4 FILE MANAGEMENT | 5 SWITCH APPS | 6 SAVE FILES
7 CHANGE SCREEN RESOLUTION | 8 EXIT APPS | 9 USE ADDITIONAL APPS | 10 USE HELP

The following step opens the Word Help window. *Why? You might not understand how certain commands or operations work in Word, so you can obtain the necessary information using help.*

1

- Run an Office app, in this case Word.
- Click the Blank document thumbnail to display a blank document.
- Press F1 to open the app's Help window (Figure 108).

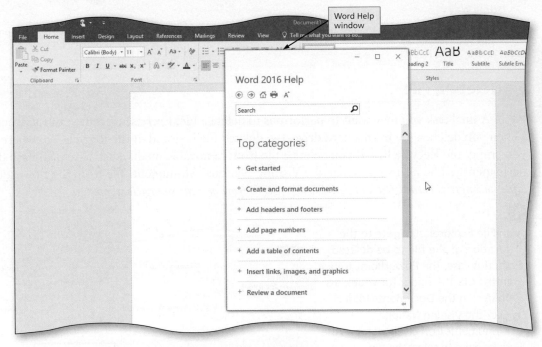

Figure 108

Moving and Resizing Windows

At times, it is useful, or even necessary, to have more than one window open and visible on the screen at the same time. You can resize and move these open windows so that you can view different areas of and elements in the window. In the case of the Help window, for example, it could be covering document text in the Word window that you need to see.

To Move a Window by Dragging

1 SIGN IN | 2 USE WINDOWS | 3 USE APPS | 4 FILE MANAGEMENT | 5 SWITCH APPS | 6 SAVE FILES
7 CHANGE SCREEN RESOLUTION | 8 EXIT APPS | 9 USE ADDITIONAL APPS | 10 USE HELP

You can move any open window that is not maximized to another location on the desktop by dragging the title bar of the window. *Why? You might want to have a better view of what is behind the window or just want to move the window so that you can see it better.* The following step drags the Word Help window to the upper-left corner of the desktop.

- Drag the window title bar (the Word Help window title bar, in this case) so that the window moves to the upper-left corner of the desktop, as shown in Figure 109.

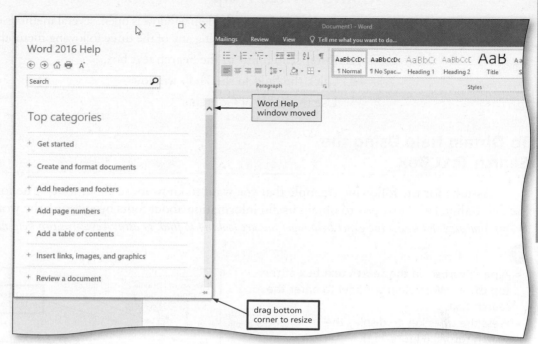

Figure 109

To Resize a Window by Dragging

1 SIGN IN | **2 USE WINDOWS** | 3 USE APPS | 4 FILE MANAGEMENT | 5 SWITCH APPS | 6 SAVE FILES
7 CHANGE SCREEN RESOLUTION | 8 EXIT APPS | 9 USE ADDITIONAL APPS | 10 USE HELP

A method used to change the size of the window is to drag the window borders. The following step changes the size of the Word Help window by dragging its borders. *Why? Sometimes, information is not visible completely in a window, and you want to increase the size of the window.*

- If you are using a mouse, point to the lower-right corner of the window (the Word Help window, in this case) until the pointer changes to a two-headed arrow.
- Drag the bottom border downward to display more of the active window (Figure 110).

Q&A Can I drag other borders on the window to enlarge or shrink the window?
Yes, you can drag the left, right, and top borders and any window corner to resize a window.

Q&A Will Windows remember the new size of the window after I close it?
Yes. When you reopen the window, Windows will display it at the same size it was when you closed it.

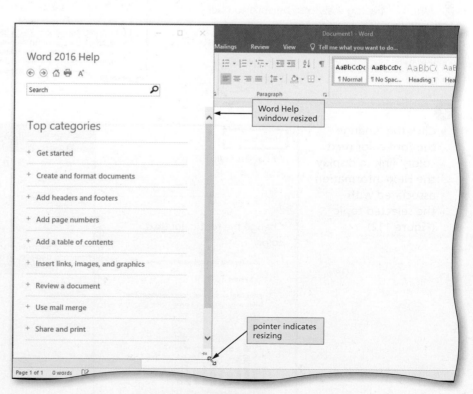

Figure 110

Using Office Help

Once an Office app's Help window is open, several methods exist for navigating Help. You can search for help by using any of the three following methods from the Help window:

1. Enter search text in the Search text box.
2. Click the links in the Help window.
3. Use the Table of Contents.

To Obtain Help Using the Search Text Box

1 SIGN IN | 2 USE WINDOWS | 3 USE APPS | 4 FILE MANAGEMENT | 5 SWITCH APPS | 6 SAVE FILES
7 CHANGE SCREEN RESOLUTION | 8 EXIT APPS | 9 USE ADDITIONAL APPS | 10 USE HELP

Assume for the following example that you want to know more about fonts. The following steps use the 'Search online help' text box to obtain useful information about fonts by entering the word, fonts, as search text. *Why? You may not know the exact help topic you are looking to find, so using keywords can help narrow your search.*

- Type **fonts** in the Search text box at the top of the Word Help window to enter the search text.
- Press the ENTER key to display the search results (Figure 111).

Q&A Why do my search results differ?
If you do not have an Internet connection, your results will reflect only the content of the Help files on your computer. When searching for help online, results also can change as material is added, deleted, and updated on the online Help webpages maintained by Microsoft.

Q&A Why were my search results not very helpful?
When initiating a search, be sure to check the spelling of the search text; also, keep your search specific to return the most accurate results.

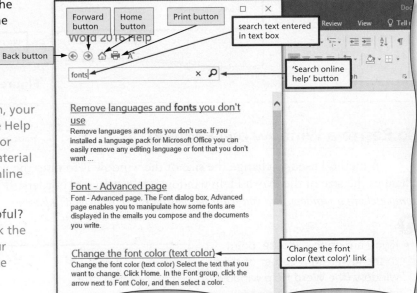

Figure 111

- Click the 'Change the font color (text color)' link to display the Help information associated with the selected topic (Figure 112).

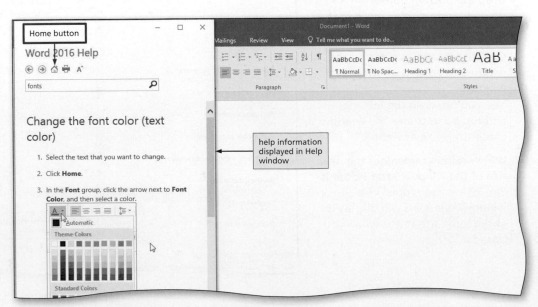

Figure 112

3
- Click the Home button in the Help window to clear the search results and redisplay the Help home page (Figure 113).
- Click the Close button in the Word 2016 Help window to close the window.

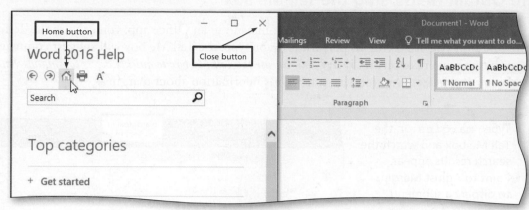

Figure 113

Obtaining Help while Working in an Office App

Help in the Office apps provides you with the ability to obtain help directly, without opening the Help window and initiating a search. For example, you may be unsure about how a particular command works, or you may be presented with a dialog box that you are not sure how to use.

Figure 114 shows one option for obtaining help while working in an Office app. If you want to learn more about a command, point to its button and wait for the ScreenTip to appear. If the Help icon and 'Tell me more' link appear in the ScreenTip, click the 'Tell me more' link or press the F1 key while pointing to the button to open the Help window associated with that command.

Figure 115 shows a dialog box that contains a Help button. Clicking the Help button or pressing the F1 key while the dialog box is displayed opens a Help window. The Help window contains help about that dialog box, if available. If no help file is available for that particular dialog box, then the main Help window opens.

As mentioned previously, the Tell Me box is available in most Office apps and can perform a variety of functions. One of these functions is to provide easy access to commands by typing a description of the command.

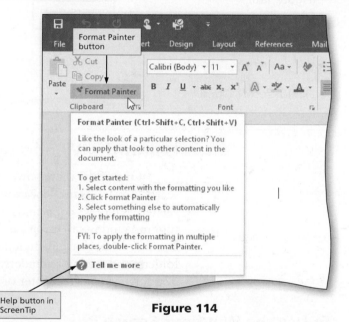

Figure 114

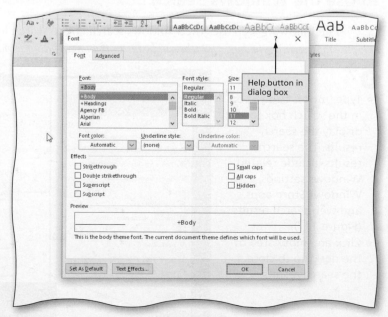

Figure 115

To Obtain Help Using the Tell Me Box

If you are having trouble finding a command in an Office app, you can use the Tell Me box to search for the function you are trying to perform. As you type, the Tell Me box will suggest commands that match the search text you are entering. **Why?** *You can use the Tell Me box to quickly access commands you otherwise may be unable to find on the ribbon.* The following step finds information about margins.

- Type **margins** in the Tell Me box and watch the search results appear.
- Point to Adjust Margins to display a submenu displaying the various margin settings (Figure 116).
- Click an empty area of the document window to close the search results.

- Exit Microsoft Word.

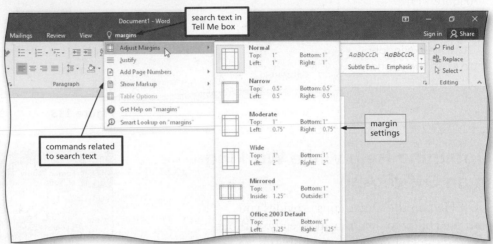

Figure 116

Using the Windows Search Box

One of the more powerful Windows features is the Windows search box. The search box is a central location from where you can type search text and quickly access related Windows commands or web search results. In addition, **Cortana** is a new search tool in Windows that you can access using the search box. It can act as a personal assistant by performing functions such as providing ideas; searching for apps, files, and folders; and setting reminders. In addition to typing search text in the search box, you also can use your computer or mobile device's microphone to give verbal commands.

To Use the Windows Search Box

The following step uses the Windows search box to search for a Windows command. **Why?** *Using the search box to locate apps, settings, folders, and files can be faster than navigating windows and dialog boxes to search for the desired content.*

- Type **notification** in the search box to display the search results. The search results include related Windows settings, Windows Store apps, and web search results (Figure 117).
- Click an empty area of the desktop to close the search results.

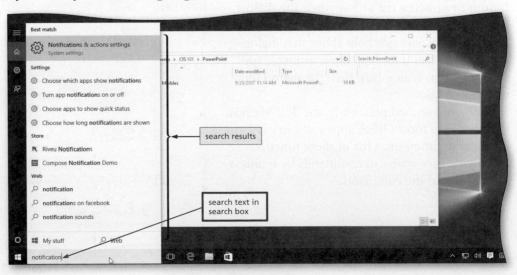

Figure 117

Summary

In this module, you learned how to use the Windows interface, several touch screen and mouse operations, file and folder management, some basic features of some Microsoft Office apps (including Word, PowerPoint, Excel, and Access), and discovered the common elements that exist among these different Office apps. You also were introduced to additional Office apps, including Outlook, Publisher, and OneNote. Topics covered included signing in, using Windows, using apps, file management, switching between apps, saving files, changing screen resolution, exiting apps, using additional apps, and using help.

CONSIDER THIS: PLAN AHEAD

What guidelines should you follow to plan your projects?

The process of communicating specific information is a learned, rational skill. Computers and software, especially Microsoft Office 2016, can help you develop ideas and present detailed information to a particular audience and minimize much of the laborious work of drafting and revising projects. No matter what method you use to plan a project, it is beneficial to follow some specific guidelines from the onset to arrive at a final product that is informative, relevant, and effective. Use some aspects of these guidelines every time you undertake a project, and others as needed in specific instances.

1. Determine the project's purpose.

    a) Clearly define why you are undertaking this assignment.

    b) Begin to draft ideas of how best to communicate information by handwriting ideas on paper; composing directly on a laptop, tablet, or mobile device; or developing a strategy that fits your particular thinking and writing style.

2. Analyze your audience.

    a) Learn about the people who will read, analyze, or view your work.

    b) Determine their interests and needs so that you can present the information they need to know and omit the information they already possess.

    c) Form a mental picture of these people or find photos of people who fit this profile so that you can develop a project with the audience in mind.

3. Gather possible content.

    a) Locate existing information that may reside in spreadsheets, databases, or other files.

    b) Conduct a web search to find relevant websites.

    c) Read pamphlets, magazine and newspaper articles, and books to gain insights of how others have approached your topic.

    d) Conduct personal interviews to obtain perspectives not available by any other means.

    e) Consider video and audio clips as potential sources for material that might complement or support the factual data you uncover.

4. Determine what content to present to your audience.

    a) Write three or four major ideas you want an audience member to remember after reading or viewing your project.

    b) Envision your project's endpoint, the key fact you wish to emphasize, so that all project elements lead to this final element.

    c) Determine relevant time factors, such as the length of time to develop the project, how long readers will spend reviewing your project, or the amount of time allocated for your speaking engagement.

    d) Decide whether a graph, photo, or artistic element can express or enhance a particular concept.

    e) Be mindful of the order in which you plan to present the content, and place the most important material at the top or bottom of the page, because readers and audience members generally remember the first and last pieces of information they see and hear.

How should you submit solutions to questions in the assignments identified with a symbol?

Every assignment in this book contains one or more questions with a ✳ symbol. These questions require you to think beyond the assigned file. Present your solutions to the question in the format required by your instructor. Possible formats may include one or more of these options: write the answer; create a document that contains the answer; present your answer to the class; discuss your answer in a group; record the answer as audio or video using a webcam, smartphone, or portable media player; or post answers on a blog, wiki, or website.

CONSIDER THIS

Apply Your Knowledge

Reinforce the skills and apply the concepts you learned in this module.

Creating a Folder and a Document

Instructions: You will create a PowerPoint Assignments folder and then create a PowerPoint presentation and save it in the folder.

Perform the following tasks:

1. Open the File Explorer window and then double-click to open the Documents folder.
2. Click the New folder button on the Quick Access Toolbar to display a new folder icon and text box for the folder name.
3. Type `PowerPoint Assignments` in the text box to name the folder. Press the ENTER key to create the folder in the Documents folder.
4. Run PowerPoint and create a new blank presentation.
5. Enter `Technology Update` in the title text placeholder (Figure 118).
6. Click the Save button on the Quick Access Toolbar. Navigate to the PowerPoint folder in the Documents folder and then save the document using the file name, Apply 1 Presentation.
7. If your Quick Access Toolbar does not show the Quick Print button, add the Quick Print button to the Quick Access Toolbar. Print the presentation using the Quick Print button on the Quick Access Toolbar. When you are finished printing, remove the Quick Print button from the Quick Access Toolbar.
8. Submit the printout to your instructor.
9. Exit PowerPoint.
10. ✱ What other commands might you find useful to include on the Quick Access Toolbar?

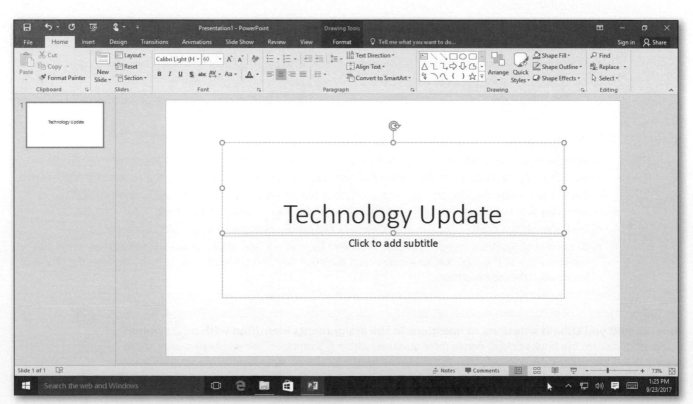

Figure 118

Extend Your Knowledge

Extend the skills you learned in this module and experiment with new skills. You will use Help to complete the assignment.

Using Help

Instructions: Use Office Help to perform the following tasks.

Perform the following tasks:
1. Run Word.
2. Click the Microsoft Word Help button to open the Word Help window (Figure 119).
3. Search Word Help to answer the following questions.

    a. What are the steps to create a hanging indent?

    b. What is mail merge?
4. With the Word app still running, run PowerPoint.
5. Click the Microsoft PowerPoint Help button on the title bar to open the PowerPoint Help window.
6. Search PowerPoint Help to answer the following questions.

    a. How can you create a Venn diagram?

    b. How do you add slide numbers to each slide?
7. Exit PowerPoint.
8. Run Excel.
9. Click the Microsoft Excel Help button to open the Excel Help window.
10. Search Excel Help to answer the following questions.

    a. What different types of charts are available in Excel?

    b. What is Flash Fill?
11. Exit Excel.
12. Run Access.
13. Click the Microsoft Access Help button to open the Access Help window.
14. Search Access Help to answer the following questions.

    a. What is a query?

    b. What are data types?
15. Exit Access.
16. Type the answers from your searches in a new blank Word document. Save the document with a new file name and then submit it in the format specified by your instructor.
17. Exit Word.
18. ✷ What search text did you use to perform the searches above? Did it take multiple attempts to search and locate the exact information for which you were searching?

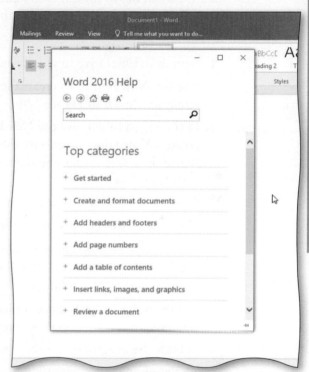

Figure 119

Expand Your World
Creating Office Online Documents

Create a solution that uses cloud or web technologies by learning and investigating on your own from general guidance.

Instructions: Create the folders shown in Figure 120. Then, using the respective Office Online app, create a small file to save in each folder (i.e., create a Word document to save in the Word folder, a PowerPoint presentation to save in the PowerPoint folder, and so on).

Perform the following tasks:

1. Sign in to OneDrive in your browser.

2. Use the New button to create the folder structure shown in Figure 120.

3. In the Word folder, use the New button to create a Word document with the file name, Reminders, and containing the text, Lunch with Lucas on Tuesday.

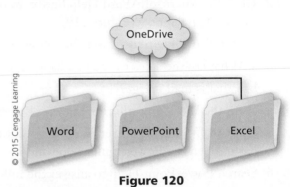

Figure 120

4. Save the document and then exit the app.

5. Navigate to the PowerPoint folder.

6. Create a PowerPoint presentation called Widget Sales with one slide containing the title text, Online Presentation, and then exit the app.

7. Navigate to the Excel folder.

8. Create an Excel spreadsheet called Widget Sales Analysis containing the text, Sales Cost Analysis, in cell A1, and then exit the app.

9. Submit the assignment in the format specified by your instructor.

10. ✳ Based on your current knowledge of OneDrive, do you think you will use it? What about the Office Online apps?

In the Labs

Design, create, modify, and/or use files following the guidelines, concepts, and skills presented in this module. Labs 1 and 2, which increase in difficulty, require you to create solutions based on what you learned in the module; Lab 3 requires you to apply your creative thinking and problem-solving skills to design and implement a solution.

Lab 1: Creating Folders for a Bookstore

Problem: Your friend works for a local bookstore. He would like to organize his files in relation to the types of books available in the store. He has seven main categories: fiction, biography, children, humor, social science, nonfiction, and medical. You are to create a folder structure similar to Figure 121.

Perform the following tasks:

1. Click the File Explorer button on the taskbar and display the contents of the Documents folder.

2. In the Documents folder, create the main folder and name it Book Categories.

3. Navigate to the Book Categories folder.

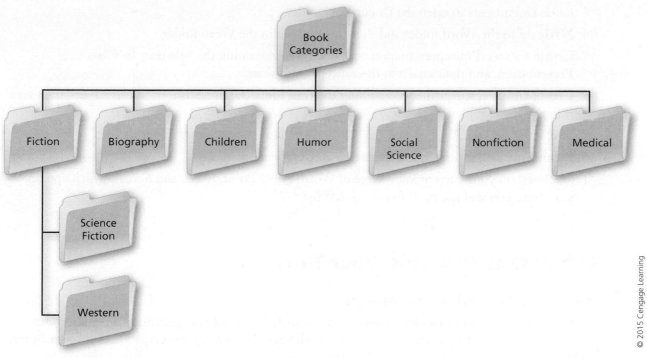

© 2015 Cengage Learning

Figure 121

4. Within the Book Categories folder, create a folder for each of the following: Fiction, Biography, Children, Humor, Social Science, Nonfiction, and Medical.

5. Within the Fiction folder, create two additional folders, one for Science Fiction and the second for Western.

6. Submit the assignment in the format specified by your instructor.

7. ✱ Think about how you use your computer for various tasks (consider personal, professional, and academic reasons). What folders do you think will be required on your computer to store the files you save?

Lab 2: Creating Office Documents and Saving Them in Appropriate Folders

Problem: You are taking a class that requires you to create a Word, PowerPoint, Excel, and Access file. You will save these files to folders named for four different Office apps (Figure 122).

Perform the following tasks:

1. Create the folders shown in Figure 122.

2. Create a Word document containing the text, Week 1 Notes.

3. In the Backstage view, click Save As and then click This PC.

4. Click the Browse button to display the Save As dialog box.

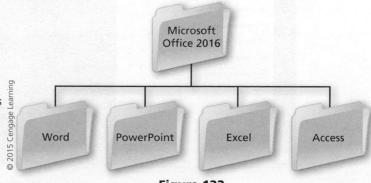

© 2015 Cengage Learning

Figure 122

5. Click Documents to open the Documents folder.

6. Navigate to the Word folder and then save the file in the Word folder.

7. Create a PowerPoint presentation with one slide containing the title text, In-Class Presentation, and then save it in the PowerPoint folder.

8. Create an Excel spreadsheet containing the text, Financial Spreadsheet, in cell A1 and then save it in the Excel folder.

9. Save an Access database named, My Movie Database, in the Access folder.

10. Submit the assignment in the format specified by your instructor.

11. ✸ Based on your current knowledge of Word, PowerPoint, Excel, and Access, which app do you think you will use most frequently? Why?

Lab 3: **Consider This: Your Turn**

Performing Research about Malware

Problem: You have just installed a new computer with the Windows operating system. Because you want to be sure that it is protected from the threat of malware, you decide to research malware, malware protection, and removing malware.

Part 1: Research the following three topics: malware, malware protection, and removing malware. Use the concepts and techniques presented in this module to use the search box to find information regarding these topics. Create a Word document that contains steps to properly safeguard a computer from malware, ways to prevent malware, as well as the different ways to remove malware or a virus should your computer become infected. Submit your assignment in the format specified by your instructor.

Part 2: You made several decisions while searching for this assignment. What decisions did you make? What was the rationale behind these decisions? How did you locate the required information about malware?

Figure 123

Index

Note: **Boldfaced** page numbers
indicate key terms

A

Access, **OFF 8**, **OFF 59**, OFF
59–60
creating databases, OFF 61–62
running, OFF 59–60
unique elements in, OFF 60–63
Access work area, **OFF 60**
accounts
email. *See* email accounts
Microsoft. *See* Microsoft accounts
signing in, OFF 6–7
active cell, **OFF 57**
active tab, **OFF 16**
add-in software, **PA-10**
address bar, **OFF 27**
Adobe Reader, OFF 23
Advanced Find features, OUT 216
animation emphasis effects, **PA-8**
app(s), **OFF 2**
exiting Office, OFF 41–42, OFF
53, OFF 59, OFF 63
Office Mix, PA-12
running and using. *See* running
apps
switching between, OFF 30–31
appointment(s), **OUT 60**
area, OUT 60
changing status, OUT 81
creating in appointment area,
OUT 73–74
creating using Appointment
window, OUT 77–78
creating using natural language
phrases, OUT 88–89
deleting single occurrence, OUT
91–92
moving, OUT 89–90
one-time, **OUT 73**, OUT 73–74
recurring. *See* recurring
appointments
setting reminder, OUT 81–82
status, OUT 78
Appointment window
creating appointment using,
OUT 77–78
creating one-time events,
OUT 92–94
creating recurring events,
OUT 95–97

attachment(s), **OUT 17**
adding to contact, OUT 132–134
attaching files to messages,
OUT 36
changing, OUT 134
opening, OUT 19, OUT 21
previewing and saving, OUT
19–20
Protected View in Microsoft
Word, OUT 21
removing from contact, OUT
134–135
Attachment Preview, **OUT 19**
attendees, meetings, **OUT 100**
Augmented reality with Office Mix,
teaching, PA-13
Auto Account Setup feature,
OUT 15
AutoArchive settings, OUT
239–240
automatic replies set up, OUT
238–239

B

BACKSPACE key, error
correction, OFF 21
Backstage view, **OFF 22**
account information in, OUT 9
closing, OFF 31
closing Office using, OFF 52
creating new documents from,
OFF 50–51
Info tab in, OFF 50
opening recent files using, OFF
52–53
backups, **OUT 21**
blank space between paragraph,
OFF 21
blinking bar, OFF 21
blue wavy underline, OUT 31
Business Card view, **OUT 136**

C

Calendar, **OUT 58**
adding cities to Weather Bar,
OUT 64–65
adding group, OUT 75
adding holidays to default, OUT
70–72
advantages of digital, OUT 59

appointments. *See* appointment(s)
changing time for reminders,
OUT 242–243
changing work time on, OUT
241–242
color for, OUT 63
configuring, OUT 59
creating folder, OUT 61–63
customizing, OUT 240–248
deleting, OUT 72
deleting items permanently,
OUT 58
distributing, OUT 112
entering locations, OUT 78
events. *See* events; one-time
events; recurring events
in Exchange ActiveSync accounts,
OUT 62
items, **OUT 60**. *See also*
appointment(s); events;
meeting(s); one-time
appointments; one-time events;
recurring appointments;
recurring events
meetings. *See* meeting(s)
Month view, **OUT 68**
multiple copies, OUT 110
natural language phrasing, OUT
87–89
navigating to specific dates, OUT
65–66
overview, OUT 58
printing. *See* printing calendars
saving as iCalendar file, OUT
112–113
Schedule View, **OUT 68**, OUT
68–69
School, OUT 102
sharing, OUT 113–114
time zone settings, OUT 243–245
using, OUT 58
Week view, **OUT 67**
Work Week view, **OUT 66**,
OUT 66–67
Calendar Tools Appointment
Series tab, OUT 87, OUT 98,
OUT 100
calendar view, **OUT 65**
Calendar window, OUT 59–60
options, OUT 80
card, **PA-6**
Card view, **OUT 136**
categorizing tasks, OUT 175–182

creating new category, OUT 175–177

deleting category, OUT 195

multiple, OUT 178–179

remaining tasks, OUT 179

renaming category, OUT 180–181

setting Quick Click, OUT 181–182

steps, OUT 177–178

cell, worksheet, **OFF 56**

cell reference, **OFF 57**

cell reference C6, OFF 57

Change Account dialog box, OUT 15

charts, **OFF 53**

cleanup tools, OUT 239

clip, **PA-11**

Clutter feature, **OUT 231**

color categories, organizing calendar, OUT 75–77

adding, OUT 75–76

assigning to appointment, OUT 77

for email account, OUT 75

color-coded category, contacts, OUT 135

column heading, **OFF 56**

command, **OFF 9**

composing email messages, OUT 2, OUT 11–13

configuring Outlook Calendar, OUT 59

'Connect to Internet' button, OFF 6

contact card, OUT 127

contact group, **OUT 122, OUT 142**

adding name to, OUT 147–148

adding notes to, OUT 148–149

creating and editing, OUT 142–150

creating from existing contacts, OUT 143–145

creating from existing email message, OUT 145–147

removing name from, OUT 149–150

contact list, **OUT 122**

advantages, OUT 123

creating, OUT 123–129

with groups, OUT 122–123

previewing, OUT 151–153

printing, OUT 153

sorting, OUT 137–138

viewing, OUT 136–137

contact record, **OUT 122**

Contact view, print styles, OUT 150

contacts

adding attachment to, OUT 132–134

adding tag to, OUT 135

creating from email messages, OUT 126–128

creating new, OUT 124–125

deleting, OUT 132

editing, OUT 129–132

filing, OUT 136

importing from external sources, OUT 129

managing in Outlook, OUT 121

Outlook, OUT 122

Outlook window, OUT 123–129

printing, OUT 150–153

removing attachment from, OUT 134–135

using search to find, OUT 138–142

contextual tabs, OFF 14

Cortana, **OFF 74, PA-14**

in Microsoft Edge, PA-14–16

Course Work category, OUT 178

Creative Commons license, **PA-7**

D

database(s), **OFF 59**

creating Access, OFF 60–61

database management system, **OFF 59**

Date Navigator, **OUT 59,** OUT 67

default calendar, adding holidays to, OUT 70–72

default language, setting, OUT 9

desktop (Windows 10), OFF 7

destination folder, **OUT 42**

Dialog Box Launcher, **OFF 15**

dialog boxes, navigating in, **OFF 34,** OFF 34–37

digital calendar, advantages of, OUT 59

Docs.com, Microsoft, **PA-8**

document(s)

electronic image of, OFF 24

method for distributing, OFF 23

printing, OFF 23–24

document properties, **OFF 22**

changing, OFF 22

purpose, OFF 22

document window, **OFF 12**

domain name, **OUT 4**

Drafts folder, OUT 33–35

drawing canvas, **PA-3**

E

'Ease of access' button, OFF 6

email (electronic mail), **OFF 64, OUT 2,** OUT 11–16

adding hyperlink to message, OUT 212–213

assigning signature to single message, OUT 227–228

attachments. *See* attachment(s)

capital letters, OUT 12

categorizing messages, OUT 182–183

checking spelling and grammar, OUT 31–33

composing, OUT 2, OUT 11–13

contact group from existing, OUT 145–147

creating contacts from messages, OUT 126–128

creating new search folder, OUT 217

customizing messages, OUT 212–219

deleting messages, OUT 45–46

forwarding messages, OUT 38–40

hard copy of, OUT 21

importance level, OUT 37–38

inserting image into message, OUT 215

message area parts, OUT 11

message formats, OUT 29–30, OUT 218–219

misspelled words in, OUT 31

moving messages, OUT 41–45

opening attachments in, OUT 21

opening messages in window, OUT 18–19

opening saved messages, OUT 35

printing messages, OUT 21–22

Quick Parts, OUT 214

replying to message, OUT 26–28

responding to messages, OUT 26–39

saving and closing messages without sending, OUT 33–34

search using Advanced Find, OUT 216

from sender to receiver, OUT 15–16

sending messages, OUT 2, OUT 15–16

Sensitivity level, **OUT 10**, OUT 10–11

signature, OUT 13

sort by conversation, OUT 219

tag in, OUT 38

themes, OUT 14

typing error, OUT 13

viewing messages in Reading Pane, OUT 17–18

voting options, OUT 216

working with mailbox, OUT 46–48

email accounts, **OUT 2**

adding account to Outlook, OUT 5

adding and customizing options, OUT 210

adding new, OUT 211–212

multiple, OUT 212

removing, OUT 6

email address, **OUT 2**

blocking specific, OUT 231

parts of, OUT 4–11

email client, **OUT 2**

email service provider, **OUT 2**

email thread, **OUT 46**

error correction, BACKSPACE key, OFF 21

events, **OUT 60**. *See also* one-time events; recurring events

Excel, **OFF 8**, **OFF 53**, OFF 53–56

charts, OFF 53

creating new documents from File Explorer, OFF 54–55

entering worksheet titles, OFF 57–58

exiting, OFF 59

formula bar, **OFF 57**

ribbon, OFF 57

running from File Explorer, OFF 55–56

saving files, OFF 58–59

tables, OFF 54

unique features of, OFF 56–59

web support, OFF 54

workbook, **OFF 53**

worksheets, **OFF 53**, OFF 56–57

Exchange server, OUT 80

F

file(s), **OFF 7**, OFF 23

closing, OFF 62

deleting, OFF 69

moving, OFF 68–69

opening existing, OFF 63

organizing, OFF 25, OUT 128

renaming, OFF 68

saving, OFF 31–34, OFF 49–52

type, OFF 23

File Explorer

creating new documents from, OFF 54–55

running apps from, OFF 55–56

window, OFF 27

file management, **OFF 67**

file names, **OFF 23**

saving existing files with same file name, OFF 58

saving with new file name, OFF 59

File tab, OFF 36

fixed formats, OFF 23

Flag Message dialog box, OUT 235

flagged word, OUT 31

folder(s), **OUT 40**

collapsing, OFF 29–30

copying to OneDrive, OFF 42–43

creating, OFF 26–28

creating in Inbox folder, OUT 40–41

Drafts, OUT 33–35

expanding, OFF 29–30

within folders, creating, OFF 28

moving email messages to, OUT 41–42

OneNote, **OFF 67**

organizing, OFF 25, OUT 19, OUT 85, OUT 128

saving files, OFF 31–34, OFF 49–52

scrolling through contents, OFF 29–30

folder windows, **OFF 27**

formatting, email messages, **OUT 29**

formula bar, **OFF 57**

free-response quiz, **PA-12**

Full Screen mode, **OFF 17**

G

gallery, **OFF 14**

gesture, **OFF 3**

grammar, checking in email messages, OUT 31–33

green computing, **OFF 23**

green wavy underline, OUT 31

gridlines, **OFF 57**

group (ribbon), **OFF 14**

H

hard copy (printout), **OFF 23**, **OUT 17**

high importance, email messages, **OUT 37**

HTML (Hypertext Markup Language), **OUT 29**

in title bar, OUT 12

Hub, **PA-14**

hyperlink, **OUT 17**

to email message, OUT 212–213

inserting, OUT 11

I

iCalendar, **OUT 100**, OUT 112

.ics (individual calendar) file format, OUT 112

importing files, OUT 101–102

saving calendar as, OUT 112–113

importance level, email messages, **OUT 37**

Inbox folder, OUT 8, OUT 40–41, OUT 61

Info tab in Backstage view, OFF 50

InfoBar, **OUT 19**

Ink to Text button, **PA-3**

Inked handwriting, **PA-3**

Inking toolbar, **PA-15**

insertion point, OFF 21

Instant Search text box, **OUT 216**

Internet service provider (ISP), OUT 2

item, Calendar, **OUT 60**.
  See also appointment(s);
  events; meeting(s); one-time
  appointments; one-time events;
  recurring appointments;
  recurring events
  emailing, OUT 89
  status options, OUT 80

J

junk email, **OUT 17**, OUT
  228–229
  adding domain to safe senders list,
    OUT 229–231
  blocking specific email address,
    OUT 231
  managing, OUT 228–231

K

keyboard shortcut, **OFF 5**
KeyTips, **OFF 16**

L

landscape orientation, **OFF 48**
language preferences, OUT 9
layouts, **OFF 48**
lecture in OneNote, recording,
  PA-4
List view, Calendar
  changing calendar view to, OUT
    110–111
  printing in, OUT 111
List view, contacts, **OUT 136**
live preview, **OFF 14**
lock screen, **OFF 5**
low importance, email messages,
  OUT 37

M

mailbox, working with, OUT
  46–48
Map It button, OUT 129
maximizing windows, **OFF 11**,
  OFF 11–12
meeting(s), **OUT 60**
  cancellation, OUT 107–108
  changing time, OUT 106–107

creating and sending meeting
  requests, OUT 104–106
importing iCalendar files, OUT
  101–102
Peek feature, OUT 103–104
replying to meeting requests,
  OUT 107–108
viewing calendars in overlay
  mode, OUT 102–103
meeting organizer, **OUT 100**
meeting request, **OUT 100**
  creating and sending, OUT
    104–106
  declining, OUT 107
  error message, OUT 106
  invitation in Inbox, OUT 107
  proposing new meeting time,
    OUT 108
  replying to, OUT 107–108
menu, **OFF 9**
message area, **OUT 11**
message format, **OUT 29**, OUT
  29–30, OUT 218–219
message header, **OUT 11**,
  OUT 18, OUT 38, OUT 105
message list, **OUT 16**
message pane, **OUT 16**
Microsoft Access 2016. *See* Access
Microsoft accounts
  area, OFF 16
  signing out of, OFF 37
Microsoft Edge, PA-14
  annotating webpages, PA-15
  browsing web with, PA-14
  inking with, PA-16
  locating information with
    Cortana, PA-14–15
  tools, PA-14
  using Cortana in, PA-16
Microsoft Excel 2016. *See* Excel
Microsoft Office 365. *See* Office
  365
Microsoft Office 2016, **OFF 7**
  apps. *See* Office apps
  Help window, OFF 70–74
  suites, OFF 8
Microsoft Office Online, **OFF 8**
Microsoft OneNote 2016. *See*
  OneNote 2016
Microsoft OneNote Mobile app,
  PA-2
Microsoft Outlook 2016. *See*
  Outlook 2016

Microsoft PowerPoint 2016. *See*
  PowerPoint
Microsoft Sway. *See* Sway
Microsoft Word 2016. *See* Word
mini toolbar, **OFF 15**
  turning off, OFF 16
minimized window, **OFF 34**, OFF
  34–35
Month view, Calendar, **OUT 68**
mouse operations, OFF 4
My Calendars pane, **OUT 60**

N

Name box, **OFF 57**
natural language phrase, **OUT 87**,
  OUT 87–89
  capitalization, OUT 89
  creating appointment date and
    time using, OUT 88–89
navigating Calendar, OUT 65–72
navigating in dialog boxes,
  OFF 34, OFF 34–37
Navigation bar, changing options,
  OUT 6–7
Navigation Pane, **OFF 28**, OUT 8
notebook, OneNote, **OFF 67**
notes
  changing view of, OUT 199
  creating, OUT 197–198
  deleting, OUT 199
  as sticky notes, OUT 197

O

object tabs, **OFF 60**
Office 365, **OFF 8**
Office apps, OFF 7–8, OFF 45–63
  exiting, OFF 41–42, OFF 53,
    OFF 59, OFF 63
  Help in, OFF 73–74
  opening Help window, OFF 70
Office Help
  opening window, OFF 70
  using Search text box, OFF 72–73
  using Tell Me box, OFF 74
  while working in apps, OFF 73–74
Office Mix, PA-10
  adding to PowerPoint, PA-10
  capturing video clips, PA-11
  inserting quizzes, live webpages,
    and apps, PA-12

marketing travel destination with, PA-13
for OneNote, PA-13
sharing presentation, PA-12
teaching augmented reality with, PA-13
on-screen keyboard, OFF 7
one-time appointments, **OUT 73**, OUT 73-74
one-time events
    creating in Appointment window, OUT 92-94
    deleting, OUT 95
OneDrive, **OFF 8**
    account, unlinking, OFF 44-45
    copying folder to, OFF 42-43
    saving on, OFF 32, OFF 35-36
OneNote 2016, **OFF 8**, **OFF 66**, OFF 66-67
    converting handwriting to text, PA-3-4
    creating notebook, PA-2
    creating Office Mix for, PA-13
    organizing research paper, PA-5
    recording lecture, PA-4
    syncing notebook to cloud, PA-2-3
    taking notes, PA-3
    window, OFF 67
Online Sway Newsletter, creating, PA-9
opening attachment, email messages, OUT 21
operating system (OS), **OFF 2**
outgoing email server, **OUT 15**
Outlook 2016, **OFF 8**, **OFF 64**, **OUT 2**, OUT 57
    advanced options, OUT 240
    Calendar. *See* Calendar
    contact photo, OUT 8
    creating and managing tasks with, OUT 161
    customizing, OUT 210
    email. *See* email (electronic mail)
    expanding folder pane, OUT 6
    Help, OUT 46, OUT 87, OUT 138
    language preferences, OUT 9
    navigation bar options, OUT 6-7
    opening data file, OUT 7-8
    Options dialog box, OUT 218
    overview, OUT 2
    People Pane, OUT 22-25

Quick Steps, OUT 43-45
    running, OUT 5-6
    screen resolution, OUT 61, OUT 150
    Sensitivity level, **OUT 10**, OUT 10-11
    setting up, OUT 3-11
    tasks, OUT 162
    using more data file, OUT 124
    window, OFF 64-65, OUT 2
Outlook contacts, OUT 122
    managing, OUT 121
    window, OUT 123-129
overlay mode, viewing calendars, OUT 102-103

P

pages, OneNote, **OFF 67**
paragraphs, black space between, OFF 21
password, **OFF 5**
path, **OFF 25**
Peek feature, Outlook, **OUT 103**, OUT 103-104
People Pane, **OUT 22**
    to change view of, OUT 22-24
    updating contact information, OUT 24
People view, **OUT 136**
personal storage table (.pst file), **OUT 7**
Phone view, **OUT 136**
Picture Tools Format tab, OFF 14
placeholders, **OFF 48**
Plain Text format, OUT 29-30
pointer (touch screen), OFF 4
POP3, **OUT 15**
Post Office Protocol (POP), **OUT 15**
postal code, searching city, OUT 64
PowerPoint, **OFF 8**, OFF 46-48
    adding to Office Mix, PA-10
    closing using Backstage view, OFF 52
    creating new documents from Backstage view, OFF 50-51
    entering content in title slides, OFF 49, OFF 51
    exiting, OFF 53
    opening recent files using Backstage view, OFF 52-53

saving files in folders, OFF 49-50
    window and ribbon, OFF 48-53
presentation (PowerPoint), **OFF 46**
    creating Sway, PA-6-7
    sharing Office Mix, PA-12
Previous Locations arrow, **OFF 27**
Print Layout view, **OFF 12**
print styles, **OUT 108**, **OUT 150**
    Contact view, OUT 150
printing calendars, OUT 108-111
    changing Calendar view to List view, OUT 110-111
    changing settings before, OUT 111
    in List view, OUT 111
    in weekly calendar style, OUT 109-110
printout, **OFF 23**
publication types, **OFF 65**
Publisher, **OFF 65**
    running, OFF 65
    window, OFF 65-66

Q

Quick Access area, **OFF 28**
Quick Access Toolbar, **OFF 16**
    customizing, OFF 20-21
    relocating, OFF 19-20
Quick Click category, **OUT 175**
    setting, OUT 181-182
Quick Parts, **OUT 214**
    creating and inserting, OUT 214
Quick Steps, **OUT 43**
    moving email messages using, OUT 43-45

R

Reading Pane, **OUT 17**
    hiding, OUT 25
    repositioning, OUT 24-25
    viewing email messages in, OUT 17-18
Reading view, **PA-14**
    viewing online news with, PA-16
Really Simple Syndication (RSS). *See* RSS feeds
recurrence pattern, **OUT 77**
recurring appointments, **OUT 73**, OUT 83-87
    adding, OUT 86-87

Index

deleting single occurrence, OUT 91–92

moving, OUT 90

saving, OUT 84–85

setting recurrence options, OUT 83–84

recurring events

creating in Appointment window, OUT 95–97

deleting, OUT 100

double arrow symbol, OUT 98

moving, OUT 98–100

recurring task, OUT 172–174

Recycle Bin, **OFF 7**

red wavy underline, OUT 31–32

Refresh button, **OFF 27**

reminder, Calendar, **OUT 77**

changing time for, OUT 242–243

customizing sound, OUT 82

default time, OUT 82

setting, OUT 81–82

responding to email messages, OUT 26–39

business *vs.* friend's response, OUT 26

options, OUT 26

responsive design, **PA-6**

Restart command, OFF 6

restoring windows, OFF 34–35

ribbon, OFF 12–15, **OFF 28**

Access, OFF 61

collapsing and expanding, OFF 17–19

customizing, OFF 57

displaying tabs, OFF 16–17

Excel, OFF 57

in PowerPoint, OFF 48

and screen resolution, OUT 6, OUT 22, OUT 59, OUT 163, OUT 211

to stay open, OUT 11

Room Finder, OUT 80

router, **OUT 15**

row heading, **OFF 56**

RSS feeds, **OUT 245**

deleting, OUT 247–248

reset time zone setting, OUT 248

subscribing to, OUT 245–247

working with, OUT 245–248

rule(s), **OUT 232**

AutoArchive settings, OUT 239–240

automatic replies set up, OUT 238–239

creating new, OUT 232–235

deleting, OUT 237–238

running, OUT 236–237

working with, OUT 232–240

running apps, OFF 9–12

Access, OFF 59–60

from File Explorer, OFF 55–56

using Search box, OFF 47–48

using Start menu, OFF 9–11

S

saving files

existing files with same file name, OFF 58

in folders, OFF 31–34, OFF 49–52

naming, OFF 32

on OneDrive, OFF 32, OFF 35–36

purpose, OFF 34

Schedule View, Calendar, **OUT 68**, OUT 68–69

Scheduling Assistant, **OUT 100**

School Calendar, OUT 102

screen clipping, PA-15

screen recording, **PA-11**

screen resolution, **OFF 38**, OFF 38–45, OUT 6

changing, OFF 39–41

Outlook, OUT 150

ribbon and, OUT 6, OUT 22, OUT 59, OUT 163, OUT 211

ScreenTip, **OFF 14**

scroll arrows, **OFF 4**

scroll bar, **OFF 4**, OFF 12

scroll box, **OFF 4**

search box, **OFF 27**

running apps using, OFF 47–48

Windows, OFF 74

Search text box, Office Help using, OFF 72–73

search to find contact, OUT 138–142

from Outlook window, OUT 141–142

refining, OUT 140–141

searching for text, OUT 138–139

sections, OneNote, **OFF 67**

sending email messages, OUT 2, OUT 15–16

Sensitivity level, **OUT 10**, OUT 10–11

server information, OUT 211

sheet tab, **OFF 56**

shortcut menu, **OFF 19**

commands, displaying, OFF 39

Show As box, OUT 94

Shut down command, OFF 6

sign-in screen, **OFF 5**

signature (email), **OUT 219**

adding image to, OUT 222–223

assigning to single email message, OUT 227–228

configuring options, OUT 224

creating, OUT 220

formatting, OUT 221–222

previewing message changes, OUT 226

signing out of Microsoft accounts, OFF 37

Sleep command, OFF 6

slide, **OFF 48**

Slide Notes, **PA-11**

slide recording, **PA-11**

slide show, **OFF 46**

SMTP (Simple Mail Transfer Protocol), **OUT 15**

solid state drive (SSD), OFF 23

source folder, **OUT 41**–42

spam, **OUT 17**

spelling, checking in email messages, OUT 31–33

correctly typed word, OUT 31–32

misspelled text, OUT 32–33

Start button, **OFF 9**

Start menu, **OFF 9**

running apps using, OFF 9–11

starting Windows, OFF 5–7

stationery, **OUT 219**

customizing, OUT 225–226

status bar, **OFF 12**

status report, **OUT 184**

sending, OUT 191–192

storage medium, OFF 23

Storyline, **PA-6**

stylus, OUT 23

subject line, **OUT 11**

suite, **OFF 8**

Sway

adding content to build story, PA-7

creating presentation, PA-6–7

creating Sway resume, PA-9

designing, PA-8

presentation, PA-9

publishing, PA-8

sharing, PA-8

Index

Sway site, **PA-6**
syncing, **PA-2**

T

tab (ribbon), **OFF 14**
tables, **OFF 54**
task(s), **OUT 162**
   additional, OUT 171–172
   advantages, OUT 163
   assigning, OUT 187–189
   attaching file, OUT 185–187
   categorizing, OUT 175–182
   changing view of, OUT 195–196
   copying and moving, OUT 182
   creating, OUT 161, OUT
      163–174
   creating new, OUT 164–166
   with due date, OUT 166–167
   forwarding, OUT 189–190
   managing, OUT 161, OUT 162,
      OUT 184–194
   marking it as complete,
      OUT 193
   options, OUT 174
   Outlook, OUT 162
   printing, OUT 196–197
   with priority, OUT 168–169
   recurring, OUT 172–174
   with reminder, OUT 170–171
   removing, OUT 194
   sending status reports, OUT
      191–192
   with status, OUT 167–168
   updating, OUT 184–185
   using To-Do List Pane, OUT 174

task pane, **OFF 15**
Tell Me box, **OFF 15**
   Office Help in, OFF 74
text, **OFF 57**
   box, OFF 6
   entry in documents, OFF 21
   finding contact by searching for,
      OUT 138–139
time zone setting, Calendar
   changing, OUT 243–245
   reset, OUT 248
Time Zones button, OUT 80
title bar, **OFF 11**
Title Slide, **OFF 48**
   entering contents in, OFF 49,
      OFF 51
to-do item, **OUT 162**
To-Do list
   creating, OUT 164–174
   window, OUT 163
To-Do List Pane, task using,
   OUT 174
tool tabs, **OFF 14**
Touch Keyboard button, OFF 12
touch mode, OFF 15
touch screen, OFF 3–4, OUT 6
   differences, OUT 73, OUT 129,
      OUT 212
   gestures, **OFF 3**
   pointer, OFF 4

U

user account, **OFF 5**
user icon, **OFF 5**, OFF 6
user name, **OFF 5**, **OUT 4**

W

Weather Bar, adding cities to,
   OUT 64–65
Web Note, **PA-15**
web support, Excel, **OFF 54**
Week view, Calendar, **OUT 67**
weekly calendar style, printing
   calendars, OUT 109–110
windows, **OFF 11**
   dragging to move, OFF 70–71
   dragging to resize, OFF 71
   maximizing, **OFF 11**, OFF 11–12
   minimizing, OFF **34**, OFF 34–35
   OneNote, OFF 67
   Outlook, OFF 64–65, OUT 2
   PowerPoint, OFF 48–53
   Publisher, OFF 65–66
   restoring, OFF 34–35
   To-Do list, OUT 163
   worksheet size and, OFF 56
Windows 10, **OFF 2**, OUT 5
   desktop, OFF 7
   keyboard shortcuts, OFF 5
   overview, OFF 2
   scrolling, OFF 4
   search box, OFF 74
   starting, OFF 5–7
   touch screen and mouse,
      OFF 3–4
Word, **OFF 7**, OFF 9–12
Work Week view, Calendar,
   OUT 66, OUT 66–67
workbook, **OFF 53**
worksheet, **OFF 53**, OFF 56–57
   size and window, OFF 56
   titles, OFF 57–58

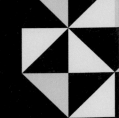

Microsoft Office 365™
OUTLOOK® 2016

INTERMEDIATE

Contents

Productivity Apps for School and Work
Introduction to OneNote 2016 — PA 2
Introduction to Sway — PA 6
Introduction to Office Mix — PA 10
Introduction to Microsoft Edge — PA 14

Microsoft **Office 2016 and Windows 10**

Office 2016 and Windows 10: Essential Concepts and Skills
Objectives — OFF 1
  Roadmap — OFF 1
Introduction to the Windows 10 Operating System — OFF 2
  Using a Touch Screen and a Mouse — OFF 3
  Scrolling — OFF 4
  Keyboard Shortcuts — OFF 5
  Starting Windows — OFF 5
  To Sign In to an Account — OFF 6
  The Windows Desktop — OFF 7
Introduction to Microsoft Office 2016 — OFF 7
  Microsoft Office 2016 Apps — OFF 7
  Microsoft Office 2016 Suites — OFF 8
Running and Using an App — OFF 9
  Word — OFF 9
  To Run an App Using the Start Menu
    and Create a Blank Document — OFF 9
  To Maximize a Window — OFF 11
  Word Document Window, Ribbon, and
    Elements Common to Office Apps — OFF 12
  To Display a Different Tab on the Ribbon — OFF 16
  To Collapse and Expand the Ribbon and
    Use Full Screen Mode — OFF 17
  To Use a Shortcut Menu to Relocate
    the Quick Access Toolbar — OFF 19
  To Customize the Quick Access Toolbar — OFF 20
  To Enter Text in a Document — OFF 21
Document Properties — OFF 22
  To Change Document Properties — OFF 22
Printing, Saving, and Organizing Files — OFF 23
  Printing a Document — OFF 23
  To Print a Document — OFF 23
  Organizing Files and Folders — OFF 25

To Create a Folder — OFF 26
Folder Windows — OFF 27
To Create a Folder within a Folder — OFF 28
To Create the Remaining Folders — OFF 28
To Expand a Folder, Scroll through
  Folder Contents, and Collapse a Folder — OFF 29
To Switch from One App to Another — OFF 30
To Save a File in a Folder — OFF 31
Navigating in Dialog Boxes — OFF 34
To Minimize and Restore a Window — OFF 34
To Save a File on OneDrive — OFF 35
To Sign Out of a Microsoft Account — OFF 37
Screen Resolution — **OFF 38**
To Change the Screen Resolution — OFF 39
To Exit an Office App with One Document Open — OFF 41
To Copy a Folder to OneDrive — OFF 42
To Unlink a OneDrive Account — OFF 44
Additional Microsoft Office Apps — **OFF 45**
PowerPoint — OFF 46
To Run an App Using the Search Box — OFF 47
The PowerPoint Window and Ribbon — OFF 48
To Enter Content in a Title Slide — OFF 49
To Save a File in a Folder — OFF 49
To Create a New Office Document
  from the Backstage View — OFF 50
To Enter Content in a Title Slide of a Second
  PowerPoint Presentation — OFF 51
To Save a File in a Folder — OFF 51
To Close an Office File Using the Backstage View — OFF 52
To Open a Recent Office File Using the
  Backstage View — OFF 52
To Exit an Office App — OFF 53
Excel — OFF 53
To Create a New Blank Office
  Document from File Explorer — OFF 54
To Run an App from File Explorer
  and Open a File — OFF 55
Unique Features of Excel — OFF 56
To Enter a Worksheet Title — OFF 57
To Save an Existing Office File
  with the Same File Name — OFF 58
To Save a File with a New File Name — OFF 59
To Exit an Office App — OFF 59

Access   OFF 59
To Run an App   OFF 59
Unique Elements in Access   OFF 60
To Create an Access Database   OFF 61
To Close an Office File   OFF 62
To Open an Existing Office File   OFF 63
To Exit an Office App   OFF 63
Other Office Apps   **OFF 64**
Outlook   OFF 64
Publisher   OFF 65
OneNote   OFF 66
Renaming, Moving, and Deleting Files   **OFF 67**
To Rename a File   OFF 68
To Move a File   OFF 68
To Delete a File   OFF 69
Microsoft Office and Windows Help   **OFF 70**
To Open the Help Window in an Office App   OFF 70
Moving and Resizing Windows   OFF 70
To Move a Window by Dragging   OFF 70
To Resize a Window by Dragging   OFF 71
Using Office Help   OFF 72
To Obtain Help Using the Search Text Box   OFF 72
Obtaining Help while Working in an Office App   OFF 73
To Obtain Help Using the Tell Me Box   OFF 74
Using the Windows Search Box   OFF 74
To Use the Windows Search Box   OFF 74
Summary   **OFF 75**
Apply Your Knowledge   **OFF 76**
Extend Your Knowledge   **OFF 77**
Expand Your World   **OFF 78**
In the Labs   **OFF 78**

To Open an Attachment   OUT 21
To Print an Email Message   OUT 21
Using the Outlook People Pane   OUT 22
To Change the View of the People Pane   OUT 22
To Reposition the Reading Pane Using
   the Tell Me Search Tool   OUT 24
Responding to Messages   **OUT 26**
To Reply to an Email Message   OUT 26
Message Formats   OUT 29
To Change the Message Format   OUT 29
Checking Spelling and Grammar   OUT 31
To Check the Spelling of a Correctly Typed Word   OUT 31
To Check the Spelling of Misspelled Text   OUT 32
Saving and Closing an Email Message   OUT 33
To Save and Close an Email Message
   without Sending It   OUT 33
To Open a Saved Email Message   OUT 35
To Attach a File to an Email Message   OUT 36
To Set Message Importance and
   Send the Message   OUT 37
To Forward an Email Message   OUT 38
Organizing Messages with Outlook Folders   **OUT 40**
To Create a New Folder in the Inbox Folder   OUT 40
To Move an Email Message to a Folder   OUT 41
Outlook Quick Steps   OUT 43
To Move an Email Message Using Quick Steps   OUT 43
To Delete an Email Message   OUT 45
Working with the Mailbox   OUT 46
To View Mailbox Size   OUT 46
Summary   **OUT 48**
Apply Your Knowledge   **OUT 49**
Extend Your Knowledge   **OUT 50**
Expand Your World: Cloud and Web Technologies   **OUT 51**
In the Labs   **OUT 53**

Microsoft Office 365 & Outlook 2016

MODULE ONE
Managing Email Messages with Outlook
Objectives   **OUT 1**
Roadmap   OUT 1
Introduction to Outlook   **OUT 2**
Project — Composing and Sending
   Email Messages   **OUT 2**
Setting Up Outlook   **OUT 3**
Parts of an Email Address   OUT 4
To Run Outlook   OUT 5
To Change the Navigation Bar Options   OUT 6
To Open an Outlook Data File   OUT 7
To Set Language Preferences   OUT 9
To Set the Sensitivity Level
   for All New Messages   OUT 10
Composing and Sending Email messages   **OUT 11**
To Compose an Email Message   OUT 11
To Apply a Theme   OUT 14
To Send an Email Message   OUT 15
How Email Messages Travel from
   Sender to Receiver   OUT 15
Working with Incoming Messages   **OUT 16**
To View an Email Message
   in the Reading Pane   OUT 17
To Open an Email Message in a Window   OUT 18
Opening Attachments   OUT 19
To Preview and Save an Attachment   OUT 19

MODULE TWO
Managing Calendars with Outlook
Objectives   **OUT 57**
Managing Calendars with Outlook   **OUT 57**
Roadmap   OUT 57
Introduction to the Outlook Calendar   **OUT 58**
Project — Appointments, Events, and
   Meetings in Calendar   **OUT 58**
Configuring the Outlook Calendar   OUT 59
Calendar Window   OUT 59
Calendar Items   OUT 60
To Create a Calendar Folder   OUT 61
To Add a City to the Calendar Weather Bar   OUT 64
Navigating the Calendar   OUT 65
To Go to a Specific Date   OUT 65
To Display the Calendar in Work Week View   OUT 66
To Display the Calendar in Week View   OUT 67
To Display the Calendar in Month View   OUT 68
To Display the Calendar in Schedule View   OUT 68
To Add Holidays to the Default Calendar   OUT 70
Creating and Editing Appointments   **OUT 72**
Creating Appointments in the Appointment Area   OUT 73
To Create a One-Time Appointment
   Using the Appointment Area   OUT 73
Organize the Calendar with Color Categories   OUT 75
To Add Color Categories   OUT 75
To Assign a Color Category to an Appointment   OUT 77

Creating Appointments Using the
    Appointment Window   OUT 77
To Create an Appointment
    Using the Appointment Window   OUT 78
Setting Appointment Options   OUT 80
To Change the Status
    of an Appointment   OUT 81
To Set a Reminder for an Appointment   OUT 81
Creating Recurring Appointments   OUT 83
To Set Recurrence Options
    for an Appointment   OUT 83
To Save an Appointment   OUT 84
To Add More Recurring Appointments   OUT 86
Using Natural Language Phrasing   OUT 87
To Create an Appointment Date and
    Time Using Natural Language Phrases   OUT 88
Editing Appointments   OUT 89
To Move an Appointment to a Different
    Time on the Same Day   OUT 89
To Move an Appointment to a
    Different Date   OUT 90
To Delete a Single Occurrence
    of a Recurring Appointment   OUT 91
Scheduling Events   **OUT 92**
To Create a One-Time Event in the
    Appointment Window   OUT 92
To Delete a One-Time Event   OUT 95
To Create a Recurring Event Using the
    Appointment Window   OUT 95
To Move a Recurring Event to a
    Different Day   OUT 98
Scheduling Meetings   **OUT 100**
To Import an iCalendar File   OUT 101
To View Calendars in the Overlay Mode   OUT 102
To View and Dock the Peek Calendar   OUT 103
To Create and Send a Meeting Request   OUT 104
To Change the Time of a Meeting
    and Send an Update   OUT 106
To Reply to a Meeting Request   OUT 107
Printing Calendars in Different Views   **OUT 108**
To Print the Calendar in Weekly
    Calendar Style   OUT 109
To Change the Calendar View
    to List View   OUT 110
To Print the Calendar in List View   OUT 111
Saving and Sharing the Calendar   **OUT 112**
To Save a Calendar as an iCalendar File   OUT 112
To Share a Calendar   OUT 113
Summary   **OUT 114**
Apply Your Knowledge   **OUT 115**
Extend Your Knowledge   **OUT 116**
Expand Your World: Cloud and Web Technologies   **OUT 117**
In the Labs   **OUT 118**

MODULE THREE
**Managing Contacts and Personal Contact
Information with Outlook**
Objectives   **OUT 121**
**Managing Contacts and Personal Contact
    Information with Outlook**   **OUT 121**
Roadmap   OUT 121
Introduction to Outlook Contacts   **OUT 122**

Project — Contact List with Groups   **OUT 122**
Creating a Contact List   **OUT 123**
Contacts – Outlook Window   OUT 123
To Create a New Contact   OUT 124
To Create Contacts from Email Messages   OUT 126
Editing a Contact   **OUT 129**
To Edit a Contact   OUT 129
To Delete a Contact   OUT 132
To Add an Attachment to a Contact   OUT 132
To Remove an Attachment from a Contact   OUT 134
Viewing and Sorting a Contact List   **OUT 136**
To Change the Current View   OUT 136
To Sort Contacts   OUT 137
Using Search to Find a Contact   **OUT 138**
To Find a Contact by Searching for Text   OUT 138
To Refine a Search   OUT 140
To Find a Contact from Any Outlook Window   OUT 141
Creating and Editing a Contact Group   **OUT 142**
To Create a Contact Group from
    Existing Contacts   OUT 143
To Create a Contact Group from
    an Existing Email Message   OUT 145
To Add a Name to a Contact Group   OUT 147
To Add Notes to a Contact Group   OUT 148
To Remove a Name from a Contact Group   OUT 149
Printing Your Contacts   **OUT 150**
To Preview a Contact List   OUT 151
To Print a Contact List   OUT 153
Summary   **OUT 154**
Apply Your Knowledge   **OUT 155**
Extend Your Knowledge   **OUT 156**
Expand Your World: Cloud and Web Technologies   **OUT 157**
In the Labs   **OUT 158**

MODULE FOUR
**Creating and Managing Tasks
with Outlook**
Objectives   **OUT 161**
Creating and Managing Tasks with Outlook   **OUT 161**
Roadmap   OUT 161
Introduction to Outlook Tasks   **OUT 162**
Project — Managing Tasks   **OUT 162**
Creating a Task   **OUT 163**
To-Do List Window   OUT 163
Creating a To-Do List   OUT 164
To Create a New Task   OUT 164
To Create a Task with a Due Date   OUT 166
To Create a Task with a Status   OUT 167
To Create a Task with a Priority   OUT 168
To Create a Task with a Reminder   OUT 170
To Create More Tasks   OUT 171
To Create a Recurring Task   OUT 172
To Create Another Recurring Task   OUT 174
Categorizing Tasks   **OUT 175**
To Create a New Category   OUT 175
To Categorize a Task   OUT 177
To Categorize Multiple Tasks   OUT 178
To Categorize Remaining Tasks   OUT 180
To Rename a Category   OUT 180
To Set a Quick Click   OUT 181
Categorizing Email Messages   **OUT 182**
To Categorize an Email Message   OUT 183

Managing Tasks **OUT 184**
To Update a Task OUT 184
To Attach a File to a Task OUT 185
To Assign a Task OUT 187
To Forward a Task OUT 189
To Send a Status Report OUT 191
To Mark a Task Complete OUT 193
To Remove a Task OUT 194
Choosing Display and Print Views **OUT 195**
To Change the Task View OUT 195
To Print Tasks OUT 196
Using Notes **OUT 197**
To Create a Note OUT 197
To Change the Notes View OUT 199
To Delete a Note OUT 199
Summary **OUT 200**
Apply Your Knowledge **OUT 201**
Extend Your Knowledge **OUT 202**
Expand Your World: Cloud and Web Technologies **OUT 203**
In the Labs **OUT 204**

MODULE FIVE
Customizing Outlook
Objectives **OUT 209**
Roadmap OUT 209
Introduction to Customizing Outlook **OUT 210**
Project — Adding a New Email Account and Customizing Options **OUT 210**
Adding New Email Accounts **OUT 211**
Customizing Email Messages **OUT 212**
To Add a Hyperlink to an Email Message OUT 212
To Create and Insert Quick Parts OUT 214
To Insert an Image into an Email Message OUT 215
To Search Using Advanced Find OUT 216
To Create a New Search Folder OUT 217

To Display Outlook Options OUT 218
To Set the Message Format OUT 218
Creating Signatures and Stationery **OUT 219**
To Create an Email Signature OUT 220
To Format an Email Signature OUT 221
To Add an Image to an Email Signature OUT 222
To Configure Signature Options OUT 224
To Customize Stationery OUT 225
To Preview Message Changes OUT 226
To Assign Signatures to a Single Email Message OUT 227
Managing Junk Email Options OUT 228
To Add a Domain to the Safe Senders List OUT 229
To Block a Specific Email Address OUT 231
Working with Rules OUT 232
To Create a New Rule OUT 232
To Run Rules OUT 236
To Delete a Rule OUT 237
To Set AutoArchive Settings OUT 239
Customizing the Calendar **OUT 240**
To Change the Work Time on the Calendar OUT 241
To Change the Time for Calendar Reminders OUT 242
To Change the Time Zone Setting OUT 243
Working with RSS Feeds OUT 245
To Subscribe to an RSS Feed OUT 245
To Delete an RSS Feed OUT 247
To Reset the Time Zone Setting OUT 248
Summary **OUT 249**
Apply Your Knowledge **OUT 250**
Extend Your Knowledge **OUT 251**
Expand Your World: Cloud and Web Technologies **OUT 252**
In the Labs **OUT 253**

Index **IND 1**